Policy Forum Series No. 42

The 2009 Federal Budget

Challenge, Response and Retrospect

Edited by
Charles M. Beach, Bev Dahlby
and Paul A.R. Hobson

John Deutsch Institute for the
Study of Economic Policy

Queen's University

Published in cooperation with
McGill-Queen's University Press
Montreal & Kingston • London • Ithaca

ISBN: 978-1-55339-165-4 (pbk.), ISBN: 978-1-55339-166-1 (bound)

Queen's University, Kingston, Ontario K7L 3N6
Telephone: (613) 533-2294 FAX: (613) 533-6025
Printed and bound in Canada

Library and Archives Canada Cataloguing in Publication

The 2009 federal budget : challenge, response and retrospect / edited by Charles M. Beach, Bev Dahlby, and Paul A.R. Hobson.

(Policy forum series)
Includes bibliographical references.
ISBN 978-1-55339-165-4 (pbk.).--ISBN 978-1-55339-166-1 (bound)

1. Budget--Canada. 2. Fiscal policy--Canada. 3. Finance, Public--Canada. 4. Canada--Economic conditions--1991-. 5. Canada--Politics and government--2006-. I. Beach, Charles M. II. Dahlby, B. G. III. Hobson, Paul A. R. (Paul Alexander Robert), 1953- IV. John Deutsch Institute for the Study of Economic Policy V. Series: Policy forum series.

HJ2054.T867 2010 336.71 C2010-903972-6

TABLE OF CONTENTS

Session Seven
Wrap-Up Panel: The Big Picture

Contributors

List of Publications

PREFACE

The 2009 Federal Budget: Challenge, Response and Retrospect is the twelfth in a series of post-budget conferences and volumes published by the John Deutsch Institute for the Study of Economic Policy (JDI) at Queen's University. Since its inception as a policy research arm of the Economics Department at Queen's, the JDI has provided periodic evaluations and appraisals of Canadian federal budgets.

The 2009 budget forum was held at Queen's University on May 7-8, 2009. A list of contributors appears at the end of this volume. The 2009 federal budget occurred following dramatic financial shocks across major nations; the onslaught of a sharp economic recession that continues to have major effects in the United States, Europe and elsewhere; dramatically changed fiscal health of the major Canadian provinces; and the installation of a new political regime in Washington with a changed policy perspective. So there is a need to examine and evaluate how the federal budget responded to those challenges. This is also the fourth Harper Conserative budget. So it provides the opportunity to identify distinctive fiscal priorities and impacts of the Harper budgets in contrast to the previous Liberal government budgets. This volume thus evaluates how well the 2009 budget addresses current economic conditions and political realities, and seeks to understand the fiscal direction and priorities of the current government.

The papers in this volume examine the political and economic context informing the 2009 budget and provide a quantitative evaluation of the impact of the overall budget package on the Canadian economy. Special attention is devoted to the size and mix of the economic stimulus and stabilization provisions in the budget, specific tax policy changes, fiscal sustainability of the budget deficits, cost-sharing and federal-provincial fiscal relations, federal equalization transfers since the O'Brien Report, Canada's declining social safety net and EI reform, social policy and anti-poverty provisions, alternative approaches to environmental protection and green initiatives, and emerging fiscal challenges.

The contributors to this volume include Robin Boadway (Queen's), Tom Courchene (Queen's), Robert Fairholm (Centre for Spatial Economics), Janice MacKinnon (Saskatchewan), Chris Matier and Stephen Tapp

(Parliamentary Budget Office), Kevin Milligan (British Columbia), Nancy Olewiler (Simon Fraser), Lars Osberg (Dalhousie), Chris Ragan (McGill), William Scarth (McMaster), Michael Smart (Toronto), Tracy Snoddon (Wilfrid Laurier), Lindsay Tedds (Victoria), Sherri Torjman and Ken Battle (Caledon Institute), and Frances Woolley (Carleton).

As with all JDI activities and publications, the person who gets things done is Sharon Sullivan. She manages the conference arrangements, coordinates the process of compiling the final versions of the papers, and then orchestrates the production of the final volume. The editors very much wish to express their sincere thanks to her for her excellent work at all these stages of production.

It is also a pleasure to thank Stephanie Stone for her editing skills and the Queen's School of Policy Studies' Publication Unit for its valuable support in preparing the cover graphics and other publication aspects of the volume.

Finally, we wish to acknowledge the excellent co-operation we received from the contributors to this volume.

Charles M. Beach
Queen's University

Bev Dahlby
University of Alberta

Paul A.R. Hobson
Acadia University

INTRODUCTION

Charles M. Beach, Queen's University; Bev Dahlby, University of Alberta; and Paul A.R. Hobson, Acadia University

For about 30 years, the John Deutsch Institute at Queen's University has organized conferences about every three years commenting on and appraising recent federal budgets in Canada. This volume contains papers presented at a May 2009 conference held at Queen's on the 2009 federal budget. This budget was a singular event. The Canadian economy had rapidly entered its first recession in more than 15 years, and this recession had the potential to be severe because of its widespread nature across Canada's major trading partners and especially the United States, and because its source – a dramatic financial crisis starting in the United States mortgage market – was quite different from other post-war recessions and hence posed a challenge for appropriate policy responses. The minority Conservative government under Prime Minister Stephen Harper had just come through a major challenge by a coalition of the three opposition parties over an earlier economic statement of November 2008. This made government more responsive to public concerns about the rapidly worsening economy, stability of the Canadian financial sector, the large jump in unemployment rates, and regional differences in exposure to the recession. This was also the fourth Harper Conservative budget presented by the Finance Minister, Jim Flaherty, and it provides an opportunity to identify distinctive fiscal priorities and impacts of the Harper budgets in contrast to the previous Liberal regimes. Hence, the title of the conference (and this volume) is "The 2009 Federal Budget: Challenge, Response and Retrospect". The objectives of the conference and the papers in this volume are (i) to review and evaluate how well the 2009 budget addressed economic conditions and policy needs, and (ii) to better understand the fiscal directions and priorities of the Harper government.

Major Themes of the Budget and Conference

The 2009 federal budget, more than any other since the mid-1990s, was not a vehicle for implementing major planks from a previous election, but rather was a response to a quite sudden and severe downturn in the Canadian (and world) economy. There was a strong public pressure for a substantial fiscal policy response. The particular mix of policy responses, though, was very much at the discretion of the government.

Specific details of the budget[1] are noted in the next section, along with an overview of the individual papers in the volume. It would be useful, though, to characterize some of the major themes of the budget and of the conference presentations on the budget.

a) The Fiscal Stimulus Action Plan – The basic numbers of the budget involve $39.9 billion of federal stimulus spending over two years, to be matched by $11.7 billion in provincial and municipal spending, for a total of $51.6 billion in stimulus spending over two years. The federal deficit – driven both by fiscal stimulative measures as well as a fall-off of government tax revenue from the economic downturn – is estimated in the budget at $33.7 billion in 2009–10, $29.9 billion for 2010–11, and $13.0 billion for 2011–12, decreasing down to a slight surplus by 2013–14. The resulting federal debt-to-GDP ratio is estimated to rise from 29% to 32% by the end of 2010–11 and thereafter slowly decline.

The budget contains major provisions in its Extraordinary Financing Framework for stabilizing the Canadian financial sector and helping to restore the flow of credit to the financial system. While some fiscal stimulus is provided through tax cuts and enhanced credits within the personal income tax system, the main focus of the budget's stimulus package is on new funding for physical infrastructure construction. While the budget is based on the assumption that all such allocated expenditures will be taken up within two years, there are some concerns that this may not actually occur. While prospective projects are supposed to be "shovel-ready" so they can be completed within two years, there are likely to be delays in getting large construction projects going, especially if there are multiple levels of governments involved and environmental reviews to be undertaken. So every dollar committed may not actually get spent within two years. The budget figures are also based

---

[1]The papers in this study look only at the provisions of the budget itself and not at the additional legislative changes appearing in the budget-implementing legislation.

on the assumption of full take-up of the planned provincial and municipal matching funding, but provinces may have difficulties coming up with the matching funds, and some provinces may reduce their expenditures on other things in order to acquire federal matching funds. The speed of recovery of the Canadian economy coming out of the recession depends a very good deal on the strength of the US recovery. As gathering evidence indicates that the US recovery is much slower than earlier expected, this too calls into question whether the stimulus impact and budget deficit figures are likely to be met. The Chris Matier/Stephen Tapp paper in this volume also raises the concern of a persistent structural deficit created by a slow recovery combined with the permanent personal income tax cuts instituted by the budget.

b) Infrastructure Funding as a Stimulus Priority – While a strong case can be made for active stimulus spending by the federal government in a sharp recession when monetary policy may be relatively weak and only partially effective, it is not clear that expenditure on physical infrastructure is necessarily the best option. Previous Harper Conservative budgets (as have some previous Chrétien Liberal budgets) have indeed favoured major spending on infrastructure. The 2007 Harper budget, for example, set up the Building Canada Plan for major infrastructure funding of $33 billion over seven years. The 2009 budget's guiding principles were that the stimulus expenditures be timely, targeted (to those most in need) and temporary. As a result, the focus was on infrastructure projects being shovel-ready and such stimulus expenditures being closed-ended and terminate after two years. But as Robert Fairholm's paper highlights, one should also want such expenditures to provide long-run benefits and increase Canadian productivity (such as improving the electricity grid or investing in urban public transport). Such large projects are likely to stretch well beyond two years. Fairholm also argues that focusing stimulus expenditures on physical infrastructure and hence on the construction sector is not as effective in terms of short-run increases in output and employment as investing in a number of other sectors, such as education and child care (outside the home), which could also provide longer-run human capital benefits. Stimulus investments in schools, education, and renewable energy, for example, were major components of the Obama economic stimulus package in the United States.

c) Incrementalism and Missed Opportunities – Economic crises provide opportunities for major policy initiatives and program rethinks. The recent international financial meltdown and subsequent rapid recession indeed gave rise to the 2009 budget's Extraordinary Financial Framework initiative along with the infrastructure stimulus measures, including investment in social housing. But on the whole, the budget follows its immediate predecessor in making numerous relatively small scattershot changes and introducing no large innovative redesigns of programs. The papers by Lindsay Tedds and Kevin Milligan consider various business tax and personal income tax-based changes, and Nancy Olewiler lists numerous specific environmental initiatives, each worthwhile in its own right, but seemingly without an overarching vision. As the contributions by Kevin Milligan and Frances Woolley note, many of these changes move the personal income tax system incrementally toward Conservative social values of universality of benefits, more reliance on parental care of children, and greater personal responsibility for earning a living in the labour market.

Several contributors to this volume, including Thomas Courchene, Robin Boadway, Nancy Olewiler, and Sherri Torjman and Ken Battle, remark on the missed opportunities in the budget to address some major concerns. There is no effective policy to address climate change. There is no carbon pricing or cap-and-trade proposal or regulation of greenhouse gas emissions, as climate change policy is put on hold until a common system can be worked out with the United States. Again, while the Obama stimulus package for the United States included major investment in renewable energy resources, the Canadian budget included only marginal efforts in this direction. The budget could also have used the occasion to initiate and encourage human capital investment, such as in early childhood development, K–12 schooling improvements, and greater post-secondary education availability, again similar to Obama's approach in the United States or Australia's budget emphasis on "Building the Education Revolution". Finally, poverty and income inequality have been increasing, and the budget offers little to the very poor. In the name of greater universality of benefits, there is less targeting of benefits to the very poor. The largest beneficiaries of the various income tax savings go to those with upper incomes. Increased use of non-refundable tax credits reduces average tax rates for middle- and higher-income households, but provides no benefit to those whose incomes are not high enough to pay income taxes. Raising the clawback threshold and benefit rates on the Working Income Tax Benefit (WITB) helps those whose earnings are high enough to qualify, but the access threshold was not reduced in the budget. If the tax credits had been made refundable and income-tested, for example, this would indeed have benefited those with very low incomes.

d) Employment Insurance and the Social Safety Net – A number of authors in this volume – as well as many media commentators – express concern about how well Canada's current Employment Insurance (EI) program and social safety net are able to deal with this recession. Compared to the last major recession Canada experienced in the early 1990s, EI is playing a much weaker role as an economic shock absorber or automatic stabilizer because a far smaller fraction of unemployed in this recession are eligible for EI benefits. There is a strong sense of unfairness in a system where all workers pay in but fewer than half can get access to benefits and where eligibility criteria and benefit duration vary considerably across the country. It can be argued that the current EI system should be made more effective and fair in protecting individual workers from large cyclical earnings losses. The current system has the effect of off-loading cyclical earnings risk onto families (which EI was originally designed to protect against) and downloading the fiscal burden of unemployment onto provinces and municipalities, who bear the burden when the ineligible unemployed land on social assistance. At the same time, social assistance in many provinces (such as Ontario) is far less generous than in the previous recession because of major cutbacks in the 1990s.

The response in the budget to the onset of recession in terms of EI system changes was, in the words of one commentator, tepid. EI contribution rates were frozen for two years, the maximum benefit duration was lengthened by five weeks, and enhanced training expenditures financed out of existing EI funds were announced. There were no changes to eligibility rules or EI benefit levels in the budget.

Several contributors in this volume offer a range of recommendations for dealing with these concerns with EI and Canada's currently frayed social safety net. For immediate attention, the Caledon Institute recommends loosening the EI eligibility requirements, lengthening benefit duration periods, changing to a more uniform and fairer set of rules on eligibility and duration period, and increasing the earnings-replacement rate up from its current 55% of insurable earnings. Thomas Courchene, in his paper, proposes several more transformative measures, including (i) a fundamental reform of EI to return it to basic insurance principles; (ii) converting personal and spousal amounts and credits in the federal income tax system into refundable and income-tested benefits, thus in effect creating a negative income tax (NIT) or guaranteed annual income (GAI) system; and (iii) integrating the current WITB into the tax-back provisions of the proposed NIT/GAI system.

Overview of the Papers

The first two contributions to this volume provide political and economic background to the 2009 federal budget.

In "The Prospect of a Hanging? The Political Context for the 2009 Federal Budget", Janice MacKinnon examines the changing economic and political environment that resulted in the about-face by the Conservative government between November 2008, when it released the document *Protecting Canada's Future: Economic and Fiscal Statement* (EFS), which projected five balanced budgets into the future, and January 2009, when it tabled *Canada's Economic Action Plan: Budget 2009*, which then projected four deficit budgets. While the EFS stressed funding cuts and tax measures, the budget just two months later proposed the largest peace-time economic stimulus package in Canadian history. In MacKinnon's words, "how important was the prospect of a hanging by the opposition parties in explaining the radical change in the Harper government's position?"

MacKinnon notes that the government did not sufficiently justify some of its actions in the EFS or lay out the groundwork for some of its proposed policy changes, such as "modernizing" the federal pay equity regime or abolishing public subsidies to political parties, which was viewed as a threat to the opposition parties. Polls interpreted such proposals as unduly partisan. Then, as the economy turned south, the EFS seemed to reflect a lack of empathy for those who were impacted by the recession. With a rapidly deteriorating economic situation and the coalescing of the three opposition parties to block such budgetary changes from a minority government, the 2009 budget dramatically changed direction. The EFS initiatives were dropped. Instead, the budget reflected broadly based public desire for an economic stimulus budget involving a major deficit and "political stability in a time of crisis". There was little choice but to spend billions of dollars to support the auto sector, concentrated in Ontario. However, financial aid was also provided for a number of other industries, such as agriculture, forestry, shipbuilding, and the space industry, in the name of regional fairness for other parts of the country. Federal expenditures on infrastructure – a core focus of the budget – had to be cost-matched by provinces and municipal governments, which brought in a fiscal downloading aspect to the budget. And a number of popular relief measures were adopted, including funding for social housing for low-income Canadians and enhancements to EI, to elicit support in the House of Commons and, more broadly, across the country. "The prospect of defeat … taught the government that partisan games had to be set aside in favour of moderation, inclusiveness, and consensus building."

In "A Federal Budget Designed for the Times: The *Economic Action Plan* of 2009", Christopher Ragan looks at the *economic* motivation for the budget and provides some economic assessment. The immediate cause of the onset of recession leading up to the budget was the collapse of the US housing market, rising delinquencies of US sub-prime mortgages, and losses in complex investment products based on these mortgages incurred in the US financial sector. The immediate result was a seizing-up of credit markets and shortage of liquidity to the United States and other economies. With the collapse, takeover, and effective nationalization of several major financial institutions in the United States and elsewhere, a government priority became insuring the stability of the financial system and the availability of credit to the economy as a whole. Economic activity slowed down sharply in late 2008. A G20 summit in Washington agreed that monetary policy would not be sufficient to deal with the rapidly worsening economic situation, and the IMF recommended simultaneous fiscal stimulus packages in the range of 2% of each country's GDP. While the Canadian financial system had far less exposure to sub-prime mortgage-backed financial assets, Canadian households were less indebted than US households, and the Canadian federal government's debt-to-GDP ratio of 29% in 2008 was substantially lower than for most other major economies, the Canadian economy was still in a fragile situation because of its large external trade exposure during a time of global recession and the collapse of raw material commodity prices in 2008 which resulted in a dramatic decline in Canada's terms of trade.

Ragan focuses his comments on the budget itself around three broad themes: financial market measures, the need for fiscal stimulus, and the importance of maintaining fiscal prudence. A set of measures, called the Extraordinary Financial Framework, sought to improve the Canadian financial system's operations and restore credit availability to the economy — for example, by CMHC buying up to $125 billion of insured mortgages from Canadian banks, thus improving their liquidity. Fiscal stimulus was designed to help assist those most likely to bear the brunt of the recession, to make use of measures with larger short-run fiscal multipliers, and to be as timely as possible through emphasis on shovel ready infrastructure projects. Ideally projects would be completed within the two-year time frame, so that such expenditures were reversible once recovery set in. The fiscal cost to the federal budget was estimated to be $22.7 billion in 2009-10 and $17.2 billion in 2010-11. And to protect some of the most vulnerable individuals, a set of tax and transfer changes were instituted, such as doubling the tax relief provided by the WITB and extending the maximum EI benefit period by five weeks. Overall, the budget projected an increase in the federal government's debt-to-GDP ratio to 32% by the end of 2010–11 and thereafter a slow decline. In Ragan's view, the government

> therefore designed a budget that focused on financial-market measures aimed at restoring the flow of credit, infrastructure spending aimed at dampening the magnitude of the recession, and targeted tax breaks and EI changes aimed at protecting those Canadians most vulnerable to the effects of the economic downturn.

The next three papers in this volume examine in more detail the analytics of economic stimulus objectives and simulated fiscal and economic impacts of the 2009 federal budget.

William Scarth takes a more analytical approach in "Stabilization Policy Debates: Assessing the Case for Fiscal Stimulus", and outlines the economic arguments for fiscal stimulus, the channels by which fiscal stimulus measures can operate and the economic environments in which stimulus measures are more or less effective. Scarth begins by examining the economy's self-correction mechanism and the role of monetary policy within the classical tradition in economics. He finds that when a zero interest rate is binding, monetary policy and quantitative or credit easing may not be sufficiently effective to stabilize the macro economy. This provides a rationale for Keynesian-type fiscal policy to help stimulate the economy. He then considers the operation of fiscal policy and the degree to which it may have only limited effect because of possible crowding-out of private sector expenditures. Once one takes account of how fiscal stimulus measures are financed, he finds that Keynesian stimulus expenditures result in short-run gain for longer-run pain in that the current recession is made smaller, but the subsequent recovery occurs at a slower pace than it would have in the absence of such stimulus. He thinks that the one-year government expenditure multiplier during a world-wide recessionary period is about 1.5. He concludes then "that fiscal policy can make some contribution to combating today's recession, and so a prudent government would embrace fiscal stimulus".

In "PBO Perspectives on Budget 2009", Chris Matier and Stephen Tapp provide analysis from the Parliamentary Budget Office (PBO) of impacts of the 2009 federal budget. According to the PBO, the budget was indeed designed essentially for economic stimulus purposes following the guiding principles that measures taken would be timely, targeted and temporary. It sought to meet Canada's G20 commitment to provide fiscal stimulus of around 2% of GDP and to enhance the availability of credit within a stable financial system in Canada. The budget proposed $39.9 billion of federal stimulus measures, to be matched by $11.7 billion in provincial and municipal leveraged contributions, for a total of $51.6 billion in incremental initiatives over the two years. These measures were estimated in the budget to increase real GDP by 1.9% and employment by 1.1% by the end of 2010. The budget also predicted a return to a federal budget surplus position by the end of the 2013-14 fiscal year.

Some of the PBO budget simulation analyses, however, show different results. The PBO projects continuing budget deficits beyond 2013-14 because of less optimistic assumptions, particularly with respect to revenue projections. They feel that the degree of stimulus incorporated into the budget may be overstated in part because it is contingent on matching expenditures of the other levels of governments. The PBO does find the stimulus measures broadly consistent with the three guiding principles of the budget, though in the past, approximately one-third of announced infrastructure funding does not get spent and lapses. They also remark that, historically, recessions caused by financial crises are generally deeper and have slower recovery periods than typical post-war, inventory- or trade-related recessions. So the Canadian economy could remain below its potential output for an extended period. The paper looks at several longer-run considerations and whether Canada's automatic stabilizers have become less effective since the last major recession due to personal and corporate tax rate cuts and to changes to EI and equalization programs. The authors conclude that the heightened interest in the budget's stimulus measures offers a great opportunity to improve budget transparency, oversight, and reporting on the budget initiatives to Parliament on an ongoing basis.

In the next contribution, Robert Fairholm asks, "Is Shovel Ready Good Enough?" Fairholm begins by reviewing major features of the economic crisis facing Canada by early 2009, such as the IMF estimate that the advanced economies were facing a 7.5% rate of drop in output in the final quarter of 2008 and the implications of falling commodity prices. In an environment where the effectiveness of monetary policy is blunted by seized-up credit markets and interest rates that are close to zero, fiscal stimulus becomes an important policy tool. Fairholm then reviews the broad numbers of the budget's stimulus action plan. He finds that only half the stimulus measures help to raise productive capacity, productivity, or labour mobility, and that the beneficiaries of these measures are overly concentrated in the construction sector despite the widespread pain being experienced across the economy.

Fairholm examines two questions: is the stimulus provided in the budget enough, and is the construction-sector focus of the stimulus package the right type of stimulus? He finds the construction-related output multipliers in the budget similar to results from his own macro model, but the stimulus initiatives may take longer to be implemented and impact the economy. Whether the budget is providing sufficient stimulus to counter the economic shocks it is facing depends on the size of the external shocks and the effectiveness of monetary policy undertaken. From his economic model, he concludes that

> If monetary policy is 50% effective and the external shock is worth 3.2% of GDP, then the federal fiscal stimulus (plus [provincial and municipal] and consumer leverage) based on the budget's estimates and monetary stimulus to date will offset this shock. … If monetary policy is less effective or the shock is bigger, then the economy will suffer a significant contraction. If consumers and business pull back and fiscal stimulus is only 80% effective, then fiscal and monetary policy will not be able to offset [a larger IMF-estimated global shock of 5.2% of GDP].

With respect to the second question, Fairholm argues that preferred measures are those that stimulate the economy more in the short run and that encourage long-term economic growth. Because of the widespread shocks from the recession, he argues for a more diversified portfolio of spending across a range of sectors. In terms of short-run GDP multipliers and employment multipliers by industry, those for construction and manufacturing are relatively low on the list, whereas those for education and child care (outside the home) are at or near the top of the list. Thus, a broader range of stimulus measures focused more on education and child care spending would have larger short-run effects than concentrating on construction as well as providing longer-run human capital benefits.

The next two chapters of this volume address tax policy changes in the budget. In "Tax Policy Changes in the 2009 Budget: Much Ado About Stimulus?", Lindsay Tedds describes the tax policy changes in the budget, their perceived economic effects, and more specifically their stimulus effects on the economy. She looks at, respectively, changes to stimulate business investment and housing construction, and to help Canadians and household spending stimulus. Measures to stimulate business investment include raising the small business tax threshold (in effect, reducing their average tax rate and helping to support the growth of small businesses), extending the mineral exploration tax credit for an additional year, temporarily increasing the capital cost allowance rates for computer equipment and systems software and for production machinery and equipment (in order to help boost long-term productivity and growth), and permanently eliminating tariffs on importing machinery and equipment (with the same objective in mind). The estimated budgetary cost of such measures is $1.0 billion by the end of 2010–11.

Measures to stimulate housing construction include introducing a temporary home renovation tax credit to undertake new renovation projects and to help offset the decline in the new housing construction, increasing the maximum that can be withdrawn from RRSPs to purchase or build a home without incurring a tax liability, and introducing a non-refundable first-time home buyers' tax credit. The budget estimated the cost to the government of these sets of measures at $3.4 billion by the end of the 2010–11 fiscal year. Finally, the measures to provide income protection for Canadians to stimulate household spending include freezing EI premium rates for two years, increasing the personal exemption amount and lower threshold levels of the personal income tax (PIT) system, increasing the non-refundable age credit for seniors in the PIT, raising the threshold levels at which the Canada Child Tax Benefit and the National Child Benefit Supplement are clawed back, and increasing the available tax credit under the WITB program. The estimated budgetary cost of these measures by the end of 2010–11 is $9.0 billion. Tedds concludes overall that the first three business investment measures are relatively inefficient at doing this job and accelerating the corporate tax rate cuts would have been better. In her view, the housing construction measures are likely to have a low "bang for the buck", and the measures to help Canadians and stimulate personal spending offer little help to the homeless and the non-working poor, including many single mothers.

Kevin Milligan's contribution in "What Have Four Conservative Budgets Done to Personal Income Taxes?" tries to identify patterns and directions in tax policy over the four years of Harper Conservative budgets for 2006 to 2009. He finds, first of all, very little change in the ratio of income taxes to personal income over this period or in personal income tax share of total federal tax revenue. This stability may have arisen because the increase in taxes that are levied on higher incomes within a progressive income tax system may have been offset by the increases in tax credits that have occurred. A key feature of tax policy over this period, though, has been the incrementalism of income tax changes centred around the introduction of many relatively small non-refundable tax credits, such as for public transit use or child fitness. These add to the complexity and administrative costs of the tax system without making it more efficient since lost revenue has to be raised elsewhere. Using his Canadian Tax and Credit Simulator package, Milligan looks at who has benefited from these accumulated income tax changes. He finds that average tax rates across individual income levels show very little change between 2005 and 2009. However, he does find quite strong changes by family composition and senior status.

> The largest identifiable beneficiaries of the Conservative income tax policy have been families with children, and specifically those with a stay-at-home parent. In addition, [he] found a large gain for seniors with substantial pension income as a result of the introduction of pension income-splitting in 2007. Whether these changes to personal income taxes represent an improvement to the Canadian economy will depend on one's assessment of the merits of shifting the tax burden in these directions.

The next two papers in this volume examine the implications of the budget for intergovernmental fiscal arrangements in Canada, again from a longer-run perspective. The contribution by Tracy Snoddon and Paul Hobson considers "Cost-Sharing and Federal-Provincial Fiscal Relations". They point out that, recently, there has been a resurgence of federal-provincial cost-sharing arrangements around infrastructure spending, to the extent that such infrastructure funding should now be viewed as a new fourth pillar of Canadian fiscal federalism, after Equalization, the Canada Health Transfer and Canada Social Transfer, and the federal-provincial Tax Collection Agreements. The authors present a brief history of cost-sharing and block grant fiscal arrangements in Canada, with a focus on health and welfare transfers and major infrastructure funding. In contrast to the previous Paul Martin government's focus on health transfer arrangements, the current Harper government has focused more on changes to the Canada Social Transfer to help support post-secondary education and child care.

The 2007 Harper budget instituted the Building Canada Plan for major infrastructure funding of $33 billion over seven years, with both provincial/territorial and municipal components, and more recent budgets have expanded on it. For example, the 2009 budget accelerated planned provincial/territorial base funding for infrastructure for the three years 2011-12 through 2013-14 to the more immediate period 2009-10 through 2010-11. It also set up a $4 billion Infrastructure Stimulus Fund for shovel-ready shared-cost projects with the provinces for 2009-10 and 2010-11. The authors review economic rationales for (closed-ended) matching infrastructure grants rather than the block grant under fiscal arrangements. They note, though, that matching grants for infrastructure may be difficult to scale up in a short time frame, some provincial or local governments may have difficulty finding funds for matching-grant initiatives in a recession, and matching grants are now being focused on infrastructure rather than on health or people.

In "The Evolution of Federal Transfers Since the O'Brien Report", Michael Smart reviews the major changes to federal transfer programs since 2007, concentrating on recent changes to the federal-provincial Equalization program, and examines arguments for and against the changes. Because of its hit in the recent recession, Ontario – for the first time – qualifies for Equalization payments beginning in 2009–10. The potential exposure to a major increase in these expenditures led the federal government to impose a ceiling on the rate of growth of total Equalization payments, such that they do not exceed the annual growth rate of nominal GDP (expected at 4.2% for 2009–10). This major change in effect converted the Equalization program from an open-ended grant to a closed-ended one, so that the program is now essentially similar to the closed-ended Fixed Framework for Equalization in place under the previous government during 2004–06. Smart concludes that

> The entry of Ontario into the program has the potential to change political support for Equalization as well – arguably, the median voter now lives in a receiving province. ... The federal budget will be in deficit for several years to come and the return to budget balance is likely to be a struggle. With major transfers to the provinces approaching 25% of federal program spending, it is not difficult to imagine that fiscal retrenchment will involve further restraint on transfers. ... Grappling with fiscal arrangements in coming years is therefore going to require decisions about the relative priority of vertical versus horizontal grants, and an articulation of what each of the grants is intended to achieve.

The other major change to the Equalization program is the change in treatment of natural resource revenues under the Equalization formula confirmed in the 2009 budget. Following recommendations of the O'Brien panel, the Equalization formula in 2007 included only 50% of provinces' natural resource revenues in the formula's definition of a province's "fiscal capacity", and a fiscal capacity cap was introduced to ensure that a receiving province's fiscal capacity would not end up being raised above that of any non-receiving province. The 2009 changes to the Equalization program involved redefining the cap in terms of the average fiscal capacity of the receiving provinces. The effect was to markedly reduce the role of resource revenues in actual Equalization payments. The budget also instituted a floor payment whereby no province would face a year-over-year fall in Equalization payments.

The next three papers examine the 2009 budget in terms of social policy changes and Canada's stretched social safety net.

In "Social Investments, Economic Returns", Sherri Torjman and Ken Battle characterize the budget as The Red-Ink Budget of 2009, as it was the first in more than a decade to run a deficit. They note that social programs in times of recession both provide fiscal stimulus to the economy as well as act as shock absorbers or automatic stabilizers, particularly in the form of income security benefits going to lower-income households. The authors organize their comments around the headings of income security and social infrastructure. In terms of income security, they comment on changes to a number of programs in the budget. The WITB, aimed at the working poor was enhanced by increasing benefits and broadening its eligibility at its top threshold. But the WITB still will not reach all working-poor Canadians. Positive changes were made to the Canada Child Tax Benefit and the National Child Benefit Supplement, but the increases were very modest, and the poorest families received no gains. No initiatives were introduced in the area of child care and child care services, a major lacking of the budget in the view of the authors. As already mentioned in previous papers, the budget also made a number of changes to personal income taxes, with the effect of slightly reducing average tax rates. But the size of the tax breaks increases with higher incomes, and the poorest Canadians get no benefits since they are already below the tax-paying threshold. With respect to EI, the authors point out how this program has become markedly less generous since major reforms in the 1990s, to the point where EI coverage of the unemployed has fallen from 83% in 1990 to only 43% in 2008, its lowest level in more than 40 years, and maximum regular weekly benefits have also declined in real terms. The 2009 budget froze EI contribution rates for 2009 and 2010 and introduced some training initiatives. Torjman and Battle argue, however, that it would have been more useful to allow more unemployed workers to qualify for the EI benefits in the first place. "EI coverage has shrunk to the [point where] EI can hardly be billed any more as the viable 'social insurance' that it originally was intended to be."

With respect to social infrastructure, Torjman and Battle strongly applaud the government's investment in affordable housing as a centrepiece of the 2009 budget. However, the commitment of $1 billion over the next two years is viewed as only a one-time initiative. The large infrastructure component of the budget is certainly appropriate in light of economic recession, but the authors would have preferred a greater focus on the social side of such stimulus investment, such as affordable housing, schools, libraries, and recreation centres that contribute to community well-being. Overall, the authors conclude that

> While the 2009 Budget made some important social policy investments, it could have directed more assistance to low- and modest-income households in order to have an even stimulative punch.

In "Canada's Declining Social Safety Net: EI Reform and the 2009 Budget", Lars Osberg looks at Canada's EI system in comparative perspective (historically and compared to other developed countries) and comments on how well the provisions of the 2009 budget address the concerns raised. He remarks how much rarer it is for the unemployed in this recession to receive EI benefits than in the previous recession, where the recipiency rate in 2009 is only about half that in 1990. This means that a larger portion of cyclical earnings risk is being borne by individuals and families, and this will be especially so for disadvantaged Canadians. It also means that more families in this recession will have to rely on social assistance (SA), offloading a larger share of the burden of maintaining the social safety net onto the provinces. Furthermore, over the last two decades, the federal government has generally shifted training expenditures from the Consolidated Revenue Fund into the UI/EI account and expanded funding of maternity, sickness, and compassionate benefits within the EI system so that by 2009, only about 60% of EI expenditures actually represent a cyclical social safety net. Thus, the role of EI as an automatic stabilizer has been seriously eroded.

As mentioned by others, the 2009 budget did make some EI changes in acknowledgement of the current recession – such as extending the maximum duration of EI benefits as a temporary measure, freezing EI premium rates for two years, and enhancing EI-financed training expenditures by $2 billion over two years – but Osberg views these measures as "distinctly tepid" in light of a worldwide synchronized recession. Neither of these latter two measures addresses lost wages as a result of the recession. He concludes

> In access, benefit duration, and income replacement levels, EI in Canada is far below OECD norms and the levels of Canadian unemployment insurance in past recessions. Budget 2009 did little to change that. Eligibility and benefit levels remained unchanged, while benefit duration was increased by only five weeks.

In "Ending Poverty Through Child Benefits: Hitting the Wall?", Frances Woolley looks at the direction of social policy in Canada since the Conservatives took office in 2006. She notes that the National Child Benefit (NCB) program had been the cornerstone of social policy under the Liberals. But the Conservatives let the NCB stagnate and focused instead on a Universal Child Care Benefit (UCCB) of $1,200 per child under the age of six (set up in the 2006 budget) and the WITB as a form of wage subsidy program (also set up in 2006 and enriched in the 2009 budget). Woolley argues that these major initiatives illustrate that, under the Conservatives, child policy and income support policy are now being separated. Child policy reflects a shift "towards universality of benefits, a trend toward universal recognition of the cost of children: every Canadian child now generates some tax benefits for his or her parent(s)". The WITB provides greater incentives to work in the labour market and provides the same benefits, independent of presence or number of children.

> The policies introduced by the Conservative government are consistent with a belief in the importance of personal responsibility, a social conservatism that values intact families, parental child care, and a concern with men's social roles.

Such policies bring greater horizontal equity within the tax system and offer potential efficiency benefits – another Conservative objective stated in previous budgets.

Woolley then offers an extensive critique of both the UCCB and the WITB. The UCCB provides potential benefits to all families with children. But the way it is introduced within the personal income tax system, higher-income families benefit more while lowest-income families get no benefits, and one-earner two-parent families benefit substantially more than other types of family structures. The fact that the UCCB is taxable for the lower earner in a household means that for a one-earner two-parent family, there are no taxes on UCCB payments. The design of the UCCB thus reduces the tax system's "discrimination against single-income families with children" and helps support the Conservative preference for parental child care. The WITB provides incentives for low-income Canadians to work, but it does not "kick in" until labour market earnings reach $3,000, and it is not generous enough to move an average low-income single worker out of poverty. She remarks that "One could see integration of the WITB with other social programs as a long-term social policy goal".

In "The 2009 Federal Budget and the Environment: Missed Opportunities and Misguided Directions", Nancy Olewiler assesses the 2009 budget from an environmental perspective. She focuses her comments on four areas: infrastructure investment, energy efficiency, greenhouse gases (GHGs) and climate change, and meeting environmental targets. By way of background, the major seven-year Building Canada Plan infrastructure investment program of the 2007 budget had a "Clean Environment" component and extended the Gas Tax Fund (GTF) of federal fuel excise tax revenue to be allocated to provinces and municipalities to support environment infrastructure projects. The 2008 budget extended funding for public transit as a one-time expenditure and made the latter fund permanent at $2 billion annually. In the 2009 budget, the keystone stimulus-driven infrastructure program could indeed include environmentally friendly projects such as public transit and "clean energy" projects, but only so long as they were shovel-ready. The budget did target the environment by setting up two funds at $1 billion each spread over five years: a Clean Infrastructure Fund and a Clean Energy Fund, where the latter is targeted at large-scale carbon capture and storage technology. The budget also included a number of small initiatives, such as continuation of homeowner grants for the Eco-energy Retrofit program and funding toward safe drinking water for First Nations.

In assessing the environmental contributions of the budget, Olewiler remarks that they are worthwhile as far as they go, but many programs would be much more effective if they were combined with an environmental pricing scheme as well, and some initiatives such as cleaning up Canada's many toxic sites were simply a "drop in the bucket" compared to what is needed. The focus of the budget's Economic Action Plan on shovel-ready projects means that it is not clear how much funding will go to environmental projects, and the Action Plan does not provide any contribution to ongoing operating expenses of public transit systems. She notes that energy pricing in Canada does not include associated environmental costs. If the government were to introduce a pricing scheme for carbon or GHGs, for example, incentives for use would be better aligned to reflect such costs, GHG emissions would be reduced, and various energy-related subsidies could be scrapped. The budget has not done this. The government has not brought in explicit initiatives to fully price and regulate GHG emissions. She concludes

> What is missing in Budget 2009 is the sense of environmental leadership in the areas of climate change and protecting our valuable natural capital. Environmental initiatives are present basically only if

they are part of infrastructure spending and programs to enhance energy efficiency.

The final two chapters of this volume take on a "big think" perspective on the budget and offer suggestions for the directions or issues that federal policy really needs to address as long-run priorities. The first is by Robin Boadway on "Budget Priorities for Canada: Time for Some Big Ideas?" He notes that recent federal budgets have not really addressed the big challenges ahead, and he argues that it is now time for some "transformative and visionary policy changes". He identifies five major fiscal challenges for which he feels policy options need to be considered. The first challenge is income inequality and poverty in Canada, as inequality and poverty rates are rising and are now above the OECD average. He suggests that the tax-transfer system could be made more distributionally effective, by emphasizing targeting more and universality less as guiding principles. All tax credits could also be made refundable and income-tested, thus converting the federal tax system into a negative income tax vehicle. The second challenge is income tax reform. Here he points to the potential benefits of a dual income tax system, introduced by the Nordic countries, where different tax schedules apply to capital income and to earnings and transfer income. This way, a progressive rate schedule could apply to the latter and a flat rate tax to the former.

The third challenge identified by Boadway is the encouragement of human capital investment in today's knowledge economy, especially by disadvantaged persons. To this end, he recommends a much enhanced Canada Student Loan program to help address equality of opportunity objectives and including a system of income contingent loans to help address uninsured risk and liquidity constraints. His fourth challenge involves Canada's huge natural resources and their uneven location across provinces, resulting in large horizontal fiscal imbalances among provinces. One approach might be to integrate the system of social transfers (CHT and CST) with the Equalization system so that federal social transfer payments are contingent on provincial fiscal capacity. Boadway's fifth challenge involves the need for bringing about a nationwide scheme for carbon pricing. Such a scheme could be based on a carbon tax or on a cap-and-trade system, and Boadway identifies a number of issues involved in implementing either scheme. He ends with a plea for basing policy on research and recommendations on basic principles rather than on short-term political considerations.

The final paper is a "big think" contribution by Thomas Courchene, aptly titled "Looking Forward: Some Immodest Proposals". In it, he remarks on the budget transition from surpluses to deficits to "fiscalamity" in such a short time. A signal feature of the budget is its downloading of deficits onto the provinces. This operates through the federal stimulus effect, requiring major shared-cost provincial involvement, and through "the impending fiscal nightmare for the provinces when these unemployed Canadians exhaust their EI benefits and are forced to turn to provincial welfare". Courchene argues that the stimulus package in the 2009 budget was too "shovel heavy" and should have been more directed to investing in human capital rather than physical capital. The infrastructure program does not focus enough on those areas that will lead to success in a knowledge-based economic environment. In the United States and Australia, corresponding stimulus packages had major education and health components. Indeed, Prime Minister Paul Martin recognized that the areas of national success in the new global order increasingly fall within provincial jurisdiction. But the 2009 federal budget makes no effort to address this.

Courchene then offers comments on rethinking three major policy areas: climate change and carbon pricing, enhancing horizontal fiscal equity, and EI. He feels that the Clean Energy Fund in the 2009 budget focused primarily on carbon capture and storage, but this should have been part of a broader portfolio of green policy initiatives. He suggests three areas where Canada should play a lead advocate role in the run-up to the upcoming Kyoto II conference. Second, in order to introduce more horizontal equity into the Equalization program, Courchene also suggests bringing the federal-provincial cash transfer programs (CHT and CST) into the Equalization framework so that these transfers become revenue-tested based on provincial fiscal capacity. He refers to this as overarching horizontal equity, or OHE for short. Third, Courchene argues that "Canada is unable and will continue to be unable to develop a state-of-the-art social envelope suitable for knowledge-based society unless and until we undertake a fundamental reform of EI". He discusses four tenets such reform should take:

- returning EI to insurance principles;
- introducing a negative income tax (NIT) or guaranteed annual income (GAI) by converting personal and spousal amounts and credits into refundable and income-tested benefits within the federal income tax system;
- increasing access to EI benefits; and
- increasing labour-force participation incentives by integrating the WITB with the tax-back provisions of the NIT/GAI.

Courchene concludes

I labelled the budget "shovel heavy" and failing on the transformative front. The massive stimulus package was a once-in-a-lifetime opportunity to chart a new course and embrace the dictates of a knowledge-based economy and society. By focusing on boards and mortar infrastructure, we … riveted our attention on what worked in the previous paradigm.

Session One
BACKGROUND CONTEXT AND MAJOR THEMES

THE PROSPECT OF A HANGING?
The Political Context for the 2009 Federal Budget

Janice MacKinnon, University of Saskatchewan

Introduction

A lot can happen in two months in politics. However, it is hard to find another time in Canadian politics when a government has done such a dramatic about-face as the government of Prime Minister Stephen Harper did between November 27, 2008, and January 27, 2009. On November 27, 2008, the Harper government released *Protecting Canada's Future: Economic and Fiscal Statement* (EFS), which projected five balanced budgets and outlined some cost-cutting measures to help achieve them. Two months later, the same government tabled *Canada's Economic Action Plan: Budget 2009*, which projected four deficit budgets and a broad array of spending measures and tax cuts that represented the largest stimulus package in peace-time Canada. What can account for the dramatic shift in the Harper government's position? What role did politics play in the about-face by the government and in the choices made in the budget? In this paper, I will discuss the political context for the 2009 budget by considering the factors that caused the government to change course and the role played by politics in some of the choices made in the budget. A key question is: how important was the prospect of a hanging by the opposition parties in explaining the radical change in the Harper government's position?

The Economic and Fiscal Statement

The differences in the content and language of the EFS and the 2009 budget are striking. The EFS painted an ambiguous picture of Canada's position in a deteriorating global economy. The document conceded the challenges, but added important qualifiers. It stated that "the financial crisis has sparked a global recession", but only conceded that Canada is in a "technical recession", meaning that in the last quarter of 2008 and the first quarter of 2009, Canada experienced negative growth (Finance, 2008a, 10). The EFS acknowledged that in a deteriorating global economy, Canada would face three major challenges: tighter credit, declining export markets, and falling commodity prices. At the same time, the document celebrated the strength of Canada's banks and the relative fiscal strength of its governments, households, and corporations. The EFS stated that there was significant uncertainty and volatility about the economic future; it pointed out that forecasts for nominal GDP growth ranged from -2.5 to +2.5%, and it conceded that the risks for the future were on the "downside" (ibid., 43, 10). At the same time, the document attempted to buy time for the government: as well as committing to implementing the government's long-term plan to enhance the competitiveness of the Canadian economy, the EFS stated that the government would monitor the fiscal and economic situation and consult with the provinces (ibid., 9).

The G20 Summit in Washington, D.C. was a reference point for both the EFS and the 2009 budget, but there was a dramatic difference in the G20 commitments that were referenced. The EFS cited Canada's G20 "responsibilities to ensure financial sector stability" and "strengthen our world-leading financial system in line with our G20 commitments" (ibid., 46, 9). These parts of the G20 Statement were used to support the government's decision to focus on strengthening Canada's financial system and enhancing the availability of credit. The EFS outlined past actions taken by the government and the Bank of Canada to support Canada's financial institutions and ensure continued access to affordable credit. Future actions announced in the EFS included providing temporary relief to seniors with Registered Retirement Income Funds and to federally regulated private pension plans and enhancing the credit available to business through two federal Crown corporations, the Export Development Bank, and the Business Development Bank of Canada. The government also took the opportunity to make the case for reform of Canada's securities regulation, arguing that having 13 securities regulators was "cumbersome and unwieldy when quick and decisive action is needed" (ibid., 75).

As well as focusing on strengthening Canada's financial system and ensuring access to credit, the EFS emphasized "maintaining and bolstering Canada's solid fundamentals" and protecting its "hard-won fiscal advantage" (ibid., 6). It trumpeted the fact that Canada was in the strongest fiscal position of any G7 country, and the government took credit for reducing the country's debt by $37 billion in three years. However, the current fiscal and economic challenges meant that there would be deficits over the next three years unless the government acted; in fact, the EFS conceded that even with government action, surpluses were "not assured" (ibid., 46).

Rather than acknowledging that deficits were inevitable, the EFS outlined measures to cut expenses. The document confirmed that equalization would be capped and its growth tied to increases in nominal GDP. The EFS also stated that departments would be expected to manage spending and there would be ongoing strategic reviews of departmental spending with the goal of enhancing efficiency. Moreover, department and corporate assets were to be reviewed to determine whether some assets should be sold. Another measure to cut costs was the plan to use legislation to limit salary increases for public servants, members of Parliament, cabinet ministers, and senators. Finally, pay equity was to be changed to make it less expensive, and the subsidy to political parties was to be eliminated as of April 1, 2009. After factoring in these changes, the EFS projected balanced budgets for the next five years.

While the EFS stressed spending cuts, balanced budgets, and measures to improve access to credit, it said little about stimulating the economy. Previously announced tax cuts were touted as examples of stimulus, and there was a commitment to expedite already announced infrastructure funding and to support workers needing retraining and communities hit especially hard by the downturn. Beyond these measures, there was only a vague commitment to "monitor the economic situation" and "continue to take necessary actions to support the economy, balancing the economic benefit of such actions with the impact on the fiscal situation" (ibid., 9).

Assessment of the Economic and Fiscal Statement

Adopting a "wait and see" approach in November 2008 could have been justified on various grounds. A major economic unknown was whether the global and Canadian downturn would stabilize or worsen. Watching the trend line for a few more weeks was a reasonable strategy for the government. One political unknown was what a change in administration in the United States from President George W. Bush to President Barack Obama would mean. A case could have been made that it was wise for the Canadian government to wait and find out the approach that would be adopted by the new Obama administration. To cite one example, if the Obama administration provided financial support for the ailing Canadian-American auto sector, then Canada would have little choice but to follow suit or risk losing its production to the United States.

A case could also have been made for taking the time to consult with the provinces, stakeholders, and the public before acting. It could even have been argued that it made sense to tighten government spending on travel and administration so that such savings could be redirected to spending that provided better stimulus for the economy. And it might have been reasonable for politicians to set an example – as they had in the 1990s – by limiting their own salaries and benefits in difficult times.

There was also a sound case to be made for capping equalization payments and tying the increase in entitlements to growth in nominal GDP. Despite the prospect of declining federal revenues as a result of the economic downturn, the federal government maintained its commitment to increasing transfers to the provinces: the Canada Health Transfer would be increased by 6%, and the Canadian Social Transfer would rise by 3%. However, as the budget pointed out, equalization had grown by 56% since 2003-04 (Finance, 2009a, 190). The cost of the program for the federal government was not the only problem with rapidly growing equalization payments. Since Ontario has about 40% of Canadian taxpayers, about 40% of the money for equalization comes from Ontario. However, Ontario's entitlement of $347 million pales in comparison with the entitlements of provinces like Quebec, which was $8 billion, or Manitoba, at $2 billion. At a time when Ontario is reeling under the weight of recession and deficit budgets, it cannot afford to have money redistributed from its taxpayers to those in other provinces, some of which have superior social programs and are in better economic and fiscal shape.

Thus, there were sound reasons for some of the decisions in the EFS, and there were reasonable explanations for not providing immediate stimulus and focusing instead on financial institutions, access to credit, and certain kinds of spending restraint. Unfortunately, the Harper government did not make the arguments justifying its actions to the public, at least not consistently or persuasively. Another major problem with the EFS was that it reflected no empathy for Canadians suffering from the economic downturn or worried about what the future might hold. It was as if the government was oblivious to the struggles of those Canadians who were already experiencing the effects of the tough economic times.

To make matters worse, some of the decisions in the EFS reflected a phenomenon that can cause major political problems for governments: solutions without problems. That is, governments that act boldly to change policies without laying the groundwork with the public and media by outlining the problem that has to be addressed often find themselves in political trouble.

There were at least three contentious policies in the EFS that riled the opposition but did not rally public support for the government since there was no broadly based public understanding of them. The government promised to "modernize" the pay equity regime (ibid., 46). The existing approach to pay equity, which allowed pay equity complaints to be filed with the Canadian Human Rights Commission after collective agreements had been signed, was described as being "litigious, adversarial, complaints based" and expensive. Instead, the government proposed to adopt the process that existed in provinces like Ontario, which would incorporate pay equity into the collective bargaining process (ibid., 55). There was an argument to be made that settling pay equity issues outside of collective agreements led to unnecessary litigation and was an expensive way for the federal government to deal with the problem. But did the public and media understand the problem and see why it had to be addressed during an economic downturn? The opposition pounced on the proposed policy change and portrayed it as a betrayal of women's rights to equality in the workplace.

The EFS also committed the government to passing legislation to limit the annual wage increases for public servants, members of Parliament, cabinet ministers, and senators. The rationale was that public sector wage increases were higher than in the private sector, and there was a need to make them "affordable" (ibid., 54). Legislation can be used instead of collective bargaining to set public sector salaries. But was there any reason for political observers to believe that such legislation was warranted in November 2008? There had not been lengthy strikes by public sector unions that disrupted services to the public. Rather than rallying public support for the government, this proposal left the impression that the government was being heavy-handed.

One short paragraph that was inserted into the discussion of departmental restraint stated that the government intended to abolish subsidies to political parties as of April 1, 2009. Members of the public might have been bewildered by how such a policy change related to the economic downturn, but opposition parties had no doubt that the Harper government was motivated by partisanship. It is true that, since subsidies to political parties are based on the number of votes they receive, the Conservatives stood to lose the most money. But it is also true that the Conservatives are the most effective fundraisers; hence, they relied the least of all of the parties on the subsidies. On the other hand, the Liberals had not mastered the task of fundraising from individual donors, which was required after recent changes to electoral financing laws, and they depended heavily on the political subsidy, especially since the party was in significant debt. Similarly, the Bloc Québécois and, to a lesser extent, the New Democratic Party relied heavily on the subsidy for their political activities.

The Proposed Coalition

The proposal was a major threat to all three opposition parties and united them in their determination to force the government to back down. Within hours, the New Democrats and Liberals were talking to each other about defeating the government and asking the Governor General to turn over the reins of government to a coalition that would have the support of the Bloc Québécois. Though the government backtracked on its most contentious proposals within days, the coalition was announced publicly and was poised to defeat the government. The government was saved only after the Governor General agreed to the Prime Minister's request to prorogue Parliament until January, when an early budget was to be presented.

One of the reasons why the government came so close to being defeated is that it was operating on the basis of faulty political assumptions. The assumption was that the government could take a "wait and see" approach to a stimulus package and play partisan politics with the EFS since it had time on its side. From its perspective, the government had won a decisive victory in the 2008 federal election. While the Conservatives had not won a majority, the party had increased its popular vote and won 19 more seats. Just as important, the official Opposition had lost ground: the Liberals' seat count had gone from 103 to 77, and its share of the popular vote had shrunk from 30% to 26%. Moreover, the election had occurred just over six weeks before the release of the EFS.

Defeat in the House of Commons and another election did not seem possible.

Moreover, there was no reason for the government to fear a coalition. Although a coalition between the Liberals and the NDP had been mentioned during the 2008 election campaign, the idea had been rejected by the Liberal leader. Also, the math did not work for a Liberal-NDP coalition. When the 77 Liberal seats were combined with the 37 NDP seats, the resulting 114 seats left the two parties well short of a majority in the 308-seat House of Commons. Moreover, while Canadians had experience with minority governments involving two parties, the idea of three parties working together took both the Canadian government and the public completely by surprise.

The 2009 Budget

Fear for their survival might have been the initial spark that united the opposition parties, but their message to the public was the need for a stimulus package to kick-start the flagging economy and help Canadians struggling with the effects of the economic downturn. Thus, the government's task was straightforward: present a stimulus budget that would gain the support of at least one opposition party or risk defeat in the House of Commons in January.

The 2009 budget differed dramatically in its approach, its assessment of the economic problems facing Canada, and its proposed solutions. The groundwork for a less partisan, more inclusive, and consensus-based approach to the budget was laid on January 26, 2009, in the Speech from the Throne, which stated, "it is imperative that we work together, that we stand beside one another and that we strive for greater solidarity" (Speech from the Throne, 2009). The empathy for the anxieties of Canadians that was lacking in the EFS was highlighted in the budget, which acknowledged that Canadians in all regions were feeling the effects of the recession and were worried about their "jobs, their hard-earned savings and their homes" as well as being concerned about "their families, their businesses and their communities" (ibid., 9). Rather than the solutions without problems that had characterized the EFS, the budget was based on an extensive consultation process that was buttressed by the advice of a high-profile advisory committee chaired by Carole Taylor, the former Liberal finance minister from British Columbia.

Instead of hedging its bets about the severity of the economic situation, as it had done in the EFS, in the budget the government described the global economy as being "in the most synchronized recession in the post-war period", and the "ongoing financial market crisis" was considered to be the worst since the 1930s (Finance, 2009a, 14). The document also stated, "It is now clear that Canada has entered a recession" (ibid.).

The G20 was cited, but not to support measures to enhance credit, as was the case in the EFS. Instead, the government stated that its actions in the budget "fulfill Canada's commitments at the recent G20 leaders' summit to provide timely stimulus to domestic demand" (Finance, 2009b, 3). The government also claimed that the budget was fulfilling Canada's obligations to comply with the International Monetary Fund's suggestion that countries present fiscal stimulus packages equivalent to 2% of GDP. The budget claimed that the total stimulus spending in the budget, including the cost-matching funding for infrastructure programs by provincial and municipal governments, was $30 billion, or 1.9% of GDP.

Political Choices and the 2009 Budget

The budget projected four years of deficits, with a broad array of spending measures, many of which reflected political as well as economic choices. From an economic perspective, it was clear that the government would have little choice but to aid the ailing auto sector, especially after the Obama administration signalled that the Americans intended to do so. However, providing billions of dollars to an industry concentrated in one province presented a political problem for the government. Premiers like Gordon Campbell of British Columbia pointed out the regional unfairness of providing financial support for the auto industry without providing any assistance to the equally troubled forestry sector. To address the political issue of regional fairness, the budget provided financial aid for industries across Canada. There was financial support for agriculture, forestry, shipbuilding, and the space industry (Finance, 2009a, 170–174), and, in a section aptly titled "Helping All Regions Prosper", the government outlined measures to support economic development in the North (ibid., 182–186). Although the financial assistance packages to these industries may not have been justified on economic grounds, they were important in quelling potential political problems for the government.

There was also a political dimension to the $12 billion being spent over two years on infrastructure, which was the centerpiece of the Budget. The government had to find "shovel ready" projects that could begin in the upcoming construction season. Also, to reach the International Monetary Fund's target of a stimulus package equal to 2% of GDP, the government had to ensure that its funds were cost-matched by provincial and municipal governments. Moreover, it was important that the provincial and municipal governments be required to provide their share of the infrastructure funding to lessen the pressure for a continuation of the spending after the two-year deadline. For all of these reasons, the majority of the federal infrastructure projects came from lists provided by the provinces or the municipalities. The idea of a partnership among federal, provincial, and municipal governments might have had political appeal. But this also meant that the projects were more like a hodge-podge of local, traditional infrastructure projects rather than investments in the kind of infrastructure that would lay the foundations for the economy of the future.

The budget was also political in the sense that it provided relief to those in need and built upon the broadly based consensus of the pre-budget meetings by presenting measures that would be widely supported not just in the House of Commons but also among Canadians from various backgrounds and regions. There was significant funding for social housing and support for seniors, Aboriginals, and low-income Canadians. There were enhancements to Employment Insurance, more money for training, and increased support for culture. It was hard to find an interest group that did not receive some kind of assistance. Thus, in political terms, it was easy to build broadly based support for a budget that seemed to be "all things to all people".

Politics played a role in forcing the government to come out with an early consensus-based budget, and many of the choices in the budget reflected political considerations. But how significant was the role played by politics?

Explanations for the Government's About-Face

The about-face by the government was bold and unprecedented, but was it precipitated solely by the prospect of a hanging, or were there other factors that explain the dramatic shift? Shortly after the budget was released, Finance Minister Jim Flaherty argued that the government's change in approach could be explained by the rapid and dramatic deterioration of the economy. He pointed out that at the time of the EFS, forecasters were still projecting positive economic growth for Canada in 2009 (Flaherty, 2009, 5). It is true that forecasts for American, global, and Canadian growth plummeted between September 2008 and January 2009. For example, consensus survey forecasts for real Canadian GDP growth declined from 2.0% in September 2008 to 0.5% in November to -0.1% by December and -0.8% by January 2009 (Finance, 2008b, 3; Finance, 2009a, 56). With such a rapid and consistent deterioration in the economic situation, the government had little choice but to join other G20 countries and inject a jolt of stimulus into a seriously flagging economy.

Another factor explaining the government's change in direction was the historic amount of consultation that occurred in a short period of time in December 2008 and January 2009. There were meetings with the provinces, municipalities, industry groups, and Aboriginals, as well as the traditional pre-budget roundtables, and there was advice from the newly appointed advisory committee. I attended the first pre-budget round table meeting in Saskatoon on December 18, 2008. What was most surprising was that among the 20 to 30 people representing groups from Alberta, Saskatchewan, and Manitoba, there was a broad consensus that the government had to craft a stimulus budget and had no choice but to run a deficit. In fact, the group's recommendations resembled the main elements of the 2009 budget. When fiscally conservative business groups, like some of those at the December meeting in Saskatoon, were advocating a deficit budget with a stimulus package, it was easier for members of a Conservative government to believe that they could present such a budget without betraying their principles. At meeting after meeting, the government found broadly based support for significant economic stimulus and a willingness to accept a deficit budget.

Just as the economic situation was changing almost daily, so was the political one: by January, it was not clear whether defeat of the budget would represent a hanging for the Conservatives or the resurrection of their hopes for a majority government. Just as the government was surprised by the proposed coalition, so were Canadian voters, and the majority were not impressed. If solutions without problems are a major problem in politics, the idea of replacing the newly elected Conservative government with a coalition was the ultimate solution without a problem. Polls showed that many Canadians were upset with the partisan approach taken by the government in the EFS. However, for the majority of voters, the solution to the problem of a partisan government was not to hand power over to a coalition government headed by Liberal leader Stéphane Dion.

A poll done by the Strategic Counsel on December 3, 2008, found that 58% of Canadians opposed the coalition, while only 37% supported it. Other polls showed similar results. Polls also showed that if an election were held, the Conservatives would win a majority government. Opposition to the coalition was strong in Ontario but overwhelming in Western Canada, where people were angrier than they had been during the National Energy Policy. In the recent election, the Liberals had won only seven of 92 seats in Western Canada (two of these seats had been won by less than 100 votes) and had placed third, behind the NDP, in every Western province. Many in Western Canada were outraged to find that within weeks of an election in which Liberal leader Stéphane Dion had been soundly rejected by voters, especially in the West, a scheme was afoot to make him prime minister.

In light of the widespread public opposition to the coalition, especially in Western Canada, what would the Governor General have done if the government's budget had been defeated in the House of Commons in January 2009? Would she have called upon the opposition coalition to form the government and risk facing the wrath of many Canadians, or would she have agreed to the Prime Minister's request for an election, which polls showed would have been won by a substantial margin by the Conservatives? In short, by January 2009, from a strictly political perspective, the prospect of a hanging by the opposition was a less pressing concern for the government than it had been in early December.

The Prospect of a Hanging?

There is no evidence that the government contemplated taking advantage of the favourable polls by engineering an election. To do so would have been irresponsible. If the defeat of the budget had led to an election, then the country would have been plunged into uncertainty and deprived of a government that could take decisive action during the campaign. If, on the other hand, the Governor General had denied the Prime Minister's request for an election and called on the coalition to govern, then there would have been intense regional divisions and serious questions raised by some about the legitimacy of Canada's constitutional system. No responsible government could have taken Canada down either of these roads and compounded an economic crisis with a political or even a constitutional crisis.

The about-face by the government between November 2008 and January 2009 can be explained by the rapidly deteriorating economic situation, the emergence of a broadly based consensus in favour of a stimulus deficit budget and the need for economic action and political stability in a time of crisis. The prospect of a hanging was not *the* decisive factor in determining the government's approach to the economic crisis.

The old saying is that nothing concentrates the mind like the prospect of a hanging in the morning. In this sense, the coalition was effective. It forced the government to focus on the economic crisis and its effects on Canadians. Without the coalition, there probably would not have been such broadly based consultations or an early budget. The prospect of defeat, however short-lived, also taught the government that partisan games had to be set aside in favour of moderation, inclusiveness, and consensus-building.

References

Finance, Department of, Government of Canada. 2008a. *Protecting Canada's Future: Economic and Fiscal Statement*, November 27.

__________. 2008b. *Economic and Fiscal Update 2008*, December 17.

__________. 2009a. *Canada's Economic Action Plan: Budget 2009*, January 27.

__________. 2009b. *Canada's Economic Action Plan: The Budget in Brief 2009*.

Flaherty, J. 2009. "It's all about confidence" (interview with Jim Flaherty), *Policy Options* 30(3) (March).

Speech from the Throne, Government of Canada. 2009, January 26.

A FEDERAL BUDGET DESIGNED FOR THE TIMES:
The *Economic Action Plan* of 2009

Christopher Ragan, McGill University and Department of Finance

The Canadian federal budget of January 27, 2009, involved several "firsts". It was the first budget in over a decade that embodied planned deficits over a five-year forecast horizon. It was the first budget in a generation proposed by a minority government facing a genuine threat of defeat at the hands of an unusually consolidated political opposition. And it was the first federal budget in over 25 years (and maybe far more) to be presented to the House of Commons during a remarkably synchronized global economic and financial crisis.

This paper offers my assessment of the 2009 federal budget and how it was motivated by the economic context of the time. My position as the Clifford Clark Visiting Economist at the federal Department of Finance has allowed me to witness parts of the budget-making process as an insider, and in my paper, I will try to provide my take on some of the thinking and motivation for the key policy actions taken.

The paper is divided into four sections. First, I describe the global economic situation as it appeared in January 2009. As you are well aware, the current recession has its roots in events that occurred outside Canada. Reviewing these events is crucial because the global nature of the recession played an important role in shaping the government's budget actions. Second, I turn to the Canadian economic context. In many ways, the Canadian economy was in better shape than the economies of the United States and Europe. All the same, and despite what was suggested by some commentators at the time, the nature of globalization implied that any global recession would inevitably be felt in Canada.

In the third section, I turn to the budget itself and explain how the policies adopted by the government were tailored to fit the economic context. Because the budget incorporated several significant measures aimed at improving the functioning of financial markets, I argue that Budget 2009 was more than a conventional budget. I provide an interpretation of the government's chosen mix of new spending and tax measures, as well as the decision to balance the needs for short-run stimulus and long-run fiscal prudence. The fourth section contains a brief summary, including some comments regarding the actions taken by the government to ensure that the budget policies would be implemented as quickly as possible.

One final introductory comment is necessary. I intentionally avoid commenting on the political realities that the government faced during the preparation of Budget 2009. I make no claim that political considerations played either no role or even one subservient to the economic necessities; Janice MacKinnon addresses these issues directly in her paper. In what follows, I present my perspective only on how the budget reflected the *economic* context of the times.

The Global Economic Context, January 2009

The rising delinquencies of US sub-prime mortgages, caused in part by the collapse of US housing prices, was the proximate cause of the problems that emerged in the fall of 2007. Large-scale securitization of these mortgages, however, meant that the losses would not be concentrated among the initial issuers of these questionable mortgages. Nor would the losses be contained to these specific securities: financial contagion spread quickly across a range of investment products, with the result being a general seizure in credit markets. With globalized capital markets, however, the interruption in the flow of credit was not confined to the United States. What began as a US housing problem soon became a global credit crisis.

Through the summer of 2008, the perception by most policy-makers was that the fundamental problem was one of *liquidity*, even though one could not ignore the role played by some reckless financial institutions. Government policy took the approach of using targeted interventions aimed at assisting those specific institutions in trouble, with the UK nationalization of Northern Rock and the US government-assisted takeover of Bear Stearns being the most prominent examples.

On the monetary side, central banks recognized that straightforward reductions in policy interest rates were necessary but probably not sufficient for dealing with the evident lack of liquidity. The counterparty risks associated with the uncertain location and quality of what we now call "toxic assets" had led to a collapse in the credit market and to a significant increase in corporate spreads. Any attempt to increase the flow of credit through interest-rate reductions would thus be ineffective so long as the monetary pipes remained plugged. Central banks therefore began implementing a series of targeted and less conventional (and sterilized) policies aimed not so much at reducing interest rates (or increasing the money supply) but at unclogging these monetary pipes and thus restoring the flow of credit.

By the end of September, however, it became clear that the real problem was one of *systemic stability*. Even financial institutions once viewed as solvent were threatened by the failure of others that were either sufficiently large or sufficiently "interconnected" or both. With the effective nationalization of Fannie Mae and Freddie Mac; the Fed's bail-out of AIG; the collapse or takeovers of Lehman Brothers, Washington Mutual and Wachovia; and the conversion of the remaining investment banks to "ordinary" commercial banks; the US financial system was dramatically transformed virtually overnight. The financial carnage radiated outward from the United States to envelope most of the developed world.

Large-scale re-capitalization of financial institutions then became a government priority, both in Europe and in the United States. Debate raged about the best way to accomplish this re-capitalization. One option involved governments purchasing a significant equity position in the companies, perhaps even a controlling interest; another involved governments purchasing the toxic assets from the institutions and concentrating them in a "bad bank", much as had been done in the United States with the Resolution Trust Company following the savings and loan crisis in the mid-1980s.

Since the middle of 2007, it has become commonplace to hear economists speak of the financial markets separately from the "real" economy, almost as if the former are merely a sideshow to the latter. I admit to being puzzled by this language. Nobody would ever suggest that the markets for labour or raw materials could be separated from the "real" economy, so why a separation for financial markets? And if there has ever been an illustration of how financial markets are an integral part of the overall economy, and how credit is a crucial input to the production process, surely it is the events of the last 18 months.

With the banking sector reeling, the "shadow" (i.e., non-bank) financial system seizing up, and stock markets collapsing, it should surprise nobody that the financial crisis quickly affected production and employment. And given the global nature of financial markets, it is also unsurprising that the economic slowdown occurred globally (see Figure 1). Indeed, the remarkable synchronicity of the various national recessions is testimony to the centrality of financial markets generally, and the flow of credit specifically, in the smooth operation of modern economies.

Central banks, especially the US Federal Reserve, began to respond in a much more aggressive manner. The financial world watched in awe as the size of the Federal Reserve's balance sheet doubled in just a few months. With policy rates near zero and the pace of the economic decline increasing, the terms "quantitative easing" and "credit easing" soon appeared in the lexicons of economists and policy-makers. Would it soon be necessary elsewhere to directly purchase financial assets with freshly printed money, thus fighting against the financial sector's panic and the

Figure 1: World Economic Growth

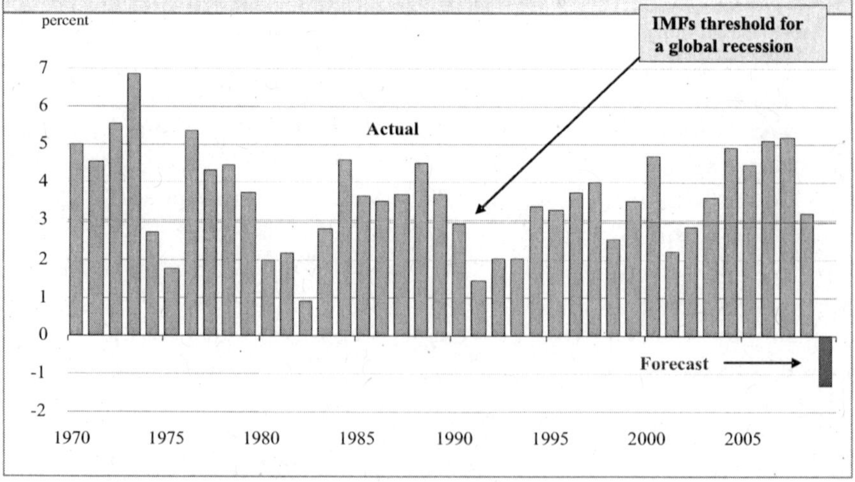

Note: World real GDP growth on a purchasing-power parity basis.
Source: International Monetary Fund *World Economic Outlook*, April 2009.

associated collapse in the money multiplier? Central banks began discussing what such a policy approach might look like, whether it would be necessary, and whether it would be effective at stimulating the economy.

As global economic activity slowed sharply in the fall of 2008, however, it was becoming clear that monetary policy – even in its more creative and aggressive forms – would be insufficient to deal with the global recession. First, at the heart of the economic problem was an overly indebted household and business sector, especially in the United States, but also in other developed countries. Second, the speed and magnitude of the economic slowdown, combined with the shattering of the financial sector, had led to a massive decline in consumer and business confidence. For both reasons, lower interest rates and more accessible credit were unlikely to be sufficient to restore aggregate demand. Something else would be needed.

To make matters worse, there was a growing recognition of two facts. First, based on historical experience from around the world, recessions associated with financial crises tend to be both deeper and more protracted than more "usual" recessions. Second, the extent to which this recession was synchronized across countries suggested that one of the standard channels of economic recovery – exports – would not be available this time round. After all, if *all* economies are experiencing roughly the same scale of recession, who is available to pull others out of the downturn through an increase in their own domestic demand?

The global and synchronized nature of both the financial crisis and the economic slowdown led to a remarkable international effort to design a broadly coordinated policy response. At the first-ever G20 leaders' summit in Washington in November 2008, there was agreement that monetary policy would be insufficient for dealing with the growing recession. The IMF had recommended the *simultaneous* adoption of fiscal stimulus packages in the range of 2% of GDP, and the G20 leaders accepted this recommendation, recognizing that a simultaneous fiscal expansion would provide greater stimulus than would unilateral action because of the reduction in import leakages. Furthermore, the leaders agreed to take whatever actions would be necessary to stabilize the financial system and also to have their countries work together to improve financial-market regulations to prevent the recurrence of such dramatic financial crises in the future.

It is worth emphasizing the level of uncertainty among economists and policy-makers in late 2008 regarding both the scale and the pace of the then coming global recession. In the summer of 2008, most forecasts still showed healthy GDP growth for a large selection of countries. By October, these forecasts had been revised downward to show slower growth, but still predicted no recession for the near future. By Christmas, however, the forecasts showed deep recessions across the developed world (see Figure 2). Many economists were sufficiently shaken by the speed of the economic deterioration that they were nervous just opening their morning newspapers for fear of what other shoes might have dropped during the night. One could easily feel this anxiety within the Department of Finance.

The Canadian Economic Context, January 2009

During the fall of 2008, there was some confusion surrounding the extent to which Canada would be caught up in the global financial and economic crisis. While Canada clearly had some advantages over other countries, it was equally clear that our links to the global economy would transmit both the financial-market events and the "real" slowdown into the Canadian economy.

Figure 2: Mean of Private-Sector Forecasts for 2009 Real GDP Growth

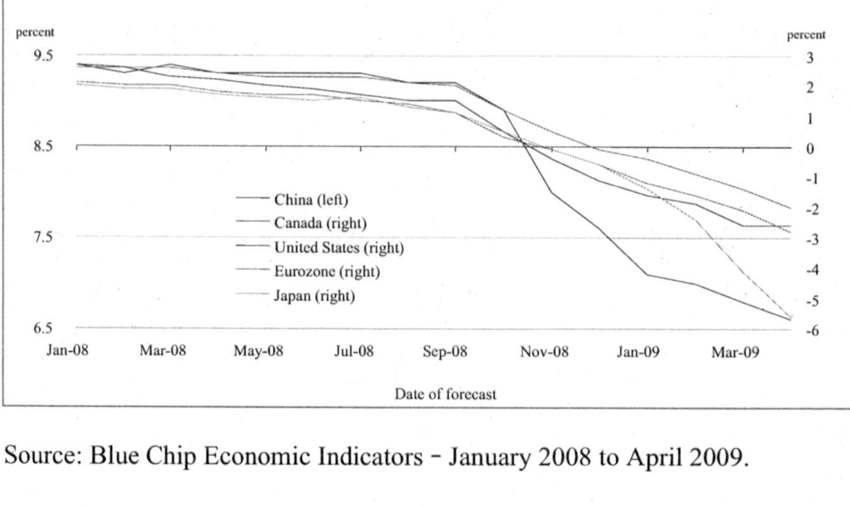

Source: Blue Chip Economic Indicators - January 2008 to April 2009.

The Canadian banks were more capitalized and less highly leveraged than were the banks in the United States and Europe (see Figure 3). In addition, they were less exposed to the toxic assets that were wreaking havoc elsewhere. As a result, there was no danger of any significant bank failure in Canada; as we all know, our banking regulations are now held up as the model to be replicated by those countries desperately in need of regulatory reform. As sound as the Canadian banks were, however, the non-bank "shadow" financial system was still adversely affected by the global financial crisis, testimony to the globalized nature of financial markets. The markets for corporate bonds and asset-backed securities, both of which play a crucial role in the overall provision of credit, were hamstrung with credit spreads far above the levels seen before 2007 (see Figure 4).

Canadian households were also less indebted than were their American counterparts, and the reduction in net worth as a fraction of disposable income in Canada was smaller than the collapse that occurred in the United States (see Figure 5). As a result, the amount of de-leveraging

Figure 3: Bank Leverage Ratios

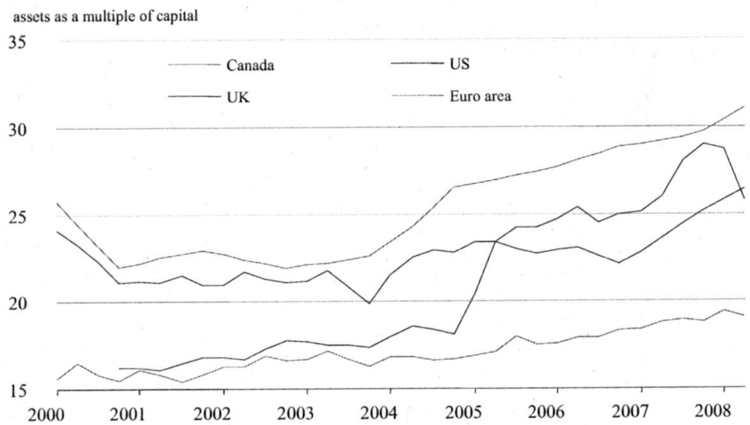

Note: Based on data for the big six Canadian banks, seven major banks from the Euro area, six major UK banks, and five large US commercial banks. Canadian data are based on the regulatory ratio of assets (including some off-balance sheet items) to adjusted Tier 1 and Tier 2 capital. Leverage for other countries is measured as the ratio of balance-sheet assets to shareholders' equity.
Sources: Bloomberg; financial statements.

Figure 4: Credit Spreads

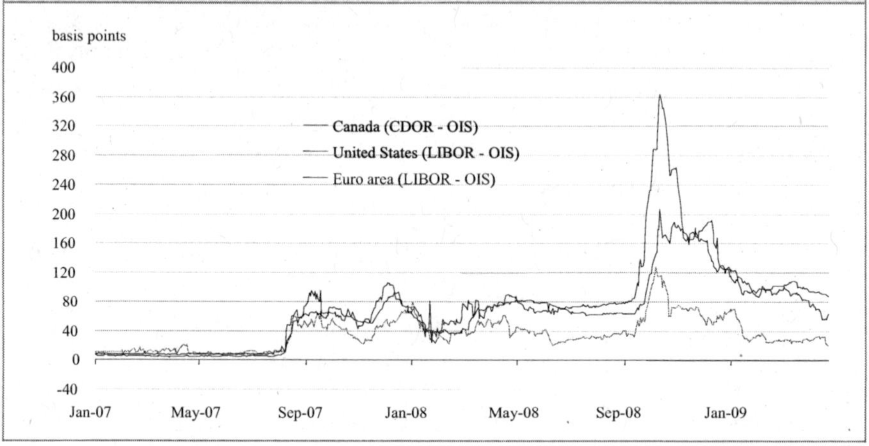

Note: The rate on the overnight-indexed swap (OIS) is used as a proxy for expected overnight rates. LIBOR is the London Interbank Offered Rate. CDOR is the Canadian Dealer Offered Rate. Daily data up to and including April 24, 2009.
Source: Bloomberg.

Figure 5: Ratio of Net Worth to Personal Disposable Income

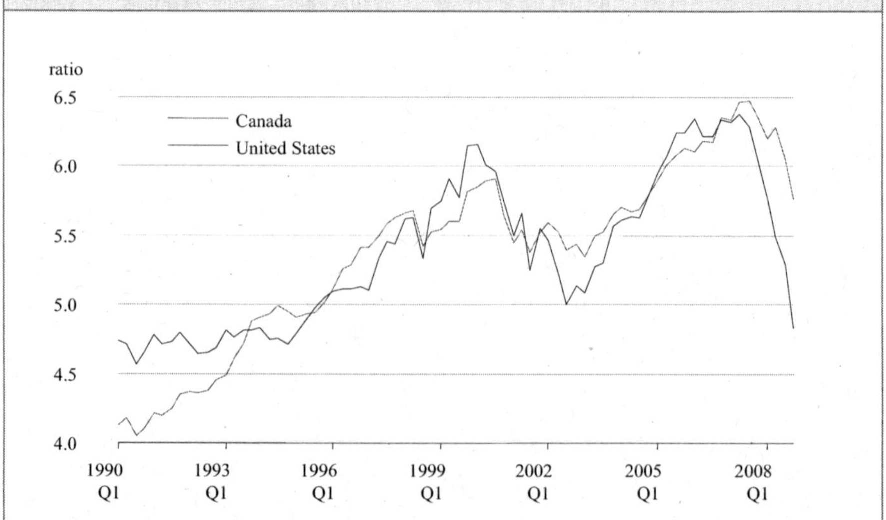

Sources: Statistics Canada; Department of Finance.

that would be necessary was smaller in Canada. That being said, the decline in Canadian household wealth was still large enough that some retrenchment of Canadian consumers was going to take place, especially when combined with the collapse in confidence that had occurred (see Figure 6). Overall, Canadian households might have been in better shape than their American friends, but the road ahead would nonetheless be rough.

Canada's sound public fiscal position was also held up as a strength, but perhaps in a way that confused the message. It is undoubtedly true that the federal government's low debt-to-GDP ratio of 29% in 2008 gave it ample flexibility with which to respond to the economic crisis. Even planned budget deficits of 2 or 3% of GDP for three years in a row would raise the debt ratio to levels far below the high point of 68% attained in 1995. Thus, Canada's past efforts at debt reduction had paid off handsomely by now providing the government with considerable room to manoeuvre. But contrary to what some seemed to be suggesting at the time, the strong fiscal position of the government could not offer Canada safe harbour from the global economic storm.

Figure 6: Consumer Confidence

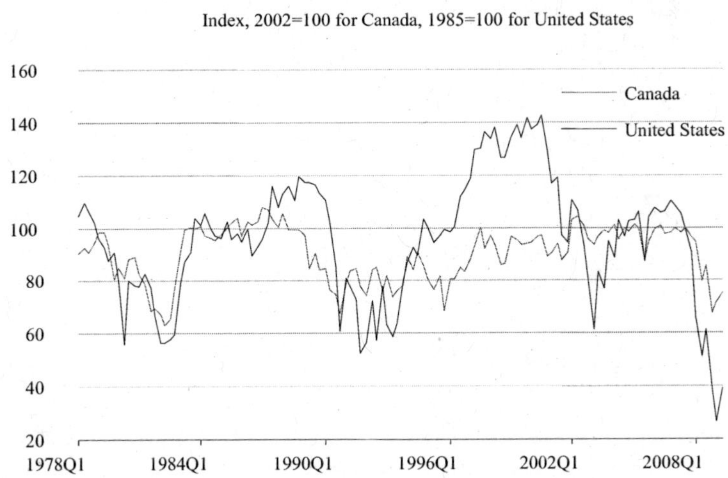

Note: 2009Q2 data is preliminary as it includes only April 2009.
Sources: The Conference Board of Canada; The Conference Board.

However strong Canada's economic position was at the beginning of 2009, the openness of Canada's economy meant that Canada could not avoid the coming global recession. The global integration of capital markets meant that financial-market disruptions originating elsewhere spilled over into Canadian markets, thus inhibiting the flow of credit domestically. Canada's dependence on exports to the United States, for a wide range of goods and services but notably for automobiles and forestry products, meant that any recession there – especially one centred on housing and automobiles – would have the usual dramatic (though lagged) effects here (see Figure 7).

Canada's resource firms sell to a world usually hungry for raw materials. But the collapse of commodity prices in 2008, reinforced (if not caused) by the global recession, meant not only a reduction in activity in one of Canada's most dynamic sectors but also a dramatic decline in Canada's terms of trade, with the implied reduction in Canada's gross domestic income (see Figure 8). Finally, employment in Canada had already begun to decline by late 2008. From its peak in September, Canadian employment had fallen roughly 1% by January. In the United States, the decline had started a year earlier, and by January the cumulative decline was a much larger 3% (see Figure 9). Given the usual lagged transmission from US to Canadian economic events, more employment losses were certain to be in Canada's future.

Figure 7: Growth in US Final Domestic Demand and Canadian Exports

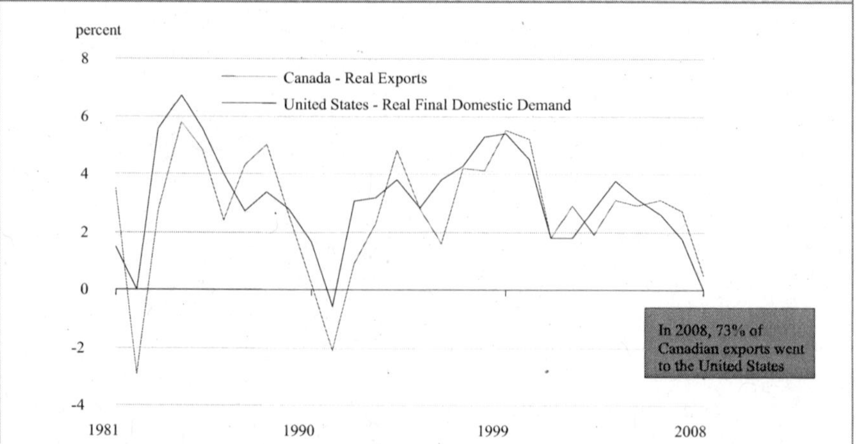

Sources: Statistics Canada; US Bureau of Economic Analysis.

Figure 8: Commodity Prices (in US dollars)

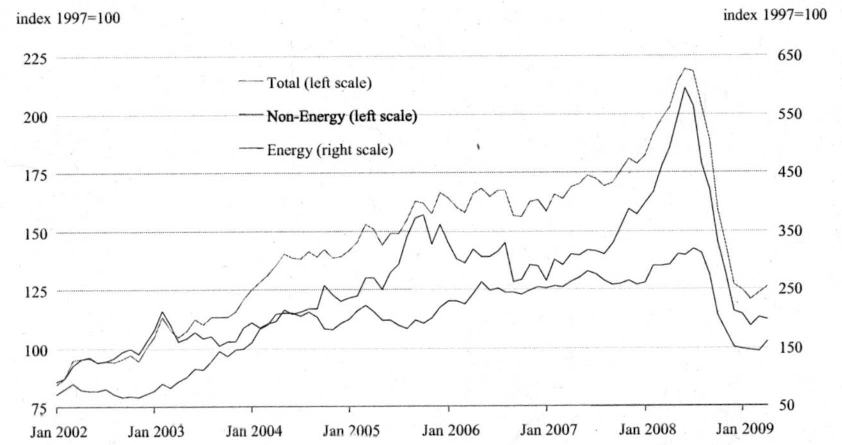

Note: April 2009 includes data up to April 24, 2009.
Source: Department of Finance Commodity Price Index.

Figure 9: Employment-to-Population Rates

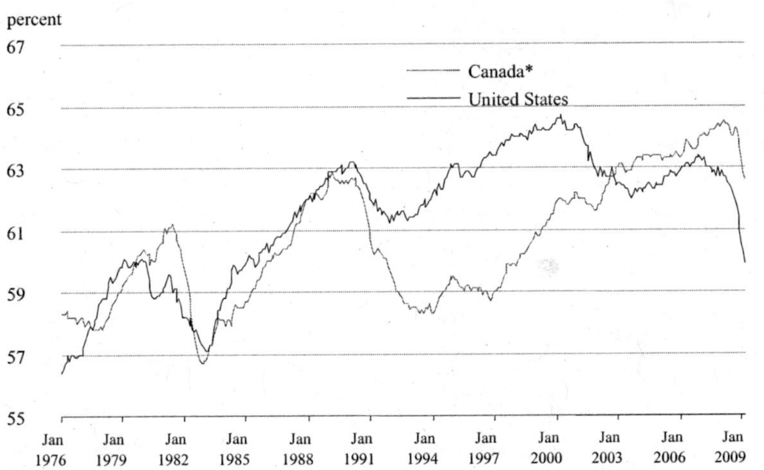

Note: * Calculated using US methodology.

A Budget Designed for the Times

Given this global and Canadian economic context, what was the federal government's policy response? Note that the 2009 federal budget is called an "economic action plan" rather than just a budget. While some of this labelling may be political spin, it does reflect something genuine about the budget. The 2009 budget contains more than the "usual" fiscal measures because the Canadian economy faced more than the "usual" economic challenges.

The government was mindful of many downside risks for different segments of the Canadian population, and thus it was led to design a budget containing a large number of policy actions. In a world of extreme policy uncertainty, it was probably necessary to take many policy measures in order to have even a modest number of policy successes. As a result, most readers find it easy to get lost in the many budget details and to lose sight of the bigger picture. In what follows, I offer my sense of this bigger picture, but do so by omitting a great many policy details. I focus on three general themes: financial-market measures, the dual need for fiscal stimulus, and the importance of maintaining fiscal prudence.

Financial-Market Measures

The government's starting point was to ensure a sound and well-functioning Canadian financial system. Properly functioning financial markets are necessary for the operation of monetary and fiscal policies, and thus it would have made little sense to produce a budget of conventional fiscal measures without first tackling the existing financial problems. Disruptions in the financial system lay at the heart of the global recession and illustrated to all the extent to which credit is the lifeblood of modern economies. Typical recessions begin with well-functioning financial markets, but rising bankruptcies occurring during the recession put obvious strains on financial institutions; subsequent recoveries occur despite the weakened state of these institutions. The current downturn, however, began with weakened financial markets and institutions, and the depth and length of the recession was likely to generate significant "negative feedback", perhaps threatening their solvency. The shoring up of these markets and the restoration of the normal flow of credit was thus viewed as a *sine qua non* for a solid economic recovery.

Some might reasonably argue that the government's financial-market policies are the most important part of the 2009 budget; but the general lack of understanding of financial markets, combined with the absence of the measures' direct fiscal costs, probably explain why these policies received much less press coverage than did the more familiar taxation and expenditure policies. The entire set of financial policies, called the Extraordinary Financing Framework (EFF), was designed to enhance the operation of Canada's financial markets and to restore the flow of credit to something approaching normal, all while exposing the Canadian taxpayer to a minimum of risk. The Insured Mortgage Purchase Plan (IMPP) involved the CMHC buying up to $125 billion in insured mortgages from Canadian banks, thus providing liquidity to the banking system. Capital injections to the Business Development Bank (BDC) and Export Development Canada (EDC) permitted these financial Crown corporations to expand their borrowing and thus their provision of credit to the private sector by an estimated $13 billion. In an effort to restart the market for asset-backed securities, which are crucial forms of finance for vehicle- and equipment-leasing companies, the Canadian Secured Credit Facility (CSCF) will eventually allow BDC to purchase up to $12 billion of these securities, thereby improving market liquidity.

In an economy in which the flow of credit is both crucial and temporarily impaired, the motivation for these measures is clear. Of course, one can criticize these actions on the grounds that such active government involvement in the provision of credit is bound to create inefficiencies, and perhaps worse. But the likely government response to such criticisms (consistent with my own) is that the current priority is to keep credit flowing in an economy in which gaps in the market are pervasive, even if some of the newly provided credit would not have been provided in even a well-functioning market. Or, to paraphrase James Tobin's quip about Harberger triangles and Okun gaps, unemployment trumps efficiency in the current economic context. The policy challenge for the future, and it is not a small one, is to judge when credit markets have returned to "normal" (perhaps a "new" normal) and thus when these extraordinary measures can be pulled back; put differently, the policy challenge is to determine the government's best exit strategy from these extraordinary financial-market measures.

The Dual Need for Fiscal Stimulus

As Bill Scarth notes in his paper, a growing consensus has emerged in recent years that monetary policy is better able than discretionary fiscal policy to provide timely and effective economic stabilization. As I argued above, however, by late 2008, it was recognized in Canada and elsewhere that in this recession, monetary policy could not be relied upon to do all of the heavy lifting, for two reasons. First, the magnitude of the shock suggested a need to use both monetary and fiscal stimulus to dampen the recession. Second, both linkages of the traditional monetary policy transmission mechanism had been weakened. Events in the financial markets had distorted the link between the policy interest rate and other market interest rates. And the need for private-sector deleveraging, and the collapse of consumer and business confidence, called into question the link between market interest rates and aggregate demand (see Figures 10 and 11). With monetary policy in such a weakened state, it was clear that fiscal stimulus would have to step up.

Fiscal policy was not just necessary as a means of dampening the extent of the economic slowdown, however. It was equally important to adopt fiscal measures to help Canadians cope with the decline in income and loss of jobs that would inevitably occur. In particular, there was a need to implement carefully designed fiscal measures to provide assistance to those Canadians who would bear the brunt of the recession. The dual tasks of providing aggregate stimulus and protecting economically vulnerable Canadians implied that the budget needed to contain a mix of targeted spending and tax measures.

Figure 10: Consumer Confidence

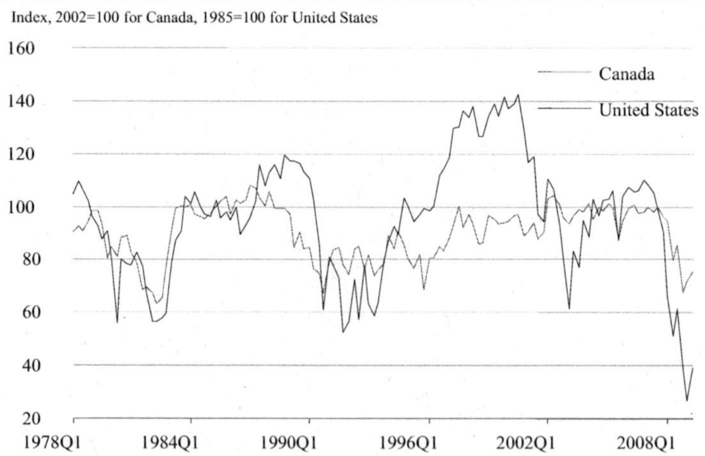

Note: 2009Q2 data is preliminary as it includes only April 2009.
Sources: The Conference Board of Canada; The Conference Board.

Figure 11: Business Confidence

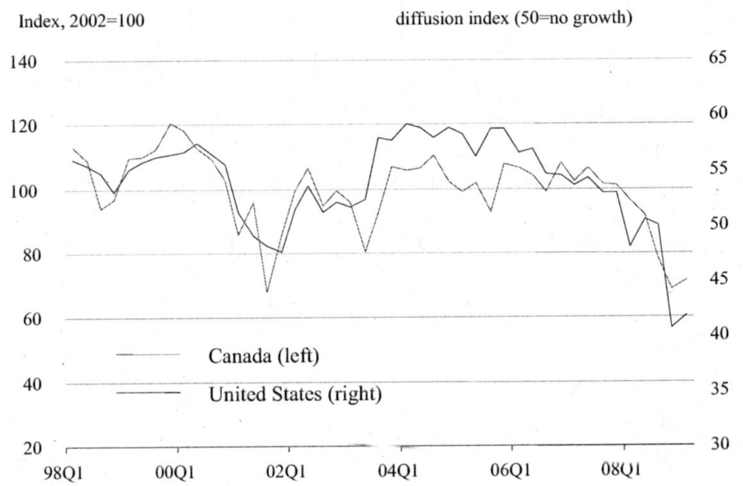

Sources: The Conference Board of Canada; Institute for Supply Management (ISM) non-manufacturing survey.

As regards the need for aggregate stimulus, the government accepted the familiar and sensible claim that new spending tends to have a larger short-run fiscal multiplier than do tax reductions, even permanent ones. As a result, the government's new measures focused on spending for broadly defined infrastructure, including the construction and renovation of social housing, new structures and maintenance for universities and colleges, public infrastructure projects for all levels of government, critical community services for First Nations, and incentives for individuals to purchase and renovate private homes. There was a natural emphasis on funding only "shovel-ready" projects so that the economic stimulus would be felt as soon as possible; at the same time, however, there was a recognition that it is difficult to construct a list of genuine and sensible projects that can be completed quickly, and so there was also a recognition of a likely trade-off between "sensible" spending and "timely" spending. As the fiscal stimulus was in its design phase, there was an inevitable relearning of some of the key limitations of large-scale discretionary fiscal stabilization policy.

The recognition that not everything could be done on the spending side contributed to the economic and political pressures for some of the aggregate stimulus being delivered through tax reductions. And the previously mentioned need to protect Canada's most vulnerable individuals suggested personal income-tax reductions targeted at low- and middle-income households. In addition to increases in the basic personal amount, which provide tax relief for all taxpayers, the government also increased the generosity of the existing child benefits and age credits. Perhaps most significant was the policy to double the tax relief provided by the Working Income Tax Benefit (WITB), a measure introduced in 2007 and designed to lower the "welfare wall" by reducing the work disincentives created by the high marginal tax rates facing low-income Canadians.

Recalling the speed at which Canadian employment had begun to decline in the last few months of 2008, it is no surprise that in the government's desire to assist vulnerable Canadians, the budget also introduced several labour-market measures. To reduce the costs and increase the benefits of employment insurance, the EI contribution premiums were frozen for two years, and the maximum benefit period was extended by five weeks. In addition, access to the federal EI work-sharing program was improved, and the maximum benefit period was extended from 38 to 52 weeks. Finally, more resources were provided to a whole range of labour-force training programs, including those provided through the EI system.

Overall, the fiscal cost of the budget measures was estimated to be $22.7 billion in 2009–10 and $17.2 billion in the following year (see Table 1). These figures do not include the financial-market measures, which have no direct fiscal cost (if the acquired assets retain their value). With provincial leverage coming both from the income-tax system and from partnership on infrastructure spending, these numbers increase to $29.3 billion and $22.3 billion, respectively. So the estimated size of the total fiscal stimulus is 1.9% of GDP in 2009–10 and 1.5% in 2010–11, numbers consistent with the agreement reached in Washington among the G20 leaders.

These estimated measures of the size of the fiscal stimulus, however, are only part of the estimated budget *deficits*. Even in the absence of new discretionary fiscal measures, the economic slowdown was quickly pushing the government's books into the red. For 2009–10, the estimated deficit would have been $11 billion in the absence of new policies; the budgetary measures increased this planned deficit to just under $34 billion. For the 2010–11 fiscal year, the total estimated deficit was increased by the new policy actions to just under $30 billion.

Table 1: The Budget Numbers

	2009	2010	Total
	(billions of dollars - cash basis)		
EI changes, Personal tax reductions, Skills and Training	**5.9**	**6.9**	**12.8**
Tax measures to support housing, Social housing investments	**5.4**	**2.3**	**7.8**
Infrastructure programming	**6.2**	**5.6**	**11.8**
Tax and Tariff changes, Sectoral adjustment measures	**5.3**	**2.3**	**7.5**
Total Federal Stimulus	**22.7**	**17.2**	**39.9**
Total Stimulus (with Leverage)	**29.3**	**22.3**	**51.6**
As a share of GDP (%)			
Total federal stimulus	1.5	1.1	2.5
Total stimulus (with leverage)	1.9	1.4	3.2

Tax measures account for $10.1 billion of total stimulus

Spending measures represent $29.9 billion of total stimulus

Note that the government was intentionally conservative in its forecasts of revenue over the budget period, using a forecast for nominal GDP growth (which largely determines government tax revenues) significantly less than the mean of the private-sector forecasts. This conservatism reflected the government's belief that most of the risks to the budget forecast were on the downside; as a result, the economy could get worse than many forecasted without causing an increase in the planned deficit. As many now suspect, however, the actual recession will prove to be even deeper and sharper than what was built into the conservative budget forecast, and so the actual deficits for the 2009-11 fiscal years may be even larger than the estimates appearing in the budget.

The Importance of Fiscal Prudence

In designing the 2009 budget, the government faced a trade-off between the short-term need for fiscal stimulus and the longer-term need to maintain fiscal prudence, a concept probably best reflected by the size of the debt-to-GDP ratio. The government did not want to sacrifice

Canada's hard-won gains, achieved over the previous decade, with the debt ratio falling from a high of 68% in 1995 to 29% in 2008 (see Figure 12).

Some argue that Canada's past performance on debt reduction gave the government the flexibility to do even more than it proposed in the 2009 budget. As Rick Harris has argued at the budget conference, the uncertainty of the economic situation suggests a case for erring on the side of over- rather than under-stimulating the economy by means of fiscal policy. Surely the government could tolerate seeing the debt ratio rise back up to 35% or even 40% before resuming its downward path. Put differently, the government could easily have designed the budget to contain a fiscal stimulus double the actual numbers, thereby further dampening the size of the recession and offering even more protection to vulnerable Canadians. Or would this have been so easy?

In order to provide *additional* stimulus that does not threaten the government's longer-term fiscal prudence, any additional tax or spending measures must satisfy two conditions. First, new budget measures must be easily *scalable*; that is, it must be feasible to significantly increase the current scale of the policy measures. If this is not straightforward, then increasing the size of the overall stimulus is difficult. Second, the

Figure 12: Canada's Federal (Net) Debt-to-GDP Ratio

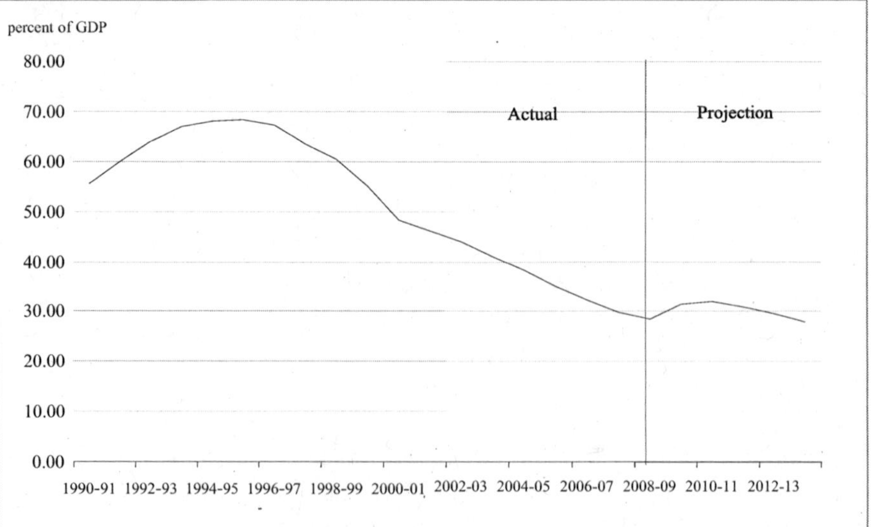

additional budget measures must be *reversible* during the inevitable future recovery. If such reversal is not feasible, for either economic or political reasons, then a much stronger case exists for keeping the stimulus package small. As it turns out, it is difficult to find policy measures that are *both* scalable and reversible. Consider the two broad categories of infrastructure spending and tax reductions.

One big advantage of placing infrastructure spending at the core of a fiscal stimulus package is that it is relatively easy to reverse the spending when the economic recovery occurs. As long as the spending is committed on a project-by-project basis rather than by establishing new programs that take on a life of their own, there can be considerable confidence that the spending will simply stop once a project is finished. The problem with infrastructure is that it is not easily scalable.

The often heard difficulties associated with infrastructure spending should be taken seriously. Simply put, it is extremely hard to find good projects that can be sensibly conceived, formally approved, carefully designed, environmentally cleared, and efficiently constructed in short order – especially if we want to avoid spending the money on things for which there is little long-run value. As one individual from southern Alberta said at a pre-budget consultation I attended in January, "The last thing we need is another cowboy museum!" Compounding these difficulties are the political complexities of reaching agreements with multiple levels of government, including the playing of various spending and taxation games that inevitably take place. So there are real limits to how much fiscal stimulus can be provided through infrastructure spending.

Any desire to increase the size of the fiscal stimulus, therefore, leads inevitably to a search for deeper tax reductions. Changes in taxes are trivial to scale up: one can just as easily reduce any given tax rate by 3% as reduce it by 1%. But with tax reductions, we quickly encounter the problem of reversibility. There is a general feeling among many economists that temporary tax changes are much less effective as stimulus measures than are permanent ones. In a model with purely Ricardian consumers (which requires some extreme assumptions), one gets the sharp prediction that temporary tax changes generally have no effect at all. But even in less extreme settings, the same general logic points to a reduced effect on aggregate demand if households know that tax changes will be reversed in the near future. So in order to be an effective stimulus, the tax reductions need to be permanent. (However, we should also recognize the logical possibility that with seriously impaired credit markets, we are likely to have more liquidity-constrained households, and thus temporary tax cuts may be almost as effective as permanent ones!) But if they are to be permanent, how does the government balance the budget or produce a surplus once the economy starts on the path to recovery? And even if one were convinced that a temporary tax cut would be stimulative, the political forces working to lock in such tax cuts are enormous. As Milton Friedman once famously suggested, nothing is so permanent as a temporary tax cut.

One other consideration argued against designing a larger fiscal stimulus. To the extent that credit is an input to the production process, it is quite likely that the financial-market adjustments due to occur over the next few years – including a more accurate re-pricing of risk – will lead to a reduction in the growth rate of potential output. If so, we cannot expect tax revenues to return to their pre-recession path. Instead, real (and nominal) GDP, and therefore the government's tax revenues, can be expected to grow more slowly as a long-run average. Restoring fiscal balance over the medium term will thus be that much more difficult, even with unchanged tax rates.

Mindful of these concerns, the government struck a pragmatic balance. It pushed infrastructure spending about as far as it could go. (Indeed, we may learn a year from now that it was simply unable to spend the amount it budgeted for this purpose.) It chose some modest and permanent tax cuts that are effective in offering modest relief to individuals and, at the same time, are affordable over the longer term. The five-week extension to EI benefits was billed as a temporary measure, but only time will tell whether the federal government (this one or some other) has the courage to reverse this policy in the future.

The budget shows the government's debt-to-GDP ratio rising to a peak of 32% by the end of 2010-11, at which point it slowly resumes its downward path toward some notional target of 25% or even lower. With the economy now probably worse than expected at the time of the budget, the peak may well be higher and occur later than suggested in the budget. Fortunately, the government's solid fiscal position coming into this recession means that there is ample room to manoeuvre. That we have any room to manoeuvre is, of course, the current payoff from the federal government's past actions in reducing the debt ratio – it is part of what a few years ago we called the "fiscal dividend". The 2009 budget strives to maintain this budget flexibility as much as possible into the medium term by keeping the debt ratio relatively low.

Given Canada's coming demographic challenges, such fiscal flexibility will be essential in the future. The aging of the baby-boom generation implies that, beginning roughly in 2020 and continuing for about 30 years, there will be declining labour-force growth and rising health-care expenditures. The declining growth in the labour force will imply, for unchanged productivity growth, a decline in the share of GDP that can be collected as tax revenues (for given tax rates). At the same time, the increased demand on health-care services suggests that, unless Canadian governments are able to reduce other types of public spending, there will be an increase in the share of GDP spent by governments. Thus, we have a coming "fiscal squeeze", which will create both economic and political challenges and almost certainly require a further increase in the government's debt-to-GDP ratio. Addressing these significant economic and political challenges will require careful government planning, effective communication with the Canadian people, and unpleasant policy decisions. Facing these challenges will be far easier with a lower debt ratio than with a higher one.

Final Words

The sharp and sudden decline in the pace of economic activity demanded that the government's fiscal actions be effective and timely. The economic situation also demanded, as did the political pressure from the opposition parties, that the government take extraordinary actions to implement its budget measures as quickly as possible.

To accelerate the funding of measures in the *Economic Action Plan*, the government introduced the *Budget Implementation Act, 2009*, in the House of Commons on February 6, 2009. The Act provided funding authority for $7.6 billion in spending for a range of measures, many of which would normally be funded through the annual appropriations process but were included in the Act this year in order to facilitate their rapid parliamentary approval. In addition, this year the Act was passed by the House of Commons and the Senate in just over a month, significantly faster than the nearly four months it took to receive royal assent for the 2008 budget.

To ensure that the budget measures would be implemented as quickly as possible, the government created a new central vote in the Main Estimates. This vote allowed up to $3 billion in funding to be provided to departments for budget measures until formal authority for these initiatives could be obtained through the Supplementary Estimates. The government also planned to table spring Supplementary Estimates in late May to provide funding authority for the majority of the remaining budget measures. Funding for budget measures is not usually appropriated until December. Finally, the government streamlined the federal approval process for infrastructure projects to ensure that infrastructure funding could be spent during the next two construction seasons.

***

In sum, the economic environment as of January 2009 demanded that the federal government take timely and dramatic actions on many fronts. It therefore designed a budget that focused on financial-market measures aimed at restoring the flow of credit, infrastructure spending aimed at dampening the magnitude of the recession, and targeted tax breaks and EI changes aimed at protecting those Canadians most vulnerable to the effects of the economic downturn. It selected a combination of policy actions both feasible and affordable, thus preserving Canada's hard-won fiscal prudence. The government indicated that it was prepared to do more if the need should arise. As of the middle of May, some individual signs of a nascent recovery were apparent, and thus, with a little luck, such additional budget measures will not be necessary. Only time will tell.

Session Two

ECONOMIC STIMULUS OBJECTIVES AND FISCAL IMPACTS OF THE BUDGET

STABILIZATION POLICY DEBATES: Assessing the Case for Fiscal Stimulus

William Scarth, McMaster University

Introduction

According to the classical tradition in economics, fiscal policy is meant to focus on society's equity and efficiency objectives. Concerns about macroeconomic stabilization are either best left to the economy's self-correction mechanism or to monetary policy. Clearly, most governments today have followed Keynes and rejected this tradition, as major stimulus packages have been the reaction to the recession. The purpose of this essay is to review the debates that have waged on this issue so that readers can achieve some confidence in arriving at their own view on this central topic. The next section explains why the self-correction mechanism, while reliable in many circumstances, can fail – even when it is enhanced by monetary policy. The Keynesian response is to rely on fiscal initiatives in these circumstances; but in the third section, we explain why such efforts may be counterproductive. Then, in the fourth and fifth sections, we explain which fiscal measures are most likely able to avoid these pitfalls and why it important for us to pursue this strategy – given the coordination problem that society faces. Finally, following brief conclusions in the last section, the Appendix provides details on models that are used in the second and third sections.

The Economy's Self-Correction Mechanism and Monetary Policy

As noted, our first line of defence when a drop in aggregate demand occurs is the economy's self-correction mechanism. Slack in labour markets should lead to lower wages; competition among firms then induces producers to pass on these cost savings in lower prices, which – assuming that the demand curve for goods is downward-sloping – stimulate increased purchases. This automatic process – that deflation itself can close the initial "deflationary gap" between actual and long-run-sustainable output – is the self-correcting mechanism.

But what makes the demand curve for the nation's entire output downward-sloping? The standard argument that applies for an individual product is that buyers reduce purchases of other goods that have become relatively more expensive. But for the whole economy, the only "other" goods are those produced in other countries. As the prices of our goods fall relative to those in the rest of the world, demand for domestically produced goods can be expected to rise. But in the present circumstance – when there is a drop in demand in all our trading partners' economies at the same time – our prices cannot be expected to fall more. So, roughly speaking, we may as well reason in terms of a closed economy when asking how we can expect our aggregate demand curve to have a negative slope.

The traditional answer to this concern is to appeal to the existence of a wealth effect (emphasized by Pigou, 1943) – that falling prices lead to an increase in the real value of assets that are based in nominal terms. But Irving Fisher (1933) had already considered this issue – in a way that did not abstract from differences between borrowers and lenders, as Pigou's analysis did. Considering private banks, Fisher focused on loans and deposits separately. With bank reserves being a very small proportion of bank assets, the loan and deposit totals are roughly the same magnitude. Since the value of *both* is increased by deflation, and since borrowers have a higher propensity to spend than do lenders, the net effect of deflation – according to Fisher – is that current spending is *decreased*, not increased. That is, focusing on wealth effects alone, Fisher argued that the aggregate demand curve is positively sloped.

Standard policy-oriented macro modelling avoids this threat to the viability of the self-correction mechanism by inserting an ongoing reaction function on the part of the central bank into the system. The simplest way of doing this is to posit that the bank lowers the interest rate whenever the price level falls below the bank's target value. Then as deflation occurs, interest rates fall, and the resulting decrease in borrowing costs is what stimulates higher aggregate demand. But this avenue for achieving a negative slope to the aggregate demand curve is not available if the central bank is unable to lower interest rates, and this is precisely the concern today – since short-term nominal interest rates have reached essentially zero.

It can be shown that – in a simple model that abstracts from Pigou, Fisher, and open-economy effects – this zero-lower-bound constraint on interest rates makes the aggregate demand curve become vertical in the lower price range of the aggregate supply and demand diagram. We can see the implications in Figure 1. The economy is initially in full equilibrium in the upper range of the diagram – with actual output equalling its sustainable level. We then consider an exogenous shift to the left in the demand curve's position. With prices given in the short run, the economy's observation point moves to the left along the initial short-run aggregate supply (*SRAS*) line, and a recession occurs. But then, as prices gradually fall (shown by the position of the *SRAS* drifting down over time), the economy's observation point shifts down the demand curve until it reaches the natural rate line again. Thus, the diagram verifies the efficacy of the self-correction mechanism – as long as the initial drop in demand is not "too big". This possibility is also illustrated

Figure 1: The Self-Correction Mechanism

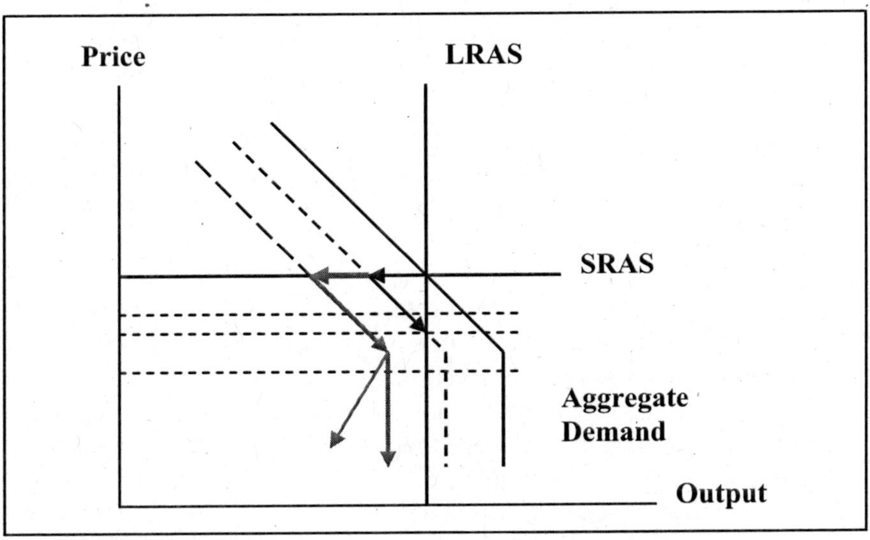

in Figure 1 by the further shift in the demand curve's position to the left. In this case, price decreases just move the economy forever down the vertical region of this demand curve, so the economy does not automatically move back to the natural rate of output. The self-correction mechanism fails in this case; deflation does not eliminate the output gap.

Can deflation actually be harmful? Keynes (1936) argued in the affirmative, and his reasoning was based on an expectations effect. He argued that people in this situation will certainly come to realize that prices can be expected to keep falling. Then they will decide to postpone part of their spending with a view to waiting for the expected price decreases. This further reduction in current demand must be shown as yet another shift to the left in the position of the current aggregate demand curve. With this expectations effect included, then, the trajectory that indicates the economy's time path during deflation is not just south – it is southwest. Deflation actually *widens* the output gap in this case, so what was supposed to be the automatic correction mechanism has become a destabilizing force. Keynes' suggested remedy was for the government to use program spending increases, and/or tax cuts, to shift the aggregate demand curve to the right.

Interested readers are encouraged to consult the Appendix, where a formal version of this scenario is summarized. Following convention, Keynes' expectations effect is introduced by distinguishing the real interest rate (which affects spending decisions) from the nominal interest rate (which is what the central bank adjusts) since the difference is the expected rate of inflation/deflation. The algebraic analysis indicates that the automatic-correction mechanism fails if the central bank's aggressiveness parameter (in lowering the interest rate in response to a price level that is below target) is smaller than the rate at which private agents revise their expectations of deflation. This result implies that, while the zero-lower-bound constraint (which forces the bank's aggressiveness parameter to zero) is sufficient to ensure that the deflation process involves instability, this outcome emerges *even before* this absolute limit is reached.

Broadly speaking, there have been four reactions to this concern. First, the analytical structure that has led us to be concerned about monetary policy losing its power can be questioned – with the result that we may come to the view that the potential macro instability worry is very much overblown. Second, we can continue to embrace the conventional analytical framework and – within that – think of ways of removing the zero-lower-bound constraint in the short-term financial market. Third, we can shift monetary policy so that it operates in the long-term bond markets. Finally, we can embrace an active fiscal policy approach (the Keynesian recommendation that – as noted – has been embraced by many governments today). We now consider each of these reactions in turn.

Monetarists have long been critical of the narrow view of the monetary-policy transmission mechanism that exists in conventional analysis. Their view is that households manage a portfolio of assets that includes money, financial claims, and consumer durables. When portfolios become out of balance – with too much money – households reallocate by acquiring more financial claims *and* durables. The effect of money on the goods market does not have to "go through" the bond market. In the monetarist view, there are direct money-to-goods reallocations within the portfolio. According to this view, a lower bound on bond rates is simply not relevant, and the best thing that the central bank can do is to ensure that money growth remains vigorous at times such as the present. For example, Laidler (2009) has recommended an annual growth rate for the *M1+* money supply measure of about 7%, although he admits that it is difficult to be precise since the relationships that link the growth in any one monetary aggregate to the economy's performance indicators are imprecise. Taylor (2009) argues that this strategy was central to Japan's eventual recovery from its problems in the 1990s.

Returning to the zero-lower-bound issue, Edlin and Jaffe (2009) have documented that commercial bank excess reserves in the United States have skyrocketed in recent months; they rose from a "fairly normal" level of $2 billion in August 2008 to $798 billion in January 2009. It is tempting to accept their interpretation that this appears to be a Keynesian "liquidity trap" in action. Edlin and Jaffe wonder why the Fed is paying interest on these bank reserves when the Fed would prefer that banks make more loans. They draw attention to suggestions such as that made by Hall (1983) – that interest be paid on reserves in an amount equal to the expected inflation rate. In deflationary times, this would involve a tax on excess reserves, which could be expected to stimulate lending (ending the liquidity trap problem) and to at least partially internalize an externality – that the social return of more lending exceeds the private return. With the precarious position of banks in the United States today, however, this would not seem to be the time to add a further challenge for their re-acquiring profitability. Nevertheless, as part of the new set of regulations for banks in the future, it would seem that serious consideration should be given to such structural changes.

Several major central banks have recently embraced what they refer to as quantitative easing. They are trying to affect long interest rates more directly than they have in the past (when they limited their intervention to manipulation of the short rate, hoping that the yield curve would cause some of this change to be felt at the long end). The general strategy is to operate in such a way that the zero-lower-bound problem at the short end becomes irrelevant. One method of trying to do this involves only a small departure from past practice. The bank can simply promise to keep the short rate low for a significant time into the future. This is what the Bank of Canada has just recently done – apparently committing itself, unless conditions change – to leaving the overnight rate at its present value until June 2010. Since we believe that the long rate is a weighted average of expected future short rates, this strategy may be able to "talk" long rates down somewhat. However, if the long rates that matter for spending decisions are for terms to maturity that exceed 15 months, this strategy may have limited success. This would especially be the case if market participants focus on the "conditional" nature of the Bank's commitment. In any event, as Andersson and Hofmann (2009) have documented, there has been very little success with this very strategy when several other central banks have tried it. They estimate that long rates were pulled down by just four basis points. Surely we must conclude that, if quantitative easing is to be pursued, central banks will have to do so much more explicitly.

In the Appendix, I have extended the standard stability analysis to allow for the distinction between short- and long-term bonds and for the expectations theory of the term structure. This analysis confirms the intuition that the central bank cannot completely avoid the zero-lower-bound constraint for the short rate just by conducting its open market operations in the long market. The term-structure arbitrage condition ensures that the constraint on the short rate still gets in the bank's way. Indeed, macro stability is still very much threatened. Further, in a separate note (Scarth, 2009a), I have provided a sensitivity test. This further analysis involves "new" micro-based demand and supply specifications, model-consistent expectations, and a monetary policy based on inflation-rate, not price-level, targeting. This new-neoclassical-synthesis approach leads to the same skepticism that is reported here. Overall, this work does not support the notion that quantitative or credit easing brings sufficient new ammunition to the central bank to allow it to operate effectively when the zero-lower-bound constraint is binding. A more monetartist view of the transmission mechanism is necessary if we are to remain optimistic in this regard.

We end this section by agreeing with DeLong (2009): "When you have only two tools left, neither of which is perfect for the job, the rational thing is to try both – credit policy and fiscal policy – at the same time." But we have yet to consider the fiscal-policy part of this conclusion. How might it help – despite the "disruptive side-effects" that DeLong acknowledges? It is to this question that we turn in the next section.

Fiscal Policy and the Crowding-Out Problem

As already noted, the idea with fiscal policy is to bring some spending forward in time so that the current position of the aggregate demand curve can be shifted to the right – making the economy less reliant on its self-correction mechanism and monetary policy. But there are several possible impediments: If the government offers a tax cut, will households and firms choose to spend the increase in disposable income, or will they be so worried about income prospects that they choose to save these funds instead? If the government raises spending on such items as infrastructure, will implementation lags so delay the stimulus that much of it will occur well after the recession is largely behind us? Whatever the initiative chosen by the government, the resulting budget deficit will raise the national debt. If the higher debt remains indefinitely, distortionary taxes will need to be levied to cover the interest payment obligations, and these distortions will lower living standards. Alternatively, if the debt is worked down later, that contractionary stance of future fiscal policy will slow the economy's recovery. These concerns are addressed in the remaining sections of the paper. Which specific fiscal initiatives can best eliminate implementation lags and minimize uncertain private-sector responses are considered in the next section. Questions concerning how initiatives are financed are the present focus.

Let us begin by considering a lump-sum tax cut financed by issuing new government bonds. If some households are liquidity-constrained – spending their entire disposable income as they live "hand to mouth", as Mankiw (2000) puts it – the current tax cut will increase aggregate demand. Mankiw estimates that roughly half of US households live hand to mouth. But what reaction can we expect on behalf of the remaining households? If they are not liquidity-constrained, and their decisions are made on an ongoing family-dynasty basis, the permanent-income theory of consumption applies. For these households, higher bond holdings represent both an opportunity to receive higher interest payments and an obligation to pay higher future taxes to cover those interest payments –

with both these incoming and outgoing flows of funds having the same present value. Thus, the exchange of present taxes for future taxes involves no change in net wealth, so nothing of interest in the macro economy will be affected by such a fiscal policy – as far as these households are concerned. This particular implication of the permanent-income hypothesis is known as the Ricardian Equivalence proposition. Of course, this proposition cannot be literally true since (as already noted) some households are not able to borrow and others have no children. As a result, these individuals do not value future taxes as much as they do current taxes. The relevant issue is whether Ricardian Equivalence is approximately true.

Despite the direct evidence provided by Mankiw, a more common method of examining this question is by running regressions based on Blanchard's (1985) extension of Ramsey's (1928) version of the permanent-income hypothesis:

$$C_{t+1} = (1 + r - i)C_t - d(d + i)B_t$$

This relationship involves next period's consumption, *C*, depending on this period's consumption and this period's non-human wealth (in this case, the stock of government bonds held by households, *B*). The three parameters are *r*, *i*, and *d*: the interest rate, the rate of impatience, and the death probability (respectively). In Ramsey's model, all agents live forever, or it is as if they do, since they love the next-generation individuals just as much as they do themselves, so $d = 0$. Blanchard's extension allows us to consider a small death probability; for example, if 2% is the annual death rate of members of the population that do not value the lives of those in the next generation that replace them, then $d = 0.02$. In addition, if all individuals have an annual rate of time preference, *i*, equal to 4%, then the coefficient on the government bond variable in the above equation can be expected to be (0.02)(0.02 + 0.04) = 0.0012. The standard test for the applicability of Ricardian equivalence is whether this regression coefficient is statistically significantly different from zero. It is asking a lot of aggregate time series regressions to distinguish a tiny number like 0.0012 from zero, so it is not surprising that this is the result that is usually found. This is taken as support for Ricardian Equivalence. But when pooled time series and cross-section evidence is used (Evans, 1993), the increased variation in the data is sufficient to reject Ricardian Equivalence. Nevertheless, evidence shows that temporary income tax changes affect saving, not spending, to a significant degree so that – despite Ricardian Equivalence being rejected

– this particular fiscal policy is not recommended. So let us now focus on government spending.

The traditional concern with higher government spending is that it may simply replace pre-existing private-sector spending – instead of adding to aggregate demand. In contrast to the "irrelevance" of the fiscal policy proposition discussed in the previous two paragraphs, this concern depends on the belief that Ricardian Equivalence is *not* empirically important. This particular argument is known as the "crowding out" effect, and it is regarded as a fundamental constraint by analysts at the Fraser Institute (see Veldhuis, Lammam, and Palacios, 2009). They state that "any increase in spending will be offset by less activity in other areas of the economy". Because the "stimulus" spending is financed by deficits, they argue that "the government will take money from some Canadians (those buying government bonds), who will then have less to spend and/or invest in the private market". It appears that Fraser analysts discount the relevance of Blinder and Solow's (1973) classic analysis entitled "Does Fiscal Policy Matter?" They considered what was then the standard model of aggregate demand – *IS-LM* – and combined it with a government budget constraint (bond issue at each point in time must equal the current deficit). Since they did not assume Ricardian Equivalence, Blinder and Solow focused on what had been left out of traditional Keynesian demand theory – the fact that both the *IS* and *LM* curves must shift up as more government bonds are issued. (More bonds raise the size of households' asset portfolios, thereby increasing the demand for all normal assets including money. An increase in money demand relative to supply shifts the *LM* Curve to the left, putting upward pressure on interest rates. More intuitively, higher interest rates are required for wealth portfolios to absorb more government bonds.)

Blinder and Solow noted Friedman's prediction (echoed by the Fraser Institute) – that the end point of this process would likely be one that was essentially perfectly above the initial one. If true, this would mean that an attempt to provide fiscal stimulus would result in just pushing up interest rates and having no lasting effect on the level of overall spending. Blinder and Solow showed that such an outcome is not logically possible within the model. Either fiscal policy has to be expansionary or the economy must be unstable. Their reading of empirical-applicability questions caused them to focus on the must-be-expansionary outcome. This was unfortunate since we now know that such models – assuming as they do that the interest rate exceeds the growth rate – involve instability. Perhaps this is why critics of fiscal stimulus today write as if the Blinder-Solow analysis never appeared.

Given the disconnect summarized in the previous paragraph, it is important that we consider an updated version of Blinder and Solow, so this is what is reported in the remainder of this section of the paper. In contrast to the earlier work, the present analysis involves variable prices, model-consistent expectations, an up-to-date Taylor-rule specification for monetary policy, and dynamic stability. As a result, it is hoped that it can be less readily dismissed by fiscal-stimulus skeptics. The formal model is sketched in the Appendix, and more extensive discussion is available in Scarth (2007). Here, I explain just the broad outline of the analysis.

I focus on the most basic question in Keynesian economics: should the government balance the budget at all times or over the time frame of one full business cycle? I consider a one-time permanent drop in aggregate demand and compare two fiscal regimes. Neither involves any change in the tax system, so Ricardian Equivalence issues are not the focus. In the first regime, the government rejects Keynes and maintains its commitment to balanced budgets by cutting government spending at the very time that the private-sector drop in demand occurs and causes the government to lose revenue. This response makes the size of the initial recession bigger. But as the economy recovers and tax collections start rising again, the government in this regime is able to bring program spending back up, and this speeds the recovery from the temporary recession.

In the second regime, the government follows Keynesian advice. It does not cut program spending when tax collections deteriorate in the recession. By maintaining higher spending (that is, by providing stimulus) compared to the other regime, the government ensures that the initial recession is smaller. But since the deficit has to be covered by bond issue, the government needs to work the debt level back down later on. This results in program spending being smaller than otherwise as the recovery proceeds, and this slows down the recovery. Overall, the Keynesian regime involves short-term gain for longer-term pain, and this is summarized in Figure 2.

The outcome in the Keynesian regime is shown by the solid output time path, while that for the always balanced-budget regime is shown by the dashed output time path. The Keynesian policy makes the initial recession smaller, but this recession dissipates at a slower rate. In the short run, people would prefer to live under the Keynesian regime, but later on, they would prefer the alternative. Since the model can be calibrated in a simple and reasonably non-controversial way, I have used

Figure 2: Implications of Keynesian Policy

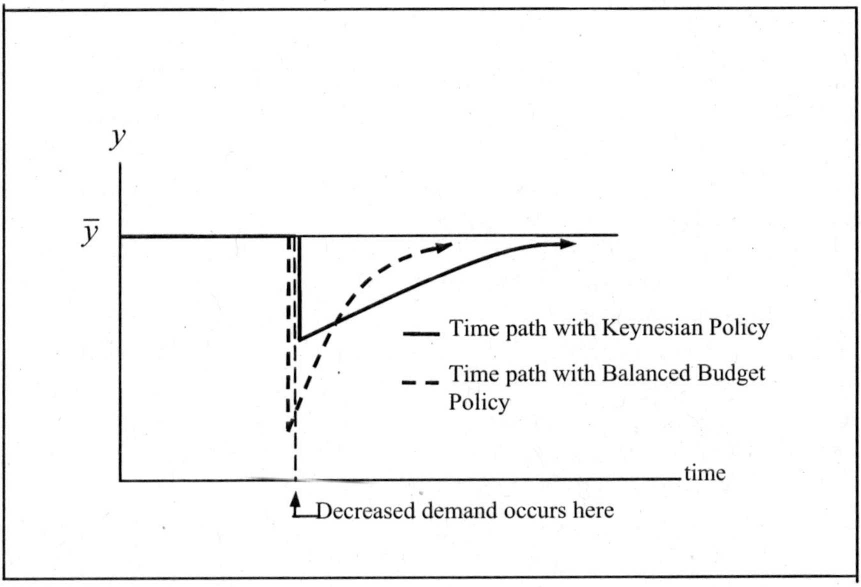

it – along with representative parameter values – to calculate the two areas shown in Figure 2 – that between each actual real output time path and the natural-rate line. The initial recession turns out to be 33% larger when the Keynesian policy advice is rejected, but the overall output loss over the entire time period is almost the same in this case. Thus, *if* the future is *not* discounted relative to the present, the short-term gain involved in the Keynesian approach is fully cancelled by the long-term pain, so there is only modest support for the Keynesian approach. Nevertheless, we *should* discount, so the analysis does support Keynes.

Perhaps a more convincing way to defend this conclusion is to switch our focus to *ongoing* changes in demand. Instead of considering just one permanent drop in demand (as above), we can assume that an exogenous component of spending follows a sine curve time path. In this setting, the more distant effects of any one change are dominated by the more immediate effects of the more recent change in autonomous spending. Our calibrated analysis indicates that the amplitude of the ongoing cycle in real output is 25% larger when the Keynesian approach to fiscal policy is rejected. This analysis provides a robustness check on related work at the OECD (2009). Analysts there have performed simulations with a number of large macro models (as well as with an aggregate dynamic stochastic general equilibrium model). Their overall conclusion is that one-third of the output volatility is removed by embracing the Keynesian approach. I conclude, therefore, that fiscal policy can make some contribution to combating today's recession, and so a prudent government would embrace fiscal stimulus.

Before closing this section, it is worth commenting on the assumed size of the fiscal policy "multiplier" that is used in various analyses. The calibrations I have reported above imply a one-year government spending multiplier on overall real output of 1.5 (an assumption shared by Finance Canada and the Centre for Policy Alternatives). According to Barro (2009a), this assumption is also used by Team Obama, and Barro regards such a number as dramatically too big – so much so, that he borrows the "voodoo" economics label that was applied to supply-siders in the 1980s and attaches it to those currently backing fiscal stimulus. Barro estimates that the extra military spending that occurred for a few years in the 1940s resulted in a temporary rise in real *GDP* above trend equal to about 80% of the government spending increase. Thus, he thinks that 0.8 is as high as we should go with a multiplier estimate and that we would not go too far wrong if we opted for a zero value. This would make stabilization policy analysis consistent with the standard assumption involved in benefit-cost analysis applied to a fully employed economy. Going this far is inappropriate, however, since resources are available in a recession. Barro's estimate from the 1940s can be questioned, both on the grounds that there were no idle resources in the United States at that time and on the grounds that households were strongly encouraged through an appeal to patriotism to save their incomes during the war.

The Canadian evidence on the estimated one-year government spending multipliers is summarized in Mankiw and Scarth (2008, 336-338). Early estimates were in the 1.5 range, but more recent results indicate a multiplier in the range of 0.50 to 0.75. These estimates are smaller than many analysts expect, for at least two reasons. First, with monetary policy increasingly focused on targeting inflation, the Bank of Canada can be counted on to keep the output gap equal to what they think is needed to deliver the desired inflation rate. If anything – such as an increase in government spending – closes that gap "too much", the Bank immediately takes steps to open it again. This very much limits the government spending multiplier. The second consideration is exchange-rate crowding-out. The Mundell (1963)-Fleming (1962) result – that fiscal policy has very little effect in a flexible exchange rate setting – has become increasingly relevant as Canada has more fully embraced truly floating exchange rates and the more fully mobile capital has become internationally.

I have calibrated the model presented in the Appendix so that it is consistent with the earlier multiplier estimate of 1.5 for two reasons. First, it is not reasonable to expect the Bank of Canada to offset fiscal initiatives at this time; second, with a similar recession (and similar fiscal initiatives being applied) throughout the Western world, there is no reason to expect Canadian interest rates to rise along with our stimulus. As a result, the exchange-rate crowding-out mechanism is not likely to be important in the present situation. Since OECD analysts expect high precautionary saving at this time, and since they have not discounted the current applicability of the Mundell-Fleming analysis, their multiplier estimates are somewhat smaller. Nevertheless, the support for active fiscal policy (that respects the need to control debt growth) emerging from their analysis is quite similar.

Alternative Fiscal Instruments: Some Guiding Principles

One of the central applied questions concerns whether fiscal stimulus should involve temporary tax cuts or temporary spending increases. As already noted, the permanent-income hypothesis is an important consideration. It implies that temporary reductions in income taxes will go mostly to higher savings. Since only limited higher spending can be anticipated, this initiative is not recommended. Indeed, the more temporary an income tax change is, the less it affects a household's long-run average income, so the more households use variations in their savings as a buffer that permits them to smooth consumption and avoid disruptions to their living standards. And all evaluations of the US initiative in 2008 indicate that the big effect was on saving, not on consumption. But does this clear verdict apply to all tax-policy initiatives? The answer is "no". As an alternative, the government can offer temporary changes in sales taxes. This fiscal policy is not designed to affect households by changing their perception of their long-run average income. Instead, it is designed to affect the *timing* of their replacement expenditures on durables. In this case, the more temporary are the tax changes, the more they affect the timing of expenditures that were going to be made fairly soon in any event.

It has been said that – to be appealing – a fiscal stimulus should be temporary, timely, and targeted: *temporary* – since the recession will not last indefinitely; *timely* – so that the initiative kicks in now when we need it, not later on when aggregate demand has largely recovered; and *targeted* – so the government's limited funds can be directed to those most in need. It would appear that vouchers – that have value only as waivers for *GST* obligations – and that expire (say) by mid-2010 – would do the trick. They are temporary (and can be believed to be temporary), and they can be targeted – since they can be distributed only to relatively poor families. Finally, they can be timely as well since they can be distributed without much lag and new administrative arrangements. With public expenditure projects, on the other hand, even though they can be temporary and targeted to very desirable goals, they are almost never timely. The evidence is that it takes an average of 18 months passing before actual spending starts (given lags in tendering, etc.). In comparison, the suggested *GST* policy seems particularly appealing.

GST-waiver vouchers represent a convenient way of implementing the standard proposition that what we need in a recession is *expectations of inflation*. *GST*-waiver vouchers that expire in the near future generate precisely these expectations, and they are all the more necessary if households and firms have come to doubt how monetary policy that is constrained by the zero-lower-bound problem is relevant for forming their expectations of inflation. It must be acknowledged, of course, that it is precisely on expectations grounds that some analysts have expressed skepticism about ongoing fiscal policies of this sort. If households know that a cut in the sales tax is coming, they are likely to postpone spending on durables until this policy is delivered. This delay of spending can make a recession worse in the first place so that – despite its good intentions – the suggested fiscal strategy can be destabilizing. This general concern has been investigated in the past (for example, Scarth, 1988), and the conclusion that has emerged is that – on balance – such ongoing fiscal policies *are* stabilizers. That earlier analysis focused on the potentially destabilizing expectations effects that accompany investment-incentive programs for firms. I have checked that similar conclusions follow when the policy involves ongoing cyclical variation in the sales tax rate (in a new-neoclassical-synthesis analysis) in Scarth (2009b).

All in all, it seems difficult to avoid the conclusion that – by opting for unjustified permanent cuts in the *GST* in earlier budgets instead of focusing on temporary cuts in the most recent budget – the government has missed an important opportunity for pursuing better fiscal policy.

Other fiscal-policy suggestions score well on the targeted and timely criteria but less well on the temporary maxim. For example, Edlin and Phelps (2009) emphasize Phelps' long-standing call for tax credits paid to companies for their employment of low-wage personnel. They like this initiative since it focuses on job creation, it allows the private sector to identify the jobs, and it puts upward pressure on the level of market wages for unskilled individuals generally. I like it too, since in Scarth (2005), I showed how this policy – *even* when financed by a distortionary tax on interest income – could help us pursue *both* our equity and efficiency goals simultaneously. In a simple endogenous growth model with unemployment, this policy is pro-efficiency since it attacks the labour-market failure at source. With lower unemployment, physical capital has more human capital with which to work, so the pre-tax interest rate rises and the ongoing growth rate of living standards for both rich and poor increases. It is worth noting that the government's Working Income Tax Benefit (which was expanded in this budget) is not a perfect substitute for Phelps' policy suggestion since it gives a tax break on the supply side (not the demand side) of the labour market. This difference is enough to make it the case that the Working Income Tax Benefit does not generate the same "win-win" outcome in the endogenous growth analysis just referred to. Nevertheless, as much as I favour Phelps' initiative, I must admit that it scores poorly on the temporary criterion. Surely the merits of Phelps plan for addressing poverty lead to our wanting to embrace it on a permanent basis. Thus, to move ahead with it now, we must simultaneously identify how it would be financed in an ongoing way.

Fiscal Policy and Confidence Effects

According to Barro (2009a), the fundamental problem with any fiscal stimulus is that it is based on the proposition that "the government is better than the private market at marshalling idle resources to produce useful stuff". Barro thinks that this proposition is obviously false. One reason why Barro's view may be appealing is that there is no crowding-out effect associated with private expenditures such as firms' investment activity. Firms finance much of such expansion by issuing equities. For one thing, there are no required interest payment obligations associated with this method of finance (as there are with government bonds). For another thing, firms dilute the ownership of the firm only when proportionately more funds can be raised than are necessary to finance that expansion (that is, when Tobin's stock market valuation ratio exceeds unity). But that is just the point: Tobin's q does not exceed unity during recessions, so the private sector is *not* better at marshalling *idle* resources.

In a comment on Barro's paper, Hill (2009) notes that "the problem now facing us is the lack of a truly comprehensive futures market in which firms with excess capacity and workers with excess leisure could make conditional commitments". In his rejoinder, Barro (2009b) indicates that such a vague appeal to a multiple-equilibria model, in which fiscal policy might help select a desirable equilibrium, is unappealing. But explicit models of this sort *have* been worked out (for example, Woodford, 1991; and Howitt and McAfee, 1992). These analyses involve thoroughgoing micro-foundations and rational expectations. In these models, the elimination of cycles is welfare-improving, and it may be possible for the government to achieve this outcome solely by committing to intervene if ever necessary. Knowledge of that commitment may be sufficient to cause agents to expect (and therefore achieve) a non-cyclical equilibrium. In short, Barro's dismissal of this work is unconvincing, and it is especially surprising given his fundamental contributions in a related literature – the role of commitment in defining a dynamically consistent monetary policy (Barro and Gordon, 1983).

Conclusions

This essay has summarized the debates surrounding the need for fiscal stimulus at this time. It has accepted the proposition that stabilization policy is best left as much as possible to the economy's self-correction mechanism and to monetary policy. Further, central attention has been given to the complications that accompany fiscal stimulus – such as the undesirable effects of the increase in government debt that must accompany deficit-financed initiatives. Despite these biases, we conclude that a prudent government should embrace a stimulus policy at this time. While the recent budget is therefore supported by the analysis in this broad sense, we have identified at least one particular policy option that would have been a preferred way to implement the stimulus.

Appendix

The following equations define the models that are referred to in the text. The notation and the rationale for each relationship is explained following the list of equations.

$$(y-\overline{y})=-\alpha(R-\overline{R}-\pi)+\beta(g-\overline{g})+\gamma(a-\overline{a}) \tag{1}$$

$$r=\overline{r}+\theta(p-\overline{p}) \tag{2}$$

$$\dot{p}=\phi(y-\overline{y})+\pi \tag{3}$$

$$\dot{\pi}=\lambda(\dot{p}-\pi) \tag{4}$$

$$\dot{R}=\overline{R}(R-r) \tag{5}$$

$$(g-\overline{g})=(\tau/\beta)(y-\overline{y}) \tag{6a}$$

$$(g-\overline{g})=-((1-\tau)\delta/\beta)(b-\overline{b}) \tag{6b}$$

$$\dot{b}=-(\overline{R}\tau/\delta)(y-\overline{y}) \tag{7}$$

$$a=\overline{a}+\varepsilon\sin(t) \tag{8}$$

y, p, a, g, and b denote the logarithms of real output, the price level, autonomous spending, government program spending, and the stock of government bonds, while r, R, τ, and π denote the levels (not the logarithms) of the short-term nominal interest rate, the long-term nominal interest rate, the proportional income tax rate, and the expected inflation rate. All slope coefficients are positive, and dots and bars above variables stand for time derivatives and full-equilibrium values (respectively).

Aggregate demand depends inversely on the long-term real interest rate and positively on both autonomous and government spending (equation (1)). Monetary policy is defined in equation (2): the short-term nominal interest rate is set above (below) its full-equilibrium value whenever the price level is above (below) target. Actual inflation is determined by a standard expectations-augmented Phillips curve (equation (3)), and expectations of inflation are revised adaptively (equation (4)). These are the only four relationships involved in the initial analysis of monetary policy and the economy's self-correction mechanism. In this basic case, I set $a = \overline{a}$ and $g = \overline{g}$ and follow Tobin (1975) in equating the short and long bond rates. As a result, the only difference is that the monetary authority sets the interest rate in pursuit of a price-level target here, while in Tobin's analysis, the central bank sets a constant money supply. The model's stability condition is $\theta > \lambda$, and this condition cannot be satisfied if the lower-bound-constraint limits the central bank's ability to decrease the interest rate during a recession.

I consider the long and short interest rates not being identical as a sensitivity test. The former is what affects aggregate demand, while it is the latter that has – up until now – been what is manipulated by the central bank. I follow the convention in macro modelling by assuming that the long bond is a consol. In this case, when the standard term-structure relationship (that the long rate is a weighted average of all expected future short rates) is differentiated with respect to time and a linear approximation of the result is taken, we get equation (5).

Finally, I adapt the specification of monetary policy so that it is consistent with what central banks are now starting to do. In this case, the bank enters the long bond market (with open market operations there in an attempt to affect the long rate directly there), instead of entering the overnight market in an attempt to affect the long rate indirectly. This re-specification involves replacing r with R in equation (2). Once again, the stability condition is $\theta > \lambda$ as long as the lower-bound constraint is not binding, and once again, stability is not possible if it is. Central banks have been hoping that by shifting their focus to the long bond market in this way (that is, by embracing quantitative easing), they can have additional ammunition for dealing with the zero-lower-bound problem. The present analysis does not provide support for this hope, nor does evidence concerning Operation Twist (United States, 1961) and the Conversion Loan (Canada, 1958) policy episodes. As noted in the text, Scarth (2009a) shows how this skepticism remains when a more up-to-date macro model is used to investigate this issue.

The remaining equations are added to allow the model to be used to defend the conclusions reported in the text concerning bond-financed fiscal policy (in the third section). Since this application involves an additional source of dynamics – that the change in the stock of government bonds outstanding must equal that period's budget deficit – I have simplified the dynamics in the basic model slightly. In particular, π in equation (1) has been replaced by $\dot{p}$, π in equation (3) has been replaced by $\dot{\bar{p}}$, and equation (4) has therefore been dropped. For a full explanation of the equations that define fiscal policy (equations (6) and (7)), readers are referred to Scarth (2007) section 7.5, but I provide a brief summary here.

Two fiscal policy regimes are compared. In the first, the government rejects the Keynesian approach and balances its budget at every instant by cutting program spending during recessions and raising spending during booms (equation (6a)). In this case, the stock of government bonds is constant. In the second policy regime, program spending varies less over the cycle; it varies just enough to keep each period's budget deficit independent of any change in the pre-existing level of interest payment obligations. This ensures that the standard stability problem that emerges with bond-financed fiscal policy in settings involving a positive interest rate and zero growth is not relevant here. Nevertheless, in this (responsible version of a) Keynesian regime, the government runs a deficit when output falls below the natural rate, and it works the correspondingly higher debt level back down later on. Equation (6b) defines the adjustment in program spending that is undertaken to limit the initial growth in debt to avoid stability problems. Equation (7) defines the ongoing set of changes in the stock of bonds that is set in motion once a disturbance pushes the economy away from the natural rate. Parameters β and δ are the full-equilibrium ratios of program spending and government interest-payment obligations to *GDP*.

I consider both once-and-for-all and ongoing changes in aggregate demand. In the former case (a one-time permanent cut in the target price level), I calculate three summary measures in each of the two fiscal regimes. I derive the size of the immediate effect on real output, the speed with which this temporary recession dissipates, and the cumulative undiscounted output loss (the ratio of the first two measures). There is both a benefit and a cost of adopting the Keynesian policy over the constantly balanced budget approach. The "good news" is that the initial recession is smaller in the Keynesian case since the traditional "built-in stabilizer" feature of a cyclically changing budget balance is allowed to operate. But what this dynamic analysis clarifies is that there is "bad news" as well since the higher government debt must be worked down later on, and this contractionary influence slows the speed of the economy's recovery. The expressions that emerge allow me to illustrate the magnitudes of these competing effects since only a few (not particularly controversial) parameters are involved in the multiplier and adjustment-speed formulae. In line with standard calibrations in the literature, I assume the following representative parameter values: $\phi = \tau$

= 1/6, α = 2, $\overline{R}$ = 0.05, and θ = 1. These values make the impact multiplier 33% larger in the balanced-budget fiscal regime, but the cumulative output effect is 2% smaller in this case. This illustrates that the "bad news" aspect of the Keynesian regime is roughly as big as the "good news" feature. Nevertheless, since the good news arrives early and the bad news arrives later on, this analysis provides some support for the Keynesian approach to fiscal policy.

More support is provided by the analysis of ongoing changes in autonomous spending – as specified by equation (8). Following the procedure explained in Scarth (2007, 32–34), and using the same calibration reported in the previous paragraph, I find the amplitude of the cycle in real output to be 25% larger when the Keynesian policy is rejected. As noted, this analysis supports fiscal stimulus at this time.

References

Andersson, M. and B. Hofmann. 2009. "Gauging the Effectiveness of Central Bank Forward Guidance". Presented at the Viessmann European Research Centre Conference on Central Bank Communication, Decision Making and Governance, Wilfred Laurier University. At www.wlu.ca/viessmann/Conference_9.htm (accessed April 2009).

Barro, R. 2009a. "Voodoo Multipliers", *Economists' Voice* (February). At www.bepress.com/ev (accessed April 2009).

__________. 2009b. "Letter: Notes on Keynes and a Reply to Greg Hill", *Economists' Voice* (February). At www.bepress.com/ev (accessed April 2009).

Barro, R. and D. Gordon. 1983. "Rules, Discretion and Reputation in a Model of Monetary Policy", *Journal of Monetary Economics* 12, 101–122.

Blanchard, O. 1985. "Debt, Deficits and Finite Horizons", *Journal of Political Economy* 93, 223–247.

Blinder, A. and R. Solow. 1973. "Does Fiscal Policy Matter?" *Journal of Public Economics* 2, 319-337.

DeLong, B. 2009. "Four Ways Out", *Economists' Voice* (February). At www.bepress.com/ev (accessed April 2009).

Edlin, A. and D. Jaffe. 2009. "Show Me the Money", *Economists' Voice* (February). At www.bepress.com/ev (accessed April 2009).

Edlin, A. and E. Phelps. 2009. "Getting Serious about Job Creation: Part I", *Economists' Voice* (February). At www.bepress.com/ev (accessed April 2009).

Evans, P. 1993. "Consumers are Not Ricardian: Evidence from Nineteen Countries", *Economic Inquiry* 31, 534–548.

Fisher, I. 1933. "The Debt-Deflation Theory of Great Depressions", *Econometrica* 1, 337-357.

Fleming, J. 1962. "Domestic Financial Policies Under Fixed and Floating Exchange Rates", *International Monetary Fund Staff Papers* 9, 369-379.

Hall, R. 1983. "Optimal Fiduciary Monetary Systems", *Journal of Monetary Economics* 12, 33-50.

Hill, G. 2009. "Letter: Misunderstanding Keynes: Robert J. Barro's 'Voodoo Multipliers'", *Economists' Voice* (February). At www.bepress.com/ev (accessed April 2009).

Howitt, P. and P. McAfee. 1992. "Animal Spirits", *The American Economic Review* 82, 493-507.

Keynes, J.M. 1936. *The General Theory of Employment, Interest and Money.* London: Macmillan.

Laidler, D. 2009. "The Bank of Canada Needs to Nurture those Green Shoots of Recovery", C.D. Howe Institute e-brief, April. At www.cdhowe.org (accessed April 2009).

Mankiw, G. 2000. "The Savers-Spenders Theory of Fiscal Policy", *The American Economic Review Papers and Proceedings* 90, 120-125.

Mankiw, G. and W. Scarth. 2008. *Macroeconomics, Third Canadian Edition.* New York: Worth Publishers.

Mundell, R. 1963. "Capital Mobility and Stabilization Policy under Fixed and Flexible Exchange Rates", *Canadian Journal of Economics and Political Science* 29, 475-485.

OECD. 2009. "The Effectiveness and Scope of Fiscal Stimulus", *OECD Economic Outlook Interim Report, March 2009*, Chapter 3, 105-150. At www.oecd.org/oecdEconomicOutlook (accessed May 2009).

Pigou, A. 1943. "The Classical Stationary State", *Economic Journal* 53, 343-351.

Ramsey, F. 1928. "A Mathematical Theory of Saving", *Economic Journal* 38, 543-559.

Scarth, W. 1988. "Built-In Stabilizers", *Canadian Journal of Economics* XXI, 747-758.

__________. 2005. "Fiscal Policy Can Raise Both Employment and Productivity", *International Productivity Monitor* 11, 39-46.

__________. 2007. *Macroeconomics: An Introduction to Advanced Methods, Third Edition.* Toronto: Thomson Custom Publishing.

__________. 2009a. "A Skeptical Note on Quantitative Easing and the Zero Lower Bound Problem", mimeo. At socserv.mcmaster.ca/scarth/.

__________. 2009b. "Sales Taxes and Stabilization Policy: A New Neo-Classical Synthesis Analysis", mimeo. At socserv.mcmaster.ca/scarth/.

Taylor, J. 2009. "The Lack of an Empirical Rationale for a Revival of Discretionary Fiscal Policy", *American Economic Review: Papers and Proceedings* 99, 550-555.

Tobin, J. 1975. "Keynesian Models of Recession and Depression", *The American Economic Review Papers and Proceedings* 65, 195-202.

Veldhuis, N., C. Lammam, and M. Palacios. 2009. "An Irresponsible Budget: Federal Fiscal Plan is a Step Backward for Canada", *Fraser Forum* (March), 5-7.

Woodford, M. 1991. "Self-Fulfilling Expectations and Fluctuations in Aggregate Demand", in G. Mankiw and D. Romer (eds.), *New Keynesian Economics*. Cambridge: MIT Press.

PBO PERSPECTIVES ON BUDGET 2009

Chris Matier and Stephen Tapp,
Parliamentary Budget Office

Introduction

The Parliamentary Budget Office (PBO) began operations in March 2008 with a mandate to provide independent analysis to Parliament on the Canadian economy and federal budget issues. This note provides analysis and observations from the PBO on Budget 2009. We begin with some brief background on the situation leading up to the budget,[1] then address specific budget issues, discuss developments and the revised outlook since the budget, and conclude by highlighting some longer-term considerations.

Brief Background

After several years of strong growth, the global economy began to slow at the end of 2007, with the US economy entering recession in December and global growth weakening significantly throughout 2008 (Figure 1). While real growth in the Canadian economy was sluggish throughout the first half of 2008, record-high commodity prices that peaked in July helped partially insulate the purchasing power of households and firms in Canada.

The authors acknowledge important contributions and comments from Mostafa Askari, Russell Barnett, Jeff Danforth, Kevin Page, and Brad Recker. The authors are responsible for any errors.

[1]For additional background, see the MacKinnon and Ragan papers in this volume.

Figure 1: World and US GDP Growth 2004-2009

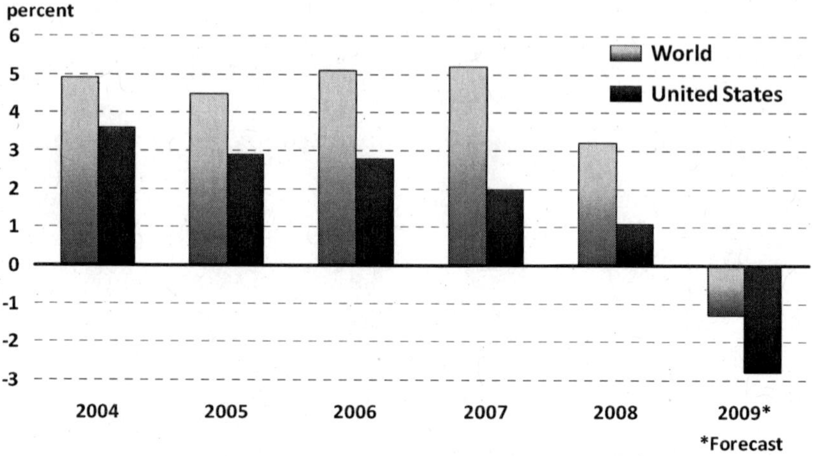

Note: World growth uses purchasing-power-parity weights.
Source: IMF.

In September 2008, global credit market strain turned into a global financial crisis with the failure of a major US investment bank. This major financial shock amplified the existing weakness in the Canadian economy and resulted in a large and rapid stock market reversal, compounding the impacts of the ongoing commodity price correction. Sharp declines in output and employment quickly followed. Consumer and business confidence collapsed owing to worsening wealth and income prospects and increased uncertainty. Overall, the deterioration in the financial and economic environment was rapid, significant, and not well anticipated. As a result, these developments led to a further downgrading of Canadian economic growth forecasts for 2009 (Figure 2).

The size of the shocks, their global nature, and the limited scope for additional conventional monetary stimulus put the onus on discretionary fiscal policy to help stabilize the Canadian economy.[2] Initially, in November 2008, the government's *Economic and Fiscal Statement* proposed mildly contractionary spending restraint aimed at achieving

---

[2]Monetary policy was thought to be constrained because the Bank of Canada had substantially reduced its policy interest rate during the preceding year (from 4.5% in November 2007 to 2.25% in November 2008) and the financial nature of the downturn had impaired the monetary policy transmission mechanism.

Figure 2: Canadian Average Private Sector Real GDP Growth Forecasts for 2009

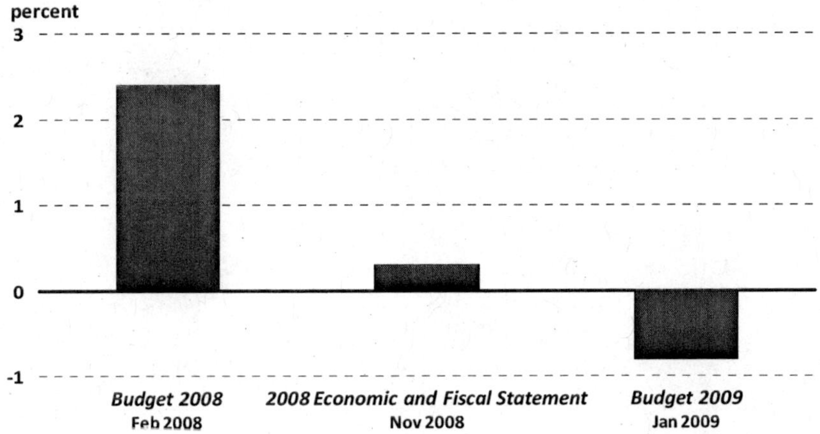

Source: Department of Finance Canada.

modest surpluses in each year of the five-year fiscal planning horizon. These policy actions were criticized by opposition parties and ultimately led to the formation of a coalition in December 2008 that threatened to defeat the minority Conservative government. This defeat was avoided by proroguing Parliament, which allowed the government time to conclude its stakeholder consultations and bring forward an early budget in January 2009.

PBO Budget 2009 Analysis

Budget 2009 was designed largely as an economic stimulus package, based on the guiding principles that its measures be timely, targeted, and temporary. The budget not only aimed to fulfill Canada's November 2008 G20 commitment to provide timely stimulus, but also to improve the availability of credit and restore the functioning of impaired financial markets. The budget reported total incremental measures at $51.6 billion (3.2% of GDP) over 2009 and 2010, based on $39.9 billion in federal stimulus and an expected $11.7 billion in provincial and municipal "leveraged" contributions.[3] The budget's stimulus impacts on the Canadian economy were estimated to increase real GDP (by 1.9%) and employment (by 189,000 jobs) by the end of 2010.

Also noteworthy was that the budget projected a return to a surplus position by the end of the forecast horizon in 2013–14. This result relied on the time-limited nature of the stimulus spending and overall spending management as well as an optimistic rebound in tax revenues toward the end of the projection period as the economy recovered.

The following sections summarize PBO analysis from pre- and post-budget reports (PBO, 2009a; and PBO, 2009b) and include expanded analysis and subsequent results. The issues covered in these sections are the fiscal projections and planning assumptions, the government's measurement of the stimulus, an assessment of budget measures relative to its guiding principles, and the quarterly budget progress reports.

Fiscal Planning Assumptions and Projection Results

In January 2009, the PBO's pre-budget briefing presented a status quo fiscal projection that relied on a similar economic outlook used for fiscal planning in Budget 2009.[4] Despite these similar economic outlooks, a key difference between the two projections was the budget balance in the outer years, where Budget 2009 featured a return to surplus by 2013–14, while the PBO's analysis projected a deficit (Table 1).[5] The difference between the two status quo projections was roughly $5 billion in 2012–13 and more than $10 billion in 2013–14.

---

[3]While Budget 2009 included important measures to improve access to financing and strengthen the financial system, the government's total stimulus estimate did not include these measures.

[4]Both the Budget 2009 and PBO status quo fiscal projections were based on surveys of private sector forecasters conducted in January 2009. PBO's projection of nominal GDP was marginally higher (+$6B) than Budget 2009's risk-adjusted forecast in 2011 but marginally lower in 2012 and 2013 (-$3B and -$7B).

[5]The differences in the near-term results is partially explained by the fact that the budget risk-adjusted its near-term nominal GDP projection, while the PBO did not risk-adjust its average scenario, instead assessing risk through an additional low-growth scenario.

Table 1: Status Quo Budget Balance Comparison ($ Billions)

	2008-09	2009-10	2010-11	2011-12	2012-13	2013-14
Status Quo Budgetary Balance ($ billions)						
Budget 2009 (risk-adjusted)	0.2	-15.7	-14.3	-8.3	-2.3	5.5
PBO January 2009 (not risk-adjusted)	0.2	-13.0	-11.6	-8.6	-7.4	-5.3
PBO January 2009 minus Budget 2009	**0.0**	**2.7**	**2.7**	**-0.3**	**-5.1**	**-10.8**

Source: Budget 2009; Parliamentary Budget Office.

Budget 2009 cited downside risks to the economic outlook that were concentrated in 2009 and 2010, owing to the possibility of more prolonged financial market problems and a weaker outlook for commodity prices. As a result, the budget prudently adjusted downward the near-term private sector forecast of nominal GDP, but returned the level of nominal GDP used for planning purposes to the private sector average by 2014 (Table 2).

There are two implications of this adjustment. First, this risk adjustment to the fiscal projection is front-end-loaded – largely affecting the near-term budget balance while having little impact on the medium term. This front-end-loaded risk adjustment differs from the treatment of economic forecast uncertainty in past budgets (prepared in the context of surpluses that grew over the projection horizon). In those budgets, "economic prudence" was back-end-loaded and grew over the projection horizon, rather than shrinking, and thereby increasingly worsened the budget balance over the projection. Second, returning to the *level* of nominal GDP in 2014 forecast average implies that nominal GDP *growth* exceeds the private sector survey average in each year after 2009 – indicating an upside risk to the private sector outlook for growth after this year.

Table 2: Budget 2009 Nominal GDP Outlook ($ Billions)

	2008	2009	2010	2011	2012	2013	2014
Nominal GDP (billions of dollars)							
January 2009 Finance survey							
Level	1,609	1,590	1,657	1,751	1,848	1,940	2,031
Growth		-1.2	4.2	5.7	5.5	5.0	4.7
Budget 2009 fiscal planning assumption							
Level	1,604	1,560	1,627	1,731	1,838	1,935	2,031
Growth		-2.7	4.3	6.4	6.2	5.3	5.0
Level Adjustment for risk	**-5**	**-30**	**-30**	**-20**	**-10**	**-5**	**0**
	2008-09	*2009-10*	*2010-11*	*2011-12*	*2012-13*	*2013-14*	
Revenue Effect of Risk Adjustment	**-0.8**	**-4.5**	**-4.5**	**-3.0**	**-1.5**	**-0.8**	

Source: Budget 2009.

In the PBO's view, incorporating larger downward adjustments to nominal GDP (or explicitly to the budget balance) in the outer years might be a more appropriate way to address the possibility that the downturn could be deeper and/or longer than private sector forecasters anticipated at the time of the budget – particularly given the global and financial nature of the recession.[6]

Notwithstanding the risk adjustment to nominal GDP, the budget's projected return to surplus was based on relatively optimistic assumptions underlying revenues in 2012–13 and 2013–14. Indeed, the different fiscal projection results between the PBO and Budget 2009 are mainly a result of differences in revenue projections ($4.5 billion in 2012–13 and $9.5 billion in 2013–14), primarily reflecting differences in corporate income tax revenues (Table 3). While Budget 2009 did not present its underlying assumptions about corporate profits, it appears to rely on a more optimistic assumption for the outer years – corporate profits as a share of nominal GDP were likely projected to remain well above their long-term historical average.[7] Other revenues, which include Employment Insurance (EI) premiums, also contributed to the differences in 2012–13 and 2013–14.

Table 3: Status Quo Revenue Comparison (Budget 2009 Minus PBO, January 2009)

	2008-09	*2009-10*	*2010-11*	*2011-12*	*2012-13*	*2013-14*
Revenues (Budget 2009 minus PBO January 2009, $ billions)						
Personal Income Taxes	0.7	-3.1	-5.6	-6.0	-4.1	-1.8
Corporate Incomes Taxes	-3.5	-1.7	2.0	5.8	6.6	7.1
Goods and Services Tax	-0.5	-1.5	-1.4	-0.7	-0.3	-0.1
Other Revenues	1.5	-1.9	0.1	0.9	2.4	4.3
Budget 2009 minus PBO January 2009 (total revenues)	**-1.8**	**-8.3**	**-4.9**	**0.1**	**4.5**	**9.5**

Source: Budget 2009; Parliamentary Budget Office.

---

[6]Recent research by Claessens, Kose, and Terrones (2008) and Reinhart and Rogoff (2009) analyze cross-country data and find evidence that financial-, credit- and housing-related recessions tend to be longer and more severe.

[7]PBO requested projection details for corporate profits and other economic variables underlying Budget 2009, but was not provided with this information because the Privy Council Office deemed it a Cabinet confidence.

Measuring the Size of the Fiscal Stimulus

Budget 2009 estimated the federal fiscal stimulus measures at $39.9 billion over 2009-10 to 2010-11. In the PBO's view, this estimate may be overstated. First, the budget estimate of federal fiscal stimulus simply offsets $5.7 billion in contractionary fiscal actions for 2009-10 and 2010-11, which were proposed only two months earlier in the November 2008 *Economic and Fiscal Statement*. Second, the budget estimate includes stimulus of $2.4 billion in 2010 from maintaining EI premiums at 2009 levels in 2010. The estimate is calculated relative to a benchmark case in which EI premiums in 2010 would have been increased to their break-even level, representing a contractionary policy response in the context of rising unemployment. Adjusting for these two considerations, results in a "net" federal stimulus of $31.8 billion, 20% smaller than reported in Budget 2009 over 2009-10 and 2010-11 (Table 4). Finally, a significant part of the government's stimulus estimate (approximately $10 billion) is contingent on matching contributions from other levels of government. If these other governments do not participate in these programs, the size of the federal stimulus falls further to $21.9 billion, 45% smaller than the Budget 2009 estimate.

Assessing Stimulus Measures Against the Budget's Guiding Principles

Budget 2009 states that the stimulus measures are based on three guiding principles – that the stimulus measures should be targeted (to trigger the largest increase in Canadian jobs and output), timely (begin by the end of May 2009), and temporary (phased out when the economy recovers to avoid long-term structural deficits). In general, the Budget 2009 stimulus measures appear broadly consistent with the government's guiding

Table 4: Estimates of the Federal Fiscal Stimulus ($ Billions)

	2009-10	*2010-11*	*Total*
Budget 2009 reported federal stimulus measures (billions of dollars)	**22.7**	**17.2**	**39.9**
Spending reductions in the November 2008 Economic and Fiscal Statement	2.9	2.8	5.7
Budget 2009 estimated cost of maintaining EI premiums at 2009 levels in 2010	0.8	1.6	2.4
Net federal stimulus	**19.0**	**12.8**	**31.8**

Source: Budget 2009.

principles, though there may be some challenges to fully achieve all these aims given that there may be trade-offs among these three objectives.[8]

Targeted

Based on Department of Finance Canada estimates of fiscal multipliers (i.e., the short-run increase in economic activity per dollar allocated to a particular policy action), Budget 2009 measures are generally targeted. The majority of the measures are allocated to "high" impact categories, with over 40% ($13.9 billion) of total federal stimulus allocated to infrastructure spending, with a multiplier of 1.6 over eight quarters – the second highest multiplier, according to Department of Finance estimates (Figure 3). That said, the highest multiplier – and possibly one of the more timely actions – measures for low-income Canadians (1.7), was allocated with fewer resources than many other categories.

Figure 3: Federal Measures 2009-2010 by Multiplier Impact ($ Billions)

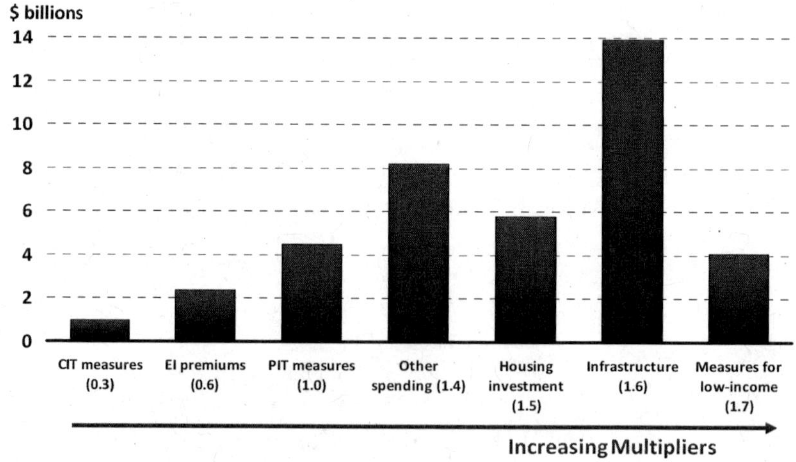

*Budget 2009 estimated multipliers shown in parentheses.
Source: Budget 2009.

[8]For example, infrastructure spending may be targeted, but not timely. Measures for low-income individuals may be timely but difficult to enact temporarily; and some temporary, targeted measures may prove to be permanent.

Timely

Budget 2009 also strives to be timely: "measures to support the economy must begin within the next 120 days". Recalling that a key, long-standing argument against the use of discretionary fiscal policy is its long time lags, implementing measures this quickly will be a significant challenge. The government's first progress report in March 2009 described some of the extraordinary measures taken to accelerate spending appropriations. However, there are some key areas of concern – particularly with respect to infrastructure funding, which accounts for the largest portion of stimulus spending. Based on recent performance, the government's infrastructure funding has lapsed (i.e., not spent) approximately one of every three dollars planned over the past two fiscal years (Table 5). Given this track record, the doubling of Infrastructure Canada appropriations in 2009–10 poses a key risk to the timely implementation of a major component of the budget.

Temporary

On a Public Accounts basis, the fiscal costs to the federal government of Budget 2009 measures over 2008–09 to 2013–14 total $49.4 billion (Table 6). While there may be political pressure to maintain some short-term actions, the majority of budget measures are planned to be temporary, with 70% of the fiscal cost incurred by 2010–11. The fiscal cost of measures is almost equally split between spending and revenue categories over the projection horizon. Spending measures are planned to be mostly temporary, with about 90% dispensed by 2010–11 ($21.6 billion). On the tax side, personal income tax cuts contribute about $4 billion to permanent fiscal costs beyond 2010–11, representing almost half of total tax measures ($11.6 billion).

Table 5: Infrastructure Canada Spending, Planned and Actual Spending ($ Billions)

	2006-07	*2007-08*	*2008-09*	*2009-10*	*2010-11*	*2011-12*
Infrastructure Canada Spending ($ billions)						
Planned	2.1	3.1	3.4	7.3	7.0	4.1
Actual	1.5	2.0	--	--	--	--

Source: Public Accounts of Canada and Infrastructure Canada's 2009-10 Report on Plans and Priorities.

Table 6: Fiscal Costs of Budget 2009 Measures (Public Accounts Basis, $ Billions)

	2008-09	*2009-10*	*2010-11*	*2011-12*	*2012-13*	*2013-14*	*Total*
Budget 2009 measures ($ billions)							
Revenue measures	1.2	6.8	5.2	3.7	4.0	3.9	**24.8**
Spending measures	0.1	11.2	10.3	1.0	1.0	1.0	**24.6**
Total measures in Budget 2009	**1.3**	**18.0**	**15.5**	**4.7**	**5.0**	**4.9**	**49.4**

Source: Budget 2009; Parliamentary Budget Office.

Budget Progress Reports

Implementing a large-scale spending acceleration in a parliamentary system in both a timely and effective manner is a difficult task. To address these concerns, a key requirement for parliamentary approval of Budget 2009 was that quarterly progress reports be provided to Parliament.

In late February 2009, prior to the release of the government's first progress report, the PBO published a discussion paper that suggested key information to be included in these reports (PBO, 2009c). In the PBO's view, the central goal of these reports should be to provide Parliament with accurate, timely, and easily understood information on three key issues: 1) the implementation and progress of budget measures; 2) recent economic and fiscal developments and prospects; and 3) assessing budget results relative to its guiding principles.

The government's first report in March 2009 focused largely on the first of these three issues – namely, on setting up the necessary authorizations to ensure that stimulus measures could begin quickly. In the first report, there was limited information provided on expected outputs and outcomes of budget measures, implementation benchmarks and timelines for specific programs, or an updated outlook for the Canadian economy and budget projection. However, if this information is provided in future reports, this may allow for a real-time assessment of program implementation and tracking of results relative to program objectives.

Tracking Stimulus Impacts and Recent Economic Developments

Budget 2009 provided detailed estimates and analysis of the short-run economic impacts of stimulus measures over 2009 and 2010. By the end of 2010, the Department of Finance estimates that the total stimulus of $51.6 billion (including leverage)[9] will increase real GDP by 1.9% and will create or maintain 189,000 jobs – equivalent to a 1.1% increase in employment relative to an unobservable baseline scenario that does not include stimulus measures. Based on this analysis, the PBO has reconstructed a baseline scenario projection (i.e., the outlook based on the January 2009 private sector survey, which does not likely reflect significant stimulus measures) with estimates of the quarterly impacts of the stimulus measures consistent with the annual and end point estimates provided in Budget 2009. This baseline scenario also serves as a useful reference point since it reflects the projected weakness in output and employment that helped prompt Budget 2009 stimulus initiatives.

The data releases to date suggest that the economy's starting point, prior to the stimulus measures, is considerably weaker than anticipated at the time of Budget 2009. With the larger than expected declines in the fourth quarter of 2008 and first quarter of 2009, the level of real GDP is now 1.6% lower than the baseline projection in the first quarter of 2009 (Table 7).

Table 7: Real GDP With and Without Budget 2009 Stimulus (Index, 2008Q4 = 100)

	08Q4	*09Q1*	*09Q2*	*09Q3*	*09Q4*	*10Q1*	*10Q2*	*10Q3*	*10Q4*
Real GDP (index, Budget 2009 2008Q4 = 100)									
With Budget 2009 stimulus	100.0	100.9	100.6	101.1	101.7	102.4	103.2	104.1	105.1
Without Budget 2009 stimulus	100.0	99.3	99.0	99.5	100.0	100.7	101.4	102.2	103.1
2008Q4 and 2009Q1 actual	99.1	97.7							

Source: Parliamentary Budget Office.

[9]The total stimulus impact assumes full take-up by other levels of government and that they do not simply divert resources from other spending priorities to take advantage of matching federal contributions.

Regarding labour market impacts, the level of employment is 0.7% (112,000 jobs) lower than the baseline projection, based on Labour Force Survey data through March 2009 (Table 8).

Looking ahead, the outlook for the Canadian economy has worsened significantly since Budget 2009 was tabled in January. Indeed, with weaker than expected real GDP growth in the final quarter of 2008 and first quarter of 2009 (relative to Budget 2009), private sector forecasters now expect[10] real GDP to decline by 2.7% in 2009 and rise by 2.0% in 2010 (versus the Budget 2009 expectations of -0.8% and 2.4%). Moreover, the current private sector outlook reflects expectations of the impact on real GDP growth of Budget 2009 stimulus measures; this implies that the downward revisions to the baseline outlook were substantial, more than offsetting any of the estimated positive impacts of the stimulus measures.

As a small open economy and commodity exporter, Canada's recovery will depend crucially on global economic and financial developments – particularly those in the United States.[11] While stimulative monetary and fiscal policies, both in Canada and abroad, will support growth, history suggests that financial-led recessions are deeper and their subsequent recoveries slower than in average recessions. These factors suggest that the global and Canadian economies could remain well below their potential production capacity for an extended period. Overall, the revised economic forecasts also imply that the current recession is expected to be more severe than recent recessions in terms of the overall amount of unrealized output (Table 9).

Table 8: Employment With and Without Budget 2009 Stimulus

	08Q4	*09Q1*	*09Q2*	*09Q3*	*09Q4*	*10Q1*	*10Q2*	*10Q3*	*10Q4*
Employment (thousands)									
With Budget 2009 stimulus	17,157	17,073	17,088	17,126	17,169	17,237	17,304	17,382	17,470
Without Budget 2009 stimulus	17,157	17,018	17,014	17,033	17,057	17,106	17,154	17,213	17,281
2008Q4 and 2009Q1 actual	17,146	16,907							

Source: Parliamentary Budget Office.

[10]Based on the May 2009 PBO survey of private sector forecasters.

[11]Vector autoregression analysis suggests that shocks to US growth are particularly important for Canada's growth through financial and trade linkages. See, e.g., Swiston and Bayoumi (2008).

Table 9: Estimated Output Gap in Recessions (% of Potential GDP)

	0	*Year 1*	*Year 2*	*Year 3*	*Year 4*	*Year 5*	*Year 6*	*Year7*
Output Gap (% of potential GDP)								
1981 to 1988	0.6	-5.1	-4.9	-1.8	0.5	0.6	2.4	4.7
1990 to 1997	1.6	-3.0	-4.1	-3.9	-1.7	-1.9	-3.1	-2.0
2007 to 2014*	0.0	-1.9	-6.7	-7.1	-6.1	-5.1	-4.4	-3.9

*May 2009 PBO Survey for real GDP growth. Potential output growth assumed to be 2.4%; lower potential output growth would result in smaller estimates of excess capacity.
Source: Department of Finance Canada; Parliamentary Budget Office.

Longer-Term Considerations

In the current environment, with the intense focus on near-term challenges, it is easy to overlook important longer-term issues. This section highlights some outstanding issues by posing three questions that may be relevant for the Canadian economy and policy-makers after the recovery takes hold – and, as such, are issues worth raising now. We conclude with three take-away observations.

Q1. Will the Current Downturn Have Longer-Term Impacts on Potential Output?

The first outstanding issue that is not well understood at the current time is the possible impacts of the current recession on potential output growth in Canada. One concern is that a severe cyclical downturn and associated restructuring of key industries could have persistent impacts on the economy's production capacity going forward. For example, in its most recent projection, in April 2009, the Bank of Canada significantly revised down its estimate of Canada's potential output growth.[12] The Bank cited capital obsolescence and labour reallocation costs resulting from structural adjustments in industries such as the automotive and forestry sectors as well as weak business investment, which would lower capital per worker. Looking forward, if these developments proved to be persistent, they could matter not only for fiscal policy-makers if they

[12]Revised down from 2.4% to 1.2% in 2009, from 2.5% to 1.5% in 2010, and from 2.5% to 1.9% in 2011.

restrain tax collections or increase spending requirements in programs such as EI, but could also have material impacts on Canadian living standards.

Q2. Is There a Risk of Structural Deficits?

Budget 2009 states a principle that stimulus measures should be phased out when the economy recovers to avoid long-term structural deficits. In practice, avoiding structural deficits may ultimately require political will and solid economic performance. Political will is required to ensure that temporary measures are in fact phased out as the economy recovers. It also means that spending remains disciplined over the medium term because, after the short-term spike in program spending, Budget 2009 plans to significantly restrain program spending so that it does not grow faster than GDP over the planning horizon. In addition, a sustained rebound in the global economy and commodity prices, and maintaining Canada's potential production capacity at high levels, will also help avoid structural deficits.

Although there is a high degree of uncertainty surrounding estimates of potential output and, therefore, structural budget balances, rough PBO calculations based on Budget 2009 projections suggest a small structural surplus position over the medium-term through 2013-14 (Table 10).[13]

Table 11 shows the impact of slower potential GDP growth on the structural budget balance estimates by assuming potential growth of 1.9% versus 2.4% annually. Lower potential growth would reduce structural revenue growth and lead to small structural deficits, equal to

Table 10: Budgetary Balance Projections ($ Billions)

	2007-08	*2008-09*	*2009-10*	*2010-11*	*2011-12*	*2012-13*	*2013-14*
Budget Balance ($ billions)							
Structural balance	9.6	3.7	-1.7	0.4	1.5	1.6	5.0
Cyclical balance	0.0	-4.8	-32.0	-30.2	-14.5	-8.9	-4.3
Budget 2009 Budgetary Balance	**9.6**	**-1.1**	**-33.7**	**-29.8**	**-13.0**	**-7.3**	**0.7**

Source: Budget 2009; Parliamentary Budget Office.

[13]Despite the government's stated fiscal objective of avoiding structural deficits, it has not yet provided estimates of structural budget balances over the projection horizon.

Table 11: PBO Estimates of Structural Budget Balances ($ Billions)

	2007-08	2008-09	2009-10	2010-11	2011-12	2012-13	2013-14
Structural Budgetary Balance ($ billions)							
2.4% potential GDP growth	9.6	3.7	-1.7	0.4	1.5	1.6	5.0
1.9% potential GDP growth	9.6	2.5	-4.2	-3.5	-3.8	-5.2	-3.6

Source: Parliamentary Budget Office.

less than 1% of GDP through 2013-14. Overall, the downward revisions to potential output by the Bank of Canada and private sector forecasters suggest downside risks to structural balance estimates over the medium term.

Q3. Will Policy-Makers Need to Re-Examine Canada's Fiscal Policy Framework?

In a previous JDI budget conference, Rick Harris (2003) made the following prediction:

> I am skeptical this Canadian value (of balanced budgets) will endure beyond the current business cycle.... Eventually a large recession will occur in Canada, a deficit will result and there will be calls for fiscal stimulus. This is inevitable. Not *if*, but only *when*.... The whole framework for fiscal policy will be revisited.

Professor Harris was right. Re-thinking the fiscal policy framework and objectives will be a key issue going forward. One aspect of this is the macroeconomic stabilization provided by fiscal policy. Internationally, the current global recession has led to a strong resurgence in support for discretionary fiscal policy among policy-makers (as part of an even broader re-examination of the role of government in the economy more generally). At the current time, it is unclear whether this support will continue or whether this response was specific to the nature of the current recession. In Canada, there may be additional forces at play rather than simply the large economic shocks and the perceived limitations of additional monetary stabilization. There is a sense that automatic stabilizers at the federal level have possibly become less countercyclical in the past decade as a result of personal and corporate income tax rate reductions and policy changes to the EI and Equalization programs.[14] If automatic stabilizers are indeed less effective, then other things being equal, that could imply an increasing reliance on discretionary fiscal stabilization measures in future recessions.

Regarding the fiscal policy framework more generally, prior to this recession, Canadian fiscal policy operated under a combination of several stated fiscal targets over differing time horizons. There was a short-term objective of paying down debt by $3 billion annually, the medium-term objectives of achieving a 25% federal debt-to-GDP ratio by 2011–12 and keeping program spending growth below that of nominal GDP growth on average, and a longer-tem goal of eliminating net total government debt by 2021 (which includes the balances of the public CPP/QPP pension plans as well as other levels of government).

As Harris predicted, a rethinking of fiscal priorities is underway, and indeed, there already appears to be a subtle adjustment of fiscal policy objectives. Budget 2009 did not reaffirm its prior specific policy targets. Instead, the budget reiterated the general goal of reducing the debt burden, stating that "as a first priority, surpluses should be dedicated to repay the deficits expected over the next four years". Also, in addition to its economic stimulus objectives, the budget appeared to suggest a new fiscal policy goal of maintaining a structural surplus/avoiding a structural deficit. This may be viewed as a move from aiming to balance the budget each year toward balancing the budget over the economic cycle – an approach generally supported by O'Neill (2005) and Dodge (1998).

Concluding Observations

With a few months passed since Budget 2009, the JDI budget conference provides the opportunity to reflect on recent developments. First, there are some important reminders on timeless issues that are easily forgotten:

1. *In policy-making discussions and for policy decisions, it is important to address near-term demands, while maintaining focus on long-term policy challenges and preserving policy credibility.*

---

[14]In fact, changes to the latter two programs may have potentially added pro-cyclical elements that could effectively amplify booms and downturns. For example, the overall size of Equalization payments is tied to GDP growth, and for EI in this recession, premiums were set to rise going forward to balance the EI account, and explicit policy actions were necessary in Budget 2009 to override this feature of the program.

One component of this is debating and articulating clearly defined exit strategies for fiscal and monetary policy for the post-recovery period. Focusing on fiscal policy, credibility was hard earned in the 1990s as many governments in Canada made great progress in reversing rising debt burdens. This required not only educating the public about the debt problem, but also making difficult policy decisions – particularly to cut spending. This progress must not be undone in the current downturn. Preserving fiscal sustainability is particularly important in anticipation of several long-run challenges, including:

- *Future demographic pressures*. Population aging will slow labour force growth dramatically, and without stronger productivity performance, living standards and public finances will come under pressure.
- *Weak productivity performance*. Canada's recent productivity performance has been weak both historically and compared to the United States.
- *Environmental problems*. Strong policy actions will be required in this area.
- *Regional and industrial adjustments*. These include the downward trend of manufacturing employment in advanced economies, will require policies that cushion these impacts while facilitating a necessary reallocation of labour from slowing regions and industries to growing regions and industries.

Overall, then, policy decisions today should attempt to clearly identify these and other key challenges and make long-term investments to address them.

2. *The global financial crisis underscores the importance of transparency in financial reporting and decision-making.*

One key contributor to the financial market crisis was a lack of transparency regarding financial assets on the part of borrowers, investors, credit rating agencies, etc. Related problems also arose in the past decade from accounting scandals in various countries in both the public and private sectors. While improving transparency in financial decision-making is not sufficient on its own to ensure sensible decision-making, improving transparency has the potential to raise warning signs sooner and possibly prevent increased speculation or poor financial management. This leads to a view of how recent developments present a unique opportunity:

3. *The heightened scrutiny of budget stimulus measures provides a unique opportunity to improve budget transparency, oversight and reporting to Parliament for Budget 2009 and beyond.*

The PBO views the introduction of quarterly budget progress reports as a welcome development. These progress reports represent a historic opportunity to strengthen budget transparency regarding the implementation, oversight, and effectiveness of government budgets. The government's first report represents an important first step toward improving interim reporting to Parliament and could ultimately strengthen Parliament's budgetary oversight role. Therefore, the PBO encourages Parliament to consider making permanent some type of progress reporting requirement to ensure that this increased level of transparency remains for future budgets.

References

Claessens, S., M.A. Kose, and M. Terrones. 2008. *What Happens During Recession, Crunches and Busts?* International Monetary Fund Working Paper/08/274.

Dodge, D.A. 1998. *Reflections on the Role of Fiscal Policy: The Doug Purvis Memorial Lecture* 24(3) (September), 275-289.

Harris, R. 2003. "Balanced Budgets as a Canadian Fiscal Value?" in C.M. Beach and T.A. Wilson (eds.), *The 2003 Federal Budget: Conflicting Tensions.* Kingston: John Deutsch Institute, Queen's University, 37-47.

O'Neill, T. 2005. *Review of Canadian Federal Fiscal Forecasting Processes and Systems.* June. At www.fin.gc.ca/activty/pubs/Oneil/PDF/Oneil_e.pdf.

PBO. 2009a. *Pre-Budget Economic and Fiscal Briefing.* January. At www2.parl.gc.ca/Sites/PBO-DPB/documents/Pre-Budget_Briefing.pdf.

__________. 2009b. *Budget 2009 Economic and Fiscal Outlook – Key Issues,* February. At www2.parl.gc.ca/sites/pbo-dpb/documents/Budget_2009_Issues.pdf.

__________. 2009c. *Key Information for the Government's Progress Reports to Assist Parliamentary Monitoring and Oversight of Budget 2009*, February. At www2.parl.gc.ca/sites/pbo-dpb/documents/Budget_2009_Progress_Report_Info.pdf.

Reinhart, C. and K. Rogoff. 2009. "The Aftermath of Financial Crisis", *American Economic Review* 99(2), 466-472.

Swiston, A. and T. Bayoumi. 2008. *Spillovers Across NAFTA.* International Monetary Fund Working Paper/08/03.

IS "SHOVEL READY" GOOD ENOUGH?

Robert Fairholm, Centre for Spatial Economics

Introduction

In order to evaluate the Canadian federal budget, it is important to consider the context under which the budget was formulated. This report will examine the external environment that Canada faced, explore the dysfunction in the financial markets that was affecting the monetary transmission mechanism at the time of the budget, identify the magnitude of fiscal stimulus required to offset the external shock given the degree of possible dysfunction in the monetary transmission mechanism, examine the budget measures, and compare the fiscal stimulus from the budget measures with other approaches that could provide both short-term stimulus to GDP and also long-term benefits to the economy.

Economic Environment Grim

External Environment

The world economy is facing a financial and economic crisis of historic proportions. The managing director of the International Monetary Fund (IMF) has indicated that the world economy is facing its worst crisis in 60 years. At the APEC summit in Lima, Peru, Prime Minister Stephen Harper stated that the financial crisis had become an economic crisis and the world was entering an economic period unlike, and potentially as dangerous, as anything we had faced since 1929.

The financial and economic crisis did not start in Canada, but Canadians are suffering from the crisis nonetheless. The financial and economic crisis is negatively affecting the Canadian economy via a number of channels, including real trade flows, terms of trade, freezing of the financial markets, and the wealth effect. There is also a considerable increase in uncertainty for businesses, consumers, and economists that could alter their behaviour. Given the magnitude of these shocks, there will be deflation for the GDP deflator and the all-items CPI. Declining prices present a grave downside risk should deflation psychology take hold.

Economic news from around the world is grim. The IMF estimates that the global economy shrank by 6.25% in the fourth quarter of 2008. Advanced economies witnessed an unprecedented 7.5% drop in output, and the emerging economies experienced a 4% drop. All of Canada's major trading partners are suffering: the United States experienced a 6.3% drop in the final quarter of 2008, output in Japan fell by an annualized rate of 12.7%, and the euro area and the United Kingdom witnessed declines of around 6%.

According to the IMF's April 2009 *World Economic Outlook*, the global economy grew by 3.2% in 2008, is expected to contract by 1.3% in 2009, and will grow by 1.9% in 2010. Given that 3% global growth is the benchmark used to represent a global recession, the world economy will be near or in recession for three consecutive years. The IMF expects that after growing by 0.9% in 2008, the advanced economies will shrink by 3.8% this year and grow by 0% next year. The US economy is forecast to contract by 2.8% in 2009 and not grow in 2010, following growth of 1.1% in 2008. The pace of growth of the advanced economies has direct implications for the pace of growth (or contraction) of Canada's real exports since these economies receive the vast majority of Canadian exports. Canada, therefore, will experience a major drop in export volumes during 2009 as a result of the global recession based on end-market growth alone.

Obviously, the United States is the most important geographic end-market for Canadian exports, with around 80% of all international exports bound for the United States before the crisis hit. The magnitude of import elasticities with respect to US output suggests that the drop in Canadian exports could be up to twice as large as a slide in the US economy.[1] Given the current economic environment, however, the output

---

[1]Chapter 3, IMF *World Economic Outlook 2007*. US import elasticities with respect to US output were reported to range from 1.7 to 2.4, depending on the time period, whether the aggregation bias is removed, and whether relative prices or the real effective exchange rate is used in the estimation.

elasticities clearly underestimate the impact on Canadian exports compared with the decline in the overall US economy because the composition of Canadian exports to the United States is heavily weighted toward wood, motor vehicles, and machinery, with a combined 33-40% share of total exports to the United States in recent years. And US expenditures for housing, motor vehicles, and capital goods are dropping dramatically during the recession in part because of the impact of the credit crunch, which made financing difficult to obtain. In their April forecast, for example, Macroeconomic Advisers forecasted that real US expenditures on new single-family dwellings would plunge by a further 43.1% in 2009, following a 36.5% drop in 2008; motor vehicle and parts would fall by 5.1% in 2009, following a 13.3% drop in 2008; and machinery excluding computers and software would fall by 20.5%, after a 6.7% drop in 2008. From these three markets alone, the impact on total Canadian exports is in the range of 3.8% in 2008 and 4.1% in 2009, using an output elasticity of one, or by 6.5% and 6.8% using an elasticity of 1.7.

Clearly, other US end-markets and, therefore, exports are being affected by the global recession, and this will magnify the impact on Canadian total exports. In addition to the direct impact on Canadian trade from the shrinkage of global markets, the financial crisis has had a major impact on trade financing. The unavailability of trade financing has directly thwarted international trade. Therefore, Canadian exporters will experience a major decline in volumes during the recession.

Terms of Trade

The developed world is not alone in experiencing the impact of the global recession. Developing economies are also experiencing a major slowdown. The IMF estimates that the emerging and developing economies will experience growth of 1.6% this year and 4.0% next year. The economic prospects for developing economies have significant implications for Canada, although not so much via direct exports as through export prices and the terms of trade.

Since the Asian crisis of 1998, there has been a high correlation between economic growth in the emerging and developing economies and global commodity prices. Using IMF data, the correlation from 1998 to 2008 in the growth in the IMF's commodity price measure "Commodity Non-Fuel Price Index, including Food and Beverages and Industrial Inputs Price Indices" deflated by the US GDP deflator was 0.77 versus the growth in developing and emerging economies, while this measure of real commodity prices had a correlation of only 0.24 versus the growth of advanced economies. This higher correlation between the growth in the emerging economies and global commodity prices is because economic growth in these countries consumes far more natural resource-intensive products than the growth in the developed world.

Weaker world growth caused a significant decline in commodity prices through the period leading up to the federal budget. For example, in its April 2009 forecast, the IMF was calling for the West Texas Intermediate (WTI) price of oil to average $52US a barrel in 2009, a 46% decrease from 2008 prices. Oil is not alone in this price correction; the IMF forecasted that non-fuel commodity prices would fall by 28% this year. The plunge in commodity prices relative to 2008 levels will be a drag on the economy because of the significant role that natural resources play in Canada. The net result is much lower investment, output, and jobs in natural resource-related sectors than what would have been the case if prices had remained at 2008 levels.

In recent months, however, there has been a bounce back in commodity prices that was unusual given the severe drop in the world economy and the weaker outlook for emerging economies. It appears that the relationship between global economic activity and commodity prices has changed because of a change in consumption patterns. According to media reports, there has been a dramatic rise in the stockpiling of oil and

Figure 1: CAD Diverges from Commodities

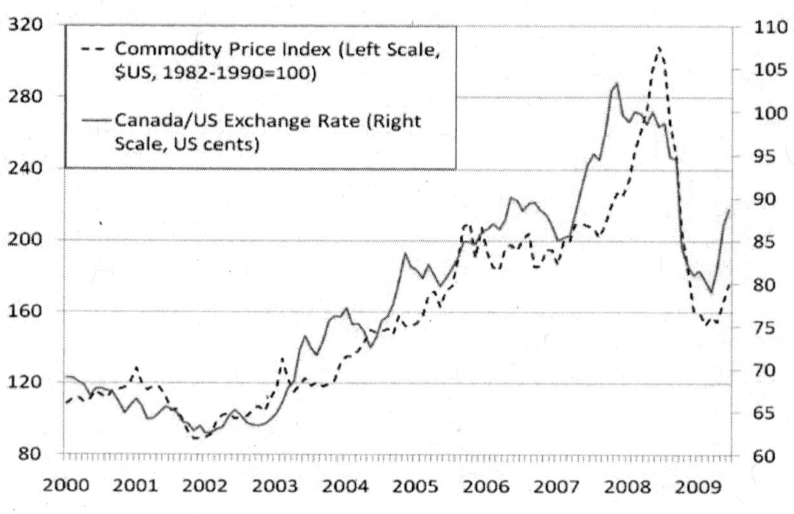

metals in China, and this has increased demand above the normal pattern relative to economic activity. Part of this inventory-building is to provide a strategic reserve for the state. But some of the inventory accumulation is being driven by individuals, such as farmers, to stockpile metals. This hoarding is being financed by the availability of cheap credit in China. Once cheap credit evaporates, the market price for these commodities could drop if these speculators have to liquidate their holdings.

Exchange Rate Effect

Based on our calculations, from the start of the crisis to the period leading up to the federal budget, the negative shock to the economy from the drop in commodity prices was offset by a concurrent depreciation in the Canadian dollar (CAD) versus the US dollar. The CAD was performing its shock absorber role. The CAD is a shock absorber no more.

One new worry for exporters is the strength of the CAD versus the US dollar. The recent run-up in the CAD is at odds with the historical pattern. In the past, the CAD was pro-cyclical – rising during periods of strong global growth and falling during periods of weak global growth – in part because the commodity price cycle is generally pro-cyclical and the CAD is closely related to commodity prices. For example, from 2000 to the end of 2008, there was a correlation of 0.98 between the CAD and the Bank of Canada's commodity price index on a quarterly basis. Recently, the CAD has risen more quickly than the bounce-back in overall commodity prices would suggest.

During this recession, a new pattern has emerged. The CAD dropped during the worst of the financial market firestorm in 2008 and into March of 2009 as risk-averse investors headed for the relative safety of the US treasury market and commodity prices generally fell. But since the end of the panic stage of the financial and economic crisis, international investors have been shifting assets toward markets outside the United States much earlier in the economic cycle than has usually been the case. Historically, the US economy was often assumed to come out of a recession first, so many investors kept assets in the US markets. This time, investors are shifting assets to other markets during the recessionary phase of the cycle, no doubt partly because of the horrendous state of the US economy, public finances, and inflationary risks.

The US dollar has experienced several waves of selling in recent months, dropping against a number of currencies, including the Canadian dollar, since early March. The rise in the CAD is clearly not related to the movements in commodity prices to the same extent as it was in the past. The CAD rose by over 17% from early March through early June, and commodity prices in aggregate rose by 12.5%. This is a stronger relative gain in the CAD versus commodity prices than usual. In comparison, the CAD rose by 58% from its trough in 2002 to its peak in 2008, while commodity prices rose by over 212%. Given the large number of problems in the US economy, there is the prospect that the CAD will remain at a high level and could move back to parity.

This large, fast, and early rise in the CAD is a large risk for the overall Canadian economy. The relatively large rise in the CAD means that Canadian exporters and import-competing firms will face a revival in international competitive pressure, which will trim real exports and boost real imports.

If this pattern between commodity prices and the dollar continues, the economy will not receive the same benefits from a large positive terms-of-trade shock as in the period from 2002 to 2008. Therefore, the short-term negatives on the economy will not be offset by the same positives from higher corporate profits, employment, and investment spending as happened during the 2002-2008 period.

Normally, the CAD rises late in the business cycle, when capacity constraints are rising. The "early" rise in the exchange rate is a problem, compared with the historic pattern, for a number of reasons. First, the negative impact on domestic prices is more of a concern during the current period of excess supply and deflationary concerns than it would be during periods when there is excess demand and inflationary pressure. Second, the negative impact on profitability from the rise in the exchange rate is more of a concern in the current environment, when there is already downward pressure on sales and profit margins, than at the peak of the cycle, when firms are experiencing capacity constraints. Third, a rising currency makes imported capital goods cheaper, and this is more in tune with the requirements of firms at the peak of the cycle, when they are looking to expand capacity. This time, the surge in the CAD is making imported capital cheaper at a time when there is excess capacity and firms are looking to cut capacity. Therefore, some of the normal benefits of the stronger CAD will be lost in the near term, and the negative short-term implications will be more evident.

Wealth Effect

The financial and economic crisis is also affecting the economy via the wealth effect. From the second quarter of 2008, when household net financial assets reached a peak of $2.83 trillion, to the first quarter of 2009, when net financial assets fell to $2.30 trillion, $521 billion of wealth has evaporated. The decline in net financial assets has wiped out close to four previous years of gains and represents almost 55% of disposable income in the first quarter of 2009. There are a range of estimates of the possible impact of changes in wealth on consumer spending.[2] Using a decline in consumption of 3 cents per dollar in asset values as a representative effect, the negative wealth effect from the drop in net financial assets could be as large as 1.6% of disposable income, or 1.8% of consumer spending, as of the first quarter of 2009.

Not all wealth is created equal in its impact on consumer spending, however. Research has often shown that changes in equity prices have less effect than changes in housing prices on consumer spending. The impact on consumption from changes in equity prices is less because equity price movements are thought to be transitory, and equities are not widely held. Given the magnitude of the equity losses held directly by households and indirectly through the high-profile losses at pension funds, there will likely be a significant impact on consumer spending and saving from changes in financial assets nonetheless.

Importantly, the economic and financial crisis had an impact on housing wealth as well as equity prices. According to the national balance sheet accounts, from the third quarter of 2008 to the first quarter of 2009, the value of residential structures dropped by $9.0 billion, and land dropped by $27.3 billion, which is the equivalent of 3.8% of disposable income, in the first quarter of 2009. Using a wealth effect of 5 cents on the dollar, the implication is that the negative impact on consumption could be as large as 0.2% of consumption as of the first quarter of 2009.

One aspect of wealth effects that is not well studied at a disaggregated level is the impact on consumption from changes in wealth from other financial markets besides equities. Financial wealth from all sources is usually combined, or equity wealth is examined directly. This topic is of

---

[2]Pichette (2004) briefly discussed the literature for Canada, with wealth effects ranging from zero to over 5 cents per dollar change in wealth. IMF (2009) reports wealth effects between 0 and 10 cents per dollar for advanced economies.

importance given the seizure of the financial markets and the implosion of the market for asset-backed commercial paper (ABCP), for example. The ABCP market was reportedly worth over $100 billion in August 2007, when it stopped functioning. And there were other markets that were hit by dysfunction in the aftermath of the financial crisis. It is an open question whether these implosions will have the same impact as the aggregate impact estimates described above or whether there will be a larger impact. It is certainly possible that the annihilation of assets that were thought to be cash equivalents might have a significantly larger impact.

Access to Capital

Clearly, the financial crisis is limiting the ability of businesses and consumers to access credit. There have been anecdotal reports of businesses being unable to find financing. And the Bank of Canada's survey of senior loan officers reported a sharp tightening in both price and non-price lending conditions from the spring of 2007 through to the winter of 2009. On the financial markets, the clearest indication of the crisis was the freeze-up of the ABCP market. At the worst of the crisis, the flow of capital through the financial markets slowed to a trickle. Unfortunately, it is difficult to quantify the magnitude of the impact of the freeze-up in the financial markets on the economy (more on this below).

Uncertainty

Given the unprecedented nature of this financial/economic crisis in modern times, we don't know how businesses and consumers will react. If consumers and/or businesses significantly change their behaviour, there is the possibility of a much larger and more protracted downturn or a slower recovery than would normally be the case, considering the stimulus that is influencing the economy. Some implications of the impact of uncertainty on the economy will be provided in the section that discusses the fiscal multipliers.

Economic Policy Flip-Flop

The likelihood of a deep global recession and prospect of the modern global depression – similar to Japan's lost decade – has pushed the discussion of methods to stimulate the economy to the forefront of the economic and policy agenda. Normally, a government should not try to stimulate an economy out of recession by massive new spending. Usually, this is a losing proposition, in part because it takes too long for fiscal measures to be enacted and start to boost economic growth. So the stimulus does not offset the downturn, but instead ends up boosting the economy when it is already recovering. Furthermore, massive government spending leads to massive government debt, and there is always the problem of weaning a government off the spending habit when the economy recovers.

Instead, the usual prescription is to allow the natural economic stabilizers embedded in the fiscal framework – unemployment insurance, welfare payments, and the income tax system – to kick into gear to help offset the slowdown and let the monetary authority counteract the downturn directly via lowering its key policy interest rate and indirectly through changes in the value of the exchange rate. Under normal circumstances, fiscal policy should focus on the supply side (and income redistribution), while monetary policy focuses on inflation via changes to aggregate demand.

This usual policy prescription needs the financial system to be working properly so that monetary policy changes are transmitted through the credit markets and influence consumer borrowing rates, corporate bond yields, and, ultimately, aggregate demand. These are not normal times.

Given the extent of the financial and economic crisis, one of the key concerns leading up to the federal budget was that the credit markets were not functioning properly, so the impact on the economy from changes in monetary policy were being blunted. Default risk drove a wedge between the policy rate and commercial interest rates, and lenders tightened up on lending standards, so that credit-worthy borrowers were finding it more difficult to obtain loans, and new issuance of debt or equity in the financial markets was all but nonexistent.

These developments raised concerns of a liquidity trap, whereby monetary policy has no influence on interest rates or aggregate demand. The risk of a liquidity trap rises as interest rates are pushed toward zero. In such a situation, the usual policy prescription is flipped on its head, and fiscal stimulus becomes the dominant policy choice. The preferred policy path, therefore, depends in part on the overall economic situation, particularly the functioning of the monetary transmission mechanism and the financial markets.

Figure 2: Lower Rates Were Not Influencing Mortgages

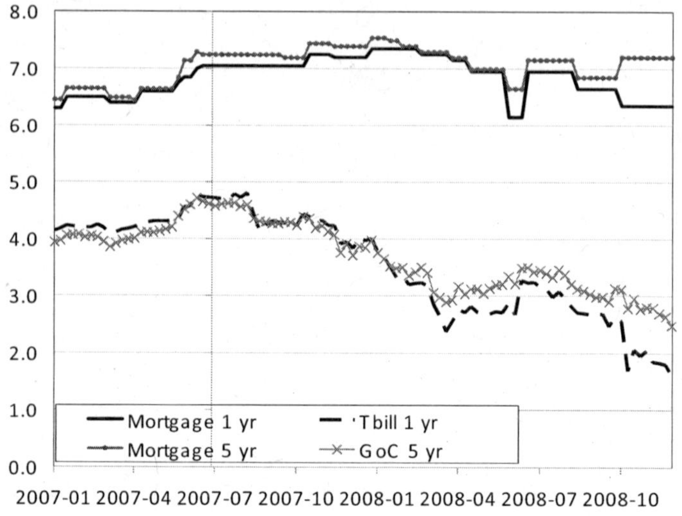

In the circumstances leading up to the Canadian federal budget, the financial markets were wounded, but not dead. Tremendous de-leveraging was occurring in the markets, and that put downward pressure on corporate bond and equity prices. Also, the evidence suggests that Canada's credit demand continued to expand, albeit at a slower pace. Consumer credit grew at an annualized 5.5% pace in the three months ending in January 2009, compared with an expansion of 8.5% over the three months ending in July of 2008. Mortgage credit expanded at an annualized pace of 8.5% in the three months to January 2009, compared with a pace of 10.4% in the previous July on the same basis. And total household credit slowed from a pace of 9.8% in the three months to July 2008 to a pace of 7.6% as of January 2009. Given that new issuance in the capital markets all but dried up, however, the credit measures of activity are misleadingly strong.

In addition to the change in the volume of credit, monetary policy affects the economy via the changes in the policy rate that are transmitted through other interest rates. From before the credit freeze in 2007 through to December 11, 2008, the Bank of Canada's policy rate declined from 4.5% to 1.5%, a drop of 3.00%. In comparison, the three-month bankers' acceptance rate fell by 2.98% over this period, suggesting that the policy rate is influencing short-term commercial interest rates. The transmission to mortgage rates, however, was less robust through to the period leading up to the federal budget. The one-year mortgage rate fell by 135 basis points over the same period, and the five-year mortgage rate was 40 basis points lower than before the crisis. The posted prime interest-loan rate reluctantly followed the overnight policy rate lower. While some of these posted rates have moved lower with the policy rate, the discounts on the prime business-loan rate that were prevalent before the crisis have vanished, and banks have started charging a premium. This suggests that the effective borrowing costs have actually risen for many borrowers even as the policy rate has declined. According to the Bank of Canada's April 2009 *Monetary Policy Report*, the effective mortgage rate fell from 5.35% at the end of July 2007 to 4.50% as of mid December 2008, for a drop of 85 basis points.

The above information suggests that leading up to the federal budget, the credit markets continued to function, and monetary policy continued to exert an influence on some interest rates, albeit with a lower degree of authority across the full spectrum of interest rates than had been the case in the past. Therefore, it is difficult to determine how much stimulus the economy was receiving directly via changes in interest rates. This suggests that other forms of stimulus, such as fiscal policy, may be more important than is traditionally the case.

Another mechanism by which the Bank of Canada can influence the economy is from changes in the exchange rate, either through changes in interest rates or via direct intervention. Since the Bank of Canada cut its policy rate by less than the 5.15% cut made by the US Federal Reserve from July 2007 through to December 2008 and Canadian short-term rates were above US rates leading up to the budget, Canadian interest rate policy did not support a devaluation of the CAD. And the Bank of Canada has a policy of permitting a floating exchange rate, so there has not been direct intervention in the currency market. Moreover, an active policy of devaluation is a non-starter in the global crisis. Obviously, not all currencies can be devalued simultaneously, and the last thing the world economy needs is a period of competitive devaluations.

Is Fiscal Stimulus Needed?

If interest rates have the same stimulating effect as historically has been the case, then the fiscal stance of the federal government in the recent budget is unwarranted since there was sufficient stimulus from the change in monetary conditions to boost the economy out of the doldrums. If there are non-linearities in the reaction of US imports with respect to US demand, or if the transmission of monetary policy has been significantly blunted, then the additional stimulus from the budget is warranted.

Given the global nature of the crisis and the anecdotal information and data available leading up to the federal budget, which suggested a very deep economic recession that had the possibility to turn into a debt-deflationary spiral, the prudent approach was to enact a major fiscal stimulus program. Obviously, there is a chance that the downside risks are exaggerated and the economy grows more quickly than expected, which later leads to a significant rise in inflation. This is a chance worth taking because the potential damage to the economy from under-stimulating the economy vastly outweighs the damage to the economy from over-stimulating the economy. That is, the risks of deflation versus inflation are asymmetric because inflation is less harmful and can be more easily dealt with than general price deflation.

Given these asymmetric risks, the IMF asked nations to provide coordinated monetary and fiscal stimulus to the world economy to reduce the risk of deflation. The head of the IMF requested that governments provide fiscal stimulus to their economies worth 2% of GDP.

Federal Budget Action Plan

Federal Finance Minister Jim Flaherty tabled a massive stimulus package that plans to inject an additional $39.9 billion into the economy over the next two fiscal years, and $51.6 billion if the provinces and municipalities (P&M) and consumers climb on board. Over the period from 2008-09 to 2013-14, total measures contained in the budget are worth $49.4 billion, with roughly $5 billion in permanent measures that extend past the next two fiscal years, roughly $4.3 billion of which are tax cuts. The principal focus of the budgetary measures is the next two fiscal years because this is the period of greatest risk to the Canadian economy from the global economic and financial crisis.

In the next two fiscal years, new spending measures are worth $18.1 billion in 2009 and $11.6 billion in 2010. Some of the major initiatives over the next two years include $11.9 billion for infrastructure, $7.8 billion for housing, $5.8 billion for sectoral aid (such as the auto industry

Table 1: Summary of Federal Budget Forecast

	2007-08	*2008-09*	*2009-10*	*2010-11*	*2011-12*	*2012-13*	*2013-14*
Revenues	242.4	236.4	224.9	239.9	259.4	276.4	294.3
Total Program Exp	199.5	206.8	229.1	236.5	235.1	244.5	254.1
Public Debt Charges	33.3	30.7	29.5	33.3	37.2	39.2	39.6
Budget Balance	9.6	-1.1	-33.7	-29.9	-13.0	-7.3	0.7

bailout), and $1.4 billion for training. Cleverly, the budget encourages additional spending by P&M and consumers to maximize the stimulus on the economy from the federal dollars. These "leveraged" amounts add up to $6.6 billion in 2009 and $5.1 billion in 2010. On the tax side, there is $2.5 billion for a freeze in the EI premium, $6.9 billion personal income tax relief, and roughly $1 billion for corporate income tax measures (accelerated CCA and removal of tariffs on equipment). Notably, the government takes great pains to stress that the income tax cuts are permanent in order to ensure the maximum short-term simulative effects from these measures; economic history shows that temporary income tax cuts tend to be saved more and spent less than permanent tax cuts. Of the measures in the budget, roughly 50% will help to boost productive capacity, productivity, or labour mobility; this is less than what I would have hoped for. And the construction sector is the greatest beneficiary, something that seems overly generous considering that the pain is widespread and there are other sectors with higher GDP multipliers.

Notably, the underlying budget balance was a sobering deficit of $11.2 billion in 2009-10, $9.8 billion in 2010-11, and $5.3 billion in 2011-12. To try to take account of a possible worsening of the economic environment, the budget includes an "adjustment for risk" worth $4.5 billion in 2009-10, $4.5 billion in 2010-11, $3.0 billion in 2011-12, $1.5 billion in 2012-13, and $0.8 billion in 2013-14. It is used to lower revenues to reflect the difference between the private sector average economic forecast, which was used as the baseline, and the nominal GDP forecasts near the bottom of the distribution of outlooks. This is an appropriate step given the economic climate.

Given the massive stimulus program, net federal debt is much higher than previously estimated. Net debt rises to $542.8 billion by 2012-13 and is $92.3 billion higher by 2013-14 than the estimate provided in the fall economic statement. As a share of GDP, net debt reaches a peak of 32.1% in 2010-11 and then falls to 28% in 2013-14. At its peak over the forecast period, the debt-to-GDP ratio remains below the level it achieved in 2006-07. In comparison, the debt-to-GDP ratio reached

Figure 3: Federal Actions Heavily Focused on Construction

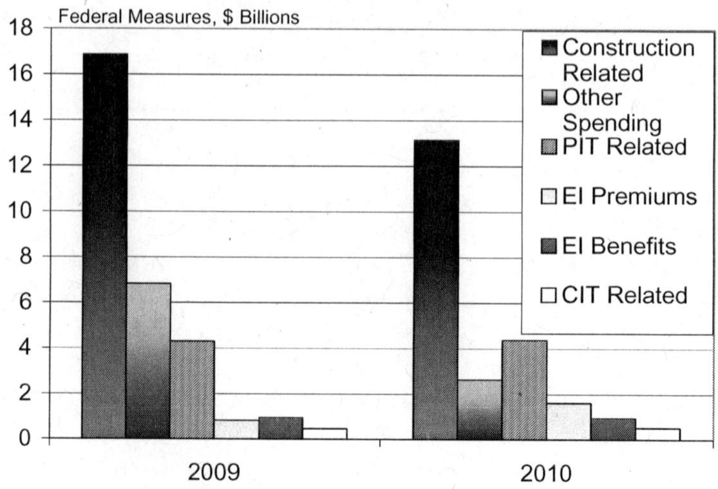

68.4% in 1995-96 at its recent height. So long as the spending stimulus measures are temporary and government does not get back onto the debt escalator, the hard-won fiscal gains of the 1990s will be largely preserved. Given the huge infusion of cash into the financial sector to unclog the system (see below), marketable debt will escalate more sharply than net debt, however.

This is a deep fiscal hole. The finance minister's plan is to provide mostly temporary stimulus and then pull the government out of deficit once the economy starts to pull out of the current economic funk. Unlike previous budgets, this budget includes a five-year outlook that shows the underlying fiscal balance rising back to a surplus of $5.5 billion by 2013-14 (a surplus of $0.7 billion, after taking account of the $4.9 billion in measures for that year).

According to the budget, this package amounts to stimulus worth 1.2% (1.6% including P&M) of GDP in 2009 and an additional 0.1% of GDP in 2010 (0.2% including P&M), plus an additional 0.2% of GDP in 2009 and 0.1% in 2010 of stimulus from the tax cuts in the 2007 economic statement, for a total of 1.8% of stimulus in 2009 and 0.3% in 2010. These amounts actually understate the stimulus from the federal government as they do not take into account the underlying increase in program spending that existed prior to the 2009 budget. After backing out the new measures from total program spending, there is an underlying 0.3% of GDP increase in spending in 2009 and 0.9% in 2010.

Therefore, total stimulus will be 2.1% of nominal GDP in 2009, including the P&M spending encouraged by the budget, and 1.2% in 2010. Notably, given the focus on construction-related spending in the budget, by our estimates the stimulus is sufficiently large to essentially offset the negative impact on that sector in 2009 and offset the worst of the downturn in 2010. Why they want to keep one sector at its cyclical peak is another question, however.

As part of the plan to ensure that the credit channels become unclogged, the government introduced an Extraordinary Financing Framework consisting of up to $200 billion of initiatives (including previous actions) designed to ease credit markets. The framework includes $50 billion of insured mortgage pools in the first half of 2009–10 under the Insured Mortgage Purchase Program (IMPP), in addition to the $75 billion already allocated, for a total program size of $125 billion. New measures include the introduction of a new Canadian Secured Credit Facility, worth $12 billion, to purchase term asset-backed securities to help consumers and businesses finance new vehicles and equipment. This is important because leasing for autos has all but shut down since the start of the credit crunch, and business access to credit is essential for the purchase of machinery. The government will also allocate $13 billion to Crown corporations, such as Export Development Canada and the Business Development Bank of Canada, to provide additional financing to businesses, and Canada Mortgage and Housing Corporation (CMHC) can provide low-cost loans to municipalities. Homeowners have also been given more flexibility to finance the purchase of new houses. Should these measures succeed and the financial system work again, then the worst of the credit crisis will be averted, and the full benefits of the low interest rate policy will flow through the economy and could provide a larger lift to the economy than the rest of the budget (see the discussion below).

Given the usual lags in the introduction of spending programs, it is likely that this budget will help to boost the economy out of recession in the latter half of 2009 and into 2010 or to boost the recovery. Given the poor outlook for global growth in 2009 and 2010, this stimulus will be needed whenever it hits the economy. The fact that there is coordinated stimulus coming from governments around the world increases the likelihood of success. Coordinated stimulus will limit the problem of import leakage, since all countries in the global economy will benefit from increased exports simultaneously. One worry is the "buy America" provisions of the US Stimulus Act. If all countries enact such policies, then the world will be worse off, and we could be going down the same trade protectionist path that made the 1930s so economically debilitating. If this happens, the fiscal stimulus provided in the budget will be swamped by idiotic beggar-thy-neighbour trade policy, and the recession will be much deeper and longer.

Assume the Worst

The budget rests on a number of economic assumptions that are useful to examine to understand the implications for the economy. There is also the basic question of whether this budget is right for the times.

The economic outlook that the Department of Finance used is the private sector average forecast from earlier in January. The outlook calls for growth of -0.8% in 2009 and 2.4% in 2010. If all of the economic stimulus listed above, but not including the stimulus that predated the budget, is added to the private sector outlook, then growth would be 0.8% (-0.8+1.6) in 2009 and 2.6% (2.4+0.2) in 2010. Compared with the private sector forecasts, there is the very big question as to what fiscal policy assumptions the private sector forecasters had concerning the 2009 budget in their forecasts already. If the private sector forecasters already had a large fiscal stimulus package, then the stimulus in the budget will not boost the forecasted output to this degree.

Figure 4: Budget Assumes Large Recession

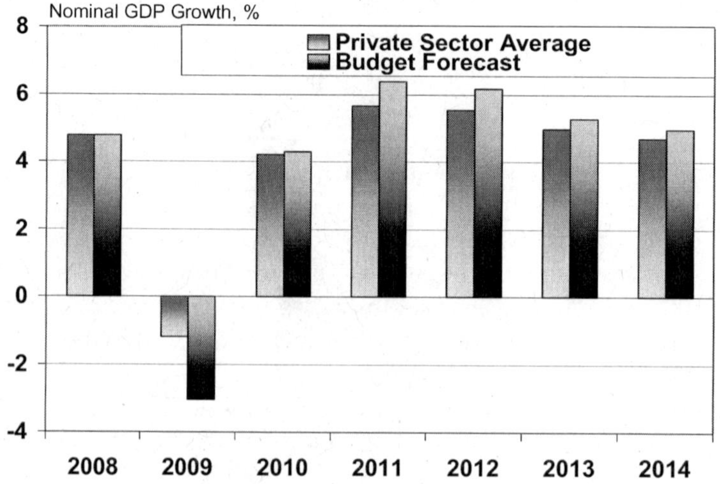

The economic path will influence revenues and economically sensitive spending, such as EI. To estimate revenues, the Department of Finance uses a more pessimistic nominal GDP forecast than the private sector average suggests to estimate revenues. The difference between the risk-adjusted nominal GDP outlook and the private sector average is 1.9% for 2009. For 2010, the outlook in the budget is for a rebound in real and nominal GDP growth that is essentially equal to the private sector forecast. So the short-term economic outlook seems reasonably conservative even considering the worsening of the outlook subsequent to the budget.

The next question is whether the revenue outlook is reasonable considering the economic outlook and the tax cuts that have been announced. Unfortunately, the budget does not show the detailed income outlook, so I used the nominal GDP outlook. Given that different taxes are related to different components of domestic income and have different elasticities, this analysis is a second-best estimate. Furthermore, over time, tax rates have changed, so some of the divergence between nominal growth and revenues is because of previous tax policy changes. To try to take this into account, I added back into revenues the tax cuts that have been announced since the 1998 budget, as indicated in various budgets and economic statements over the years, and I assumed that the tax cuts would grow by the same rate as nominal GDP past the point of the provided impact estimates. Once these calculations were done, it was

Figure 5: Federal Revenues Bounce Back After Recession …

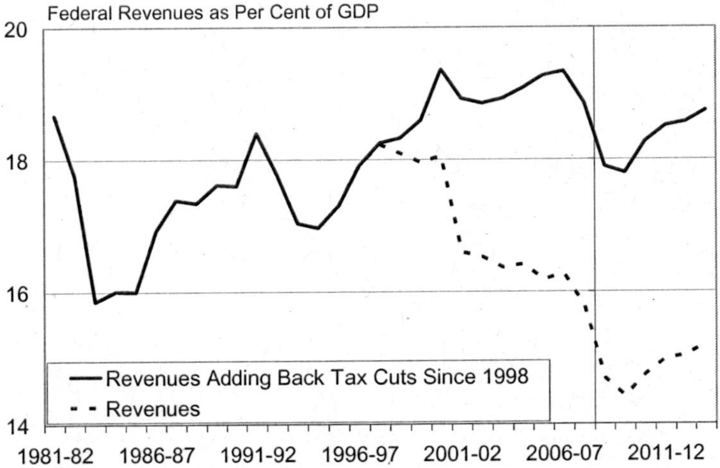

Figure 6: ... More Quickly Than in Past Recoveries

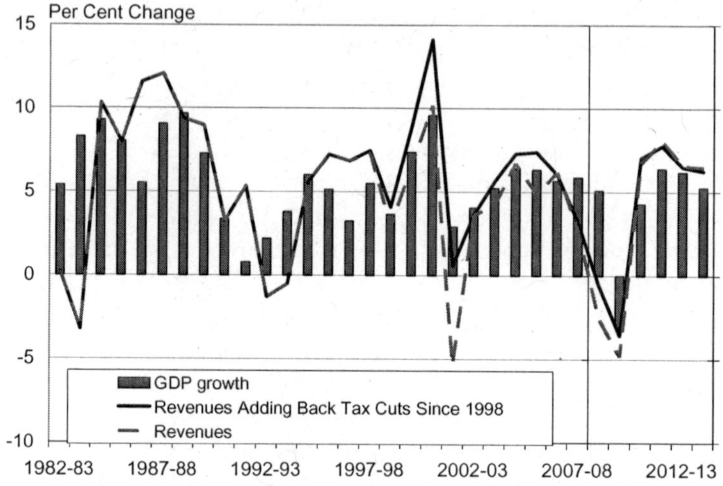

possible to get a sense of how total revenues performed versus nominal GDP in the past and compare it with the forecast. This comparison suggests that Finance is expecting revenues to snap back fairly quickly compared with past slowdowns and recessions. It is not unusual for government revenues to improve versus GDP growth later in the cycle, but typically, this does not happen in the first year after a recession. If the current downturn is the worst since the 1930s or indeed equal to the 1981-82 recession, then corporate income tax revenues, in particular, are likely to be weaker in 2010-11 than Finance suggests. If revenues grow at the same pace as nominal GDP (which is optimistic, given the usual post-recession pattern), then revenues will be $5.4 billion lower in 2010-11 than anticipated and debt $5.4 billion higher.

Over the medium term, revenues continue to grow more quickly than nominal GDP, in part because of a tax increase that is implicitly part of the budget, but is not highlighted in the impact tables and will tax away a large part of the "permanent" tax cuts by 2013-14. As is indicated in the budget, EI premiums will be frozen over the next couple of years; however, the budget also indicates that thereafter, EI premiums will be set based on ensuring that the EI account will break even over time. Compared with the fall economic statement, the EI balance is close to $2 billion higher by 2013-14, and EI revenues are $1.7 billion higher. Since the unemployment rate forecast on average over 2012-14 is 0.2% higher than in the economic statement, the implication is that employment is lower and, therefore, these gains are because of a higher premium rate than was used in the economic statement. These tax increases will reduce the beneficial effect of the $3.8 billion in tax reductions that remain by 2013–14. Higher EI premiums impact lower-income jobs more than high-income jobs because EI premiums represent a higher share of total labour costs to employers, and this will diminish the benefits of other tax cuts provided to low-income Canadians.

How Much Stimulus?

The dominant question concerning the budget is not about larger deficits but about whether the stimulus provided by the budget is enough. There are two parts to this question. First, what short-term stimulus does the budget provide, and second, how much is needed? In the budget documents, the federal government provides considerable details on the short-term stimulus from the tax cuts and spending increases. They illustrate the expenditure and tax multipliers in a table in an appendix, which shows the dollar impact on the level of real GDP from a *permanent* one-dollar increase in either spending or tax cuts. Presumably, the emphasis on the permanency of the measures is really focused on the permanency of the tax cuts because most of the spending is not permanent by design and it is known that temporary tax cuts do not provide the same boost to economic activity as a permanent change in taxes. As was discovered in the United States in the 1960s and again by the temporary tax cuts in the United States last year, temporary tax cuts don't work.

Finance's construction-related multipliers rise from 1.0 in the first year to 1.4–1.5 in the second year. One reason the multipliers are relatively high is because Finance assumes that given the deflationary pressures at work in the global economy today, there would be no ill effects from crowding out via changes in interest rates and the exchange rate. Certainly, in the current environment, with an increased appetite for the safety of government bonds and T-bills, there is every reason to agree with this assumption. In a few quick shocks to our model with the same assumptions regarding no change in interest rates and the exchange rate, I get similar multipliers for real construction-related spending by 2010, but a smaller multiplier for "other spending". Our model, however, has a larger multiplier for the first year of the simulation for each real dollar shock than what Finance assumes.

Another way to examine multipliers is to use input-output (IO) multipliers that Statistics Canada has estimated. This approach becomes particularly relevant if we assume that interest rates and the exchange rate don't change because of the economic situation and that there are no capacity constraints since the IO system cannot take these effects into account. The direct and indirect GDP multiplier for construction is 0.78 from Statistics Canada's IO model. Since this estimate does not include the induced effect (from higher employment and income), that effect should be added.

According to Statistics Canada, the employment multiplier for construction spending was 9.98 jobs per million dollars of expenditure. The Survey of Employment Payrolls and Hours shows that the average wage in the construction industry was $48.7 thousand ($935 average weekly wage times 52) in 2007. Therefore, per billion dollars of spending, there will be 9,980 new jobs created, and the total wage increase will be roughly $485.6 million (since the average wages and supplementary labour income per employee in the third quarter of 2008 was $48.5 thousand, so the non-construction-related increase in jobs will provide a similar increase in wages to that for construction jobs). Using a standard multiplier with a marginal propensity to consume (MPC) of 0.9, a marginal tax rate of 0.31 and an import leakage of 0.33, the estimate of the impact on the economy from this additional spending would result in a GDP increase of 0.68 and result in the total multiplier being 1.46, which is similar in magnitude to the macro model multipliers discussed above.

There are a couple of factors that could thwart the economic stimulus provided by the budget measures. The first is fear. If consumers and businesses become fearful, they will increase their precautionary savings, and this means that subsequent rounds of spending will experience a smaller multiplier effect. For example, based on an import leakage of 33 cents on the dollar, and using Ontario as a representative province, the difference in the multiplier effects for a middle-income person with $52,000 of income from a 0.20 change in their MPC from 90 cents per dollar increase in income to 70 cents is roughly a difference of 0.25 on the spending multiplier. This type of effect would lower the stimulus provided by the budget by 0.5% in 2009 and 0.3% in 2010. This difference in the multiplier effects underscores why shoring up consumer and business confidence is critical at this time. If consumers and business believe that monetary and fiscal authorities have taken the appropriate steps to protect Canada during this dire economic time, then the stimulus provided to the economy from the budget will be all that much larger. If Canadians become fearful, the economy could suffer from the paradox of thrift.

The second dynamic that could thwart Finance's plans is forward-looking taxpayers. Finance assumes that consumers are not "Ricardian". If consumers are Ricardian – in the sense that they are forward-looking and anticipate that a tax cut today, financed by issuing government debt, will result in higher taxes being imposed in the future – they will cut back on spending today to save for the tax increase to come. Perfect Ricardian equivalence implies that a reduction in government savings resulting from a tax cut is fully offset by higher private savings and aggregate demand is not affected (Hemming, Kell, and Mahfouz, 2002). Hemming, Kell, and Mahfouz (2002) stress that some researchers have provided reasons to conclude that perfect Ricardian equivalence is unlikely, but there are times when a Ricardian response is more likely. For example, a Ricardian response is more likely when it is perceived that the current path of government debt is unsustainable and that future tax increases will soon be required to lower the debt. Certainly, this dynamic will haunt US efforts to boost their economy. For Canada, this condition does not appear to hold, but Canada could get sideswiped through this development in the United States nonetheless.

The federal government is providing temporary stimulus. The debt-to-GDP ratio is expected to rise, but remain at relatively moderate levels compared with the past 15 years, and then to reverse course within the next five years. So there is a good chance that the short-term multipliers will remain above one, even if not at the levels suggested by Finance.

In order to reduce the risk of a Ricardian response by consumers, perhaps Finance should re-affirm their commitment to their medium term debt-to-GDP target of 25% in order to convince businesses and households that the tax cuts and spending increases are affordable. While they are unlikely to achieve their debt-to-GDP target by 2014–15, as they had earlier hoped, they could achieve it thereafter. Based on their outlook, if the debt-to-GDP continues to drop in 2014–15 and 2015–16 as in 2013–14, then they will achieve their target by 2015–16 (see Figure 7). Given the optimistic revenue outlook and size of the economic shock, this target will likely be postponed, but there is clearly the prospect of a return to a period with a falling debt-to-GDP ratio within the next five years; this may also boost confidence that the budgetary measures are affordable.

Figure 7: A Temporary Diversion in Declining Debt Ratio

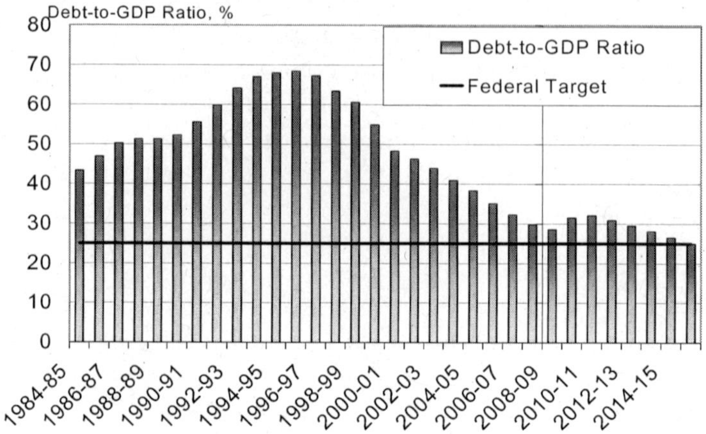

Is It Enough?

There is also the question of whether the budget is providing sufficient stimulus to the economy to help weather the global economic storm. The answer to this question depends on the size of the external shock and the effectiveness of monetary policy. Our base case outlook prior to the budget had an external shock worth roughly 1.4% of Canadian GDP based on the output gap of Canada's major trading partners (from the IMF's October outlook and the December US forecast by Macroeconomic Advisers) but the worsening of the global economy pushed this to 5.2% based on the April IMF outlook.

We also know that monetary policy has been blunted. If we assume that bank credit, except fixed-term mortgage credit, which represents roughly 12.5% of bank credit, remains well functioning, then roughly 87.5% of the bank-related monetary transmission mechanism is working (and probably somewhat less since banks swung from discounts to premiums versus their posted rates). As indicated in the Bank of Canada's April *Monetary Policy Report Update*, variable rate mortgages fell by 0.85% versus 3.00% in the policy rate since before the crisis to mid-December and by 1.55% versus 3.50% from before the crisis to late January. Other parts of the financial markets were operating, albeit at a trickle compared to earlier periods, so if we make the heroic assumption that the functioning of other markets is of similar importance as the tightening of bank lending, then we can calculate the degree of blunting of monetary policy. Since bank credit represents roughly 25% of the market, the worst that monetary policy is thwarted is by roughly 78% (100-25%*87.5%) or, in other words, monetary policy is 22% effective. Clearly, this is a very rough guess. In order to provide a range of possible outcomes, I have created a figure that shows the degree of monetary stimulus based on monetary policy actions taken to date and the effectiveness of monetary policy, added in the impact of the budget, and compared this stimulus with the externally generated shocks mentioned above (see Figure 8). The figure shows the impact of budget measures and the external shock measured as a percent of GDP (vertical axis). On the horizontal axis is the assumed effectiveness of the monetary transmission mechanism. The axis ranges from zero to 1.00 to reflect monetary policy that is zero to 100% effective.

If monetary policy is 50% effective and the external shock is worth 3.2% of GDP, then the federal fiscal stimulus (plus P&M and consumer leverage) based on the budget's estimates and monetary stimulus to date will offset this shock. If monetary policy is 22% effective, then monctary stimulus to date along with the budget measures will offset a shock of 2.6%. Or after assuming that underlying provincial and municipal spending will boost the economy by 1%, then the federal fiscal stance plus monetary policy actions to date will offset a shock of roughly 3.6% if monetary policy is 22% effective. A larger shock or more broken monetary policy will still leave the economy in the soup. For example, a shock of 5.2% will require monetary policy to be 100% effective, the

Figure 8: Stimulus from Policy Actions to Date Versus Shocks

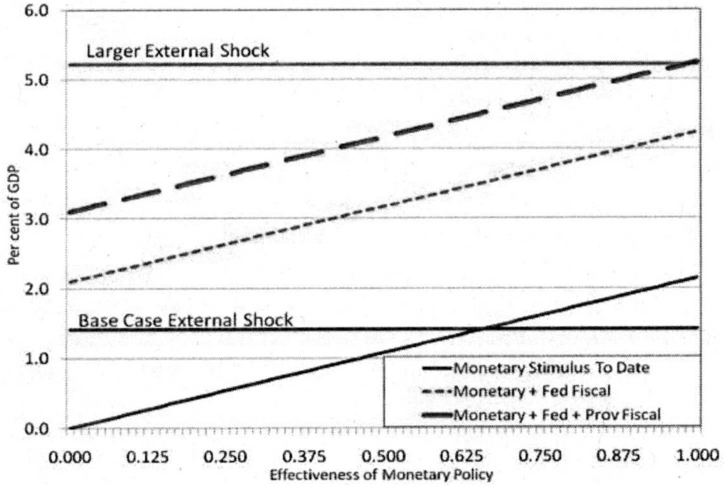

Figure 9: Stimulus: Fiscal 80% Effective and Zero Policy Rate

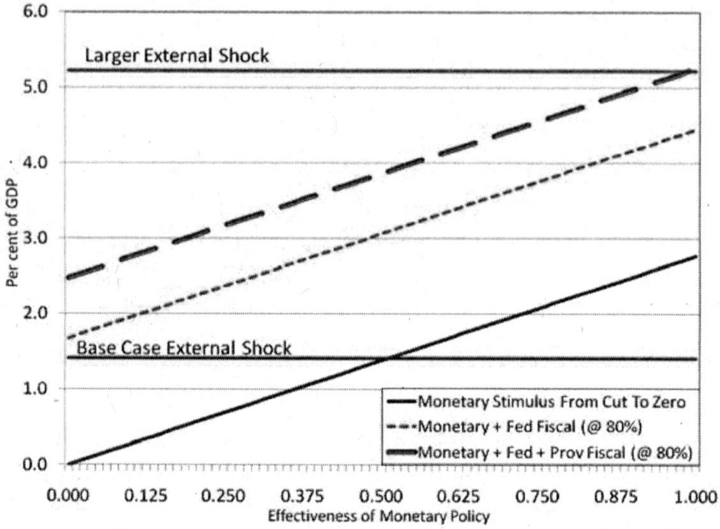

federal budget to be 100% effective, and provinces and municipalities to boost spending by 1% of GDP. Anything less will not offset the larger external shock. And if consumers and business raise precautionary savings in the face of the external shock, then the monetary and fiscal stimulus will not offset the larger external shock.

If the monetary policy rate is cut to zero, then this budget, along with a one percent of GDP increase in provincial and municipal spending, will just offset an external shock of 5.2% if monetary policy is 76% effective (see Figure 10). If monetary policy is less effective or the shock is bigger, then the economy will suffer a significant contraction. If consumers and business pull back and fiscal stimulus is only 80% effective, then fiscal and monetary policy will not be able to offset the larger shock even with the policy rate at zero and monetary policy 100% effective. Of course, the Bank has other tools at its disposal once the policy rate is cut to zero, but these measures tend to be less effective than a cut in the policy rate, and the exact magnitudes are unknown.

These figures also demonstrate the importance of the measures taken to date as well as those contained in the budget to unclog the financial markets and return the monetary transmission mechanism to full health. The difference in stimulus between a monetary system that is 22% effective and 100% effective is worth 2.1% of GDP, which is larger than the stimulus from all the other measures contained in the budget.

Figure 10: Stimulus: Zero Policy Rate and Full Fiscal Multiplier

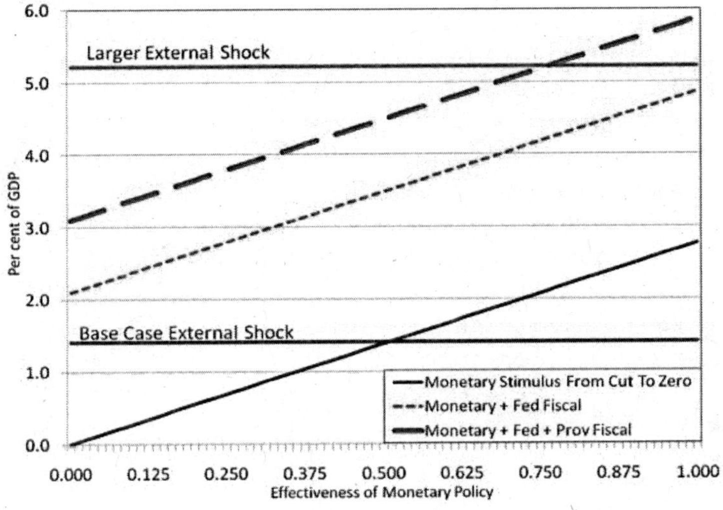

The Right Type of Stimulus?

One basic question about the budget is concerning the heavy reliance on stimulating the construction sector. This begs the question: Is this is the best way to stimulate the economy? To examine this issue, it is useful to consider both short-term multipliers and long-term effects. Given the extent of the crisis facing Canada, measures that stimulate the economy more in the short term are to be preferred over measures that stimulate the economy less in the short term. Actions that encourage long-term economic growth are preferred over measures that have no lasting impact on the productive capacity of the economy or in enhancing the flexibility of markets, including labour mobility, which will enhance the economy's ability to deal with economic shocks.

From the perspective of these principles, there are some advantages to the focus on construction, at least the infrastructure spending. Infrastructure investment provides a short-term jolt to the economy as well as boosting the economy's productive capacity. Certainly, spending on construction would provide more of a short-term jolt to the economy than encouraging machinery investment because of the high degree of import leakages in the latter, for example. But there remains the question as to whether this type of spending provides the biggest bang for the taxpayers' buck or whether a more diversified portfolio of spending would have provided a larger impact on GDP, created more jobs, or helped the economy more in the long run. Certainly, a more varied stimulus program would have spread the direct stimulus across more sectors of the economy than the concentration on construction. Although clearly the manufacturing sector, which received aid of $5.8 billion, and the financial sector benefited from massive aid to restore the functioning of the financial system.

The budget seems to focus on revenue or gross output (GO) multipliers, since some of the sectors that have high GO multipliers received significant aid (see Table 2). According to Cross and Ghanem (2006), the GO multiplier for the construction sector is 1.76 and manufacturing 1.67, both of which are relatively high; this reflects the complexity of these industries' linkages with other sectors in the economy. They indicate, however, that focusing on the GO multiplier to reflect the importance of an industry to overall economic activity and growth is a mistake. The

Table 2: Industry Multipliers per Dollar Increase in Output

Industry	*GDP Multiplier*	*Gross Output Multiplier*
Finance, insurance and real estate	0.95	1.37
Education	0.94	1.39
Retail trade	0.92	1.53
Non-profit institutions	0.92	1.42
Wholesale trade	0.90	1.56
Administrative	0.90	1.46
Other services	0.90	1.42
Government	0.90	1.48
Child care outside the home	0.90	1.35
Utilities	0.89	1.30
Professional and technical	0.89	1.53
Mining	0.88	1.41
Health care	0.88	1.40
Recreation	0.87	1.67
Transportation	0.86	1.63
Accommodation and food	0.85	1.78
Information	0.84	1.54
Forestry	0.79	1.65
Primary support	0.78	1.53
Construction	0.78	1.76
Agriculture	0.77	1.97
Fishing	0.77	1.53
Manufacturing	0.61	1.67

Sources: Cross and Ghanem (2006); CCHRSC (2009) report of a Statistics Canada IO model simulation.

GDP multiplier should be used instead. Despite having a high GO multiplier, the GDP multiplier for the construction and manufacturing industries is among the lowest of all major industries because their import leakages are relatively high. Many of the industries that have low GO multipliers have high GDP multipliers and vice versa.

If the intent is to boost revenues in a large number of industries by a large amount, then those industries with high GO multipliers should be chosen to receive stimulus. If the intent is to boost real GDP, industries that have high GDP multipliers should be selected to directly or indirectly receive stimulus. And if the intent is to boost employment, then the government should select industries with high employment multipliers (see Table 3).

Table 3: Employment Multipliers Jobs per $ Million of Gross Output

Industry	*Direct Jobs*	*Indirect Jobs*	*Total Employment Multiplier*
Child care outside the home	36.92	2.62	39.54
Other Services (Except Public)	20.40	7.16	27.55
Educational Services	24.57	2.90	27.46
Accommodation and Food Services	19.79	5.16	24.95
Arts, Entertainment and Recreation	17.29	5.98	23.27
Retail Trade	17.68	3.82	21.50
Non-Profit Institutions Serving Households	16.88	3.10	19.98
Health Care and Social Assistance	13.45	5.88	19.33
Administrative and Support, Waste and …	16.53	2.36	18.89
Crop and Animal Production	8.00	6.26	14.26
Professional, Scientific and Technical	10.05	4.16	14.21
Government Sector	8.92	4.41	13.33
Wholesale Trade	7.72	4.13	11.85
Transportation and Warehousing	6.90	3.83	10.73
Support Activities for Agriculture and …	9.34	0.85	10.20
Construction	5.70	4.27	9.98
Information and Cultural Industries	5.18	3.61	8.79
Fishing, Hunting and Trapping	5.59	2.94	8.54
Forestry and Logging	4.14	4.21	8.35
Manufacturing	3.05	3.66	6.71
Finance, Insurance, Real Estate and Rental	3.07	2.01	5.08
Utilities	2.47	1.79	4.26
Mining and Oil and Gas Extraction	1.16	1.54	2.70

Sources: Statistics Canada Employment Multipliers for 2005; CCHRSC (2009) report of a Statistics Canada IO model simulation.

Notably, these Statistics Canada multipliers explicitly exclude the induced effect on the economy of changes in income of those employed as a result of the increase in output. The induced multiplier effect will vary depending on the number of people employed, their income and their marginal propensity to consume. Generally speaking, higher-income individuals save more per dollar of increased income than lower-income individuals. Conversely, lower-income individuals will spend more per dollar increase in income. Therefore, the induced-effect multiplier will be higher when lower-income workers are hired or their hours of work and pay are increased.

For example, Dynan, Skinner, and Zeldes (2004) found for the United States that the marginal propensity to save was 3 cents per dollar for low-income households and 43 cents per dollar for high-income households. Other leakages besides savings, such as imports and taxes, will also lower the GDP multiplier. The tax leakage rises with income in Canada because of the progressive tax system. Using Ontario as a representative province, a dollar increase in wage income would boost personal income taxes payable by 21 cents for those earning an annual salary of $16,865 for 2007 (the lowest annualized average weekly earnings for a major industry from the Statistics Canada Web site). In contrast, an income earner in the top marginal tax bracket would experience a tax increase of 47 cents per dollar increase in wages. For workers who earn a mid-level of income equal to the average income of a finance industry worker of

Figure 11: Direct, Indirect and Induced GDP Multiplier

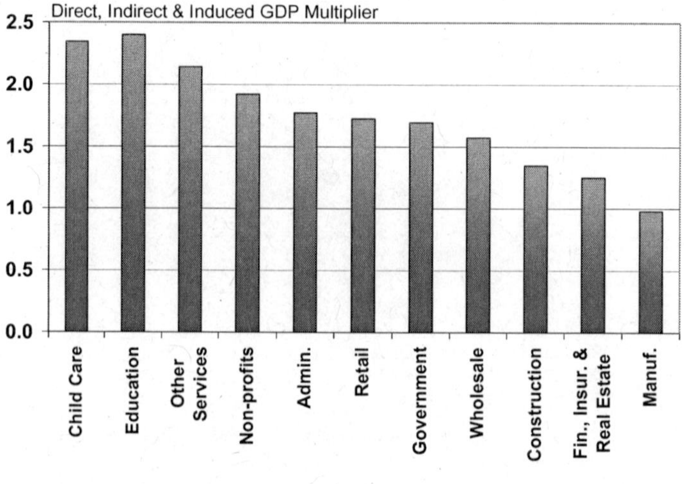

$52,000 per annum, the marginal tax rate of an extra dollar of income was 31 cents in 2007, and the marginal tax rate for mining and oil extraction workers was 37 cents per dollar increase in wage income.

Assuming a marginal import leakage of 33 cents per dollar, which reflects the aggregate imports to GDP ratio, the induced multiplier for an increase in a low-income job and wages would be 1.77 per dollar increase in employment income, compared with a multiplier of 0.97 for the top tax bracket, a multiplier of 1.36 for the low mid-level earners, and 1.27 for high mid-level earners. This means that using the same import leakage for low-income earners and low mid-level earners, the induced multiplier would be 31% higher for the former. Since higher-income workers also tend to consume more imported goods and services per dollar increase in income, the divergence between these estimates would become even more pronounced. Using an import leakage of 20 cents per dollar of spending for low income earners, 33 cents for low mid-level earners, 35 cents for high mid-level earners, and 40 cents per dollar for high-income earners, the induced income multipliers would be 2.31, 1.36, 1.24, and 0.91 respectively.

After the induced effects are taken into consideration, then there is a further reordering of the list of sectors discussed above. The sector with the highest multiplier is the education sector, followed by the child care outside the home sector and the other services industry. Construction, financial services, and manufacturing fall to the bottom of the heap in part because they generally employ average to above-average wage earners, and therefore the induced effect is less.

The implication of the above analysis is that, in terms of stimulating real economic activity in the short term, it is better to provide stimulus to those industries that have a high GDP multiplier and also employ workers with lower wages. This means that the government would get more bang for the taxpayers' buck by encouraging education or child care activity rather than mining and oil and gas, construction, or manufacturing activity in the short run, for example. Notably, similar to infrastructure investment spending, both education and child care impact the economy in the long term via changes in human capital.

The second principle described above is that stimulus should take the economy's productive capacity into account. For the budget to score the highest marks from this perspective, the supply side of the economy must be described by an AK production function, with an unusually large reliance on structures. A broader view of the production function would include many types of physical assets, research and development, the quantity of labour, as well as human capital. Boosting the accumulation of these other factors of production would also boost productive capacity and long-term economic growth. And diminishing returns suggest that a broader portfolio of spending on a range of factors of production would likely provide more long-term bang for each dollar spent than an over-reliance on spending in one area, unless that factor of production had been previously depleted excessively. After all, the standard neoclassical model tells us that to double output, you need to double all factor inputs, not just one.

A broader view of the economy could have provided a better portfolio of spending options that would boost near-term economic growth as well as helping to boost long-term economic growth. In particular, it should be noted that education provides significant short-term stimulus to GDP and also contributes to long-term economic growth through the accumulation of human capital.

The short-term impact of child care outside the home on GDP is also noteworthy. Like education, quality child care provides the accumulation of human capital that affects long-term economic growth (see Dickens, Sawhill, and Tebbs, 2006). However, in the case of child care, that human capital will influence the economy in the very long run, when those children who were in care reach the labour force. Furthermore, it should be noted that the research reviewed by CCHRSC (2009) has shown that the availability of child care has significant near-term labour supply effects because it allows parents to enter the labour force. Consequently, the provision of quality child care can have a significant short-term impact on the economy, as is evident from the high short-term multiplier; can have significant short- to-medium-term impacts on the economy via parents' labour force participation (or participation in training programs); and can have significant long-term impacts on economic growth via the accumulation of human capital by the children who use quality child care.

Considering that the research as identified by CCHRSC (2009) on child care highlights the importance of quality, and that more highly trained workers tend to provide better early learning environments, one way to leverage off both the short-term multiplier of education and child care in a temporary spending program would be to increase spending on training for those providing child care. Since out-of-home child care and training are provided throughout the country, this type of initiative would provide stimulus throughout the country. Improved training could also improve the human capital gains to the children using child care.

Conclusion

In summary, the budget is an important plan to help offset the negative impact on the economy from developments abroad that are threatening to cause the worst economic downturn in the post-Second World War period. The budget provides actions to unclog the financial markets and get credit markets operating again, and, if the plan works, they could provide more stimulus to the economy than the direct fiscal measures contained in the budget. The fiscal measures in the budget are expected to provide stimulus this year worth 1.6% of GDP and an additional 0.2% in 2010, but there is the chance that it will take longer for some of the stimulus measures to be rolled out and influence the economy. Infrastructure spending in particular can take a prolonged period, so there is the likelihood that the economy will shrink significantly in 2009, but bounce back more vigorously next year.

In some respects, what matters is not the stimulus measures themselves, but the impact these measures have on consumer and business expectations. If consumers and business believe the stimulus provided by monetary and fiscal authorities is sufficient to offset the negative shock to the economy, then they might be more willing to spend themselves and boost the economy. On the other hand, if businesses and consumers do not believe the stimulus package is sufficient, then they will hunker down and not spend; this would make the recession deeper and/or longer.

Similarly, expectations play a role in determining the short-term impact of the budget's measures. If households believe the tax cuts are permanent, they will spend a relatively large percentage of the increase in after-tax income, based on their marginal propensity to consume. However, if consumers don't believe the tax cuts are permanent, and instead consider the $98 billion in increased debt as representing future tax increases, they will not increase spending significantly despite the rise in take-home pay and could actually cut spending; this would leave the economy no further ahead despite the stimulus. Given that the government's debt-to-GDP ratio remains at a moderate level, hopefully the budget will provide the maximum short-term stimulus to the economy.

The dominant focus on construction spending in the budget is excessive. A broader range of spending measures could provide larger short-term stimulus and long-term benefits to the economy. Diminishing returns means that a broader range of spending that influences the accumulation of several factor inputs would provide for stronger long-term growth than focusing on one factor input. And the short-term GDP multipliers indicate that construction and manufacturing activity are near the bottom of the list for their impact on the economy. Education and child care-related spending both have larger short-term GDP multipliers than construction or manufacturing. Education and quality child care also provide significant long-term growth effects via the accumulation of human capital. And the provision of child care can also have short- to-medium labour supply effects. Training child care workers to improve the quality of the provision of child care services, therefore, could combine the benefits of education spending with those of child care in programs that provide temporary stimulus to the economy, but also provide long-term benefits.

References

Child Care Human Resources Sector Council (CCHRSC). 2009. "Addressing Workforce Shortages in Early Childhood Education and Care Project: Literature Review of Socioeconomic Effects and Net Benefits". Ottawa: CCHRSC.

Cross, P. and Z. Ghanem. 2006. "Multipliers and Outsourcing: How Industries Interact with Each Other and Affect GDP", *Canadian Economic Observer*, January 2006, Statistics Canada – Catalogue No. 11-010.

Dickens, W.T., I. Sawhill, and J. Tebbs. 2006. "The Effects of Investing in Early Education on Economic Growth", Working Paper, Washington, DC: Brookings Institution, 1-26.

Dynan, K., J. Skinner, and S. Zeldes. 2004. "Do the Rich Save More?" *Journal of Political Economy* 112(2).

Hemming, R., M. Kell, and S. Mahfouz. 2002. "The Effectiveness of Fiscal Policy in Stimulating Economic Activity – A Review of the Literature", IMF Working Paper WP/02/208.

IMF. 2007. "Chapter Three: Exchange Rates and the Adjustment of External Imbalances", *World Economic Outlook*, April.

__________ 2009. "Chapter Two: Country and Regional Perspectives", *World Economic Outlook*, April.

Pichette, L. 2004. "Are Wealth Effects Important For Canada?" *Bank of Canada Review*, Spring, 29-35.

Session Three

TAX POLICY CHANGES AND FINANCIAL REGULATION

TAX POLICY CHANGES IN THE 2009 BUDGET: Much Ado About Stimulus?

Lindsay M. Tedds, University of Victoria

"Adversity is a *stimulus."*
James Broughton

Introduction

The 2009 federal budget (Finance Canada, 2009) was announced amidst a global economic contraction that had followed a protracted period of significant economic growth. The objective of the budget was to "protect [Canada] from an immediate economic threat while providing the solutions we need to secure our long-term growth and prosperity" (p. 9) by delivering "potent economic stimulus to encourage growth and restore confidence in our economy" (p. 10). The mantra for the estimated $30 billion stimulus plan was that it must be: *timely* and begin within the first five months of 2009; *targeted* to produce "the largest increase in Canadian jobs and output" (p. 10); and *temporary* such that the stimuli end when the economy recovers (p. 10).

Of the $30 billion in announced spending in Budget 2009 (Finance Canada, 2009, p. 10), over one third was apportioned to tax relief: approximately $1 billion directed at simulating business investment and over $12 billion focused on stimulating individual consumption. Table 1 summarizes these tax policy changes and their estimated cost to the Government of Canada. The changes are grouped into one of three categories, depending on the general intent of the change, as follows: changes to stimulate business investment; changes to stimulate housing construction; and changes to help Canadians and spending stimulus.

This paper will describe the tax policy changes in the 2009 budget, highlighting the motivation (perceived or stated), the context, and perceived effect for each change. It will also comment, where appropriate, on the stimulus effect of the change. In reviewing the table, a general observation quickly emerges: the tax policy changes contained in Budget 2009 included not only changes that appear to have been proposed with one or more of the three criteria for its stimulus plan in mind, but also changes that reflect the government's general approach to taxation over the last decade. In particular, there are a number of changes that are neither targeted nor temporary, and several are measures that have been taken in previous budgets during a period of economic growth.

Table 1: Tax Changes and Estimated Cost

	2008-09	*2009-10*	*2010-11*	*Total*
Changes to Stimulate Business Investment				
Increasing Small Business Threshold	--	45	80	125
Mining Investment Tax Credit	--	70	-15	55
Changes to Capital Cost Allowance, Computers and M&P Machinery	--	340	355	695
Tariff Relief on Machinery & Equipment	12	76	81	169
Repealing Section 18.2 of the ITA	--	--	--	--
Subtotal	**12**	**531**	**501**	**1,044**
Stimulate Housing Construction				
Home Renovation Tax Credit	500	2,500	--	3,000
Home Buyers' Plan	--	15	15	30
First-Time Home Buyers' Tax Credit	30	175	180	385
Subtotal	**530**	**2,690**	**195**	**3,415**
Helping Canadians and Spending Stimulus				
Freezing EI Rates	693	1,381	--	2,074
Personal Income Tax Changes	470	1,885	1,950	4,305
National Child Benefit Supplement and Canada Child Tax Benefit	--	230	310	540
Working Income Tax Benefit	145	580	580	1,305
Age Credit	80	325	340	745
Subtotal	**1,388**	**4,401**	**3,180**	**8,969**
Total All Tax Changes	**1,930**	**7,622**	**3,876**	**13,428**

Note: Cost estimates taken directly from the 2009 federal budget.

Changes to Stimulate Business Investment

Small Business Threshold

Canadian Controlled Private Corporations (CCPCs) operate under a preferred tax regime over foreign-controlled and publicly traded corporations in Canada.[1] One element of the preferential tax regime is that, similar to the personal income tax system, the CCPC tax regime is progressive. For qualifying CCPCs, active business income up to the Small Business Threshold (SBT) is taxed at a lower rate than income above that amount. Budget 2009 increased the SBT from $400,000 to $500,000 (Finance Canada, 2009, p. 181). Currently, the rate applied to income below the threshold is 11%, and 19% is the rate applied to income above the threshold.[2] The change in the threshold effectively reduces taxes for qualifying CCPCs whose active business income is *above* $400,000. Specifically, the increase in the threshold translates into a tax savings of $8,000 for qualifying CCPCs whose active business income is above $400,000.

The rationale for this increase is to support the growth of small businesses by allowing them to "retain more of their earnings for reinvestment and expansion, thereby helping to create jobs and promote economic growth in Canada" (Finance Canada, 2009, p. 181). Underlying this statement is the assumption that the higher tax rate applied to business income above the SBT acts as a barrier to growth. There is some evidence to support the notion that businesses intentionally remain below the SBT.[3] Hendricks, Amit, and Whistler (1997) found that reported business income clustered just below the SBT. The percentage of businesses, however, is small, with only 3% of businesses clustering near the SBT (98.1% of businesses reported taxable income below the threshold [p. 29]). While the study is dated, examining business income reported for 1992, it remains one of the few studies in this area.[4]

---

[1]A CCPC is defined in subsection 125(7) of the *Income Tax Act* (ITA).

[2]The benefits from the SBT begin to be clawed back when a CCPC taxable capital reaches $10 million and is fully clawed back when it reaches $15 million. This clawback applies to CCPCs in all provinces except Ontario, which has its own clawback mechanism.

[3]One way for a business to target business income to just below the threshold is to pay out any income over the threshold as wages or bonuses to the owner(s).

[4]Given this discussion, it is timely to update the work in Hendricks, Amit, and Whistler (1997). In the past eight years, the SBT has been raised six times

The barrier to growth, however, is not the SBT per se but rather the steep increase in tax rates applied to income above the threshold. That is, increasing the SBT does provide incentive for firms to grow their income from $400,000 to $500,000, but it creates a disincentive to grow any further. In order to minimize the effect of the cap, the differential between the two rates, currently at 8%, needs to shrink. Table 2 summarizes the changes in the threshold and tax rates faced by CCPCs since 2002. The differential between the two rates has already shrunk from 13% in 2002 to the current 8% and is scheduled to be reduced to 4% by 2012.

In terms of meeting the guiding principles of stimulus spending, the measure is neither temporary, nor is it specifically targeted to increase jobs and output. Why might the increase in the SBT have little effect on growth? First, increasing the threshold assumes that small businesses are interested in growth. Tal (2006) found that "almost 60% of all small business owners in Canada consider themselves as 'lifestylers' that use their business as a means of generating income, while balancing other commitments or lifestyle choices" (p. 8) and are not interested in growth. In addition, Hendricks, Amit, and Whistler (1997) found that only 0.6% of businesses were able to grow their business income beyond the threshold, implying that the threshold "plays a significant role in financing growth for only a small fraction of CCPCs" (p. 10). This notion that few businesses benefit from an increase in the threshold is also borne out by the relatively low estimate of the forgone revenues of this initiative, estimated at only $80 million in 2010-2011.

Table 2: Small Business Threshold, Small Business Tax Rates, and the General Corporate Rate

	2002	*2003*	*2004*	*2005*	*2006*	*2007*	*2008*	*2009*	*2010*	*2011*	*2012*
Small Business Threshold ($000)	200	225	250	275	300	400	400	500	500	500	500
Small Business Tax Rate (%)	12	12	12	12	12	12	11.5	11	11	11	11
General Corporate Rate (%)	25	23	21	21	21	21	19.5	19	18	16.5	15

without any significant evidence that doing so supports growth amongst small businesses. Such detailed analysis should be done before any further increases are contemplated.

Second, it ignores other barriers to growth, such as business acumen, access to capital, compliance costs, labour legislation, succession planning, and, of course, demand for the businesses' goods and services. Third, raising the limit appears to benefit only a small proportion of qualifying CCPCs. In fact, one of the recommendations made by the Technical Committee on Business Taxation (TCBT) (Canada, 1998) was that the SBT should not be increased for this reason (p. 5.8). Fourth, most employment growth by small businesses results from the creation of new businesses, and not growth of existing business, and most new businesses will enter the market well below the SBT (Industry Canada, 2008; Canada, 1998, p. 5.2). Fifth, it fails to address the burden of profit-insensitive taxes, such as property taxes, payroll taxes, excise taxes, and provincial sales taxes, which have a "disproportionate impact on smaller businesses" (Canada, 1998, p. 5.5). Last, the SBT creates "distortions and incentives for tax planning" (Canada, 1998, p. 5.8).

In lieu of raising the SBT, Budget 2009 could have accelerated the planned decrease in the general corporate tax rate, shown above in Table 1. Such a change would have benefited not only CCPCs with business income above the SBT (including those that have the benefits of the SBTs clawed back), but all corporations. The research clearly shows that corporate taxes significantly influence investment decisions, and it has been shown that they negatively influence organizational form, financial structure, and dividend policy (ab Iorwerth and Danforth, 2004; Bird and Smart, 2001; Parsons, 2008; Schaller, 2007). A more pressing small business policy issue, which is tied to an aging population, is succession planning because 71% of small business owners in Canada intend to exit ownership or transfer control of their business by 2016, yet only 35% of these businesses have a succession plan, and only 7% have a formalized plan (Bruce and Picard, 2006, pp. 306-307). Without a greater policy emphasis on succession planning amongst Canadian small businesses, many businesses and associated jobs will not exist in the very near future.

Mining Investment Tax Credit

Section 66(1) of the *Income Tax Act* allows principal business corporations (certain corporations in the mining, oil and gas, and renewable energy and energy conservation sectors) to fully deduct exploration and pre-development expenses incurred in Canada from their income in the year the expenses were incurred. Many corporations with exploration and development expenses, however, are in a non-taxable position in a given tax year and are unable to deduct these expenses. Whilst unused exploration and pre-development expenses can be carried forward indefinitely, qualifying corporations can also choose to transfer these deductions to flow-through share (FTS) investors. FTSs are attractive to corporations that have difficulty raising capital to finance exploration and pre-development activities, notably junior resource corporations, which have little prospect of generating revenue in the foreseeable future and which will go out of business and not be able to use the deductions without FTS investments. They are also attractive to investors as they are permitted to fully deduct the cost of their FTSs from their income: the deduction is worth more to an individual than to a corporation since personal income tax rates are notably higher than corporate tax rates.

While FTSs are not a recent addition to the Canadian tax regime, the super flow-through share (SFTS) is. In the 2000 *Economic Statement and Budget Update* (Finance Canada, 2000), the Government of Canada announced the non-refundable Investment Tax Credit for Exploration (ITCE). It was intended to be a temporary (expiring at the end of 2003) 15% investment tax credit for investors in FTS of mineral exploration companies. The impetus for the SFTS was the low price of metals that occurred throughout the 1990s and that caused a significant contraction in mineral exploration. While metal prices rebounded to historic highs by the mid-2000s, the tax credit was renewed for additional one-year periods. It was reinstated in 2006 as the Mineral Exploration Tax Credit (METC), which was set to expire on March 31, 2009, but Budget 2009 extended the credit for an additional one-year period. Many provinces also have comparable programs. The purpose of the credit is to stimulate exploration activities.

It is useful to provide an example of how FTSs in general, and the tax credit specifically, benefit the investor. Mary is an investor located in BC who earns $250,000 a year and is taxed at the highest rate, both federally (29%) and provincially (14.7%). She decides to invest $10,000 in a mining exploration company though the purchase of FTSs. In the tax year in which she makes the purchase, she is able to deduct the $10,000 from her income. Had she not made the purchase, she would have paid $2,900 in federal taxes and $1,470 in provincial taxes on the $10,000. As a result of the deduction, Mary saved $4,370 in income taxes, making the cost of the investment to Mary only $5,630. Since Mary invested in a mining exploration company, she is also eligible for provincial and federal tax credits. The value of the BC tax credit is 20%, or $2,000. The federal METC is 15%, but is calculated on the value of the investment minus any provincial tax credit. In Mary's case, it is calculated on

$8,000, for a federal tax credit worth $1,200. Because the tax credits are in effect a grant, the value of the federal and provincial tax credit is subject to income tax, resulting in Mary incurring a tax liability of $1,390. In total, Mary garners a tax benefit of $6,180. Of the $10,000 initial investment, Mary shoulders $3,820 (38.2%) of the cost, while taxpayers bear $6,180 (61.8%) of the cost of the investment.

In order for Mary to break even (ignoring inflation and other time costs of money), she only needs to sell the $10,000 investment for $4,888.03 (the adjusted-cost basis of the shares is zero). If she sells for this amount, she will only pay $1,068.03 in capital gains taxes, leaving Mary with the initial after-tax cost of the investment ($3,820). In this scenario, the taxpayer is left with a $5,111.97 deficit. Because Mary sold at a value less than her original investment, this implies that the company's stock price decreased, and it can be assumed that it did not find any mineral deposits of value, implying no additional corporate taxes to make up the difference. In fact, in order for the taxpayer to break even (assuming no additional corporate taxes), Mary would have to sell the shares for $28,283.75, which represents an unlikely 182% return on her (and the taxpayers') investment. Clearly, the tax regime for FTSs is preferential even without the METC, and one has to wonder how much additional influence the tax credit has had on investment in mining FTSs. In addition, there is evidence to indicate that the investments in mining FTSs are predominately done for tax-planning reasons as demand for these products increases at the end of the calendar year.[5] They are also actively marketed to investors who are looking for last-minute tax deductions. An unintended cost of the SFTS regime is that it is likely shifting investment dollars away from other, less risky, and unsubsidized investments.

The Prospectors & Developers Association of Canada credits the METC with contributing significantly to mineral exploration activity and new mineral discoveries in Canada: in particular, increasing exploration expenditures from approximately $300 million in the late 1990s to an estimated $1.722 billion in 2006, the highest total for exploration and deposit appraisal expenditures since 1987 and 1988; and leading to 268 new mineral discoveries in 2005, compared with 15 in 1999 (Prospectors & Development Association of Canada, n.d.). Figure 1 plots exploration expenditures along with the Metal Price Index (MPI) from 1980 to 2007.

[5]As demand for FTSs increases, the quality of the products for sale on the market decreases, thereby increasing the likelihood that Canadian taxpayers are never reimbursed for their share of the investment in FTSs.

Figure 1: Exploration Expenditures and the Metal Price Index

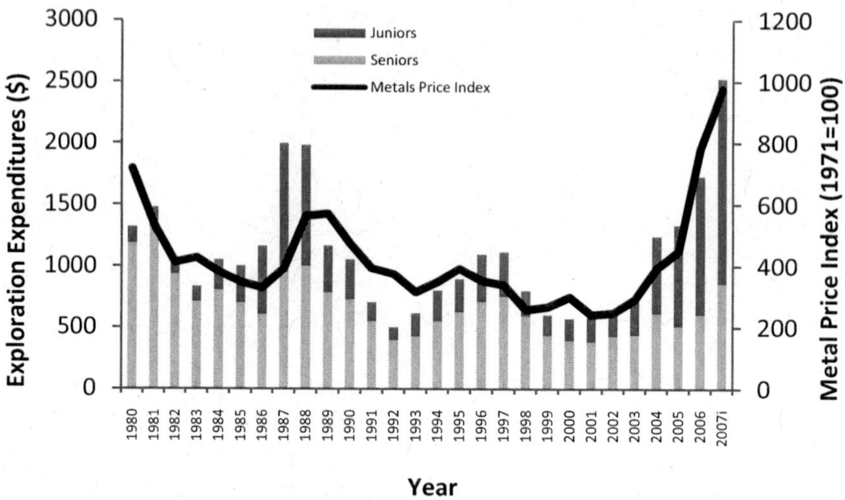

Source: Natural Resources Canada; Statistics Canada.

It shows a high correlation between expenditures and metal prices, and it is likely that the true driving force behind the expansion was the increase in metal prices.

In terms of the value of the deposits found, the value has increased from $189 million in 1999 to $556 million in 2007 in nominal terms. However, most of this increase is solely the result of the rise in prices. In real terms, the value has increased from $428 million in 1999 to $450 million in 2007. As a percentage of exploration costs, the value of the deposits dropped from 60% of exploration costs in 1999 to 24% in 2007. This indicates that the increase in exploration is not paying off in terms of an increase in the value of located deposits.

There is little evidence that the METC induces increased exploration activity over that stimulated by the existing FTS regime and the increase in commodity prices. On the investor side, the METC subsidizes high-risk investments and appears to be predominately used for tax-planning purposes by high-income taxpayers rather than for calculated investment purposes. On the administration side, the FTS regime is associated with high administrative and compliance costs, and most of the benefits accrue to tax lawyers and accountants (McKenzie, 1994; and Jog, Lenjosek, and McKenzie, 1996). Whether or not the increased exploration pays off in terms of long-term jobs and economic opportunities in northern Canada depends on how and on what the exploration costs are being spent and how many of the deposits become long-term viable mines.

Changes to Capital Cost Allowance

Generally, under Canada's tax code, costs incurred to earn income are deductible from the income earned for tax purposes. This is called the matching principle: it matches expenses with the income generated. When an expense is incurred to acquire a capital asset, the expense is typically allocated over the useful life of the capital asset since the one-time expense generates a flow of income. The capital cost allowance (CCA) rate determines how much of the cost of a capital asset may be deducted each year for tax purposes. The CCA deduction is non-refundable, and the CCA rates vary according to the useful life of the capital asset. In addition, to prevent a flurry of tax-motivated purchases at the end of a tax year, for many assets only half of the expense can be included in the purchase year for purposes of that year's CCA deduction calculation. This is commonly referred to as the half-year rate. To calculate the CCA deduction, most asset classes use the declining balance. The declining balance method produces relatively larger CCA deductions during the earlier years of an asset's life, decreasing deductions over time, and an asset balance that never reaches zero. The other method is called a straight-line method and generates equal CCA deductions each year until the balance reaches zero.

Budget 2009 included changes to the CCA system for two specific assets, the intent of which was to increase or accelerate investment in these specific capital assets. First, the CCA rate for computer equipment and systems software was temporarily increased from 55%[6] to 100% for qualifying purchases after January 27, 2009, and before February 1, 2011. In addition, the half-year rate was waived so that the expense is fully deducted in one year. The measure is intended to boost productivity through faster adoption of newer technology (Finance Canada, 2009, p. 167). Second, the CCA rate for machinery and equipment used for production is normally 30%. Budget 2007 implemented a temporary 50% straight-line CCA rate for purchases of these assets made before January 1, 2009. Budget 2008 extended this to include purchases made in 2009 and provided for a declining basis for assets acquired in 2010 and 2011. Budget 2009 waived the declining basis and extended the 50% straight-

---

[6]The CCA rate for computer equipment and systems software was increased from 45% to 55% in Budget 2007.

line CCA rate into 2010 and 2011. This means that purchases of machinery and equipment can be fully deducted in the first two years of the assets' useful life. This measure is to "assist businesses in the manufacturing and processing sector to meet the current economic challenges, boost productivity, and position themselves for long-term success" (Finance Canada, 2009, p. 168).

Increasing the CCA rate permits an asset to be depreciated more rapidly than the presumed decline in the asset's value, thereby providing an immediate tax advantage. For example, a qualifying CCPC with taxable income before CCA of $500,000 (effective tax rate of 11% in 2009) and a year-end of December 31 purchases $20,000 in computer equipment and systems software on March 15, 2009. Under the accelerated rules with the half-year rate waived, the business can deduct $20,000 from its operating income for an immediate tax savings of $2,200 in 2009. Under the normal CCA rules, with a CCA rate of 55% and the half-year rate, the total tax savings approaches $2,200, but it is spread over a number of years, as shown in Table 3.

There are several things to note about accelerating CCA rates, assuming no changes in tax rates and positive taxable business income. First, the total tax savings under an accelerated regime and the normal regime is

Table 3: Normal CCA Rules for Computer Equipment and Software (dollars)

Year	*Capital Cost*	*CCA*	*Tax Savings*
2009	20,000.00	5,500.00	605.00
2010	14,500.00	7,975.00	877.25
2011	6,525.00	3,588.75	394.76
2012	2,936.25	1,614.94	177.64
2013	1,321.31	726.72	79.94
2014	594.59	327.02	35.97
2015	267.57	147.16	16.19
2016	120.40	66.22	7.28
2017	54.18	29.80	3.28
2018	24.38	13.41	1.48
2019	10.97	6.03	0.66
2020	4.94	2.72	0.30
2021	2.22	1.22	0.13

essentially the same in nominal terms.[7] Second, the total taxes paid by a corporation under the two regimes are the same, but the accelerated regime allows the business to defer corporate taxes to future years. Third, because of the deferment, an accelerated CCA regime can be viewed as an interest-free loan from the government; but since the general corporate tax rate is scheduled to drop over the next several years, the accelerated CCA regime actually reduces overall taxes paid to corporations by allowing businesses that pay the general corporate tax rate to claim more of the deduction during years in which the tax rate is higher.

The underlying assumption is that the temporary acceleration rate will incentivize businesses to increase their investments in these assets, thereby increasing the long-term productivity and growth. Accelerating CCA rates have several key shortcomings. First, in any year, some firms will be investing in these assets regardless, and the accelerated rate simply subsidizes behaviour that would have occurred anyway.[8] Second, businesses with no taxable income in the years that the accelerated rate applies do not benefit from the change despite making the desired purchase. Third, it is assumed that accelerating the purchase of the specific assets has a bigger benefit than increased purchases of other assets. That is, accelerated rates cause investment dollars to be shifted from other asset classes that, for any given business, could have induced higher productivity growth than an investment in an accelerated class.[9] Fourth, an accelerated rate essentially subsidizes the sector that produces the asset at the expense of other sectors in the economy. In particular, the program leads to an increase in demand for certain assets and a decrease in demand for others. Further, the increase in demand will likely lead to increases in the prices of specific assets because of the increase in demand. Fifth, accelerated rates distort the matching principle underlying the Canadian tax system. Finally, as pointed out by the TCBT, "when assessing the appropriateness of certain accelerated deductions, it should be remembered that there are a number of other significant deductions,

---

[7]Though the present value of taxes paid is lower with the accelerated CCA.

[8]Of course, this is a common problem with most incentive programs, such as Scientific Research and Experimental Development (SR&ED), but any such programs should stipulate the current level of activity and the anticipated increase in activity because of the new initiative.

[9]One justification for accelerated CCA is that the specific assets generate externalities. There is some evidence that investment in machinery and equipment generates spillover effects (e.g., DeLong and Summers, 1991), but this is a highly controversial view (e.g., Auerbach, Hassett, and Oliner, 1994).

which, while recognized for financial accounting purposes can only be deducted later – perhaps many years later – for tax purposes. These rules may more than offset the advantages accruing to businesses that are able to claim capital cost deductions more rapidly than they depreciate them in their own records"[10] (Canada, 1998, p. 4.9).

A better policy for promoting investment in the short term, to ensure long-term increases in productivity without subsidizing certain businesses and sectors, would have been to accelerate the reduction in the general corporate tax rate (see Table 2).[11] Such a measure would have been a more efficient way to incentivize businesses to increase investments in capital assets.[12] Alternatively, abolishing the half-year rate or implementing a simple pro-rating system based on the purchase date for all asset classes could have been pursued. Finally, if there was still a desire to target specific assets, then an investment tax credit is a preferable tool[13] (Canada, 1998, p 4.10).

---

[10]In particular, TCBT noted that:

> These rules include:
> – provisions for the best estimate of legal claims. For accounting purposes, a company must accrue its best estimate of outstanding claims, but in general, these can only be deducted for income tax purposes when actually determined or paid.
> – provisions for obsolescence and for the decline in value in certain capital assets. While these may be required for accounting purposes, in a number of circumstances they will not be recognized for tax purposes either until actually incurred or until the disposal of the last asset in a class of similar assets.
> – provision for a post-retirement benefit for retired employees. Under current accounting proposals, these costs must be accrued, for accounting purposes, over the working lives of the individuals, so as to match these costs with the contribution that the employees make to the generation of revenue. For tax purposes, however, the costs can only be deducted as incurred (Canada, 1998, p. 4.23).

[11]As the quality of capital assets produced in the market tends to increase over time, thereby prolonging the life of many capital assets, CCA rates should be reviewed regularly to ensure that the rate continues to match the life of the asset.

[12]In the absence of spillovers from certain types of assets, most economists would agree that the preferred tax structure is one with a broad base and a low statutory rate.

[13]As articulated by the TCBT, investment tax credits:

> Are generally a more efficient incentive than accelerated allowances, because the benefit is provided up front where it can assist in financing

Eliminating Tariffs on Machinery and Equipment

As noted in Budget 2009, almost 90% of imports entering Canada are tariff-free (Finance Canada, 2009, p. 169), yet many items under the broad category of machinery and equipment are subject to tariffs ranging from 2% to 11%. Budget 2009 permanently eliminates tariffs on machinery and equipment. Tariffs raise the price of these goods, both foreign and domestic, and this reduces demand for them. In general, taxes on inputs distort production decisions, and the government revenues collected through the tariff does not offset these losses. Eliminating the tariff is consistent with the interest in encouraging Canadian businesses to purchase machinery and equipment (see the above section on capital cost rates).

Repealing Section 18.2 of the Income Tax Act

Budget 2009 contained a seemingly innocuous bullet stating that it was repealing the interest deductibility constraints in 18.2 of the *Income Tax Act*; but unlike most other budget items, no additional information or explanation was provided despite the fact that this is a significant policy change (Finance Canada, 2009, p. 162).

As noted previously, the matching principle of the Canadian tax system allows taxpayers to deduct costs incurred to earn an income from the income earned. For example, if a taxpayer borrows money for income-generating purposes (e.g., purchasing shares that pay a dividend), the interest paid on the borrowed money is tax-deductible. That is, only the income earned minus the cost incurred is taxable. There is, however, a twist when it comes to Canadian corporations with foreign affiliates. In general, Canadian corporations can invest or acquire shares in foreign affiliates, and the dividends that the Canadian corporation earns from this investment are not subject to taxation in Canada if they are earned in a country with which Canada has a tax treaty. The twist arises if the

---

the cost of the asset, rather than over some period of years. The use of investment tax credits makes the incentive more visible and therefore imposes accountability as well as avoiding distorting the income tax base. The use of federal investment tax credits instead of accelerated allowances minimizes the entanglement of federal and provincial tax systems. The cost of a federal initiative is thus borne by the federal government and not shifted in part to the provinces (through alterations in the common tax base), thus preserving the integrity of the taxable income base for both levels of government (Canada, 1998, p. 4.11-4.12).

Canadian corporation borrows money to make the initial investment. The corporation can deduct the interest for tax purposes, but does not pay tax on the associated income;[14] there is no matching income to expenses.[15] The problem that arises is that, if the foreign affiliate is located in a low or no tax region, then the tax paid on the incoming income does not approximate Canadian taxes, implying that the effective tax rate on the foreign investment income is lower than on similar income from domestic sources. The generous tax treatment of interest-funding foreign direct investment erodes tax revenues in Canada.

The Department of Finance began reviewing these tax rules in 1987, the Auditor General expressed concern with the current rules in 1992 and again in 2002, and the TCBT recommended that interest deductibility for investment in foreign affiliates should be disallowed (Canada, 1998, p. 6.18). No action was taken until Budget 2007 announced the surprise addition of section 18.2 to the *Income Tax Act*. Specifically, "interest expense on indebtedness incurred to acquire the shares of a foreign affiliate [should] no longer be deductible, unless and until the shares generate income that Canada actually taxes" (Finance Canada, 2007, p. 242). Section 18.2 was to come into force on March 19, 2007, but it was delayed until January 1, 2012, and considerably narrowed to include only "the range of affected interest expense to that which can be linked with the earning of exempt income in 'double-dip' and other 'tax-efficient' financing structures" (Edgar, Farrar, and Mawani, 2008, p. 810).

Despite the fact that section 18.2 would not come into force until 2012, Budget 2009 announced that it would immediately repeal it. Repealing section 18.2 was one of the recommendations made by the Advisory Panel on Canada's System of International Taxation, which reported in December 2008 and which favoured instead a regime that included the adoption of a specific anti-avoidance rule (Canada, 2008). Edgar, Farrar, and Mawani (2008) disagree with the recommendations made by the Advisory Panel and instead argue for the adoption of a comprehensive thin-capitalization regime. The arguments both in favour and against section 18.2 are complicated and too lengthy to be discussed here.

---

[14]The rule providing Canadian companies with the ability to deduct interest on funds borrowed to invest in domestic and foreign affiliates has been in place since the 1972 tax reform.

[15]For a more complete description of the rules regarding the exemption of foreign source income, interested readers should consult the report by the Advisory Panel on Canada's System of International Taxation (Canada, 2008).

Instead, interested readers should consult Canada (1998); Edgar, Farrar, and Mawani (2008); and Canada (2008) for a full discussion.

Stimulating Housing Construction

Home Renovation Tax Credit

According to Budget 2009, "home renovations can represent a smart investment in the long-term value of a home and generate broad-based economic activity ... to support economic growth during these challenging times, Budget 2009 proposes to introduce a temporary Home Renovation Tax Credit (HRTC). The HRTC will provide a temporary incentive for Canadians to undertake new renovation projects or accelerate planned future projects, thus providing timely stimulus to the Canadian economy" (Finance Canada, 2009, p. 127). The HRTC in a non-refundable tax credit that applies to renovations undertaken between January 28, 2009, and February 1, 2010, and applies to eligible expenditures above $1,000 but below $10,000. The maximum value of the tax credit is, therefore, $1,350.

Is there a need to stimulate home renovations in Canada? Figure 2 plots real expenditures on renovations since 1981. Expenditures on home renovations have doubled since 1999, from about $16 billion to almost $33 billion in 2008. Not only did renovation expenditures over this

Figure 2: Renovation Expenditures, 1992 Constant $

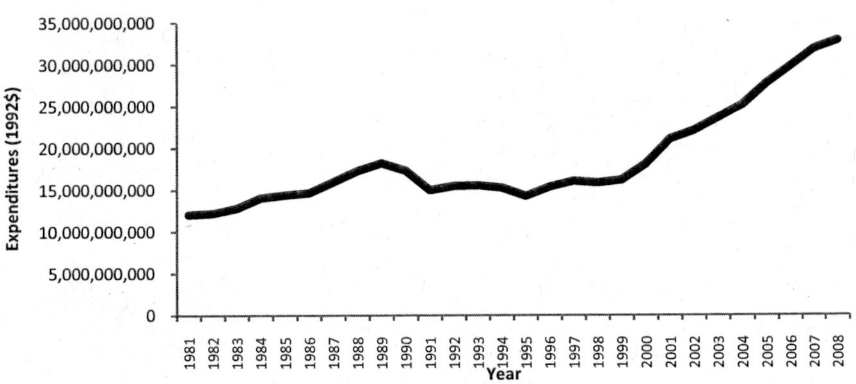

Source: Statistics Canada.

period far exceed the historical average rate, but they also surpassed growth in real GDP. Expenditures, however, began to slow in 2008, and in the first quarter of 2009, renovation activity fell 4.2%; however, the amount being spent is about 6% higher than that spent in the same quarter in 2006 (Statistics Canada, 2004). This slowing of growth appears to be more of a correction back to a more balanced growth path and is not indicative of a sector that is troubled.

Another reason for stimulating renovations was to partially offset the decline in the construction of new housing. Figure 3 plots real expenditures on new home construction since 1981. The trend is quite similar to that seen for renovations: expenditures had almost doubled between 1999 and 2008, and the growth rate was steep. Expenditures began to slow in the second quarter of 2008 as the worldwide economic decline took hold and the value of new home construction fell to a six-year low over the subsequent year. This long decline, however, has likely just recently turned a corner, with the Canada Mortgage and Housing Corporation (CMHC, 2009) noting that home constructions increased by a surprising 12.1% in August 2009.

Many of the arguments that were made against the accelerated CCA rates for computers and machinery discussed above apply to this budget item.

Figure 3: New Home Construction, 1992 Constant $

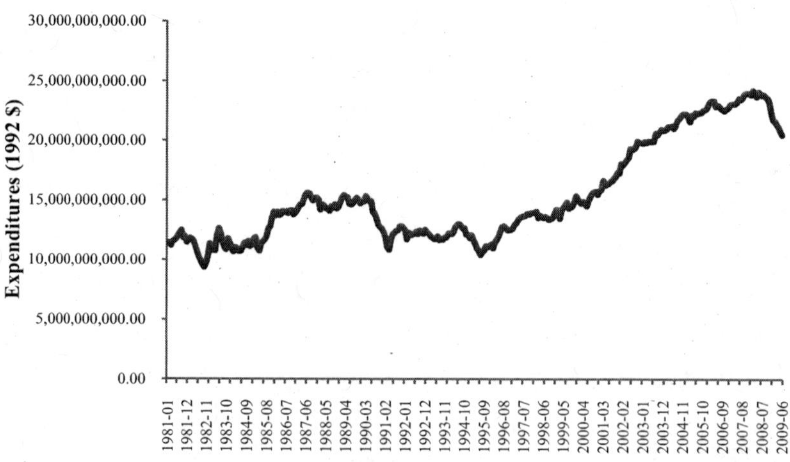

Source: Statistics Canada.

The tax credit will subsidize a significant amount of expenditures that would have occurred regardless, and it will be very difficult to disentangle how much of total expenditures was truly stimulated by the credit.[16] Individuals owing no federal tax will not benefit from the HRTC, making the credit targeted toward middle- and high-income earners. It also assumes that accelerating any planned or new renovations has a bigger benefit than other expenditures that may have been planned by the homeowner. In addition, renovations made now may also not pay off as much in the future due to the depreciation of most renovations. Many renovations only truly pay off when done within a few years of an expected sale, and accelerating renovations may not be in the long-term interests of the homeowner. For example, a kitchen renovation from the 1980s would not hold its full value into 2008. It is unclear why all Canadian taxpayers should be subsidizing an investment in an asset when the returns mostly accrue to the individual homeowner and his or her family (particularly because of the principal-residence tax exemption). Finally, the administrative costs of this initiative, particularly audit and enforcement, are likely to be quite high on the HRTC, reducing any benefit from the initiative. Income taxes are highly distortionary, and a more significant long-term benefit would have likely come from further accelerating income tax cuts, particularly to high-income earners.

Another possible benefit of the HRTC is that, because the homeowner needs to document the expenditures to be claimed, it may shift renovation expenditures from the underground economy to the observed economy. On the other hand, the tax credit is less than the price differential normally seen in this market, making underground expenditures still preferred on a price-comparison basis. Further, many persons who operate in the underground economy do so covertly such that the homeowner is still issued a receipt, albeit a generic receipt. The HRTC did not include explicit rules about the documentation requirements, and the credit will, in part, go toward expenditures made and income earned in the underground economy.

Home Buyers' Plan

The Home Buyers' Plan (HBP), introduced in 1992, permits first-time home buyers to withdraw up to $20,000 from their Registered Retirement Savings Plan (RRSP) to purchase or build a home without incurring a tax liability. If the purchase is made with a spouse or

[16]Supra footnote 8.

common-law partner, then each individual can withdraw up to the maximum amount. In this case, both individuals must qualify as first-time home buyers. Withdrawals under the HBP must be repaid with the minimum annual repayment being equal to 1/15 of the amount withdrawn. Individuals that fail to make a repayment, in full or in part, must add the shortfall amount to their taxable income. The primary motivation for the program was that first-time home buyers have more difficulty in coming up with an appropriate down payment as they do not have equity from a previous home. Budget 2009 increased the maximum withdrawal amount to $25,000. The revised withdrawal amount provides a 20% down payment on $125,000 toward the purchase price of a home. To put this into context, in March 2009, the average home price in Canada was $288,641; it ranges from $147,682 in PEI to $425,708 in BC (Canadian Real Estate Board, n.d.).

Because the taxpayer is allowed to deduct RRSP contributions from their income and a withdrawal under the HBP does not induce a tax liability, this effectively means that first-time home buyers can use up to $20,000 in pre-tax income to purchase a home. The withdrawal, however, needs to be paid back with after-tax dollars to the program, and it is likely that the individual's marginal tax rate was lower when making the contributions than when making the repayments, thereby providing no loss in tax revenues to the government. In essence, the program allows an individual to borrow from themselves. The cost to the individual is the investment return (or the benefit of losing out on an investment loss) of the withdrawn money, but, in theory, the asset they invested in (the house) should increase in value, thereby earning a return on investment outside the RRSP. Assuming the home is the individual's primary residence, upon sale the gains are not taxed, whereas had the gains accrued in the RRSP, they are taxed on withdrawal. Whether or not the investment in housing versus an investment in an RRSP yields a greater return to the individual depends on a variety of different factors, including the taxpayer's marginal tax rates when RRSP contributions and withdrawals were made.

The HBP is popular amongst first-time home buyers. According to the Canada Mortgage and Housing Corporation (CMHC, 2006), since 1992 over 1.5 million individuals have used almost $16 billion of their RRSPs to buy homes. In addition, per annum withdrawals and the number of individuals using the program have remained relatively stable since the inception of the program. Since the inception of the program, the average withdrawal under the HBP is about $10,000-$11,000 (though it varies significantly by province), or about half the original maximum amount, and approximately 130,000 individuals use the program. The plan, however, is primarily used in Ontario and Quebec, with these residents accounting for 92% of participants in the program and accounting for 97% of withdrawn amounts. A survey conducted in March 2005 of mortgage holders found that nearly half of first-time home buyers used RRSPs as a source of down payment, and for 39% of first-time home buyers, the RRSP withdrawal was the primary source of their down payment. Overall, the increase in the threshold would appear to benefit a very small proportion of first-time home buyers. In addition, as banks include the required repayments when calculating the amount of mortgage the individual qualifies for, the withdrawal decreases the maximum total mortgage the individual qualifies for.

It should be noted that Budget 2008 announced the Tax-Free Savings Account (TFSA), which allows individuals to save after-tax income and earn investment income tax-free. Some thought needs to be given to whether RRSPs are an appropriate savings vehicle over the long run for home purchases, particularly since the TFSA provides a more suitable vehicle to save for consumption expenditures such as home purchases.

First-Time Home Buyers' Tax Credit

When purchasing a home, buyers incur costs in addition to mortgage and moving costs, and some are one-time, non-recurring costs. The non-recurring costs are commonly referred to as closing costs and include legal fees and disbursements, title insurance, land survey fees, property transfer taxes, GST, mortgage processing fees, appraisal fees, and other miscellaneous costs. Closing costs tend to run in the order of up to 4% of the purchase price of the home, though it varies by jurisdiction. Budget 2009 introduced a First-Time Home Buyers' Tax Credit (FTHBTC) for homes acquired after January 27, 2009. The FTHBTC is a non-refundable tax credit that provides a maximum of $750 in tax relief. The rationale for the credit is that many first-time home buyers find it difficult to "pay these costs in addition to saving money for a down payment" (Finance Canada, 2009, p. 132). The measure is provided under the "stimulate housing construction" pillar.

Given the structure of the tax credit, the FTHBTC is unlikely to cause any changes in behaviour. Because this is being delivered through the tax system as a credit, it simply acts as a delayed partial reimbursement of costs (delayed until the home buyers receive their refund in the first or second quarter of the following year). It means that the home buyers must first pay all the closing costs up front, so home buyers must still save for their closing costs or use their available credit, assuming that by doing so they are able to afford the stream of payments, and it does reduce their approved mortgage amount. They also must wait up to a year before receiving their subsidy for buying their first home. That is, it does not reduce the amount that needs to be saved in order to purchase the home. As a consequence, the FTHBTC cannot accelerate an already planned purchase or cause other individuals to make the leap into home ownership. In other words, the FTHBTC simply subsidizes behaviour that would have occurred without the tax credit. There may be some delayed benefit amongst those who claim the FTHBTC and receive a tax refund; however, empirical evidence suggests that lump-sum payments such as a tax refund are much more likely to be used to increase savings or reduce debt than induce increased consumption (Shefrin and Thaler, 1988; Feldman, 2010).

A final comment relates to the material on the HBP discussed above: individuals can use their withdrawals under the HBP to cover their closing costs. In this case, the FTHBTC is providing a tax credit for expenditures made from pre-tax dollars. Whilst tax credits have become quite common under the Canadian and other tax systems, tax credits are normally calculated using net or taxable income rather than pre-tax income; hence, the FTHBTC as currently structured represents a significant shift in tax policy, and not for the better.

Helping Canadians and Spending Stimulus

Freezing EI Rates

Changes to EI rates can be considered a tax policy change since EI premiums are essentially a payroll tax. Budget 2009 froze EI premiums for both 2009 and 2010 at 2008 rates: $1.73 per $100 (p. 95) for the employee rate. This also effectively froze EI premiums for employers, which are calculated at 1.4 times the employee rate. On the basis that EI premiums would have been increased in 2009 in order to achieve a break-even level, this change could be viewed as a tax cut. However, as the maximum insurable earnings (MIE) rose from $41,100 to $42,300 in 2009, the net effect is that employees whose wage earnings are below the 2008 MIE threshold will pay no additional tax, while employees whose wage earnings are above the 2008 MIE will pay additional taxes. Equally, employers will pay more in EI premiums for all employees whose wage earnings are above the 2008 MIE. In total, employees earning above the 2008 MIE will pay approximately $20 (or 0.77 cents per paycheque, assuming a biweekly pay schedule) more, and employers will pay approximately $30 more, per annum in EI premiums than in 2008, thereby reducing income for both parties. That said, the additional amount being withheld during a given pay period is negligible and may not have any direct negative effects on consumption or employment and certainly has fewer negative effects than had rates been increased.

Personal Income Tax Changes

In 2009, all bracket thresholds increased 2.5% as a result of indexation,[17] but Budget 2009 included an additional increase of 5% to the exemption amount and thresholds for the first two of the four tax brackets. That is, the personal exemption and the thresholds for the first two tax brackets increased by 7.5%. To deliver the relief in a timely fashion, withholding calculations were revised effective April 1, 2009.

Table 4 summarizes the exemption and threshold amounts for 2008, the original 2009 figures based on the changes announced in the budget, the maximum tax savings, and the maximum savings per paycheque, assuming a biweekly pay schedule. The increase in the personal exemption over and above the original exemption amount for 2009 results in a tax savings of $33 for the year, or an additional $1.27 cents per paycheque for individuals in the top tax bracket. Having an additional $1,893 taxed at 15% rather than 26% results in an additional tax savings of $75.76 and a total tax savings of $108.76, or an additional $4.18 per paycheque if at the top of the threshold. And having an additional $3,788 taxed at 22% rather than at 26% provides a further tax savings of $113.64 and a total tax savings of $222.4, or an additional $8.55 per paycheque for individuals in the top tax bracket. The resulting effect is that every taxpayer will pay less tax in 2009, resulting in an

[17] Beginning January 1, 1974, the personal income tax system was indexed annually by raising the tax brackets and increasing personal exemptions by an inflation factor based on the CPI. The 1986 tax reform limited the inflation factor to the CPI less 3%. This shifted the personal income tax system in Canada from a fully indexed system to a system based on partial indexing and resulted in bracket creep: because incomes generally rise with the cost of living, many Canadians paid more taxes than they would have had the system remained fully indexed. Effective January 1, 2000, full indexation was restored. In addition, Budget 2000 announced a five-year tax reduction plan that increased the tax brackets and personal exemptions by greater than inflation in some years.

Table 4: Original and Modified Personal Income Tax Bracket Thresholds and Exemption

Tax Rates	*2008*	*Original for 2009*	*Budget 2009*	*Tax Savings*[1]	*Cumul. Tax Savings*	*Savings Per Pay-cheque*
0%	$9,600	$10,100	$10,320	33	33	1.27
15%	Up to $37,885	Up to $38,832	Up to $40,726	75.76	108.76	4.18
22%	$37,886-$75,769	$38,833-$77,664	$40,727-$81,452	113.64	222.4	8.55
26%	$75,770-$123,184	$77,665-$126,264	$81,452-$126,264	0	222.4	8.55
29%	>$123,185	>=$126,265	>=$126,265	0	222.4	8.55

[1]Calculated using the difference between the original thresholds for 2009 and those announced in Budget 2009.

overall increase in disposable income in Canada that will, at least in part, fuel increased consumption, albeit perhaps just an extra coffee from Tim Hortons for some or a venti soy chai latte and raspberry scone at Starbucks for others (and only every two weeks). An alternative use for this additional money is to offset any housing rental increases or increases in property taxes that have occurred in 2009.

This assumes, however, that taxpayers notice the difference in their take-home pay and also spend the increase. In the United States, Shapiro and Slemrod (2001) added questions onto the April 1992 Survey of Consumers following a change in withholding amounts that resulted in a small increase in take-home pay. The findings are quite interesting. Half of the respondents did not notice a change in their paycheque, which supports the findings of Krishna and Johar (1996) and Morwitz, Greenleaf, and Johnson (1998) that small credits are ignored. This also indicates that paying out tax relief in regular, small payments will also likely be ignored. More interesting is that of the half that did notice a change, half of those reported that the paycheque was reduced as a result of the change. Of those that did notice and noticed an increase, when asked what they would do with this extra money, less than 50% said they would spend it.

An alternative measure, followed in the United States, is to provide an immediate stimulus cheque to taxpayers for their annual tax relief rather than revising the withholding formula. The assumption is that by providing a large amount all at once will have a greater effect on consumption expenditures. The evidence, however, indicates that the marginal propensity to consume (MPC) out of lump sum payments is much lower than the MPC out of regular income. The MPC estimates for regular income range from 0.5 to 0. 685, but only 0.32 to 0.437 for lump sum income (Ishikawa and Ueda, 1984; Shefrin and Thaler, 1988). Out of the two ways to deliver tax relief to individuals with an expectation of a short-term stimulus effect, the method followed by Canada appears to be the preferred choice; however, increases in other taxes, such as property taxes and payroll taxes, need to be taken into account before determining the potential stimulus effect.

Age Credit

Individuals who are 65 years of age and earn an income that is below a certain threshold are allowed to claim an additional non-refundable personal credit called the age amount credit. The purpose of this credit is to help alleviate poverty amongst seniors. In 2009, seniors with a taxable income amounting to $32,311 or less receive the full credit; however, it is partially clawed back on incomes between $32,312 and $75,031 and eliminated for individuals whose income exceeds $75,032. Budget 2009 increased the age credit by $1,000 to $6,408, providing seniors with an added tax relief of $150 per annum. As noted by Kevin Milligan (2010), the age credit distorts horizontal equity across age groups in low- and moderate-income households and provides additional after-tax income to households that have already acquired consumer durables such as cars, furnishings, and homes. In this regard, they often have lower annual durable expenditure requirements than non-senior households with similar income levels. On the other hand, they may have larger overall marginal propensities to consume since they no longer need to save for retirement. Combining this information, the increase in the age credit may provide some economic stimulus. But a more broad-based measure would have been to increase the GST credit, further increasing the personal exemption (discussed below), or further enriching the Working Income Tax Benefit (WITB) (discussed below), each of which would have provided a greater stimulus effect since a greater proportion of consuming households would have been targeted.

The Canada Child Tax Benefit and the National Child Benefit Supplement

The Canada Child Tax Benefit (CCTB) and the National Child Benefit Supplement (NCBS) were implemented in 1998 and represented an integrated approach to federal and provincial child benefit programs. Budget 2009 announced changes in the payments under these programs; the changes are directly tied to the aforementioned changes in the personal income tax system. CCTB benefits are clawed back at a rate of 2% for one child and 4% for families with two or more children once family income exceeds the threshold set for the 15% income tax bracket. Because this threshold was raised to $40,726, this means that qualifying families can earn an additional $1,894 over the threshold that would have been in place through indexing alone. Equally, the clawback threshold under the NCBS was increased by the same increase as the CCTB threshold, to $23,712. The overall effect is that families earning more than $38,832 but below the amount where the CCTB is fully clawed back, and families earning more than $23,712 but below the amount where the NCB is fully clawed back, both receive an additional benefit amount over what they would have had thresholds increased by the normal indexation amount. However, these changes will have little effect on children in the poorest families in Canada.

Working Income Tax Benefit

Canada's poorest working families did, however, benefit from changes to the Working Income Tax Benefit (WITB). Budget 2007 introduced the WITB with the objective of lowering the "welfare wall" and making "work pay for low- and modest-income Canadians" (Finance Canada, 2007, p. 78). That is, the goal is to increase the labour supply of low-income Canadians. The WITB is modelled after the 30-year old American program called the Earned Income Tax Credit (EITC).

Budget 2009 increased the available tax credit from $522 to $925 for individuals and from $1,044 to $1,680 for couples and single parents. For individuals, the enhanced benefit is phased in at a rate of 25% of each dollar earned over $3,000, reaching a maximum for earned income between $6,700 and $10,500. The benefit is phased out at a rate of 15% of each additional dollar earned over $10,500 and fully eliminated at an income of $16,667. For couples and single parents, the enhanced benefit is phased in at a rate of 25% of each dollar earned in excess of $3,000, reaching a maximum for earned income between $9,720 and $14,500. The benefit is phased out at a rate of 15% of each additional dollar earned in excess of $14,500 and fully eliminated at an income of $25,700. The enhanced program provides a benefit that is closer to that originally envisioned for such a program by Liberal Finance Minister Goodale in 2005, and, in effect, the changes cut personal income taxes for those qualifying individuals.

Scarth and Tang (2008) provide a simulation of the effects of the WITB program before the enhancement. They find that the WITB reduces structural unemployment, though the magnitude is small, their market wage may be reduced, and it increases average income of beneficiaries. The overall conclusion is that the WITB does "increase the living standard of the targeted subset of the working poor" (p. 34). They also find that the WITB program has more positive effects than a comparable employment subsidy or general income tax cut. An unintended benefit of the program is that, since it has a positive effect on observed labour supply, it is likely to draw some low-income individuals out of the underground workforce, thereby providing them with access to social security programs such as CPP and EI and ensuring protection by labour regulation.

Combined, the CCTB/NCBS and WITB measures put more money into wallets and purses of households that are very likely to use it to boost consumption expenditures. In addition, the WITB, combined with personal income tax relief, the Canada Employment Credit, and changes to the Child Tax Benefit and associated supplement, are significant steps toward reducing poverty in general and child poverty in particular; however, poverty amongst the homeless and individuals not working remains unaddressed.

Conclusion

The budget contains a number of measures to stimulate consumption. In terms of stimulating business investment, increasing the small business threshold, renewing the METC, and changing the CCA are inefficient measures for stimulating investment and should have been replaced by accelerating the cuts to corporate taxes. On the other hand, eliminating tariffs is beneficial. The measures for stimulating housing construction are not substantiated by the evidence and, like many of the measures to stimulate business investment, are likely to have a low "bang for the buck" because there is no evidence that they will substantially increase spending in this area, and they are likely to simply subsidize activities that would have been undertaken in the absence of the tax measure. Instead, this money could have been used to accelerate personal tax cuts and enrich programs aimed at helping the poor. Finally, the measures aimed at helping Canadians and stimulating personal spending are beneficial but are more beneficial for poverty reduction than economic stimulus (though the two are intertwined) since the programs are not likely to be, nor should they be, temporary. That said, there has been little focus on helping the homeless and the non-working poor (many of whom are single mothers), and this represents a significant gap in current policy. Taken together, the message arising from this analysis is that the ideal economic stimuli when using the tax system are those actions that should be done, regardless of the general macroeconomic situation. Taxes are highly distortionary, and the best stimulus often comes from cutting overall tax rates and allowing individuals and firms to decide where and how to spend them.

References

ab Iorwerth, A. and J. Danforth. 2004. "Is Investment Not Sensitive to its User Cost? The Macro Evidence Revisited", Working Paper 2004-05, Department of Finance, Ottawa.

Auerbach, A., K. Hassett, and S. Oliner. 1994. "Reassessing the Social Returns to Equipment Investment", *Quarterly Journal of Economics* 109(3), 789-802.

Bird, R. and M. Smart. 2001. "Tax Policy and Tax Research in Canada", in P. Grady and A. Sharpe (eds.), *The State of Economics in Canada.* Montreal: McGill-Queen's University Press.

Bruce, D. and D. Picard. 2006. "Making Succession a Success: Perspectives from Canadian Small and Medium-Sized Enterprises", *Journal of Small Business Management* 44(2), 306-309.

Canada. 1998. *Report of the Technical Committee on Business Taxation.* Ottawa: Department of Finance.

__________. 2008. *Report of the Advisory Panel on Canada's System of International Taxation.* Ottawa: Department of Finance.

Canada Mortgage and Housing Corporation (CMHC). 2006. *Housing Now.* Ottawa: Public Works and Government Services, July.

__________. 2009. *Preliminary Housing Start Data.* Ottawa: Public Works and Government Services, September.

Canadian Real Estate Board. n.d. *MLS Statistics.* Retrieved May 5, 2009, from www.crea.ca/public/news_stats/statistics.htm.

deLong, J.B. and L. Summers. 1991. "Equipment Investment and Economic Growth", *Quarterly Journal of Economics* 106(2), 445-502.

Edgar, T., J. Farrar, and A. Mawani. 2008. "Foreign Direct Investment, Tin Capitalization, and the Interest Expense Deduction: A Policy Analysis", *Canadian Tax Journal* 56(4), 803-869.

Feldman, N. 2010. "Mental Accounting Effects of Income Tax Shifting", *The Review of Economics and Statistics* 92(1), 70-86.

Finance Canada. 2000. *Economic Statement and Budget Update 2000.* Ottawa: Department of Finance.

_________. 2007. *The Budget Plan: Aspire to a Stronger, Safer, Better Canada*. Ottawa: Department of Finance.

_________. 2009. *The Budget Plan: Canada's Economic Action Plan*. Ottawa: Department of Finance.

Hendricks, K., R. Amit, and D. Whistler. 1997. *Business Taxation of Small and Medium-Sized Enterprises in Canada*. Working Paper 97-11. Prepared for the Technical Committee on Business Taxation. Ottawa: Department of Finance.

Industry Canada. 2008. *Key Small Business Statistics*. Ottawa: Industry Canada, January.

Ishikawa, T. and K. Ueda. 1984. "The Bonus Payment System and Japanese Personal Savings", in M. Aoki (ed.), *The Economic Analysis of the Japanese Firm*. Amsterdam: North Holland.

Jog, V., G. Lenjosek, and K. McKenzie. 1996. "Flow-through Shares: Premium Sharing and Cost-Effectiveness", *Canadian Tax Journal* 44(4), 1016-1051.

Krishna, A. and G. Johar. 1996. "Consumer Perceptions of Deals: The Biasing Effects of Varying Deal Prices", *Journal of Experimental Psychology: Applied* 2(3), 187-206.

McKenzie, K. 1994. "Refundability and the Incentive Effects of Flowthrough Shares", *Canadian Tax Journal* 42(4), 1100-1114.

Milligan, K. 2010. "What Have Four Conservative Budgets Done to Personal Income Taxes?", this volume.

Morwitz, V., E. Greenleaf, and E. Johnson. 1998. "Divide and Prosper: Consumers' Reactions to Partitioned Prices", *Journal of Marketing Research* 25 (November), 453-463.

Parsons, M. 2008. "The Effect of Corporate Taxes on Canadian Investment: An Empirical Investigation", Working Paper 2008-01, Department of Finance.

Prospectors & Developers Association of Canada. n.d. "PDAC's Position on Canada's 'Super' Flow-Through Program". Retrieved May 5, 2009, from www.pdac.ca/pdac/advocacy/financial/flow-through.html.

Schaller, H. 2007. "The Long-Run Effect of Taxes, Prices, and the Interest Rate on the Capital Stock", Working Paper. Ottawa: Carleton University.

Scarth, W. and L. Tang. 2008. "An Evaluation of the Working Income Tax Benefit", *Canadian Public Policy* XXXIV(1), 25-36.

Shapiro, M.D. and J. Slemrod. 2001. "Consumer Response to Tax Rebates", NBER Working Paper No. W8672. At ssrn.com/abstract=294721.

Shefrin, H.M. and R.H. Thaler. 1988. "The Behavioral Life-Cycle Hypothesis", *Economic Inquiry* 26, 609-643.

Statistics Canada. 2004. "Canadian Economic Accounts", *The Daily*. March 2. Statistics Canada. At www.statcan.gc.ca/daily-quotidien/090302/dq090302a-eng.htm. Acccessed May 5, 2009.

Tal, B. 2006. *Small Business in Canada: Trends and Prospects*. CIBC World Markets Economics and Strategy, September.

WHAT HAVE FOUR CONSERVATIVE BUDGETS DONE TO PERSONAL INCOME TAXES?

Kevin Milligan, University of British Columbia

Introduction

Since the Conservatives won the federal election of 2006 and formed the government, Finance Minister Jim Flaherty has delivered four budgets. While the constraints of a minority government and a strategy of incremental politics have limited changes to tax policy, the accumulated weight of four budgets may still reveal interesting patterns and some sense of direction for Conservative tax policy. In this paper, I describe and analyze the personal income tax policy changes of the 2006 through 2009 budgets. The analysis starts by fitting the changes into a conceptual framework and then proceeds to an empirical study of tax burdens by income group, as well as by marital status, the presence of children, and whether there are seniors present.

For context, I begin with the aggregate trends in personal income tax collection at the federal level. In Figure 1, I take an annual series of federal personal income tax revenue and divide it by the personal income series taken from the national accounts.[1] The tax revenue data is on a fiscal year basis, while the national accounts are based on calendar years. However, the resulting series should be informative for picking out any trend breaks in the share of personal income taken by the federal

---

I thank conference participants and especially Bev Dahlby for many helpful comments.

[1]Personal income in the national accounts comprises income received by Canadian residents, whether from factor income or government transfers.

Figure 1: Personal Income Tax as a Percentage of Personal Income

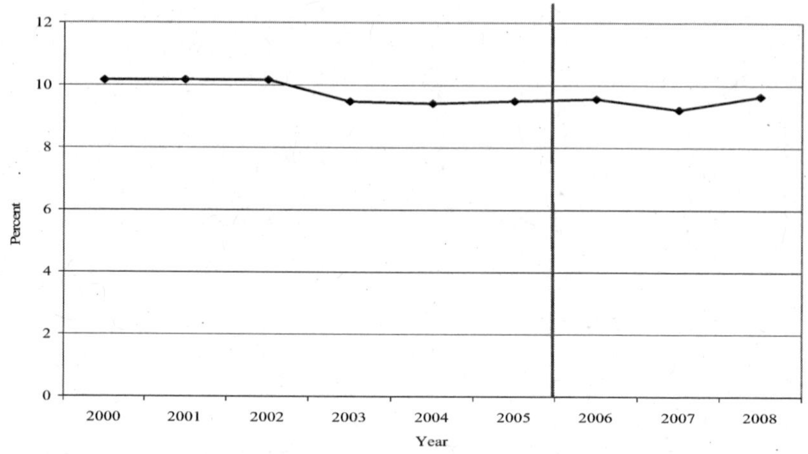

Source: Personal income tax is on a fiscal year basis and is taken from CANSIM v156116. Personal income is on a calendar year basis and is taken from CANSIM v691801.

government in taxes. For context, I show the years 2000–2005 under the Liberal governments of prime ministers Chrétien and Martin, as well as the 2006–2008 data for the Conservative government of Prime Minister Harper. Data for the fiscal year ending in 2009 is not yet available.

The series shows a surprising lack of movement. Actual personal income tax revenue grew in nominal terms by 20.5% from $98.4 billion in 2005 to $118.6 billion in 2008. However, personal income grew by almost the same percentage, leaving the share of personal income taken by federal taxes at about 9.5%. This suggests that whatever changes have been made, they have been proportional in aggregate. So, up to 2008, there was no noticeable change in aggregate fiscal policy through personal income taxation. Normally, one would expect higher incomes to be translated through the progressive personal income tax into a higher percentage of personal income being taken through taxes. However, the increases in tax credits may have more or less offset this trend.

Even if personal income taxes remained proportionally similar between 2005 and 2008, a shift in other forms of taxation could lead to important changes in the tax mix. In particular, many economists and commentators have discussed the implications of cutting the Goods and Services Tax from 7% to 5%. To this end, Figure 2 examines the share of federal tax revenue coming from different sources. I categorize the

Figure 2: Changes in the Federal Tax Mix

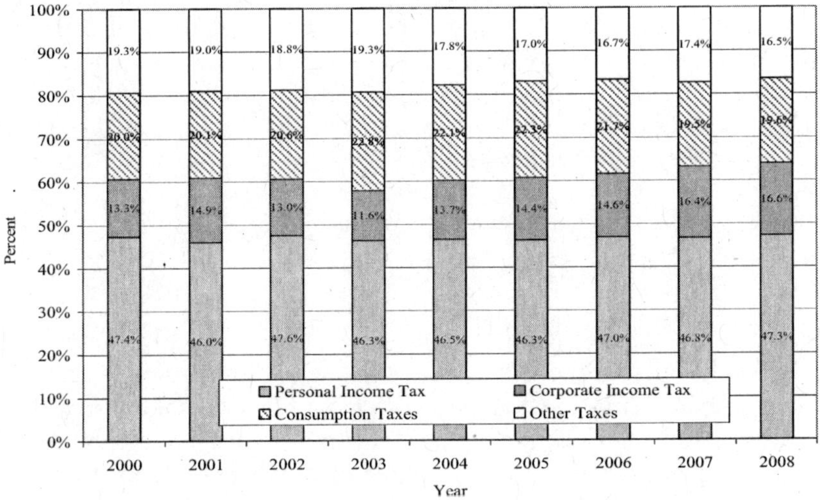

Source: CANSIM Matrix 3850002.

revenue sources into personal income taxes, corporate income taxes, consumption taxes, and other taxes.[2]

Total federal revenue in 2005 was $212.2 billion, rising 18% to $250.8 billion in 2008. The share of this revenue brought in by the personal income tax increased slightly from 46.3 to 47.3%, but this remained in the range seen from 2000 to 2004. There was a sizeable drop from 22.3% to 19.6% in consumption taxes, as sales tax revenue stayed flat in nominal terms owing to the cut in the Goods and Services Tax rate from 7% to 5%. Corporate income tax revenue jumped two percentage points, owing more to buoyant corporate profits than policy changes. While this does indicate some change in the tax mix, these changes do not represent a substantial shift in the tax mix at the federal level.

This preliminary analysis of aggregate trends suggests little change to either the overall share of activity captured by the personal income tax

---

[2]Consumption taxes include general sales taxes (the Goods and Services Tax), alcoholic beverages and tobacco taxes, amusement taxes, gasoline and motor fuel taxes, remitted gaming profits, custom duties, and other consumption taxes. Other taxes include health and drug insurance premiums, property and related taxes, contributions to social security plans, natural resource taxes and licences, interest and investment income, fines, penalties, and other revenue. The data come from CANSIM matrix 3850002.

system or to the mix of revenue sources. In the rest of the paper, I focus on the details of the changes in tax policy over the last four budgets. The next section provides a listing and brief description of all changes to the federal personal income tax over the last four budgets. Following that, I categorize and analyze these changes. Finally, I provide evidence from simulations on how these changes have affected tax burdens.

Personal Income Tax Changes

A defining feature of tax policy under the Conservative government has been incrementalism. In contrast to past party platforms, which featured marquee personal income tax cuts, the Conservative policy proposals prior to the federal election of 2006 encompassed a bundle of small, targeted tax changes. While the continued incrementalism since the 2006 election might be ascribed to the minority Parliament, it is worth noting that this incrementalism had its birth in strategic decisions made before the Conservatives knew that they would be in a minority situation. (See Flanagan, 2007, p. 282.) In this section, I provide details on all federal personal income tax changes over the 2005 to 2009 period. I exclude the important dividend tax credit changes announced in 2005 by the Liberal Government but implemented in 2006, since this was not a decision made by the Conservatives.

Rates and Brackets

There have been no changes to the rate structure, except for a 0.25% blip in the bottom tax rate from 15% to 15.25% in 2006, which was reversed in the following year.[3] The thresholds for the four tax brackets were adjusted for inflation between 2005 and 2008, but otherwise remained the same. The 2009 budget announced larger-than-inflation increases in the thresholds for the second and third brackets, but tax rates were left unchanged. These developments are summarized in Table 1.

---

[3]The previous Liberal Government announced in the 2005 Fall Fiscal Update a cut in the bottom rate from 16% to 15% retroactive to January 1, 2005. This change, however, was not legislated before the fall of the Liberal Government. The new Conservative Government recognized the change for 2005 and the first half of 2006, but set the rate at 15.5% for the last six months of 2006, making the 2006 rate effectively 15.25%. This was set back to 15% for 2007 in the 2007 budget.

Table 1: Tax Brackets and Rates 2005-2009

	Rate	*Thresholds*				
		2005	2006	2007	2008	2009
1st bracket	15/15.25/15	0	0	0	0	0
2nd bracket	22	35,595	36,378	37,178	37,885	40,726
3rd bracket	26	71,190	72,756	74,357	75,769	81,452
4th bracket	29	115,739	118,285	120,887	123,184	126,264

Source: Canada Revenue Agency tax forms, various years.

Non-Refundable Tax Credits

The bulk of the tax changes that have been implemented are adjustments to non-refundable tax credits. The dollar value of these tax credits is determined by multiplying the bottom tax rate by the credit amount. So, a $500 credit lowers the tax liability in 2009 by 15% of $500, or $75. However, the tax liability cannot fall below zero. This means that any Canadian who already has sufficient credits to push the tax liability to zero would see no benefit from additional credits. This point is not trivial – of the more than 23 million returns filed in 2006, more than 7 million of them, accounting for 31.9% of the total, were non-taxable returns.[4] Below, I list these changes and describe each briefly:

- *Canada employment amount*: Credit of $250 in 2006, then $1,000 in 2007 for earned income.
- *Children's fitness amount*: Credit of $500 for children's sports expenditures, starting in 2007.
- *Textbook amount*: An extra $65 (full-time) or $20 (part-time) added to the monthly education amount. No need to show textbook expenditures.
- *Public transit amount*: Credit for monthly transit passes introduced in 2007.
- *Pension income amount*: Increase of $1,000 to a level of $2,000 for qualified pension income in 2006.
- *Dependent children*: Credit of $2,000 per child aged 18 and under.
- *Age amount*: Increased from $3,979 in 2005 to $5,066 in 2006, then to $6,408 in 2009.

[4]Source is the 2008 Interim Statistics-Universe Data (covering the 2006 tax year), available on the website of the Canada Revenue Agency, http://www.cra-arc.gc.ca/gncy/stts/ntrm-eng.html. Non-taxable returns are defined as those with a total tax liability of less than two dollars.

- *Basic amount*: Increased from $8,839 to $9,600 in 2007, then to $10,320 in 2009.
- *Spousal amount*: Increased from $7,505 to $9,600 in 2007, then to $10,320 in 2009.

Other Changes

There have been two substantial changes to income tax-based transfers. First, the Universal Child Care Benefit was introduced in July 2006, paying $100 per month for each child under the age of six. This benefit is taxable income for the lower-income spouse, but is not included as net income for the purposes of determining entitlement to refundable tax credits such as the Canada Child Tax Benefit.[5] The other innovation to benefits is the implementation of the Working Income Tax Benefit, which provides an earned income supplement for those with earned income greater than $3,000. This benefit is implemented as a refundable tax credit on the tax form, although "pre-payment" of the benefit can be made. The 2009 budget proposed an expansion of the size of this benefit to $925 for singles and $1,680 for couples. The Working Income Tax Benefit is clawed back for those with net income (adjusted for the Universal Child Care Benefit) greater than $10,500 for singles and $14,500 for couples.

Finally, there are two changes to the definition of income. Since 2007, it became possible to elect to split certain types of pension income between spouses. This includes income from Registered Retirement Income Funds, Registered Pension Plans, and Registered Retirement Savings Plans. In some cases, this is restricted to partners age 65 or more. The second income-definition change relates to scholarship income received by students. Starting in 2006, scholarship income became excludable, undoing another piece of the 1972 reform that implemented a Carter Commission-inspired comprehensive income definition.

Assessment

The most salient change to the system is the multitude of non-refundable tax credits. While politicians tend not to distinguish between tax burden

---

[5]Specifically, line 236 Net Income has the Universal Child Care Benefit subtracted before determination of entitlement for refundable tax credits.

cuts, achieved by cutting rates, and cuts that are achieved through increasing tax credits, the economic impact of the two choices is starkly different. When rates are cut, there is a lowering of the gap between the gross and the after-tax return to work, saving, and investment. This increases, in general, economic efficiency. The cost of such cuts is typically an increase in inequality, as lower rates benefit those paying taxes more than those who don't. Thus, efficiency is helped at the cost of equity.

In contrast, the non-refundable tax credits do not change marginal tax rates and thus have no impact on the wedge between gross and after-tax returns. Holding spending constant, this means that more revenue must be raised elsewhere, leading to a decrease in efficiency. One benefit, potentially, comes from improvements in equity by having the distribution of the tax burden better reflect society's preferences about who should pay. In this way, efficiency is hindered, but equity is helped only to the extent that credit beneficiaries are those whom society views as needy. The other potential benefit is through the incentive effect of tax credits on the prices of different activities, which, if chosen wisely, may improve efficiency. I expand on these arguments below.

When Do Non-Refundable Tax Credits Make Sense?

Three arguments may be made to justify the inclusion of tax credits for specific taxpayer characteristics or for certain types of spending.[6] The first is the person's ability to pay. Certain types of spending do not enhance welfare, but merely perpetuate existence. They do not bring gratification, but instead relieve need. In this way, ability to pay should not include expenditures on such items. Spending on medical treatments and basic food and shelter are examples. Second, some expenditures represent costs of earning income. Just as a business should be taxed on profit rather than on revenue, individuals ought to be taxed on the net return to work rather than gross income. Examples here include child care expenses, commuting costs, and costs of investment in education. However, the proper treatment of these kinds of expenses is to allow a deduction from taxable income since these expenditures do not enhance ability to pay, which ought to be the basis for assessing tax burdens. Finally, in the presence of externalities or other market failures, governments may intervene through tax credits to change the price of

[6]This section draws on and incorporates the arguments about the economic definition of income found in Goode (1977).

goods. These are often called "Pigouvian" interventions, referring to Arthur Pigou's suggestion to use taxes to close the gap between social returns and market prices. Tax credits for charitable donations are an example of this type of tax treatment.

In principle, these three arguments open the door to a vast number of credits. For example, the purchase of an umbrella does not enhance my welfare; it merely keeps me in my current dry state. In practice, the complexity and administrative costs of the tax system must be balanced against these equity arguments. The basic amount (set at $10,320 for 2009) achieves this balance by granting a non-refundable amount to all tax filers that accounts for a basket of basic needs (from food to basic shelter to umbrellas), expenditures on which do not enhance ability to pay. In the presence of the basic amount, the right question when assessing a new non-refundable tax credit is whether the welfare gain, net of complexity and administrative costs, exceeds the gain that would be had by simply incorporating the proposed tax credit into the existing basic amount.

Can the Conservative Tax Credits Be Justified?

Accounts of the 2006 election focus on the deliberate strategy of targeting tax breaks at specific swing voter groups. (See Wells, 2006, p. 214; and Flanagan, 2007, p. 226.) This makes it relatively clear that the motivation behind these tax credit changes was to exercise interest group politics rather than to implement a consistent tax policy. With that in mind, it is still an interesting question to wonder whether there is *any* sound tax policy rationale for the changes made to non-refundable tax credits. The idea here is to gauge the size of the policy fig leaf with which the Conservatives hid their naked political motivation.

Table 2 provides a summary attempt to categorize the new non-refundable tax credits into the three justifications listed above. The Canada Employment Amount is an attempt to account for costs of earning income. Given its widespread application (to all with earned income), it seems unlikely to be more effective than an increase in the basic amount – and, moreover, if meant to account for expenses necessary to earn income, it should be a deduction. The Children's Fitness Amount was pitched as a way to increase children's participation in sports, perhaps in a Pigouvian way to encourage more sporting activity than would happen with market prices. However, given that non-participation is more likely at lower income levels, the non-refundability

Table 2: Assessment of Non-Refundable Tax Credits

Tax Change	*Ability to Pay*	*Cost of Earning*	*Pigouvian*
Canada Employment Amount		▪	
Children's Fitness Amount			▪
Textbook Amount		▪	
Public Transit Amount		▪	▪
Pension Income Amount			?
Dependent Children	▪		
Age Amount	?		
Basic Amount	▪		
Spousal Amount	▪		

Notes: A dot indicates that the listed tax change might be justified under the corresponding argument. A question mark indicates a more tenuous claim to justification under the argument.

of the tax credit raises the question of whether this credit is well targeted to achieve that goal. The textbook amount is really just an increase in the credits for education, as no textbook receipts are required to claim it. If education represents a cost of earning future income, this credit may help relieve the taxation of these inputs. The public transit amount could be justified as a Pigouvian intervention to improve the environment or as a reflection of the costs of earning income. However, environmental goals are likely best achieved through other, broader means (such as environmental taxes or cap-and-trade systems), which allow individuals to choose among appropriately priced transportation options rather than funnelling them into a particular choice. Recognition of pension income through the pension income amount is difficult to assess – perhaps it is meant to reduce the taxation on savings in order to encourage more saving by households.

The final four credits mentioned in Table 2 are more broadly based, reflecting increases in the recognition of basic needs that don't contribute to ability to pay. The basic amount goes to all taxable filers, while the new dependent children's credit and the spousal amount can be thought of as recognizing costs incurred by a household head to provide for family members. The age credit is a bit harder to justify here, though, as poverty among the elderly is actually much lower than among younger Canadians, and out-of-pocket expenditures on items such as housing are much lower among the elderly than younger Canadians. (See Milligan, 2007, for more on elderly poverty and Woolley, 2007, on the tax position of the elderly.) To the extent that the definition of "basic needs" is subjective across time and across people, increases in the recognition of expenditures on basic needs may be justified. But, as always, any gain in equity resulting from these changes should be weighed against the efficiency loss of the higher tax rates that must recoup the lost revenue.

Overall, and especially when viewed in aggregate, it seems difficult to see the case for many of the specific tax credits over the alternative of increasing the basic amount – especially when administrative and complexity costs are considered. The broad-based tax credits, however, may be more easily justified so long as one thinks that basic needs were not adequately covered by the existing tax credits. It is important to remember, however, that an equal-revenue cut in tax rates would have improved the efficiency of the economy – whatever the gain in equity, it does come at a cost. The next section turns to the question of how these tax changes have affected the distribution of tax burdens, in order to judge the impact of the Conservative tax changes on equity considerations.

Who Has Benefited?

In this section, I present results from simulations of the tax system over the period from 2000 to 2009. I use the Canadian Tax and Credit Simulator package (Milligan, 2009), which delivers tax liabilities and transfer entitlements for simulated individuals of different characteristics. I take the actual tax parameters for years up to 2008 and the announced parameters for the 2009 year. In the simulations, I focus on a taxpayer living in British Columbia, although repeating the exercise for other provinces makes little difference. In order to maintain the focus on federal tax changes, I "freeze" the British Columbia income tax system at its 2005 levels, increasing credit amounts and thresholds only by the inflation factor used in British Columbia and keeping all rates at the 2005 values.

Many of the tax changes described above are illuminated little by simulation – if you have earned income, you are better off by $150 ($1,000 credit times the 15% credit rate). The same applies for students, public transit users, and parents with children in sports. However, I pick out two groups that might benefit from further analysis – families with children, and seniors. Below I present simulations for these two groups to see how changes in tax policy have affected their tax burdens. I also show how burdens have changed across income levels.

By Income Levels

I begin with an exhibit of the overall changes in tax burden across income groups. Figure 3 shows the average tax rate, net of refundable tax credits and including Canada Pension Plan and Employment Insurance payroll taxes, for a single individual with no children in different years. Each line traces the progression of the average tax rate for a given year across earned income levels from $0 to $150,000. These income levels are set in 2005 dollars and adjusted for inflation for the other years, meaning that inflation alone won't shift the average tax rates if the tax system were perfectly indexed to inflation. The simulations take increments of $100, accounting for the lack of complete smoothness of the lines. The figure shows the years 2005, 2007, and 2009, with 2000 also shown for context. I assume no special expenditures, such as public transit, or special status, such as being a student.

The results show a strong difference between the 2000 average tax rates and the other three years, which are clustered together. This difference is driven by the tax rate and bracket changes implemented by the Liberals

Figure 3: Average Tax Rates Across Incomes

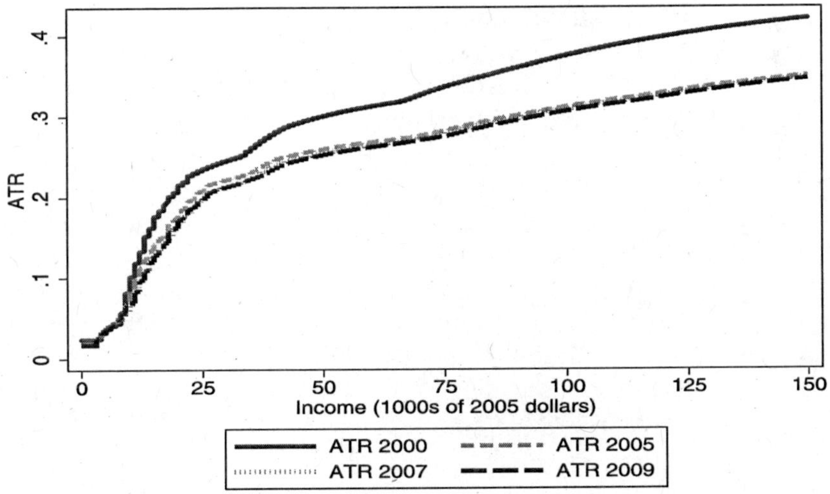

Source: Calculations made with Canadian Tax and Credit Simulator.

in 2001. This clearly had a large impact on the average tax rate across the income distribution, especially at higher income levels. At $25,000, the average tax rate drops between 2000 and 2005 from 23.3% to 20.7%, while at $100,000, it drops from 37.5% to 31.1%.

From 2005 to 2009, however, the average tax rates under the Conservative government show very little change. The slight increase in tax bracket thresholds in 2009 leads to slightly lower average tax rates in 2009 compared to 2007 at higher income levels. The increase in the basic amount from $8,648 in 2005 to $10,320 in 2009 improves the bottom line of a taxable filer by $250.80. In addition, the Canada Employment Amount delivers another $150. However, the impact of these magnitudes on average tax rates fades quickly as one moves up the income scale.

By Family Composition

Several of the changes to tax policy have an impact that differs by family composition. Those with children benefit from the new $2,000 non-refundable tax credit for children age of 18 or less. This delivers a tax break of $300 per child when multiplied by the 15% credit rate. In addition, the Universal Child Care Benefit is paid to families with children under age six, and it is taxed on the return of the lower-earning spouse. This means that parents not employed outside the home pay no tax on this income, while families with two working parents will face taxes on their payments. Finally, increases to the spousal amount from $7,344 in 2005 to $10,320 in 2009 provide a more substantial $446 boost to families with one parent not working outside the home.[7]

To investigate the impact of these changes on families, I simulate the tax burden of families of four different types. I look at a single childless individual, a single parent of two children, a married couple with two children and one parent at home, and a married couple with two children and both parents working. In all cases, I assume the children are ages three and eight, meaning that one receives the Universal Child Care Benefit and the other does not. When there is no parent at home, I assume child care costs for the three-year-old of $750 per month, which

---

[7]The Working Income Tax Benefit can also have a large (up to $1,680) impact on families with children who happen to be in the income range ($3,000 to $25,700 in 2009 for two-parent families). However, because it is a refundable tax credit, it does not have an impact on the rest of the personal income tax system, so I leave it out of this analysis.

are eligible for the Child Care Expense Deduction. To keep things simple, I look only at an average worker (earning $41,100, which is the Year's Maximum Pensionable Earnings from the Canada Pension Plan system). When both parents are working, I assign this earned income to both spouses. This level of income means that the Working Income Tax Benefit is not at play.

Figure 4 shows the results. I graph the after-tax income level for each family type for the years 2005 to 2009, normalized to 100 for 2005. The single childless person sees very little change in after-tax income, consistent with what was seen in Figure 3 earlier. When two children are added, however, the family gains more than 5% by 2007 and 6.4% by 2009. This amounts to an inflation-adjusted drop of $1,323 in the tax liability, which is 12% of the 2005 tax burden. Next, I add a stay-at-home parent. The increase in after-tax income is comparable to what was seen for the single parent. Finally, I add a two-working-parent family. In the figure, this family is graphed by one parent's income rather than the total of both, making the lines harder to compare to others. Still, it is clear that the gain in after-tax income for the two-working-parent family isn't as high. This arises because of the higher tax rate on the Universal Child Care Benefit and the fact that the two-working-parent family doesn't benefit from the spousal amount increase.

Figure 4: Disposable Incomes Across Family Types

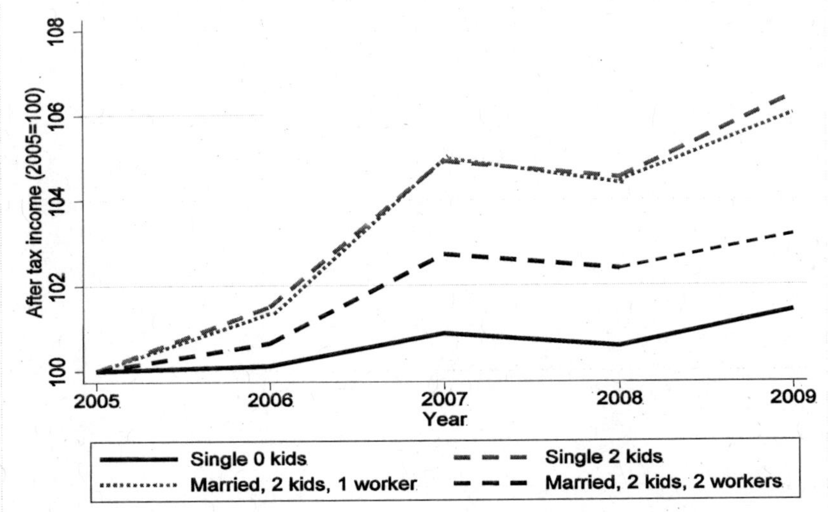

Source: Calculations made with Canadian Tax and Credit Simulator.

Seniors

A number of tax changes affected seniors directly. The age amount went from $3,976 in 2005 to $6,408 in 2009, decreasing the tax burden by $364 for taxable filers. Also, the pension income amount increased by $1,000, meaning a difference in tax burdens of $150 for those with pension income. Finally, pension income-splitting benefits couples with pension income.

To simulate the impact on seniors, I set up senior families with Canada Pension Plan and Old Age Security income, plus some Registered Retirement Savings Plan income. For the Canada Pension Plan, I assume both spouses receive the maximum pension. Old Age Security income is also assumed to come in at its maximum level. Finally, I assume Registered Retirement Savings Plan income is $2,500 per person in the couple.

Figure 5 displays the results. For comparison, I include a single childless non-senior, similar to the single childless individual in Figure 3. The other two lines are for a single senior and a married senior. The gains for the seniors are relatively small as the gain from the age amount and pension amount are not large.

Figure 5: Disposable Incomes for Seniors

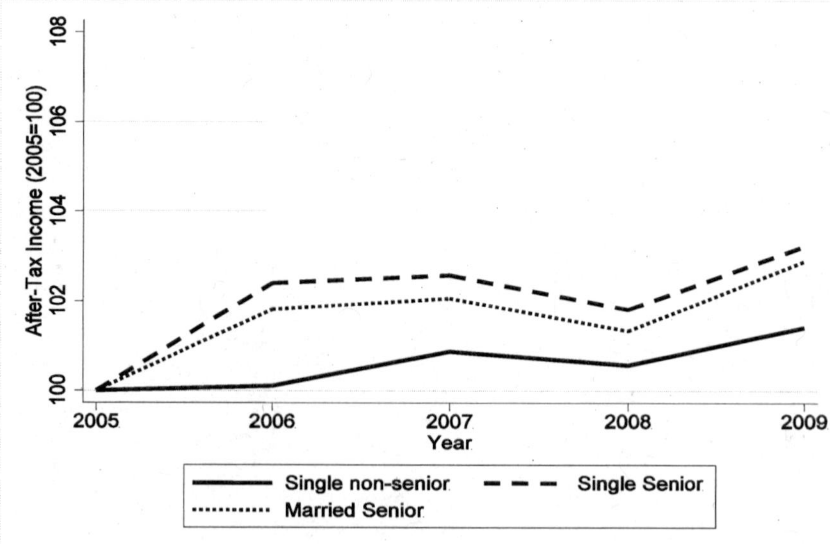

Source: Calculations made with Canadian Tax and Credit Simulator.

A more material gain is possible through the income-splitting provision introduced in 2007. Under this provision, qualified pension income can be split between the two spouses in the couple. (See Woolley, 2007, for a more complete analysis of the impact of income-splitting.) Figure 6 shows the average tax rate for a senior couple with the same income profile described above, but with an increasing amount of pension income as one moves from left to right in the graph. The years 2006 and 2007 are shown, being the last year before income-splitting and the first year after.

There is an evident substantial difference between the average tax rate in the two years. The gap reaches 4 percentage points at $50,000 of pension income. At $100,000 of pension income, the inflation-adjusted tax difference is $8,112, which is 20.2% of the total tax burden. This represents a substantial saving to the couple. However, to put this in context, only 65.9% of senior couples in the 2005 Survey of Labour and Income Dynamics have any pension income. The 75th percentile is $18,500, the 95th percentile is $47,500, and the 99th percentile is $80,000. This suggests that most of the benefit of this tax change will accrue to the small proportion of seniors with substantial pension income.

Figure 6: Average Tax Rates When Income Splitting

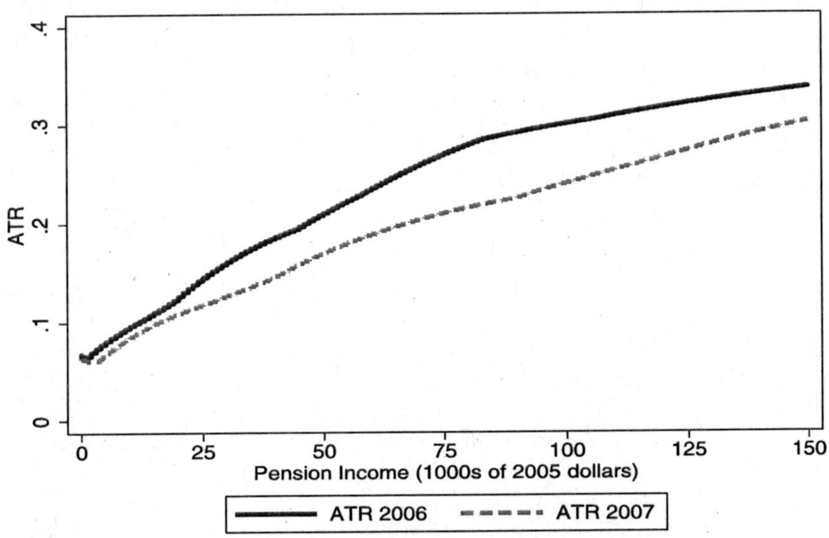

Source: Calculations made with Canadian Tax and Credit Simulator.

Conclusions

This paper has studied the overall impact of changes in personal income tax policy over the four Conservative budgets from 2006 to 2009. There has been almost no change in the proportion of personal income taken as taxes and only a small change in the share of personal income tax in revenue. The biggest change has been the introduction of many small non-refundable tax credits, which added to the complexity and administrative costs of the tax system, funding transfers to specific groups at the cost of forgone revenue. These credits contributed to a significant shift in the distribution of the tax burden. The largest identifiable beneficiaries of the Conservative income tax policy have been families with children, and specifically those with a stay-at-home parent. In addition, I found a large gain for seniors with substantial pension income as a result of the introduction of pension income-splitting in 2007. Whether these changes to personal income taxes represent an improvement to the Canadian economy will depend on one's assessment of the merits of shifting the tax burden in these directions.

Political commentary has suggested that the Conservatives view income tax policy as a political tool to increase their short-run electoral chances rather than as a tool to improve the functioning of the Canadian economy. It is far from uncommon for political parties to succumb to the vice of sacrificing good policy for electoral advantage, so one should be measured in assessing too much blame to the current government – this seems to be a persistent choice made by politicians in Canada. To the extent that there is a difference between political and policy goals, however, this difference may say more about the functioning of Canadian democracy than the politicians who exploit it.

References

Flanagan, T. 2007. *Harper's Team: Behind the Scenes of the Conservative Rise to Power*. Montreal: McGill-Queen's University Press.

Goode, R. 1977. "The Economic Definition of Income", in J.A. Pechman (ed.), *Comprehensive Income Taxation*. Washington, DC: The Brookings Institution, 1-36.

Milligan, K. 2007. "The Evolution of Elderly Poverty in Canada", *Canadian Public Policy* 34(4), s79-s94.

__________. 2009. Canadian Tax and Credit Simulator. Database, software and documentation, Version 2009-1.

Wells, P. 2006. *Right Side Up: The Fall of Paul Martin and the Rise of Stephen Harper's New Conservatism*. Toronto: McClelland and Stewart.
Woolley, F. 2007. "Liability Without Control – The Curious Case of Pension Income Splitting", *Canadian Tax Journal* 55(3), 603-625.

Session Four

IMPLICATIONS FOR INTERGOVERNMENTAL FISCAL ARRANGEMENTS

COST-SHARING AND FEDERAL-PROVINCIAL FISCAL RELATIONS

Tracy Snoddon, Wilfrid Laurier University, and Paul Hobson, Acadia University

Introduction

Over the period from the early 1970s to the mid-1990s, there was a gradual but inexorable shift away from federal cost-sharing grants to provinces in support of health and social expenditures in favour of block grants. Recently, there has been a resurgence of federal-provincial matching grants as a key feature in Canada's fiscal arrangements. The cost-sharing initiatives introduced in the past four years of Harper budgets have been directed at provincial and municipal infrastructure projects. Indeed, one might characterize infrastructure funding as a new *fourth* pillar of Canadian fiscal federalism, along with Equalization, the Canada Health Transfer and Canada Social Transfer, and the Tax Collection Agreements.

These recent initiatives raise a number of interesting questions about the rationale for the establishment of a new, fourth pillar and the decision to reintroduce cost-sharing as a key element in Canada's fiscal arrangements. The Harper budgets represent a departure from the trajectory of federal-provincial fiscal arrangements over the last few decades. Our first objective in this paper is to document this shift in federal-provincial arrangements. We do so by first presenting a brief history of fiscal arrangements in health, education, welfare, and infrastructure (two of the four pillars) and then summarizing recent federal initiatives in these areas. Our second objective is to provide some insight into the implications of this shift for federal-provincial arrangements in Canada and to briefly comment on the contribution of the fourth pillar to the federal stimulus initiatives in Budget 2009.

We focus on major transfers for health and welfare – the Canada Health Transfer (CHT) and the Canada Social Transfer (CST) – and on major infrastructure funding for provincial and municipal governments. Cash transfers under these programs are estimated to be about $42 billion in 2009/10 (see Table 1).

A Brief History of Canada's Cost-Sharing and Block Grants

Health, Education, and Welfare

Fiscal arrangements for health and welfare date back to the mid-20th century. When first introduced, these transfers took the form of matching or cost-shared grants.[1] The 1957 *Hospital and Diagnostic Services Act* provided for cost-sharing with provinces based on 25% actual per capita provincial spending and 25% national-average per capita spending on these services. The *Medical Care Act*, introduced in 1966, provided for cost-sharing with provinces based on 50% of national-average spending per capita on physician and related services. To support provincial spending on welfare, the federal government also introduced the Canada Assistance Plan (CAP) in 1966. Under CAP, the federal government shared with the provinces 50% of eligible welfare expenses. This was an open-ended matching grant that grew at the rate of growth of provincial welfare spending.

Table 1: CHT, CST, and Infrastructure Cash to Provinces and Municipalities

	2009/10 (Millions of dollars)	*Share of Total*
CHT Cash	24,000	57%
CST Cash	10,900	26%
Infrastructure	7,046	17%
Total Cash	**41,946**	

Source: *The Budget Plan 2009* (Table 3.7); *The Budget Plan 2007* (Table 5.3).

---

[1]For a history of Canada's federal-provincial fiscal arrangements, see Boadway and Hobson (1993) and Perry (1997).

The move away from cost-sharing began in 1977 with the introduction of Established Programs Financing (EPF), which rolled transfers for health care and post-secondary education into a single block fund. The idea was that a transfer be provided in equal parts through a tax transfer component and a cash transfer component. The associated EPF tax points amounted to 13.5 percentage points of personal income tax (PIT) and 1 percentage point of corporate income tax (CIT), which included some points carried over from the previous post-secondary education funding arrangements. The value of the transferred tax points was, and still is, subject to Equalization, so it might be argued that a component of Equalization payments made to provinces contributes to funding of health care and post-secondary education. As provincial economies grow, so too does the value of the tax points. Initially, the EPF cash transfer was escalated by the growth rate of per capita GNP. Thus, the total transfer was not equal per capita. Subsequently, it was the total transfer that was legislated to grow in line with the economy, converting it to an equal per capita total amount.

The shift away from cost-sharing continued when, in 1995, the federal government capped at 5% the annual rate of growth in CAP transfers to Ontario, Alberta, and British Columbia. One year later, the Canada Health and Social Transfer (CHST) was introduced to replace both EPF and CAP. As such, CHST carried with it the construct of the former EPF tax points. For 1996/97, the grant was allocated among provinces in the same proportion as combined EPF and CAP entitlements for 1995/96. It was, therefore, not an equal per capita allocation. Subsequently, CHST moved to an equal per capita total allocation.

In 2004, the CHST was restructured into two separate transfers – the CHT and the CST.

Infrastructure

Federal infrastructure funding to provinces (and municipalities) can be characterized as episodic – federal contributions are typically made to designated programs or projects with specific end dates. Perry (1997) notes that federal conditional grants in support of infrastructure-related spending can be traced back to the early 1900s. During these years, grants were limited to specific projects or parts of projects, such as railway crossings, bridges, and sections of roads. Fifty percent cost-sharing grants for the Trans-Canada Highway program were introduced in 1950. A maximum of $150 million for grants was set aside and a completion date of 1956 set. The deadline and amounts were subsequently extended and enhanced. The highway was completed in 1971 and involved $825 million in federal cost-shared contributions.[2] Perry notes that, while the program began as a uniform national program in 1963, the federal government assumed 90% of the construction costs in the Atlantic provinces beginning in that year.

In 1958, the federal government introduced the Municipal Winter Works Incentive Program. Under the program, the federal government made 50% matching grants to local governments (through provincial governments), covering direct labour costs from December to April on specific capital projects. This program was in place for 10 years. Provincial contributions were not required, although some provinces undertook them.

Wylie (1996) has described the period from the 1940s to the 1960s as a "Golden Age" for private and public infrastructure investment for Canada, comparing the robust average annual growth rate for public infrastructure capital accumulation per person-hour worked of 5.93% for the period 1947 to 1972 to the 1.21% average annual growth rate for the period from 1973 to 1991 (Wylie, 1996, pp. S351 and S352). Similar observations are made in Roy (2007). Roy calculates a 4% average annual growth in total government infrastructure capital (in 1997 dollars) for the period 1961 to 1971. The average annual growth rate declines over time, reaching a low of 0.3% for the period 1991 to 2001. After 2001, the slide is reversed, with an average annual growth rate of 1.5% for the period 2001 to 2005.

Along with the decline in infrastructure investment, there has been an increase in the average age of engineering infrastructure in Canada. Gaudreault and Lemire (2006) find that the average age of public infrastructure has increased from 14.7 years in 1973 to 17.5 years in 1999. For provincial public infrastructure, the average age rose from 14.4 years in 1963 to 18.8 years in 2003, while the average age of federal infrastructure remained fairly constant, around 21 years over this period. For municipal infrastructure, the average age increased over this period, although less so than for provincial infrastructure. Since 2001, the trend in average age of infrastructure has been reversed. For 2007, the average age was 16.3 years (see Gagnon, Gaudreault, and Overton, 2008).

---

[2]Padova (2006, p. 4). This paper also provides a historical overview of the federal government's involvement in highway construction.

There was renewed interest in infrastructure when the Canada Infrastructure Works program was introduced in 1994. Under the program, the federal government agreed to contribute one third of the costs of local infrastructure investment, with provinces and municipalities contributing the rest. Like most federal infrastructure initiatives, the program was to be of short duration, covering project expenditures over a three-year period. The program was, however, subsequently extended, resulting in $2.4 billion in federal funding. From 2000 to 2003, major federal-provincial-municipal initiatives included support for municipal infrastructure through Infrastructure Canada in 2002, the Municipal Rural Infrastructure Fund in 2004, and Gas Tax Sharing in 2005.

Current Fiscal Arrangements in Health, Education, and Welfare

Canada Health Transfer

CHT transfers are conditional, lump-sum, or block grants. These transfers are made on an equal per capita basis and include both a cash component and the associated value of the EPF tax points. The value of the CHT-related tax points equalled $13.7 billion in 2009/10 and will continue to grow in line with the economy. Legislated through 2013/14, CHT cash is $24 billion for 2009/10. Since the Liberal government's 2005 budget, CHT cash will grow at an annual rate of 6% and will reach over $30 billion in 2013/14. Table 2 shows CHT cash levels from 2006/07 to 2013/14.

Harper's Budget 2007 announced a move to equal per capita CHT cash funding beginning 2014/15 and provided transitional payments to protect provinces against declines in the years leading up to equal per capita cash.

Table 2: Canada Health and Canada Social Cash Transfers (in Millions of Dollars)

	2006/07	*2007/08*	*2008/09*	*2009/10*	*2010/11*	*2011/12*	*2012/13*	*2013/14*
CHT	20,140	21,604	22,629	23,987	25,426	26,952	28,569	30,283
CST	8,500	9,857	10,559	10,868	11,194	11,530	11,876	12,232

Source: Federal Support to Provinces and Territories, Department of Finance (www.fin.gc.ca/fedprov/mtp-eng.asp), updated January 2009; authors' calculations.

Canada Social Transfer

Table 2 also shows CST cash for the period 2006/07 to 2013/14. For 2009/10, \$3.3 billion, \$6.4 billion, and \$1.1 billion of total CST cash is notionally earmarked for post-secondary education, social programs, and children, respectively. There is a condition on CST transfers that prohibits provinces from imposing minimum residency requirements for social assistance. The provinces and territories also receive CST support indirectly through the value of the 1977 EPF tax points. This amounts to \$8.6 billion in 2009/10 and will continue to grow in line with the economy.

In contrast to the federal government's focus on health spending and related transfers under Martin, the Harper government has directed some attention to the CST transfer. Initiatives, most of which were announced in 2007, include an increase of \$800 million in base funding for post-secondary education commencing 2008/09; an additional \$250 million to support the development of child care spaces; a move to equal per capita cash for CST, effective 2007/08, with a \$687 million increase to base funding for 2007/08; and, a funding track for CST cash with an annual escalator of 3% starting in 2009/10.

New Cost-Sharing Arrangements for Infrastructure: A Fourth Pillar?

Harper's Budget 2007 introduced the Building Canada Plan, providing \$33 billion over seven years in major infrastructure funding. Most elements of the plan were new, but some pre-existing measures, like Gas Tax Sharing and the GST rebate for municipalities, were also included as part of this larger infrastructure envelope.

The Building Canada Plan's five main elements are:
1. Municipal Base Funding
2. Provincial/Territorial (P/T) Base Funding
3. Building Canada Fund (BCF)
4. Gateways and Border Crossings Fund
5. Private-Public Partnerships Fund.

Our focus is on the first three elements of the Building Canada Plan and on related infrastructure measures introduced in the 2008 and 2009 budgets.

Table 3 shows the allocation of selected infrastructure initiatives by jurisdiction for the period 2007-2014.

Municipal Base Funding: Gas Tax Fund and GST Rebate

Federal revenue-sharing with the municipalities is a new feature of Canadian fiscal arrangements, at least since the post-war devolution of the tax rental agreements. Originally introduced in Budget 2005 under Paul Martin, Gas Tax Sharing was made permanent in Harper's 2008 budget with the establishment of the Gas Tax Fund as one of the components of the Building Canada Plan. The fund is distributed on an equal per capita basis, with a minimum allotment for the smallest of jurisdictions. These transfers, intended to help municipalities fund long-term infrastructure projects, flow first to provincial governments that have discretion over how monies are actually distributed across municipalities.

Table 3: Selected Federal Infrastructure Funds by Jurisdiction, 2007-2014 (Millions of Dollars)

	1 Build Canada Fund	*2 P/T Base Funding*	*3 Municipal Base Funding - Gas Tax Fund only*	*Municipal-Rural Infrastructure Top-Up*	*Infrastructure Stimulus Fund (2009/10 and 2010/11)*	*Total*[a]
BC	1057	175	1486	24	526	3268
AB	841	175	1161	19	431	2627
SK	236	175	337	7	122	877
MN	279	175	392	8	145	999
ON	3147	175	4405	64	1553	9344
QC	1954	175	2729	40	931	5829
NB	188	175	267	7	90	727
NS	236	175	334	7	113	865
PEI	35	175	88.5	4	17	320
NF	131	175	187	5	61	559
Yukon	8	175	88.5	3	4	278
NWT	11	175	88.5	3	5	283
Nunavut	8	175	88.5	3	4	278
Total	**8,131**	**2,275**	**11,652**	**194**	**4002**	**26254**

[a] Note that the total is less than $33 billion. This is because some of the Building Canada Plan initiatives are not allocated by jurisdiction but are national in scope and are allocated on a merit basis. Also note that the Infrastructure Stimulus Fund, which is not a component of the Building Canada Plan, is included here.

Source: Building Canada Backgrounder – Infrastructure Funding (allocations by fund and jurisdiction 2007-2014), 2008 (www.buildingcanada.gc.ca); Budget 2009, authors' calculations.

Gas fund transfers, characterized as conditional, lump sum, or block grants, are set at $2 billion in 2009/10. These transfers represent about 35% of the seven-year, $33 billion Building Canada Plan commitment.

In Budget 2004, the Liberal government increased the rebate on GST paid by municipal governments from 57.14% to 100%. The aggregate value of the GST rebate is estimated at $790 million for 2009/10.

Together, the GST rebate and the Gas Tax Fund are now referred to as Municipal Base Funding under the Building Canada Plan.

Provincial Base Funding for Infrastructure

As part of the larger Building Canada initiative, a provincial/territorial (P/T) base-funding component was introduced in 2007. Eligible infrastructure projects would be cost-shared with the federal government, covering 50% of eligible provincial expenditures. The maximum allocation for each province and territory was set at $25 million per year for the next seven years. A unique feature of this funding was that it was allocated on an equal per jurisdiction, rather than an equal per capita, basis. The grant is a closed-ended matching grant. However, if some jurisdictions are unable to take up the full allotment, then the actual distribution of funds will not be equal across jurisdictions. Budget 2009 accelerated P/T base funding for infrastructure by allocating the 2011/12, 2012/13, and 2013/14 base payments to 2009/10 and 2010/11.

Table 4 shows the initial and accelerated amounts from 2007/08 to 2010/11.

Build Canada Fund[3]

Budget 2007 provided $8.8 billion over seven years to the Build Canada Fund. The fund has two major cost-sharing components – the Major Infrastructure Component (MIC) and the Communities Component (CC). The MIC is intended for projects in larger cities (with populations over 100,000). Maximum allotments are distributed on an equal per capita

---

[3]The fund supports infrastructure projects undertakén by provincial, territorial, and municipal governments and, under certain circumstances, private sector entities. Highway, water and wastewater, public transit, and green energy infrastructure projects are priorities.

Table 4: New Infrastructure Initiatives, 2007/08 to 2010/11 (Millions of Dollars)

	Budget Measure	*2007/08*	*2008/09*	*2009/10*	*2010/11*
Build Canada Fund	Budget 2007	572	926	1186	1401
	Budget 2009			250	250
P/T	Budget 2007	325	325	325	325
Base Funding	Budget 2009			495	495
Municipal Base Funding					
- Gas Tax Fund	Budget 2004 Budget 2008 made permanent	800	1000	2000	2000
- GST Rebate	Budget 2004	715	750	790	830
Infrastructure Stimulus Fund	Budget 2009			2000	2000
Total		**2412**	**3001**	**7246**	**7301**

Source: *The Budget Plan 2007*, Table 5.3; *The Budget Plan 2009*, Table 3.7.

basis, and the matching rate varies, depending on what levels of government are participating. If the project involves provincial government financing alone, then the matching rate is 50%. If both municipal and provincial governments contribute, the federal matching rate is 33.3%.

The CC funds projects in smaller communities (with populations under 100,000). The federal matching rate is 33.3%, and the maximum allotments are distributed on an equal per capita basis. Budget 2009 provided for an additional $500 million over two years for this component, as shown in Table 4.

Setting a maximum grant for both MIC and CC components for each jurisdiction converts these grants from open-ended to closed-ended matching grants.

Infrastructure Stimulus Fund

A $4 billion Infrastructure Stimulus Fund was announced in Budget 2009. This fund is not a component of the Building Canada Plan. Funds are allocated over 2009/10 and 2010/11 and will be available to provinces on a merit and project-readiness, 50% cost-sharing basis (33.3% matching if municipal financing was also involved). Maximum provincial allocations will be determined on an equal per capita basis and will be aimed at projects that have a short-run horizon and that are ready to go. These grants can also be characterized as closed-ended, matching grants.

Issues and Analysis

With the Conservative Government's introduction of the Building Canada Plan in 2007 and subsequent initiatives, infrastructure has taken on a growing presence in federal-provincial fiscal arrangements. The language and direction in Harper's budgets makes it clear that infrastructure is an important priority. Infrastructure building, cost-shared between federal and provincial partners, is not new. What is different is the magnitude and scope of the infrastructure funding under Harper. A few back-of-the-envelope calculations make the point.

Budget 2003 under Martin included new strategic infrastructure and municipal infrastructure funding, totalling $3 billion over 10 years, an average of $300 million per year. This represents about 0.2% of federal program spending in 2003/04. Harper's Budget 2007 announced $33 billion over seven years. Including only the P/T base funding and the Build Canada Fund (which are arguably new initiatives), we calculate an average of $1.48 billion per year, which represents about 0.7% of federal program spending in 2007/08. Adding to this the Gas Tax Fund component of the municipal base funding, average annual spending increases to $3.1 billion, representing about 1.6% of total program spending in 2007/08.[4]

Figure 1 shows the share of the total value of cash plus tax transfers by "pillar" for 2009/10. CHT and CST cash (pillar 2) account for the largest share, about 43%. CHT cash alone accounts for 30%. Cash transfers for Equalization (pillar 1) make up about 21% of the total cash plus tax transfers, and infrastructure grants comprise about 9%.[5]

---

[4]Comparing the average annual new infrastructure spending, as announced in budgets 2003 and 2007, annual spending under Harper is almost five times that announced in 2003. It is also useful to note that in 1994, the Canada Infrastructure Works program was initiated. Over five years, the federal government spent $2.4 billion. This amounts to average spending of $480 million a year, or 0.4% of program spending in 1996/97.

[5]Included are municipal base funding, provincial/territorial base funding, the Build Canada Fund, and the Infrastructure Stimulus Fund amounts (as well as any accelerated payments to occur in 2009/10).

Figure 1: Four Pillars of Federal-Provincial Fiscal Arrangements, 2009/10

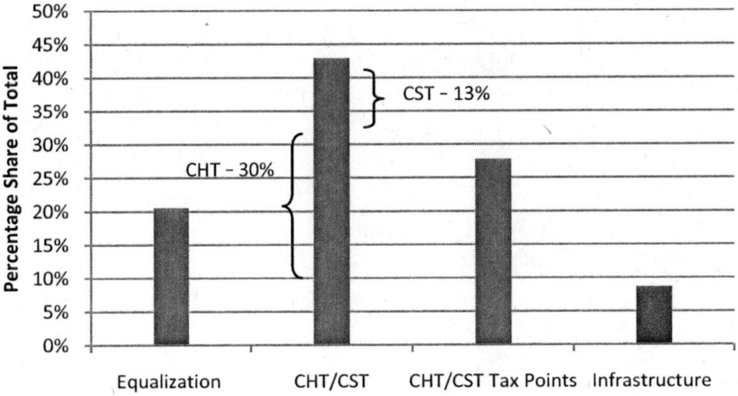

Source: Based on data from *The Budget Plan 2009* (Table 3.7) and *The Budget Plan 2007* (Table 5.3).

We argue that Harper's infrastructure funding amounts to the creation of a new fourth pillar of federal-provincial fiscal arrangements. And because much of the infrastructure funding takes the form of closed-ended, matching grants, cost-sharing is once again becoming an important dimension of federal-provincial fiscal arrangements. The creation of this new "cost-sharing" pillar raises several issues. Here, we identify and discuss key issues as we see them.

The Harper Agenda

The Harper budgets have a strong focus on the promotion of the national economic union and competitiveness. Indeed, a competitive and efficient economic union is one of the government's five guiding principles to restoring fiscal balance in Canada, as outlined in Budget 2006 (see Department of Finance, 2006, p. 150). Initiatives include a focus on education, infrastructure, a single securities regulator, and sales tax harmonization. Admittedly, some of the initiatives, like federal gas tax-sharing and the GST rebate to municipalities, were introduced under Martin. However, they have been adopted and extended by Harper. It is notable that the gas tax grants are conditional block grants. In contrast, new infrastructure initiatives under Harper, like P/T base funding and the two components of the Build Canada Fund, all take the form of closed-ended, matching grants.

Economic Rationale for Matching Infrastructure Grants

An economic argument can be made to support the federal government's choice of matching rather than block-type grants. A significant share of infrastructure, like local roads and highways, water and waste management treatment, and local public transit, for example, are areas of provincial (and municipal) responsibility. Some of the benefits of this infrastructure may spill outside the boundaries of the jurisdiction undertaking the investment. The existence of spillovers suggests that under-investment might occur if the provision decision is made at the local or provincial government level. Such externalities or spillovers can be addressed with matching grants from a higher level of government at the rate appropriate to internalize the externality.

In principle, matching rates might also take into account differences in the fiscal capacity of recipient governments and indirect revenue effects on the donor government.[6] Such considerations imply that optimal matching grants can vary across jurisdiction. In practice, however, matching rates for federal grants, including those for infrastructure, tend to be uniform across jurisdictions and to involve equal sharing. This may reflect informational and data limitations that preclude the calculation of optimal matching rates. However, it seems that equal sharing and uniform matching rates are largely political rather than economic choices.

Accountability and Transparency

Matching grants do, under most circumstances, provide an incentive to undertake more of the activity to which the grants are directed. While there is an economic argument for doing so, political considerations are also at work because the federal government under Harper has a political agenda to adopt policies, such as infrastructure investments, that promote efficiency and competitiveness. With matching grants for infrastructure, it can be seen as doing so as the grants are specific in purpose. Such grants do not necessarily ensure that total infrastructure spending increases, as it is still possible for provinces to displace the funds, substituting federal dollars in place of existing provincial infrastructure spending. Limiting displacement requires specific conditions and

[6]For a discussion of matching grants and rates, see Bird and Smart (2002), Dahlby and Wilson (2003), and Huber and Runkel (2006).

monitoring. Lazar (2008) argues, however, that overall anti-displacement efforts in federal-provincial transfers tend to be weak.

From a political perspective, the federal government can identify projects and matched dollar amounts with the added bonus that infrastructure projects are often highly visible to voters. This creates a sense of improved accountability and transparency of federal government spending even if displacement is occurring.

Open-Ended or Closed-Ended

All the matching infrastructure grants are closed-ended rather than open-ended, and, in most cases, the maximum allocation is determined on an equal per capita basis. What explains the choice of closed-ended rather than open-ended?

Information asymmetries may play a role.[7] The federal government lacks information on provincial and municipal preferences, the degree of spillovers, and so on. Thus, not only is it difficult to determine an optimal matching rate, but under an open-ended matching grant, the federal government faces uncertainty as to the size of its financial obligations. The choice to set a maximum allocation allows the federal government to better predict and control growth of its own expenditures.

It is worthwhile to note that block grants, rather than matching grants, are sometimes argued to be the "better" choice in achieving expenditure control for the donor government. Canada's recent history of federal cash transfers for health suggests that this need not be the case. Figure 2 shows cash transfers for health and social spending, actual and as announced in federal budgets, from 1996 to 2009. While cash transfers under the new CHST from 1996 onward were intended to be constrained (as indicated by the Budget 1996 grey bars), subsequent budgets have increased cash over intended levels in almost every year since. Smart (2005) argues that the move to block funding has not led to expenditure restraint. Instead, provincial expenditures, especially with respect to health, have continued to grow, and successful lobbying by provincial governments has meant that the federal government has been paying for a significant share of this growth.

[7]Huber and Runkel (2006) explore this idea.

Figure 2: Federal Health and Social Cash Transfers, Budget Announcements, and Actuals

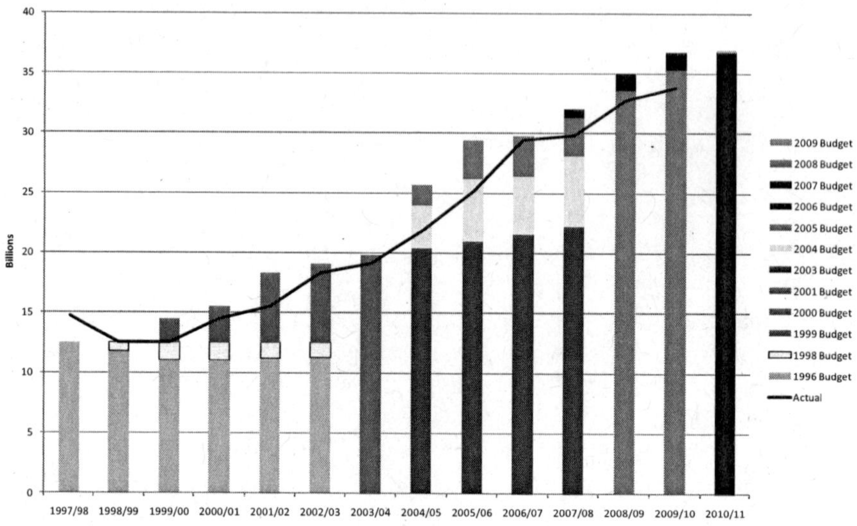

Source: Various federal budget documents. At www.fin.gc.ca/access/budinfo-eng.asp.

Matching grants help to promote spending that is desirable from the federal government's perspective. The closed-ended form may help to control growth (and reduce uncertainty) more effectively than an open-ended grant.

Provincial Perspective

Infrastructure grants create a clear incentive for provinces to shift spending in order to get their maximum share. To take advantage of the infrastructure funds, provincial governments can reduce spending in other areas, raise additional tax revenue, or incur a higher deficit. If a province receives its maximum allocation, further provincial spending generates no additional transfer dollars. There is, however, no guarantee that the maximum amount of grant available will be taken up.[8]

[8]This is easily demonstrated in the context of a standard community preferences model.

There is a serious concern about the abilities of provinces with different fiscal capacities to avail themselves of the new infrastructure funds while maintaining social programs. This might be particularly acute in our current economic climate, when demands on provincial welfare systems will increase.

Is the Status of "Fourth Pillar" Warranted?

The short answer seems to be yes. Like education, infrastructure is important to the efficient movement of labour and goods and the efficient functioning of the national economy. And while infrastructure grants are not really new, their scope and magnitude have increased sufficiently to warrant pillar status.

Is the pillar temporary? We argue that the new pillar will be around for some time. First, it is important to note that Harper's introduction of the Building Canada Plan was not motivated as a stimulus measure but as an efficiency and productivity investment. Second, the fact that the government subsequently introduced a stimulus package to address economic concerns simply added to the infrastructure agenda. Indeed, much of the stimulus introduced in Budget 2009 involved acceleration of infrastructure funds under existing components of the Building Canada Plan. The creation of a separate Infrastructure Stimulus Fund (closed-ended and matching) signals that these funds, not the main infrastructure components, are temporary. Third, federal gas tax-sharing was initially limited to a five-year period. The creation of the Gas Tax Fund signals a more permanent commitment to at least this component.

The establishment of a fourth pillar with a reliance on closed-ended, matching grants does give rise to some complaints. Unlike health, social, and Equalization grants, provincial governments actually have to spend money on infrastructure to get the federal funds. Some provinces may resent the use of the federal spending power to influence provincial spending priorities. This may be a legitimate concern if spillover effects are weak or non-existent. Cost-sharing programs also tend to be administratively costly and subject to delays.

Are Matching Infrastructure Grants the Best "Stimulus" for the Current Economic Times?

The elimination of CAP in 1996/97 marked the end of matching grants in Canadian federal-provincial fiscal arrangements. Budget 2009 provided a timely opportunity to reinstate matching grants based on provincial welfare expenditures. Matching grants of this type better reflect the differing economic circumstances of provinces/territories, although the potential problem of distinguishing between need and generosity may once again arise. Certainly, in relation to provincial welfare expenditures, equal per capita funding makes little sense. Moreover, funnelling federal stimulus funds through provincial welfare recipients would provide not only an incentive for provinces to spend more generously on welfare, but also ensure that the stimulus funds were being spent in those provinces where the need is greatest. In contrast, matching grants for infrastructure are more difficult to scale up in a short time frame. As well, it may be a slow process getting infrastructure projects off the ground, even after they have been recommended and approved.

Conclusions

We argue that infrastructure funding can be characterized as a new *fourth* pillar of Canadian fiscal federalism, along with Equalization, the Canada Health Transfer and Canada Social Transfer, and the Tax Collection Agreements. As well, these initiatives reintroduce cost sharing as an important element of federal-provincial arrangements in Canada. Notably, the share of infrastructure grants is approaching the share of CST cash in total cash plus tax transfers to provinces in 2009/10.

Politically, such grants are attractive to the federal government. Federal government spending appears targeted and transparent, improving accountability. At the same time, the closed-ended form provides the federal government with some certainty in terms of its aggregate financial commitment.

Matching grants in support of provincial and municipal infrastructure generate familiar complaints – distortions to provincial spending priorities, costly and cumbersome to administer, and potentially significant time lags in the case of infrastructure. Historically, federal infrastructure funding arrangements have been extended in order to disburse all funds or complete projects. Further channelling of federal stimulus funds into cost-sharing infrastructure grants may have little impact if there are already lags in the take-up and disbursement of monies under the Building Canada Plan. There is a potential problem with the distribution of infrastructure grants if some provinces (and municipalities) are more fiscally constrained than others and are unable to avail themselves of the maximum amounts. Finally, it is significant that the return to matching grants in Canadian federal-provincial fiscal arrangements marks a clear focus on physical infrastructure rather than health or people.

References

Bird, R. and M. Smart. 2002. "Intergovernmental Fiscal Transfers: International Lessons for Developing Countries", *World Development* 30(6), 899-912.

Boadway, R. and P. Hobson. 1993. *Intergovernmental Fiscal Relations in Canada.* Toronto: Canadian Tax Foundation.

Dahlby, B. and S. Wilson. 2003. "Vertical Fiscal Externalities in a Federation", *Journal of Public Economics* 87, 917-930.

Department of Finance Canada. 2003. *The Budget Plan 2003.* Ottawa: Department of Finance.

__________. 2006. *The Budget Plan 2006: Focusing on Priorities.* Ottawa: Department of Finance.

__________. 2007. *The Budget Plan 2007: Aspire to a Stronger, Safer, Better Government.* Ottawa: Department of Finance.

__________. 2008. *The Budget Plan 2008: Responsible Leadership.* Ottawa: Department of Finance.

__________. 2009. *The Budget Plan 2009: Canada's Economic Action Plan.* Ottawa: Department of Finance.

Gagnon, M., V. Gaudreault, and D. Overton. 2008. "Age of Public Infrastructure: Provincial Perspective," *Analysis in Brief,* Statistics Canada Catalogue No. 11-621-MWIE2006035. At www.statcan.ca/english/research/11-621-MIE/11-607-MIE2008067.htm. Accessed June 29, 2009.

Gaudreault, V. and P. Lemire. 2006. "The Age of Public Infrastructure in Canada," *Analysis in Brief,* Statistics Canada Catalogue No. 11-621-MWIE2006035. At www.statcan.ca/english/research/11-621-MIE/11-621-MIE2006035.htm. Accessed June 29, 2009.

Huber, B. and M. Runkel. 2006. "Optimal Design of Intergovernmental Grants Under Asymmetric Information", *International Tax and Public Finance* 13, 25-41.

Lazar, H. 2008. *Displacement in Federal Transfer Payments: Exploring Concept and Practice with Special Reference to the Canadian Millennium Scholarship Foundation.* Montreal: The Canadian Millennium Scholarship Foundation.

Padova, A. 2006. *Federal Participation in Highway Construction and Policy in Canada.* Ottawa: Library of Parliament.

Perry, D. 1997. *Financing the Canadian Federation, 1967 to 1995: Setting the Stage for Change*. Toronto: Canadian Tax Foundation.
Roy, F. 2007. "From Roads to Rinks: Government Spending on Infrastructure in Canada, 1961 to 2005", *Canadian Economic Observer* 20(9), Statistics Canada Catalogue No. 11-010-XIB. At www.statcan.gc.ca/pub/11-010-x/11-010-x2007009-eng.pdf. Accessed June 29, 2009.
Smart, M. 2005. "Federal Transfers: Principles, Practice and Prospects", C.D. Howe Working Paper, September. Toronto: CD Howe Institute.
Wylie, P. 1996. "Infrastructure and Canadian Economic Growth 1946-1991", *Canadian Journal of Economics* 29, Special Issue: Part 1, S350-S355.

THE EVOLUTION OF FEDERAL TRANSFERS SINCE THE O'BRIEN REPORT

Michael Smart, University of Toronto

Introduction

The 2007 federal budget enacted fundamental changes to Equalization and other transfers that were to "put all major fiscal arrangements on a long-term, principles-based track to 2013-14". Less than 18 months later, in November 2008, the Government was forced to reopen the file again, announcing that, for the first time in the history of the program, Ontario would qualify for and receive Equalization payments, beginning in 2009-10. At the same time, changes to the Equalization formula were announced that limit the growth of the program's cost and change the treatment of natural resource revenues under the formula.

These changes were subsequently confirmed in Budget 2009, which also included related changes to numerous other intergovernmental transfer and regionally targeted spending programs – including the Atlantic Offshore Accords, the Canada Health Transfer, and the establishment of a Southern Ontario Development Agency, to name but a few. The changes have naturally brought criticism from many of the other traditional Equalization-receiving provinces, which have decried the restraints on Equalization in particular as an abandonment of the principles underlying the 2007 reform, as inherently unfair to receiving provinces, and as having been effected in a unilateral and non-transparent way by the federal government – a fact in itself a violation of the principles of "open federalism" promised by the federal government in 2006 and 2007.

The main objective of this paper is to review the most significant changes to federal transfers since 2007, as well as the arguments for and against the changes. More provisionally, I also look ahead to what Equalization and other transfers might look like in the future.

While the changes are far-reaching and complex, the key change is undoubtedly the decision to impose a ceiling on the growth of total Equalization payments. This converts Equalization to a closed-ended grant – that is, one in which the total cost is a direct policy lever – in contrast to the open-ended grant that existed during 2007–08 and prior to 2004 – in which the total cost of the program was determined residually, as a function of various other policy parameters in the formula.[1] Indeed, as I argue below, with the introduction of a ceiling on the program, together with other changes in the treatment of natural resource revenues in the formula, the Equalization program is now for practical purposes very little different (though larger) than the closed-ended Fixed Framework for Equalization that was in place under the previous federal government during 2004–06. This is obviously an inconvenient fact from the point of view of a government that promised a different approach to fiscal federalism, but it is an important one for assessment of the reforms and the way forward.

The entry of Ontario into the program and its simultaneous restraint are obviously no coincidence: without changes to the formula, paying Equalization to a province as large as Ontario has the potential to be very expensive for the federal government. As I argue below, this simple fact is likely to have a significant impact on Equalization and other federal transfers for many years to come. As a means of controlling the fiscal risks to which the federal government is now exposed under Equalization – and to limit the possibly destabilizing pro-cyclical features of the program if energy revenues are to recover with the economy in future – the decision to limit Equalization growth, therefore, appears inevitable.

The reforms are not mere federal penny-pinching, however. In spite of provincial criticisms, a closed-ended equalization grant is just as much "principles-based" as the open-ended grant that existed during 2007–08 and prior to 2004. Moreover, the level of Equalization spending promised by the government for future years seems adequate as long as

---

[1]While Equalization is now a closed-ended grant for the federal government, its structure is largely unchanged from the perspective of an individual receiving province, to which annual payments may rise or fall as a function of economic conditions and fiscal choices.

fiscal disparities among provinces do not become significantly worse (as, for example, could happen if the economic decline in Ontario proves to be worse than currently forecast). On the basis of economic principle, relatively little has changed with the 2009 reforms.

Regardless of these justifications, the renewed controversy over the Equalization formula seems regrettable. Traditionally, the Equalization program has had a much lower degree of political salience and scrutiny than in the last five years – and federal-provincial relations have been different as a consequence. Lowering the political visibility of the program might improve accountability in Canadian politics if officials are more inclined to stick to their knitting and avoid blame-shifting exercises. To blame provincial budget deficits on federal transfer reform, as more than one provincial government did in 2009, seems like simple misdirection.

The political dynamics behind the program have nevertheless changed considerably, and this may affect how the program will continue to evolve in future. First, high energy revenues (which will persist for several years in the Equalization formula as a result of built-in lags in how data enter the formula) mean that Newfoundland, British Columbia, and Saskatchewan are no longer receiving provinces – so that the regional political pressures that led to the 2007 reforms in the treatment of natural resources in Equalization are for the time being at least much reduced.[2] Second, there is some suggestion that federal political calculus has changed as well, so that across-the-board enhancement of Equalization is no longer seen as a useful component of electoral strategy. Both these factors create some hope of greater peace and stability on the Equalization file in the medium-term future.

On the other hand, debate over the appropriate level and growth rate of Equalization and other transfers will surely intensify over the longer term. Provincial objections were initially muted, but are likely to increase as the cumulative impact of the ceiling increases in turn, relative to entitlements under the 2007 formula. The entry of Ontario into the program has the potential to change political support for Equalization as well – arguably, the median voter now lives in a receiving province. At the same time, pressure on the federal government to further reduce

[2]Indeed, many of the most controversial elements of the 2007 reforms – partial inclusion of resource revenues and the fiscal capacity cap – are now of little quantitative significance since resource-rich provinces are out of the program regardless.

major transfers is apt to increase as solutions to bringing federal deficits under control are sought.

With the latest changes, the federal government operates three distinct lump-sum grants as its major transfers, each allocated based on different principles and each legislated to grow at a different rate – the Canada Health Transfer (CHT), at 6% annually; the Canada Social Transfer (CST), at 3%; and now Equalization, at the growth rate of nominal GDP. Grappling with fiscal arrangements in coming years is therefore going to require decisions about the relative priority of vertical versus horizontal grants and an articulation of what each of the grants is intended to achieve.

The plan of the rest of the paper is as follows: The second section describes the changes in federal transfers since 2007. The third section offers an assessment of the main changes that have occurred to the Equalization program, and the last section concludes with a discussion of the further changes that are likely – or desirable – in future.

Changes to Federal Transfers: An Overview

The most complex and far-reaching recent changes in transfers concern the Equalization program, and the bulk of this paper is concerned with Equalization. Nevertheless, there have been changes to other transfers of importance to certain provinces, which I consider below.

At a meeting of finance ministers in November 2008, the federal government announced several important changes to the Equalization program aimed at ensuring that the cost of the program would grow (in the words of the news release) "at a sustainable rate". The changes, which do indeed reduce the cost of the program substantially below status quo projections, were confirmed in the 2009 budget and included in the *Budget Implementation Act*.

Understanding the changes requires a bit of background knowledge of the 2007 changes to the Equalization formula – many of which have been effectively reversed by the latest changes. The 2007 formula was based closely on the recommendations of the O'Brien expert panel, whose core elements were:

- Equalization payments were to be calculated by comparing the fiscal capacity of each province with the average capacity of all ten provinces ("the ten-province standard") – replacing the five-province standard operating during the 1982–2004 period that crucially excluded Alberta's fiscal capacity. The new standard was therefore higher than the old one, resulting in higher total payments and exposing the program to additional volatility, associated with the rise and fall in Alberta's energy revenues.
- Only 50% of provinces' resource revenues were to be included in fiscal capacity – and so also in the ten-province Equalization standard. The key implication of partial inclusion was to increase payments to resource-rich provinces then receiving Equalization[3] by reducing "tax-back" of their resource revenues. At the same time, partial inclusion made the reform affordable, since it meant that only half of Alberta's energy revenues were included in the standard to which provinces were being raised.
- Notwithstanding partial inclusion, a fiscal capacity cap was introduced, which ensured that Equalization would not raise the full fiscal capacity (i.e., counting 100% of resource revenues) above that of any non-receiving province. While the cap was a new element and never previously part of the Equalization formula, in effect it meant that – for resource-rich provinces subject to the cap – payments were determined by including 100% of resource revenues, and the effective Equalization standard for these provinces became the full fiscal capacity of the lowest non-receiving province – which during 2007–08 and 2008–09 was Ontario.

These changes were controversial (and expensive) when implemented and were seen as a key part of a strategy to "restore fiscal balance" with the provinces in a way that would put an end to controversy and reap long-term political gains for the government.

The latest changes, however, affect all these key elements of the 2007 formula in a fundamental way. In brief:

- The annual growth in total payments is not to exceed a specified rate (4.2% for 2009–10), and payments to all receiving provinces are reduced by an equal per capita amount to keep payments under the ceiling. This converts the Equalization program from an open-ended grant, in which the specified standard determines the total payments,

---

[3]Notably, Saskatchewan, and Newfoundland and Labrador – neither of which will receive Equalization in 2009-10.

to a closed-ended grant, in which the specified total payments in effect determine the standard. The implication is, of course, that the ten-province standard is now entirely irrelevant to payments.

- With Ontario entering the program, the "lowest non-receiving province" cap would have risen in an undesirable way. The cap has therefore been redefined to be the average fiscal capacity (including Equalization payments and 100% of resource revenues) of the receiving provinces themselves – a provision that nicely echoes the use of all-province averages elsewhere in the formula.
- While partial resource inclusion remains, its importance is now severely diminished, as most of the previous receiving provinces are now subject to the fiscal capacity cap (and so to 100% effective inclusion) – or are out of the program entirely by virtue of their high resource revenues.

As such, the 2009 Equalization program is very similar in structure to the Fixed Framework of 2004-06, which was also a closed-ended formula that legislated the total cost of the program and which counted 100% of resource revenues towards fiscal capacity. The key difference, indeed, is simply that the program is now more expensive than ever – about $1.7 billion more than the Fixed Framework would have been if it had remained in place in 2009-10.[4]

Fiscal Impacts of Equalization Changes

To understand how the 2009 changes affect all these elements, it may be useful to go through the steps of the new calculation using actual data for 2009-10, as reported in Table 1. The first row of the table reports the Equalization payment each province[5] would have received in 2009-10 based on the old (2008-09) formula. The remaining rows show the

[4]The five-province standard that operated during 1982-2004 would have generated a total payment even lower in turn.

[5]Evidently, the table excludes Saskatchewan, and Newfoundland and Labrador, as well as the other non-receiving provinces. Payments to these provinces under Equalization are zero for 2009-10 – and they would have been zero even if the formula had not been changed.

Table 1: Impact of Reforms on Equalization Entitlements, 2009-10 ($ Millions)

	PE	*NS*	*NB*	*QC*	*ON*	*MB*	*Total*
Entitlement based on 2008-09 formula	347	1,645	1,727	9,346	980	2,042	16,086
Impact of reforms:							
- Ceiling on payments	-11	-76	-61	-623	-1,033	-97	-1,904
- Receiving province cap	5	-271	29	-308	500	44	0
- Floor protections	-1	93	-6	-61	-101	74	0
Entitlements based on 2009-10 formula	340	1,391	1,689	8,353	345	2,063	14,182
Population (thousands)	138	937	746	7,641	12,679	1,186	23,328

Source: Department of Finance.

impact of each component of the new formula changes, followed by the actual payment for 2009-10.[6]

The GDP growth ceiling

The first element of the reform is a ceiling on the total cost of the program, which is now to grow from year to year at the same rate as the growth rate of nominal GDP (4.2% this year), rather than to be determined endogenously from the ten-province standard as before. As Table 1 shows, without this provision, the total cost of the program would have been $16.1 billion in 2009-10, but the ceiling constrains it to just under $14.2 billion.

In order to achieve this reduction, payments to each of the receiving provinces are in effect reduced by $81 per capita relative to what the ten-province standard would have generated, resulting in the fiscal impacts reported in row 2 of the table.[7] Furthermore, Budget 2009 clarifies that

[6]The interested reader may note that the impact figures presented in Table 1 differ substantially from the conceptually similar figures reported in the 2009 Quebec *Budget Plan*. The Quebec figures compare 2009-10 payments to the payments that had been forecast in Quebec's 2008-09 fiscal plan, whereas Table 1 is based on actual data that were subsequently released to the public by the federal Department of Finance. That is, the impacts in Table 1 are calculated by holding the underlying data constant at 2009-10 actual levels and changing only the parameters of the Equalization formula.

[7]The reported impact for Ontario at $1,033 million in fact exceeds the $980 million payment it would have received without the ceiling, a clear impossibility since Equalization payments are non-negative. In other words, the ceiling would

the ceiling on total payments is also a floor on total payments: if the ten-province standard declines in future, for example because of reductions in energy revenues, the total cost of the program will continue to increase at the same rate as nominal GDP, with equal per capita *increases* in payments made to ensure that this is so.

In other words, the ceiling provision essentially abandons the ten-province standard that was the linchpin of the 2007 reform, replacing it with an approach that is equivalent to the Fixed Framework of 2004-06.

The receiving province cap

The 2007 reform reduced the inclusion rate for resource revenues in the formula to 50% from 100% – resulting in higher payments to then-recipient provinces like Saskatchewan, and Newfoundland and Labrador. At the same time, it introduced the "fiscal capacity cap" that limited these gains by stipulating that Equalization payments could not raise a province's fiscal capacity (including 100% of resource revenues) above that of any province not receiving Equalization. In 2007, the non-recipient with the lowest fiscal capacity was Ontario, so this was for all intents and purposes an "Ontario standard" for resource-rich provinces. With the entry of Ontario into the program, the cap would under the legislation have jumped to British Columbia's fiscal capacity, about $800 per capita higher than Ontario's, resulting in higher payments to resource-rich receiving provinces, which would, under the ceiling, have been paid for by reducing payments to other provinces.

In what budget documents termed a fairness measure, the definition of the cap is to be changed. Instead of using the lowest fiscal capacity of non-receiving provinces (the BC cap), the cap is to be set at the average fiscal capacity (including Equalization) of provinces receiving Equalization. Table 1 shows the impact of this mechanism in row 3. The effect of the lower cap is to reduce Equalization paid to the receiving provinces with above-average resource revenues – Nova Scotia and Quebec. The savings are then in effect paid to all provinces in equal per capita amounts as a result of the ceiling; this explains the increased payments to the others in row 3.

---

have made Ontario once again a non-recipient province if no other changes had been made. This "excess" reduction is, however, offset by the increase reported in row 3.

The change to the cap makes sense if one accepts the fairness principles that were behind the Ontario cap in the first place. After all, it makes no sense to say that transfers to resource-rich provinces should have increased in 2009 simply because Ontario's fiscal capacity has fallen relative to the average – but that would have been the result if the definition of the cap were not changed. Furthermore, the adoption of a cap based on the average of the receiving provinces has a certain inherent appeal: other aspects of the program are already based on averaging fiscal capacity across provinces, and as an average, the new cap is likely to be far less volatile than the old one was; this helps with fiscal planning for all governments involved.

It is somewhat curious that, as Table 1 shows, choosing a higher or lower cap today principally induces transfers between the provinces of Ontario and Quebec – neither of which was a proponent of partial inclusion in the first place. While that could change if resource-rich provinces like Saskatchewan were to return to the program with lower energy revenues in future, at present the cap is a sideshow.

The floor provision

Finally, for 2009–10 only, floor payments are to be made to ensure that no province experiences a year-over-year nominal decline in Equalization payments (including payments under the Offshore Accords). In practice, this benefits only Nova Scotia and Manitoba – the former because the lower fiscal capacity cap is disproportionately binding on Nova Scotia, and the latter mainly because of the rise in Manitoba's fiscal capacity as a result of inherent economic growth. Once again, because of the ceiling, these transitional floor payments are "paid for" through a $8 per capita reduction in Equalization payments to the other four provinces.

The floor payments cannot truly be said to be based on any sound economic or social principle, nor are they small. Nova Scotia's floor payment of $99 per capita exceeds Ontario's total Equalization payment of $27 per capita by a factor of two![8] But the politicization of

[8]Furthermore, the figures presented in Table 1 and the protection payment for Nova Scotia reported there do not appear to include the additional "transition" payment of $74 million to Nova Scotia that represents compensation for the year-over-year reduction in Equalization, which is arguably already compensated by higher offset payments under the 2005 Offshore Accord – see Flaherty (2009).

Equalization in recent years seems to have contributed to the notion that no province can ever "lose" Equalization in nominal terms. This is antithetical to the underlying principles of the program – which is designed to insure provinces by responding to changes in revenue capacities (Smart, 2004) – but seems to be a necessary part of the political compromises needed to sustain reforms to the program.

Other Issues

Offshore Accords: Nova Scotia and Newfoundland

The floor provisions are particularly difficult to understand for Nova Scotia since they merely add another layer to the complex set of protections the province has obtained for its Equalization payments. While a full analysis of such protections is outside the scope of this paper, any analysis of the impact of the Equalization changes on Nova Scotia must consider how the changes interact with:

- The offset payments Nova Scotia receives annually through its 2005 Offshore Accord.
- The probability that the cumulative sum of those offset payments eventually exhausts the advance payment of $830 million received against future offsets in 2005.
- The option Nova Scotia ultimately has under its Cumulative-Best-of Guarantee to revert retroactively to having its Equalization payments calculated under the pre-2007 formula (which is not affected by the restraints on Equalization announced in Budget 2009) instead of the O'Brien formula.
- The floor payments against year-over-year declines in Equalization (but not offsets) that are part of Budget 2009.

In short, Nova Scotia's fiscal arrangements include a complex web of insurance and reinsurance, and the impact of changes in Equalization on its ultimate net entitlements are far from clear.

More controversial in 2009 were changes to the Equalization legislation that affect offset payments to Newfoundland and Labrador under its 1985 Accord, which was designed to protect the province against *year-over-year declines* in Equalization, rather than protect offshore revenues per se. Since under the 2007 Equalization arrangements, Newfoundland has the right to choose among three different Equalization formulas, and it is likely to opt for a different formula in future than it has in the past, determining how offset payments should protect it against declines is clearly complex. Nevertheless, the choices that have been made in this regard have been controversial. It is perhaps surprising that 1985 Accord offset payments matter at all, since they are credited against 2005 Accord offset payments, and all offsets are in turn clawed back through the fiscal capacity cap of Equalization. But since Newfoundland no longer receives positive Equalization or 2005 Accord payments, these intricacies of past agreements assume real importance.

Hydroelectric capacity measurement: Ontario and Quebec

The other change to Equalization of quantitative significance in 2009–10 concerns the way government business enterprises in the electricity sector are treated for purposes of measuring fiscal capacity. Under new rules coming into force for the current fiscal year, dividends paid to the government of Ontario by the Crown-owned Hydro One will no longer count in the resource revenue base for the purposes of computing fiscal capacity – in contrast to dividends paid from Ontario Power Generation, Hydro Quebec, and the other Crown-owned electricity companies in provinces (British Columbia, Saskatchewan, and New Brunswick) with significant amounts of hydroelectric generation capacity. Instead, Hydro One will be treated like other non-hydro government business enterprises (GBEs); this means that the net income of the company will be included in the business income base instead.

Since the effective tax rate at which capacity is equalized under the business income tax (BIT) base is much lower than the 50% inclusion rate for resource revenues, the effect of the change is to reduce Ontario's fiscal capacity relative to that of other provinces and to increase its Equalization entitlement. The fiscal impact of the change appears to be small relative to the overall size of the Equalization program, but large relative to Ontario's own entitlement in 2009–10 of $347 million.

The ostensible reason for the change is that Hydro One is involved in the transmission and distribution of electric power, but not its production, and so its remittances cannot be regarded as resource revenues. Considerable attention was devoted to the issue in Quebec's 2009 Budget Plan, where it is pointed out that applying the same treatment to the transmission and distribution divisions of the (vertically integrated) Hydro-Québec would increase Quebec's entitlement even more – by $250 million annually, according to Quebec's estimate.

The broader issue at stake is the appropriate measurement of rents from natural resources and, in particular, of how to achieve fairness and efficiency in the treatment of the considerable government-owned investments in electricity generation capacity.

The move to equalizing remitted profits of most provinces' electricity GBEs was instituted in 2007 on the recommendation of the O'Brien panel. The change was clearly intended as a way to increase the sensitivity of transfers to the great revenue potential of hydroelectricity in some receiving provinces – particularly Quebec. But the consequence of greater equity in the treatment of hydro may be worsened incentives for the provinces to manage their resource appropriately. Bernard and Ben Mabrouk (2009) point out that Quebec's decision to receive dividends from Hydro-Québec is already reducing its Equalization payments from Ottawa. The decision to change the treatment of Ontario's hydro GBEs has certainly raised the profile of this issue in Quebec.

However, because fiscal capacity for hydro is now measured by remitted profits, the Equalization formula acts like a cash flow tax on hydro GBEs – which effectively gives the provinces a full credit under Equalization for earnings retained and reinvested in new hydro assets. In the long run, such a tax is equivalent to a tax on pure economic rent accruing to government from water power resources. Such a tax has certain desirable features:

- It cannot be avoided in the long run by reducing dividends paid but merely deferred.[9]
- It exempts the normal return on the capital invested by the provinces to exploit the resources (since dividends reinvested and not remitted are not subject to Equalization). Therefore, receiving provinces have undiminished incentives to invest in hydroelectric generation capacity in order to sell power at market prices in other provinces or to the United States.

In reality, neither of the two approaches currently used for measuring fiscal capacity from hydro GBEs is adequate. For one thing, the distinction between the different types of companies subject to the two different approaches (and two different rates of tax-back) is somewhat arbitrary – as Quebec has argued. More important, neither approach deals

[9]The perspective described here is known as the "new view of dividend taxation", familiar from the theory of corporate taxation.

adequately with "dissipated rents", i.e., the benefits provincial residents receive from consuming power supplied by GBEs at less than its true opportunity cost. A wholesale reform would deal with both problems.

Canada Health Transfer

Budget 2009 also proposed technical changes to the Canada Health Transfer (CHT) allocation formula, which would result in effective transfers among provinces in the amount of several hundred million dollars per year – and which have the potential to change more fundamentally the equity principles that underly the allocation rule for CHT. To understand the proposed changes once again requires some history.

Since the 2004 Health Accord, total payments under the Canada Health Transfer are legislated to increase by 6% annually until renewal of the program in 2014-15. While CHT is a "vertical" grant in aid of provincial health expenditures, the program does include one significant equalizing element: cash transfers to some provinces are adjusted to reflect the unequal values of personal and corporate income tax points transferred by the federal government to the provinces in 1977. In previous years, this has meant that Alberta and Ontario (and usually British Columbia) received lower CHT cash transfers per capita than Equalization-receiving provinces, while Saskatchewan (and recently British Columbia) have received higher cash transfers per capita than Equalization-receiving provinces, in the years that they have not received Equalization.

While this arrangement appears curious, it has in fact made sense in the light of the 1977 changes to fiscal arrangements, which replaced certain cash payments to the provinces by a transfer of "tax room" under which the federal government reduced its tax rates on personal and corporate income, while the provinces simultaneously increased their own tax rates by equivalent amounts (see Courchene, 1979). In order for the tax points to have the same value for all provinces, it was decided that the tax points would be fully equalized on a net basis. Consequently, CHT cash payments to Alberta and Ontario (and usually British Columbia) have been reduced by an amount equal to the excess value of the 1977 tax points.

With Ontario's entry into Equalization for the first time in 2009-10, the logic of these adjustments has changed. For each dollar per capita that Ontario's fiscal capacity from the 1977 tax points exceeds the national average, its Equalization payment is automatically reduced by one dollar per capita: this is precisely how Equalization works for receiving provinces. To also reduce its CHT cash payments in respect of the 1977 tax point transfer would therefore constitute "double jeopardy" – and yet this is what existing legislation requires.[10] The Budget 2009 proposal would eliminate double jeopardy by raising Ontario's CHT cash to the same level as other receiving provinces.

The budget proposal, however, goes further, also eliminating over time the CHT cash premium for provinces (currently Newfoundland and Labrador, and Saskatchewan) that do not receive Equalization, but whose 1977 tax points are below average value; this now rightly triggers higher CHT cash to maintain full equalization of the tax points. As such, the proposed changes would represent an accelerated transitional step toward paying equal per capita CHT cash for all ten provinces – which the Government is committed to doing in 2014–15 anyway.

Reaction from the provinces to this measure was decidedly negative, and, perhaps for this reason, it now appears that the change will be implemented only for Ontario and not for the provinces receiving above-average payments. Furthermore, the change for Ontario will be effected, in the short run at least, in a way that avoids reducing cash payments to other provinces from inside the CHT cash envelope.[11]

Given the apparent difficulty in implementing this reform, we may anticipate that it would be similarly difficult to reduce payments to any province receiving above-average cash in 2014–15, when the move to equal per capita cash for all ten provinces is slated to occur. Top-up payments to ensure that no province loses from reallocation – just as is being done this year – are one likely solution.

Of course, if present trends continue, the prime beneficiary of equal per capita CHT cash will not be Ontario but Alberta – which would receive about $200 per capita (more than $700 million) in additional federal cash if the change were effected immediately. Regardless of how the 1977 tax-point transfer is treated in future, there are broader issues of interprovincial equity in all the major transfers that should be addressed, given the growing disparities among provinces.

---

[10]This anomaly has arisen in the legislation presumably because this is the first time a province with above-average value of 1977 tax points has received Equalization – by virtue of aggregate fiscal capacity that is below-average value.

[11]See Quebec's 2009 *Budget Plan*, pp. G15–16, for details.

Evaluation

The 2009 changes to Equalization and related transfers are controversial, far-reaching – and, thus far, subject to relatively little public scrutiny and debate. In this section, I offer an evaluation of the changes and a look at the pressures Equalization might face in future – and how perhaps it should change to respond to those pressures.

Was Restraint on Equalization Necessary?

Restraint on Equalization was advertised by the federal government as an affordability issue. That is a legitimate perspective, but it does not seem like the full story. Given that, without change, Equalization would in 2009–10 have been just $1.9 billion higher, and given the other spending initiatives undertaken by the Government in the current fiscal year, letting Equalization go would, in some sense, have remained "affordable". A slightly different perspective holds that it was the risk of further increases in future, if energy prices rebound in 2010 and beyond, that led the Government to act now to limit the program.[12] But those risks are no higher now than they were a year earlier, when the program was allowed to grow unfettered – indeed, they appear much smaller for the medium term.

Arguably, what changed in 2009–10 that necessitated restraint on the program was Ontario's transition to receiving-province status. Ontario does not present an immediate affordability challenge for Equalization – its 2009–10 payment is just $347 million, and even unrestrained, it would have been less than $1 billion. Rather, because of Ontario's large population, what has changed fundamentally is the fiscal risks to which the federal government is exposed through Equalization.[13]

---

[12]Some readers may wonder why Equalization costs are growing at all in 2009-10 given that energy prices (and thus provincial revenues) are so much lower now than they were early in 2008. The reason is that payments in each year depend on a moving average of revenues accruing two to four years earlier. Alberta's 2008-09 energy royalties will therefore continue to affect payments up to 2012-13.

[13]The same point was made by Courchene (1979) in his discussion of how the Equalization program worked in the 1977-81 period – the last time Ontario's fiscal capacity fell below the national average – and much of this section parallels the analysis there.

To understand how Ontario's entry affects volatility of Equalization payments, some discussion of the mechanics of the formula is needed. Conceptually, Equalization transfers are calculated in order that each receiving province, if it applies the national average level of tax effort, will receive the same (equalized) revenues per capita as the average of all ten provinces. Practically, under the 2007 formula, this calculation is done by dividing revenues into five categories: Personal Income Taxes, Business Income Taxes, Consumption Taxes, Natural Resource Revenues, and Property plus Miscellaneous Taxes. For each category, each province's deficiency or excess in fiscal capacity is calculated by subtracting its share of the measured tax base from its share of the national population. The province's Equalization entitlement in respect of the category is then calculated by multiplying its deficiency (or excess) percentage by the national total of revenues to be equalized for the category.[14]

For example, in 2007-08, Quebec comprised approximately 23% of the national population, but only about 18% of the tax base for personal income taxes, and total provincial personal income tax revenues for the year were about $80 billion. Thus, Quebec's population share of national total revenues would be about $18.4 billion, but its share of the actual base permits it to obtain only $14.4 billion in own-source revenues by applying national average tax effort. It therefore has an Equalization entitlement of about $4 billion – the 5 percentage-point deficiency times the $80 billion in total revenues – for the personal income tax category.[15]

Provinces' entitlements for each category are then summed, and the total, if positive, represents the province's Equalization payment before "bells and whistles" – that is, before introducing the moving average of three years' data and before determining the impact of the ceiling, the fiscal capacity cap, and the floor protection payment. Of course, a province with a negative sum of entitlements receives a payment of zero – under

[14]The reader may be more familiar with Equalization payments being determined by subtracting the province's tax base per capita from the national average level and multiplying by the national average tax rate. The two approaches are mathematically equivalent, but the one presented here shows more clearly the components of statistical risks in payments.

[15]The figures presented are not "O'Brien-ized": that is, they refer to actual data for the 2007-08 fiscal year rather than the moving average of data that determine Equalization payments for a given year under the post-2007 O'Brien formula.

Canada's "gross basis" system of equalization, these provinces do not contribute payments to the have-not provinces.

With this background, the figures in Table 2 show how Ontario's transition to receiving status affects the total payouts at this first (pre-"bells and whistles") stage of the calculation. The first (leftmost) column of figures shows the national total revenues to be equalized. The next two columns show the calculation of aggregate entitlements for the other five receiving provinces – which are the "Core Five" (PEI, Nova Scotia, New Brunswick, Quebec, and Manitoba) that have received payments in every year since the program's inception. Thus, the 7.5-percentage-point PIT base deficiency of the Core Five translates into a $5.977 billion Equalization cost for PIT and so on, with the total entitlement to these provinces being $15.807 billion. The final two columns repeat these calculations with Ontario included in the aggregate base deficiencies – and so in the aggregate entitlements column too.

Observe that Ontario's entry causes base deficiencies and so entitlements to fall for three categories – PIT, BIT, and Property Taxes – where Ontario remains a province with above-average fiscal capacity. (However, Ontario's surplus capacity has slipped considerably in recent years, particularly for the BIT category.) For Consumption Taxes, Ontario has a deficiency of 1.5 percentage points so that inclusion of Ontario for this category raises entitlements by about $1.1 billion.

But the striking feature of Table 2 is Ontario's impact on Equalization of the Natural Resources category. Without Ontario, the aggregate deficiency of receiving provinces would be 18.8%, translating into an

Table 2: The Impact of Ontario on the Equalization Formula

		Equalization Payments to:			
		Core 5 Provinces:		*Core 5 + Ontario:*	
	Revenues to be Equalized	*Base Deficiency*	*Equalization Entitlement*	*Base Deficiency*	*Equalization Entitlement*
	($ millions)	(%)	($ millions)	(%)	($ millions)
Personal Income Taxes	79,824	7.5	5,977	4.8	3,809
Business Income Taxes	26,521	9.6	2,543	8.3	2,204
Consumption Taxes	71,141	3.2	2,258	4.7	3,340
Natural Resources	11,384	18.8	2,144	56.9	6,477
Property Taxes	51,036	5.7	2,884	2.7	1,372
Total	**239,906**		**15,807**		**17,202**

Notes: The Core 5 provinces are PEI, Nova Scotia, New Brunswick, Quebec, and Manitoba. The data are for the 2007-08 fiscal year.

aggregate payment of $2.144 billion as a function of the $11.384 billion in resource revenues that are included in Equalization. But Ontario has less than 1% of the measured natural resource revenue base and 39% of the population. Its entry into Equalization, therefore, causes the aggregate base deficiency for resources to rise by about 38 percentage points and Equalization payments for the category to rise by $4.3 billion. On balance, adding positive and negative entitlements, Ontario's inclusion causes this notional calculation of Equalization to rise by $1.4 billion overall.

Whether $1.4 billion is large or small,[16] it is also clear from Table 2 that the impact of Ontario on the cost of the program could quickly become much larger – volatility of Equalization spending increases with Ontario's inclusion. The figures show that, with the Core Five receiving provinces, each $1 billion in included resource revenues accruing to a non-receiving province (like Alberta, Saskatchewan, or British Columbia) would cost the federal government $188 million in additional Equalization payments. But with inclusion of Ontario, this marginal federal cost rises to $569 million. A $1 billion annual swing in included provincial resource revenues is not large relative to its empirical distribution. Indeed, the standard deviation of annual changes in (50% of) resource revenues over the 1982-83 to 2007-08 period is $3.1 billion (in 2005 constant dollars).

Put more simply, allowing Ontario to enter Equalization while doing nothing to restrain the program would have exposed Ottawa to the risk that program costs would, with high probability, swing from year to year by $1 billion or more. Whether that would have been desirable or not is of course a matter for debate – recent developments have shown that the federal government is once again willing to use annual deficits as a means of smoothing volatility in revenues and expenditures. But it would have been a significant change in the dynamics of the program, and this would have made federal fiscal planning very difficult in any future situation in which the "no deficits" rule has been re-established as the government's fiscal anchor.[17]

---

[16] As noted, Ontario's actual pre-ceiling entitlement for 2009-10 would be still lower, due to the O'Brien moving average.

[17] It also has the potential to undermine macroeconomic stabilization.

The corollary is that Ontario is too big a province to be insured by the Equalization program as it currently operates.[18] This seems like yet another argument in favour of introducing "net basis" elements into our Equalization formula, in which revenue risks would be pooled to some extent through direct revenue-sharing transfers among the ten provinces.[19]

Is the Fixed Pool Approach Justified?

Even if Ontario's entry into the program necessitated federal action of some kind, is the return to a "fixed pool", or closed-ended grant, justified? There is a frequent sense among commentators that the fixed pool approach is inconsistent with the principles of Equalization. The O'Brien panel, in particular, wrote that: "There also is a sense that the concept of a fixed pool runs counter to the fundamental nature of Equalization – that it is intended to respond to changes in fiscal capacity of the provinces, rather than acting as a fixed entitlement over time. Establishing a fixed pool with a growth track divorces the Equalization program from the actual financial situation in provinces and the overall need for Equalization over time" (Expert Panel, 2006). The argument is echoed in the critique of the latest changes in Quebec (2009).

In fact, there does not seem to be any strong principle that suggests an open-ended equalization grant should be preferred to a closed-ended grant – particularly not when attention is confined to gross-basis equalization schemes like Canada's, which equalize up to the national average but do not require provinces with above-average capacity to pay into the system.

Under the open-ended approach, government policy determines a fiscal capacity standard to which receiving provinces are raised. Under the

[18]In principle, the federal government could pass the fiscal risks of Ontario's entry on to energy-rich provinces, thereby improving insurance arrangements, by increasing the federal tax take from the energy sector. But federal political and perhaps constitutional realities seem to preclude that.

[19]A further alternative for controlling fiscal risk is to reduce yet again the fraction of resource revenues equalized under the formula. Apart from the highly political redistribution among receiving provinces that this would entail, with current levels of energy price volatility it seems likely that the inclusion rate would have to be reduced to zero before federal fiscal risks were reduced to acceptable levels.

2007 formula, the standard was the average per capita revenues of the ten provinces (excluding half of resource revenues); under the 1982–2004 formula, it was the average revenues of a group of five provinces, and so on. Under Canada's gross-basis system, transfers do not address the fiscal disparities between receiving and non-receiving provinces, so that there is nothing special about the national average revenues as the standard to which provinces are raised. In 2009–10, the ceiling brings the effective standard for the program about 1% below the ten-province average of revenues – hardly a violation of fundamental principles of equalization.

While many countries operate transfer programs similar in structure to Equalization, Canada is quite unusual in financing open-ended equalization grants from federal spending alone. Most countries in the OECD have adopted one of two approaches to dealing with federal fiscal risks (OECD, 2007):

1. Fixing the distributable pool as a proportion of certain federal revenues or in absolute terms.
2. Relying to a greater extent on "net basis" horizontal equalization grants that are funded in part by the sub-national governments themselves.

For example:

- In Australia, 100% of the revenues from the federal Goods and Services Tax (a VAT) are earmarked for financing the main system of (vertical and horizontal) unconditional grants to the states.
- In Japan and several other countries, the growth rate of equalization grants is linked to the growth rate of total federal revenues.
- In Switzerland since 2008, equalization grants are closed-ended – i.e., fixed in units of the national currency by legislation, and the costs are shared between the federal and cantonal governments.
- In Denmark, grants are likewise closed-ended, and the total cost to the federal government changes from year to year depending on a formula that depends on the nominal growth of the economy and on expenditure needs of recipient governments – but not on sub-national revenues.
- In Germany, the federal equalization system has two main components, one of which is financed by the earmarking of certain federal taxes, while the other is a net scheme financed by contributions from rich states to poor states. Under neither component is

there a fiscal risk to the federal government that is unmatched by countervailing risks in earmarked federal revenues.

In all these cases, equalization transfers are designed to limit federal fiscal risks, either by use of closed-ended grants or grants linked to earmarked revenues, or by explicitly requiring fiscal risk-sharing with state governments through net basis equalization schemes. What is more, all this occurs in the context of countries that have much less revenue decentralization and much less regional diversity in resource revenues; this is what makes Equalization so volatile in Canada.

Is the Level of Federal Spending on Equalization Appropriate?

Regardless of how the amount was determined, Ottawa will spend $14.2 billion on Equalization in 2009-10. Is that amount appropriate? Quebec (2009) has argued that the current level of Equalization is inadequate.

The chief argument that Quebec advances for a larger Equalization pool is that the cost of the program is smaller in proportion to national GDP than historical norms. Since 1967-68, the program has averaged just over 1% of GDP, whereas it is now about 0.9%. By this metric, spending would be adequate in 2009-10 if the O'Brien formula were applied, without imposing a ceiling. There is, of course, no reason to expect an open-ended Equalization to grow in proportion to GDP; instead, it is expected to rise and fall with the extent of measured disparities in fiscal capacity among provinces. By some measures, disparities among provinces are certainly on the rise, but this has yet to be reflected in the program. The slower growth of the program in proportion to GDP reflects in part the rising fiscal capacity of resource-rich, traditional receiving provinces. When attention is confined to Core Five receiving provinces, the picture is rather different – see Figure 1, which measures Equalization payments as a percentage of GDP since 1981-82.

Concluding Remarks: The Future of Equalization

Notwithstanding the careful compromises that went into the latest revamping of the Equalization formula, the pressure for further change is almost certain to increase. Provincial objections to the November announcement were initially muted, but are likely to increase as the cumulative impact of the ceiling increases in turn, relative to entitlements

Figure 1: Equalization as a Proportion of GDP

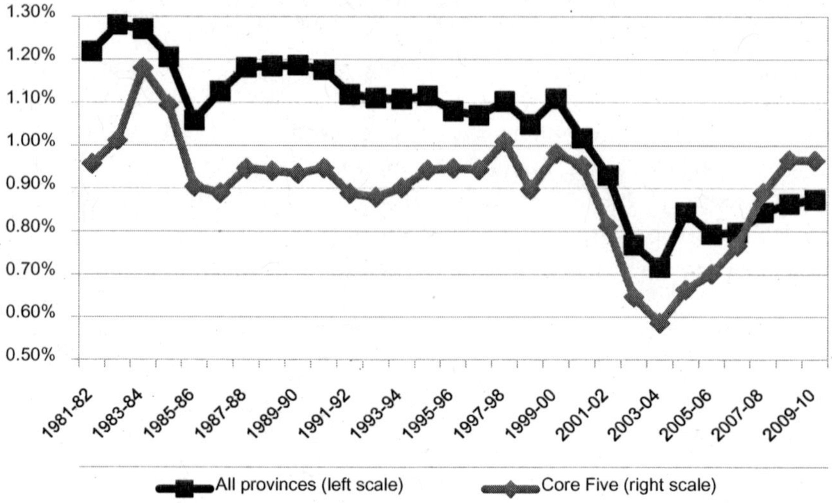

under the 2007 formula. The entry of Ontario into the program has the potential to change political support for Equalization as well – arguably, the median voter now lives in a receiving province. While receiving provinces may push for a return to the 2007 formula, without a ceiling, their efforts may come to focus more realistically on making the case for a ceiling that grows at a faster rate than has been promised by Ottawa. Such a process has the potential once again to undermine fiscal accountability among governments in Canada (Smart, 2005; Kotsogiannis and Schwager, 2008).

At the same time, developments on the federal side will be pulling the program in very different directions. The federal budget will be in deficit for several years to come, and the return to budget balance is likely to be a struggle. With major transfers to the provinces approaching 25% of federal program spending, it is not difficult to imagine that fiscal retrenchment will involve further restraint on transfers. But which transfers? With the 2009 Equalization changes, the federal government now operates three distinct lump-sum grants as its major transfers, each allocated based on different principles and each legislated to grow at a different rate – the Canada Health Transfer (CHT) at 6% annually, the Canada Social Transfer (CST) at 3%, and now Equalization at the growth rate of nominal GDP. Grappling with fiscal arrangements in coming years is therefore going to require decisions about the relative priority of vertical versus horizontal grants and an articulation of what each of the grants is intended to achieve.

If, as I have argued here, Equalization is to remain a closed-ended grant, then what is required is an understanding of what is an appropriate way of determining the level of spending on the program in future. One alternative to the current method of growing the ceiling in line with nominal GDP would be to earmark some portion of federal tax revenues for Equalization – and possibly for some of the other major transfers. Thus, for example, as in Australia and Germany, Equalization and some portion of the block transfers could be financed by dedicating all future revenues from the federal GST to the transfers.

Earmarking federal revenues to fund block grants would have evident benefits for fiscal risk management by the federal government – transfers would be tied explicitly to affordability. But to the extent that earmarking increases federal power to commit to these arrangements, it could increase predictability of transfers for the provinces as well. Correctly structured, earmarked transfers would be more stable than current arrangements, and the greater stability would be fairer to Ontario and other provinces that may move into and out of Equalization in future.

References

Bernard, J.-T. and S. Ben Mabrouk. 2009. "Péréquation et comportement stratégique des provinces bénéficiaires : un contre-exemple intriguant". Mimeo. GREEN: Université Laval.

Courchene, T.J. 1979. *Refinancing the Canadian Federation: A Survey of the 1977 Fiscal Arrangements Act.* Toronto: C.D. Howe Institute.

Expert Panel on Equalization and Territorial Formula Financing. 2006. *Achieving a National Purpose: Putting Equalization Back on Track.* Ottawa: Department of Finance.

Flaherty, J.M. 2009. *Letter to The Honourable Michael G. Baker, Minister of Finance, Nova Scotia*, January 30. Retrieved from www.gov.ns.ca/finance/site-finance/media/finance/Flaherty_re_Equalization.pdf.

Kotsogiannis, C. and R. Schwager. 2008. "Accountability and Fiscal Equalisation", *Journal of Public Economics* 92, 2336-2349.

OECD. 2007. "Fiscal Equalisation in OECD Countries", Working Paper No. 4, Network on Fiscal Relations Across Levels of Government.

Quebec. 2009. *Budget Plan.*

Smart, M. 2004. "Equalization and Stabilization", *Canadian Public Policy* 30(2), 195-208.

__________. 2005. "Federal Transfers: Principles, Practice, and Prospects", C.D. Howe Working Paper.

Session Five

SOCIAL POLICY, AUTOMATIC STABILIZERS, AND THE STRETCHED SOCIAL SAFETY NET

SOCIAL INVESTMENTS, ECONOMIC RETURNS

Sherri Torjman and Ken Battle, Caledon Institute

Introduction

For more than a decade, the Caledon Institute has been analyzing the social policy dimensions of federal budgets. In addition to assessing the impact of specific measures, we try to identify a core theme that each budget represents. There was The Down Payment Budget of 1997, The Payback Budget of 2000, The Vote or Veto Budget of 2005, The Coffee Shop Budget of 2008, and now The Red-Ink Budget of 2009.

Ironically, the 2009 budget was introduced one day after the Chinese New Year – a festive time marked by celebration and redecoration for the New Year. Tradition involves the painting of doors and window frames – bright red. Customs include hanging red-paper lanterns and distributing red packets of money to children. There is supposed to be a splash of red everywhere. This year, Canada's federal budget adopted the red theme in a big way.

It came as no surprise that the government introduced a "red-ink" budget. For several weeks, Canadians had been primed for a spending budget. In fact, red ink was actually expected in that all member nations of the G20 had been encouraged to bring in deficit financing to tackle the global economic recession.

But in this case, the colour of good luck brought no good fortune. The 2009 budget was the first in more than a decade to fall below the break-even line and enter the dreaded deficit territory. Canada has now returned officially to the red zone – after years of being the only G8 nation to have landed in the black by vanquishing our deficit.

Going back to the red sea was not a decision taken lightly. But under current circumstances, it was the right thing to do in an economic recession.

Our analysis of the 2009 budget is based on a set of proposals that Caledon had put forward in December 2008 after the publication of the *Economic and Fiscal Statement* (Battle, Torjman, and Mendelson, 2008). Prior to issuing that Statement, the federal government was reassuring Canadians that they would be able to weather the economic crisis gripping the world because the "fundamentals" of our economy were in place. Canada's debt-to-GDP ratio was the lowest in the G8 and was on a downturn trajectory; its banks were among the healthiest in the world; and the country was not experiencing the same sub-prime mortgage housing crisis seen south of the border.

In our view, however, an important ingredient was missing from this conversation about fundamentals. It had to do with the lessons of history, which have taught us that, in tough economic times, *social programs* can act as vital supports for both the economy and society. They are far from a drain on the economy, but rather act as both shock absorber and fiscal stimulus.

Social programs act as *shock absorber* when times are tough for individual households. Programs such as Employment Insurance, child benefits, public pensions, and welfare are intended to ensure that the poor, unemployed, families with children, and seniors have at least some money to pay for necessities such as food, clothing, and shelter (however lacking some of these programs may be in practice[1]).

Social programs act as *fiscal stimulus* when times are tough for the economy. Social programs put money straight into the hands of large numbers of Canadians whose collective spending can help restart the economic motor. They pump money directly into the economy.

Social programs, particularly in the form of income security benefits to low-income households, have a strong multiplier effect because they are likely to be spent immediately rather than squirrelled away in savings or spent offshore. In this sense, increases to income security benefits are effective counter-cyclical actions. Unlike other stimulus measures,

---

[1]Canada's automatic stabilizer is the seventh lowest among OECD countries at 0.38 compared to the OECD average of .44 (Girouard and André, 2005, Table 9, p. 22).

however, increases to programs such as the Canada Child Tax Benefit and the Working Income Tax Benefit should not be withdrawn after they are made. The purpose of enhancing these benefits goes beyond economic stimulus. Because a primary goal of these programs is to reduce poverty, immediate increases for stimulative impact can serve as a foundation for longer-term improvement over time.

Caledon has strongly supported the need for deficit financing during these rough economic times. Our fiscal stimulus approach favours spending increases over tax cuts. Spending injections – if delivered through income security programs targeted to low- and modest-income Canadians and the unemployed – flow cash to families and individuals who are more likely to spend it right away and thus help stimulate the economy. Income tax cuts, by contrast, are more apt to be saved or used to pay down personal debt. We have also supported investment in social infrastructure that creates jobs in the short term and helps build strong and healthy communities in the long term.

Ottawa currently has at its disposal several effective social programs that can play an important role in an economic stimulus package to combat the recession. In a paper entitled *The Forgotten Fundamentals*, we put forward proposals for boosting three geared-to-income programs – the Canada Child Tax Benefit, refundable GST credit, and Working Income Tax Benefit. We argued that the expenditure on these income-tested programs would put additional money into the hands of lower-income households, which are more likely than higher-income families to spend it immediately. The paper proposed several key reforms to Employment Insurance as well (Battle, Torjman, and Mendelson, 2008).

We also called for investment in social infrastructure in response to the need to stem the big job losses being announced daily and to create employment. This area includes investment in social housing, recreation programs and places, and high-quality affordable child care (Torjman, 2009).

Income Security

Working Income Tax Benefit

The Working Income Tax Benefit (WITB) is a promising program targeted to the working poor, who make up about half of Canada's low-income population. It has two major objectives – to reduce disincentives to work for recipients stuck behind the welfare wall and to enhance incentives to work among the working poor.

The WITB aims at lowering the welfare wall by supplementing low earnings from employment to "help make work pay", to use the British term. The WITB enables social assistance recipients to make the difficult move from welfare to work by topping up their typically low earnings.

The other aim of the WITB is to increase incentives for people to join the workforce, keep working (even for low earnings), and not have to fall back onto the tangled safety net of welfare. Some of these workers eventually will be able to climb the earnings ladder and escape poverty.

In 2008, the WITB provided a modest $510 maximum payment annually to single low-income Canadians working only part-time. Eligibility for the WITB ended at the low level of $13,081 in net income for single workers, and the maximum payment of $510 went to those between $5,550 and $9,681 – low earnings indeed. There is also a WITB supplement for low-income workers with disabilities (who qualify for the disability tax credit) worth a maximum of $255 in 2008.

The WITB is somewhat less stingy for single parents, couples, and recipients with disabilities. In 2008, single parents and couples earning between $8,100 and $14,776 received a maximum payment of $1,019, with diminishing benefits until eligibility ended at net family income of $21,576.

We argued in our pre-budget analysis that the maximum annual payment of just $510 in 2008 for single workers and $1,019 for couples and single parents was far too modest (Battle and Torjman, 2008). Moreover, the design of the WITB was problematic; it reached only poor workers employed part-time. Canadians working full-time at the minimum wage are not eligible for assistance. We recommended not only that benefits be doubled, but also that the eligible income ranges be extended to put extra cash into the hands of more Canadians who work but remain poor.

The 2009 budget took a big step in the right direction by raising the WITB's payments and broadening its reach to help more of Canada's working poor (Battle, 2009). It substantially boosted the WITB from a maximum $510 for single recipients in 2008 to $925 in 2009 – a real (i.e., inflation-adjusted) increase of 77.2%. The net income level at which eligibility for the WITB ends increased from $13,081 in 2008 to $16,667 in 2009 for single recipients.

Figure 1 illustrates the pattern of WITB benefits for single workers before and after the 2009 budget. The "before" scenario shows WITB for 2009 if the federal government had indexed the 2008 figures only to the cost of living. The "after" picture illustrates WITB as proposed in the 2009 budget.

For single parents and couples, the maximum WITB payment will rise from $1,044 in 2008 to $1,680 in 2009, for a substantial real increase of 60.9%. The net family income level above which eligibility for WITB ends will climb from $21,576 in 2008 to $25,700 in 2009. Figure 2 shows the distribution of WITB benefits to single parents and families before and after the changes made in the 2009 budget.

These improvements will address two of the key weaknesses of the original program – its lean payments and its exclusion of full-time workers earning low wages. But despite these improvements, the WITB will not reach all working-poor Canadians. Take the case of a worker living in Toronto whose earnings equal the after-tax low income cut-off, an estimated $18,670 in 2009. That amount is $2,012 above the $16,667 level where eligibility for WITB ends. To receive the maximum benefit

Figure 1: WITB for Single Persons, Before and After Budget, 2009

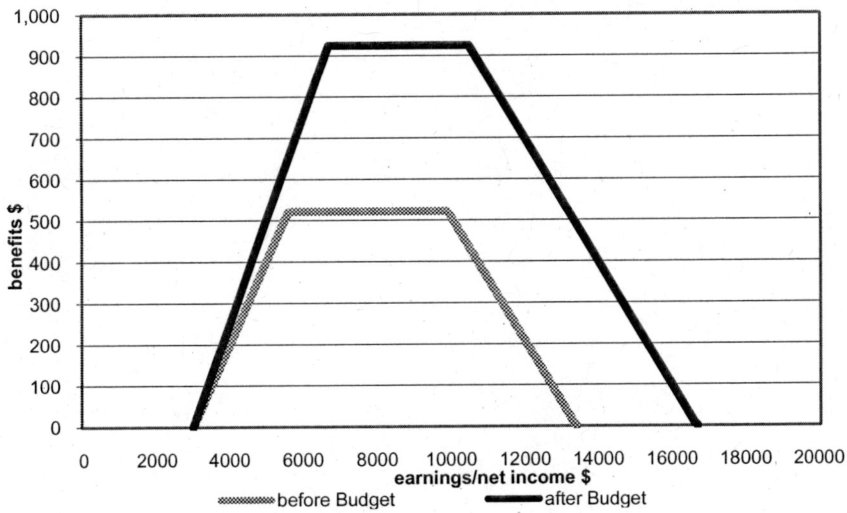

Figure 2: WITB for Families, Before and After Budget, 2009

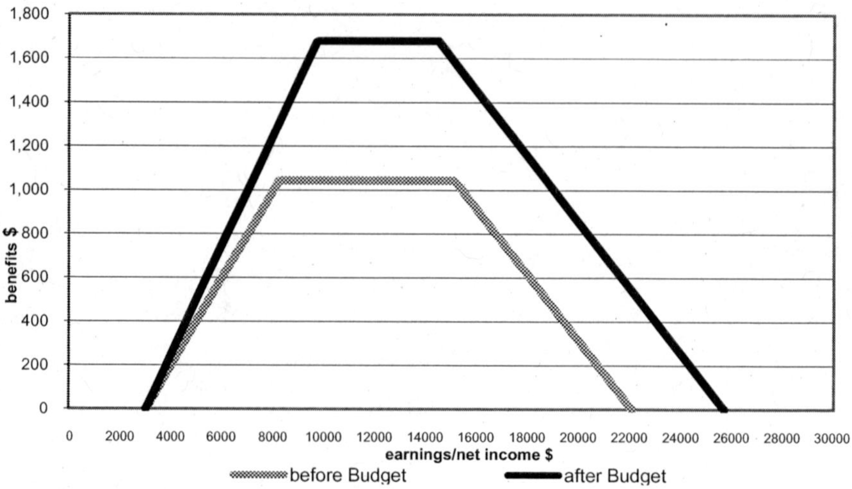

of $925 from WITB in 2009, the most a worker can make is $10,500 – far ($8,170) below the $18,670 level for someone earning at the poverty line.

The 2009 budget's proposals to enhance the WITB are laudable. They strengthen both key aims of the program – helping welfare recipients get over the welfare wall and supplementing the earnings of the working poor. The investment in WITB will foster economic stimulus by sending more money to more working-poor Canadians. However, Ottawa will need to implement further improvements to WITB over time so that it extends higher up the income ladder and becomes a major income support for Canadians who work at minimum and low wages.

Child Benefits

The 2009 budget made some small but positive changes to the Canada Child Tax Benefit. Unfortunately, the increases are too modest to count for much as economic stimulus.

Child benefits are one of the most important income transfers for families with children. As part of the federal/provincial National Child Benefit, Ottawa has substantially boosted the Canada Child Tax Benefit in recent years. Since lower-income families are more likely to spend any additional funds immediately, the Canada Child Tax Benefit packs a powerful stimulative punch. The benefit is delivered through the income tax system, and any increases can be put quickly into play.

The Canada Child Tax Benefit is composed of two parts. The base Child Tax Benefit serves almost all – nine in ten – families and is intended to help parents with their child-rearing expenses. For the current payment year (July 2008-June 2009), the maximum base Child Tax Benefit is $1,307 per child. The maximum amount is payable up to net family income of $37,885 – the same as the income tax system's first tax bracket. Above this level, payments are reduced at a rate of 2%, which means that eligibility for benefits ends at a high $103,235 in net family income (even higher in terms of gross income). For families with two or more children, benefits are reduced at the rate of 4% above net family income of $37,885.

The National Child Benefit Supplement (NCBS) sits on top of the base Child Tax Benefit and provides an additional benefit to low- and modest-income families. Currently, the maximum amount is $2,025 for the first child, $1,792 for the second child, and $1,704 for the third and each additional child.

Like the base Child Tax Benefit, the NCBS is income-tested, though more steeply. Above net family income of $21,287, the NCBS is reduced at the rates of 12.2% for families with one child, 22.7% for families with two children, and 27.8% for families with three or more children. The NCBS is aimed at the poverty reduction goal, though the base Child Tax Benefit paid to low-income families also contributes.

The net family income threshold above which the base Child Tax Benefit is reduced is set at the same level as the first income tax bracket in order to integrate the federal tax and benefit systems. Because the 2009 budget raised the bottom and second tax brackets above their normal indexation adjustment (see discussion below), it also increased the income threshold for the base Child Tax Benefit to the same level and lifted the income threshold for the NCBS in the same proportion. These changes to the Canada Child Tax Benefit will take effect in the July 2009-June 2010 payment year.

Under normal indexation, the net family income threshold above which the base Child Tax Benefit is reduced would have been $38,832 in 2009; the 2009 budget will raise this to $40,726. The net family income threshold above which the NCBS declines will rise from $21,926 to $23,820.

The changes will increase benefits in two ways. Because the base Child Tax Benefit will be reduced at a higher level ($40,726 instead of $38,832), more families will get the maximum benefit, and fewer will get the reduced benefit. Similarly, more families will get the maximum NCBS and fewer will receive the reduced amount. The net family income level when benefits disappear for families with one or two children will increase from $105,480 to $107,726.

Figure 3 shows the change in federal child benefits – the base Child Tax Benefit and the NCBS – for families with one child. The poorest families, with incomes below $21,000, will see no improvement in their child benefits. The large majority of families with low, middle, and high incomes will receive modest increases in benefits. Low- and modest-income families with incomes in the $25,000 to $40,000 range will enjoy the largest increases, ranging from $102 to $231. Families with net incomes over $40,000 will see small increases ($23 for the $40,000

Figure 3: Change in Canada Child Tax Benefit as Result of Budget, Families with One Child, July 2009–June 2010

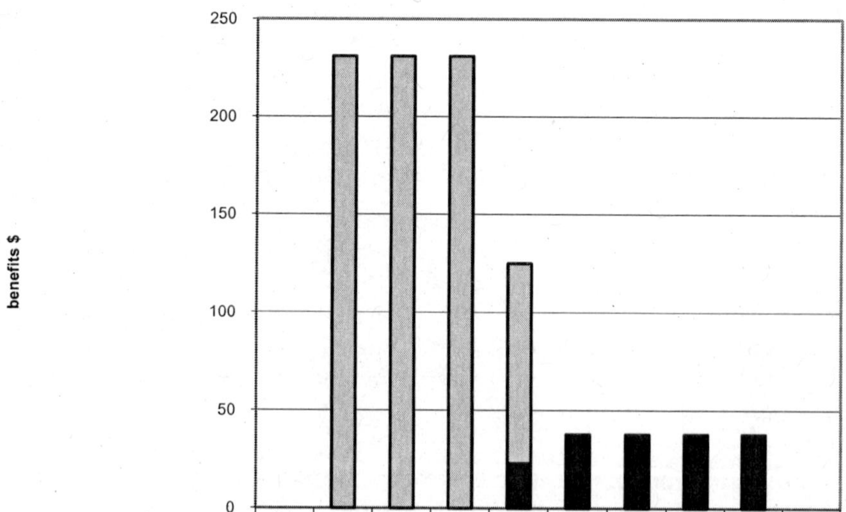

	20K	25K	30K	35K	40K	45K	50K	75K	100K	110K
National Child Benefit Supplement	0	231	231	231	102	0	0	0	0	0
base Child Tax Benefit	0	0	0	0	23	38	38	38	38	0

■base Child Tax Benefit ◘National Child Benefit Supplement

family and $38 for those above $40,000). Families with incomes over $107,000 do not qualify for the Canada Child Tax Benefit.

Figure 4 presents the results for families with two children. While the amounts differ, the overall pattern is the same as for families with one child. The poorest families see no gain, modest-income families enjoy the largest improvement (though still small relative to their total child benefits), and middle- and upper-income families receive very modest increases.

Though minimal and limited in scope, the increases in child benefits for lower-income families will enhance the poverty reduction objective; on the other hand, the poorest families gain nothing. The tiny increases for middle- and high-income families represent only symbolic improvement in the child benefit system's capacity to help parents with their child-rearing costs.

Figure 4: Change in Canada Child Tax Benefit as Result of Budget, Families with Two Children, July 2009-June 2010

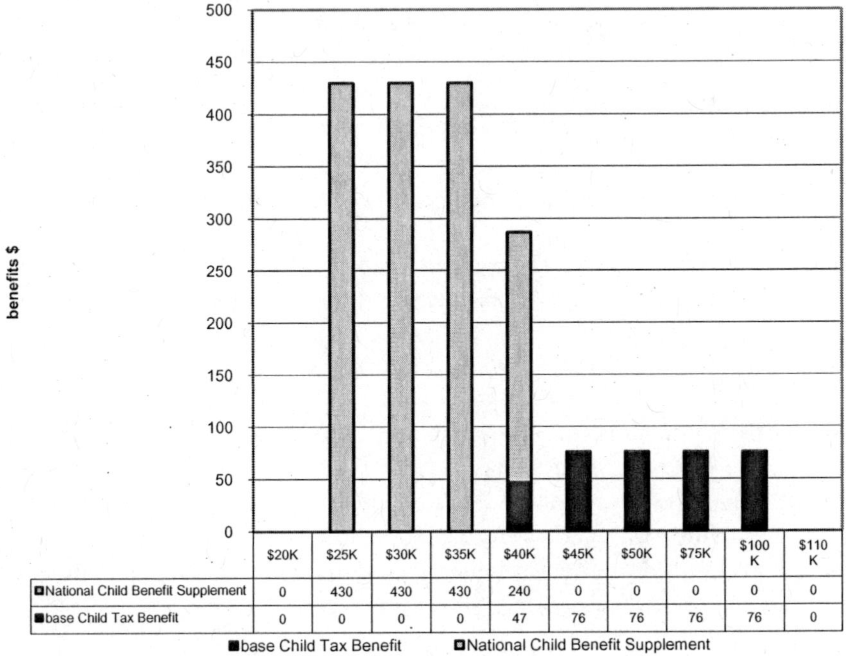

	$20K	$25K	$30K	$35K	$40K	$45K	$50K	$75K	$100 K	$110 K
National Child Benefit Supplement	0	430	430	430	240	0	0	0	0	0
base Child Tax Benefit	0	0	0	0	47	76	76	76	76	0

■base Child Tax Benefit ◘National Child Benefit Supplement

Tax Cuts

The 2009 budget raised the basic personal amount, spousal and common-law partner amount, and eligible dependant amount from $9,600 in 2008 to $10,320 in 2009. The age credit went from a maximum $5,276 in 2008 to $6,408 for 2009. The budget also raised the first income tax bracket from $37,885 in 2008 to $40,726 in 2009 and the second tax bracket from $75,769 in 2008 to $81,452 in 2009.

The budget's claim of "tax cuts for low- and middle-income taxpayers" is actually rather deceptive. The poorest Canadians will see no tax relief since they are already below the tax-paying threshold and pay no federal income tax. Lower- and middle-income taxpayers will get very small tax cuts, while those in the upper-income range will enjoy the largest tax break. But the amounts are so modest as to call into question their fiscal stimulus contribution, even if one believes that taxpayers will run out and spend their tax savings rather than bank them or pay down debt.

Figure 5 shows that the tax savings for single persons range from zero for those with income of $10,000, who are below the tax-paying threshold, to $33 for those with incomes of $20,000 or $30,000, $115 for those at $40,000, $166 at $60,000, $259 at $80,000, and $317 for taxpayers with incomes of $100,000 and $150,000 (Department of Finance Canada, 2009, p. 308). The amount of tax break increases as incomes rise.

At all income levels, the tax reductions are very small relative to total income – less than 1%. They range from a low of .11% for single tax-payers at $30,000 to a high of .32% for those at $80,000 and $100,000.

The numbers differ, but the overall pattern of results is the same for single parents with one child, one-earner couples with two children, and two-earner couples with two children. Income tax savings rise with income and represent a tiny fraction of total income.

The results for seniors are similar overall, though the federal income tax savings are generally larger than for the non-elderly because the elderly benefit from the increase in the age credit as well as the other tax changes for the non-aged. Figure 6 shows income tax savings for three elderly households – single seniors, one-pension senior couples, and two-pension senior couples – at different income levels.

Figure 5: Income Tax Savings from Budget, Taxpayers Under 65, by Household Type and Income, 2009

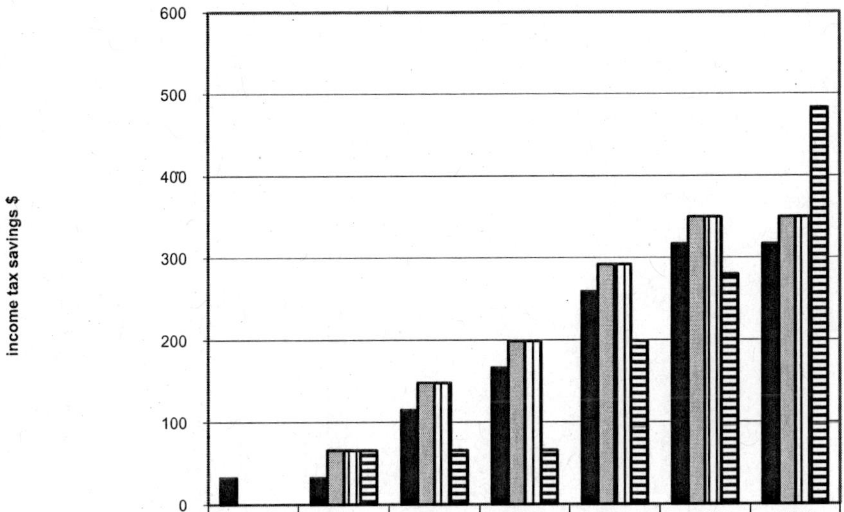

	$20K	$30K	$40K	$60K	$80K	$100K	$150K
single persons	33	33	115	166	259	317	317
single parents, 1 child	0	66	148	199	292	350	350
one-earner couples, 2 kids	0	66	148	199	292	350	350
two-earner couples, 2 kids	0	66	66	66	199	280	483

Income tax savings range from zero for poor elderly below the tax-paying threshold to $183 for those with modest incomes of $20,000 and $30,000, $316 at $40,000 and $60,000, and $317 at $80,000 and above. Measured as a percentage of income, the tax reductions range from a low of .21% for seniors with incomes of $150,000 to a high of .92% for those with incomes of $20,000. Unlike taxpayers under age 65, the larger tax cuts for seniors are progressive when measured relative to income, although not in absolute amounts.

While the income tax breaks in the 2009 budget are very small relative to Canadian taxpayers' incomes, the total cost to the federal Treasury in lost revenue is considerable, at close to $2 billion. Some of the cost reflects inflationary indexing, but the remaining cost is still significant. These tax cuts will do nothing to ameliorate the effects of the recession on individuals, since the largest amounts are going to those with the highest income.

Figure 6: Income Tax Savings from Budget, Taxpayers 65 and Older, by Household Type and Income, 2009

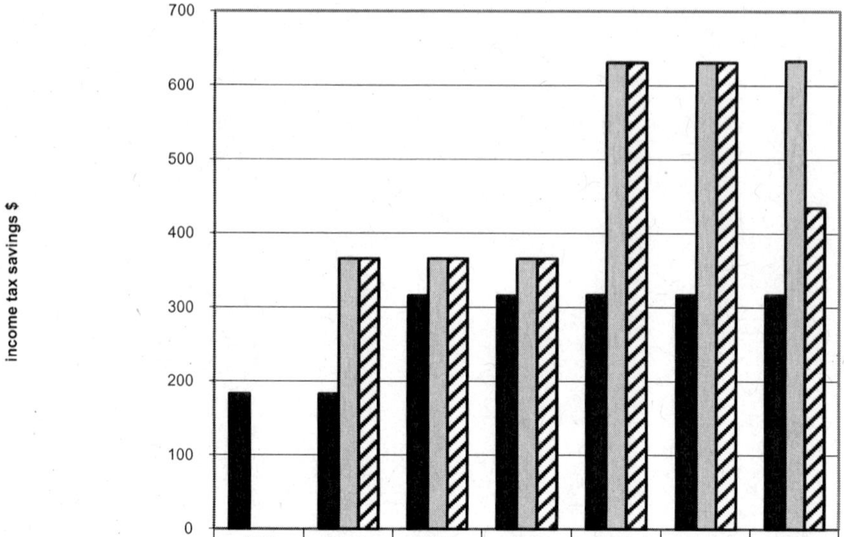

	$20K	$30K	$40K	$60K	$80K	$100K	$150K
single seniors	183	183	316	316	317	317	317
one-pension senior couples	0	366	366	366	631	631	633
two-pension senior couples	0	366	366	366	631	631	435

In our pre-budget statement *The Forgotten Fundamentals*, Caledon proposed an alternative to income tax cuts – doubling the GST credit – a refundable tax credit geared to low- and modest-income Canadians who are most likely to spend any extra money they receive (Battle, Torjman, and Mendelson, 2008). Figure 7 compares the 2009 budget's tax cuts with the Caledon proposal to double the GST credit. The contrast is striking.

Granted, doubling the GST credit would cost approximately $3.3 billion, whereas the income tax cuts will cost Ottawa $2.2 billion (Yalnizyan and MacDonald, 2009, p. 12). But boosting the GST credit would pack a much bigger stimulus punch than income tax cuts that most benefit upper-income taxpayers.

Annual maximum benefits under the GST credit are currently $242 for each eligible adult and the first child in single-parent families and $127

Figure 7: Income Tax Cuts Versus Double GST Credit, Single Parent with One Child, by Income, 2009

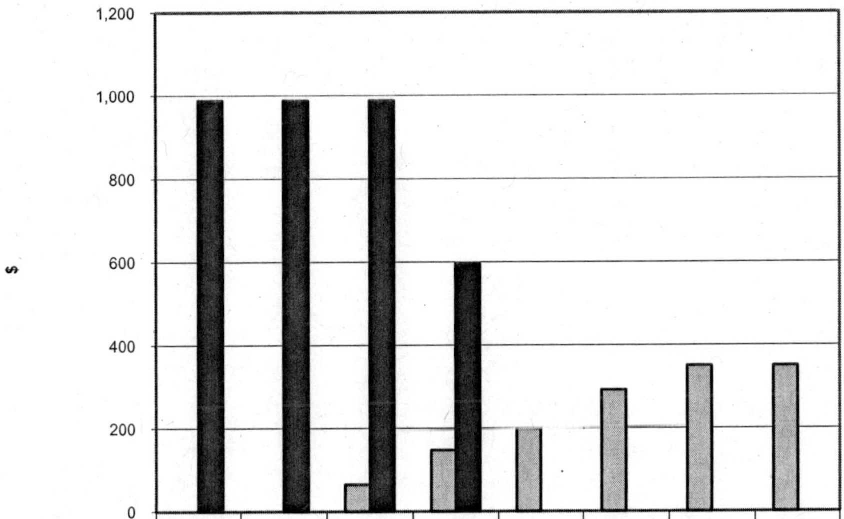

	$10K	$20K	$30K	$40K	$60K	$80K	$100K	$150K
income tax cuts	0	0	66	148	199	292	350	350
double GST credit	988	988	988	596	0	0	0	0

income tax cuts ■double GST credit

per child for other children. For example, a single parent with one child currently receives up to $484 a year.

Maximum benefits from the refundable GST credit should be doubled, so that this family would receive $968. Like the Canada Child Tax Benefit, this increase to the refundable GST credit could be put into play quickly through the Canada Revenue Agency at little or no administrative cost.

Employment Insurance

Born out of the Great Depression, Employment Insurance (EI) is another potentially powerful policy lever, especially in tough economic times. As a result of several major changes introduced in the 1990s to tighten access to EI and reduce the amount and duration of payments, the numbers of eligible beneficiaries have dropped dramatically over the years.

Figure 8 shows that only an estimated 44.0% of unemployed Canadians qualified for benefits under this so-called "social insurance" at last count (in 2007). Coverage is even lower in a number of provinces – e.g., 23.8% in Alberta, 29.0% in Ontario, 37.7% in Manitoba, 38.1% in BC, and 42.6% in Saskatchewan. All employees must pay EI premiums, but fewer than half the unemployed receive benefits in return.

Some of Canada's most vulnerable groups – older workers, part-time workers, recent immigrants, new entrants to the labour force, persons with disabilities, and low-wage workers generally – are typically excluded from EI. So too are the self-employed.

Coverage of the unemployed has fallen from 83% in 1990 to 43% in 2008, which is the lowest since 1976. There is a gender gap – only 39.1% of unemployed women received regular EI benefits in 2008 compared to 45.5% of jobless men – and it has widened in recent years from 2.0 percentage points in 1996 to 6.4 percentage points in 2008; see Figure 8.

The maximum regular weekly EI benefit is $447 in 2009 or a maximum yearly $22,350, taking into account the 2009 budget's increase of up to five weeks; in 1995, it was $595 in inflation-adjusted terms ($448 in current dollars). In 2007, average benefits for women ($298) amounted

Figure 8: Percentage of Unemployed Canadians Receiving Regular Employment Insurance Benefits, by Gender, 1976-2007

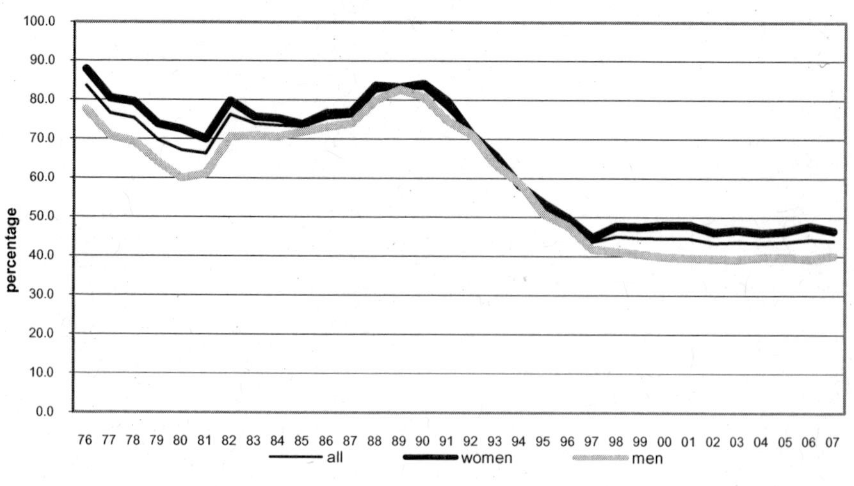

to $13,410-$4,544 below the after-tax low income cut-off (LICO) for a metro area ($17,954). Average benefits for men ($360) amounted to $16,200-$1,754 below the after-tax LICO for a metro area.

Over the past few years, we proposed that EI be restored and strengthened through the measures outlined below (Battle, Mendelson, and Torjman, 2006):

- Reduce the hours of work required to qualify for EI: uniform entrance requirement of 360 hours to replace both variable entrance requirements and the 600 hours required for special benefits (e.g., maternity and parental).
- Raise the earnings replacement rate from 55% to 70%, lifting maximum weekly benefits to $570 – their level in the previous recession. The amount of benefit should be calculated on the best 12 weeks of earnings of the previous 26 so as to allow flexibility to take part-time jobs.
- Eliminate the two-week waiting period.
- Extend the maximum duration of benefits up to 50 weeks (which Ottawa did in the 2009 budget, but only temporarily). Current EI beneficiaries, and those who lose their jobs over the next two years and meet the eligibility requirements, will draw benefits for an extra five weeks, up to a maximum of 50 weeks.

EI's financing also needs reform. The plan should now be drawing down accumulated savings from premiums collected during flush years to pump money into the economy during these lean years, thereby helping thousands of businesses to keep afloat and their workers to remain employed. Premiums should be set higher in good economic times and lower when the going gets rough.

Such measures would strengthen the program, but would still leave many unemployed without coverage. Canada's entire support system for the unemployed – welfare as well as EI – needs to be re-examined through a joint review by the federal and provincial/territorial governments.

Here is a bold new idea: Ottawa should create a new Temporary Income (TI) program to complement a strengthened EI. The new scheme would pay temporary and time-limited, income-tested benefits to unemployed workers with low or modest incomes who cannot qualify for EI. It would be financed out of general revenues. The new program would prevent tens of thousands of the unemployed from falling onto provincial welfare rolls.

Federal Assistance to Provinces and Territories

For the first time since the Great Depression, Canada's provinces and territories will be entering into a severe economic downturn without any federal programs that are responsive to added provincial/territorial costs. In the 1990s, the Canada Assistance Plan paid 50% of eligible social assistance costs to the provinces and territories. But the Canada Assistance Plan is long gone, having been replaced in 1995 by a single block transfer, the Canada Health and Social Transfer, in 2004 divided into the Canada Social Transfer and Canada Health Transfer (Battle and Torjman, 1995). The most vulnerable provinces and territories will require some assistance from Ottawa to cope with their inevitably rising spending.

Currently, Ontario gets less than an equal per capita Canada Health Transfer due to an arcane adjustment related to a decades-old tax transfer. With the recession's severe impact on Ontario, this adjustment is not fair to the taxpayers of that province, who must carry an unequal burden. One change that Ottawa could make immediately is to pay an equal per capita cash transfer to all equalization-receiving provinces, including Ontario. More generally, the federal government should consider a new program to relieve some of the cost in a province or territory whose social assistance and other social benefit spending rises above a stated percentage of its GDP.

Training

The red-ink budget builds on the opportunity embedded in the current economic adversity through investment in a variety of training measures. A better educated workforce will position Canada to take advantage of the upturn when it comes. The budget announced a new Canada Skills and Transition Strategy worth \$8.3 billion toward a range of initiatives to help Canadians weather the economic storm. While the general description sounds excellent, the fine print tells a different story.

The hefty total breaks down into three parts: \$1.9 billion to strengthen benefits to help workers find training and the right jobs, \$1.9 billion to enhance the availability of training, and \$4.5 billion to hold EI rates to \$1.73 per \$100 for 2009 and 2010. Freezing the EI rates for both employers and employees was the right thing to do during a recession. But billing this payroll tax freeze as part of a new "skills and transition strategy" is inappropriate. Moreover, the tax freeze comprises more than 50% of the cost of the new "skills" initiative – hardly a modest amount.

The skills components of the program fall into two major streams, which comprise a long list of new measures. The first has to do with *strengthening benefits for workers*. Among the many new measures was $1.15 billion for extending regular EI benefits by an extra five weeks to a maximum 50 weeks for the next two years. An additional $500 million over two years will allow the extension of EI benefits for long-term training for "long-tenured workers". These are individuals who have spent years working in a single industry or for the same employer and need to retrain for another job, possibly in a new industry.

The second set of measures in the Canada Skills and Transition Strategy to *expand the availability of training* is also worth $1.9 billion. Ottawa will increase funds for training delivered through EI by $1 billion over two years; this will top up the current annual funding of $1.5 billion used to assist EI clients in their search for new employment.

The new funds will help bolster a labour market program that had been introduced in 2007, intended explicitly for workers who do not qualify for EI benefits and thereby have limited access to the labour market measures available to EI beneficiaries. A Strategic Training and Transition Fund worth $500 million over two years will support the self-employed and others who have been out of work for an extended period and are not eligible for EI training.

The Caledon Institute fully supports the wide range of investments in training. For years, we have pointed out that a significant proportion of jobless workers have limited or no access to training or upgrading delivered through EI because they have not worked sufficient hours to qualify for the employment benefits provided by this key income support program.

The programs announced in the 2009 budget will provide a badly needed injection of funds into a hit-and-miss training system that, by many accounts, was often more miss than hit. But as in the other budget expenditures, these training announcements come with a unique set of concerns. The new programs, while welcome, represent an almost dizzying array of measures that may well benefit from some coherent integration and coordination when they are actually implemented. A considerable proportion of funds may end up in administrative overhead rather than direct programming.

It is also unclear how the new measures will mesh (or not) with existing programs run by provinces and territories as part of their respective training and welfare systems. Duplication and new layers of complexity may well result. Given that the provinces and territories are also under significant fiscal pressure, it will be important to ensure that the new federal investment does not just substitute for the money that they would otherwise have spent.

Finally, and perhaps most important, the EI extension announced as part of the Canada Skills and Transition Strategy was necessary but woefully insufficient. It will provide some badly needed assistance to those who are already receiving EI benefits but are having difficulty finding a new job – clearly a problem during an economic recession.

At the same time, changes should have been introduced – as earlier discussed – to allow more workers to qualify for the program in the first place. EI coverage has shrunk to the lowest level in its history. EI can hardly be billed any more as the viable "social insurance" that it originally was intended to be.

Social Infrastructure

Affordable Housing

We have strongly endorsed the budget's funds for affordable housing, having made the case – along with many other organizations – for this critical investment. We have pointed out in numerous reports that far too many Canadians live in substandard housing that seriously threatens their physical and mental health.

The availability of high-quality affordable housing is an essential element of poverty reduction (Torjman, 2008). While the budget made no reference to poverty or to a badly needed poverty strategy like the ones in which several provinces are now engaged, at least it supports a critical weapon in the wider war on poverty.

Investment in affordable housing was a centerpiece of the 2009 budget. The government committed a one-time $1 billion injection over the next two years for renovation and energy retrofits to improve the quality and energy efficiency of up to 200,000 social housing units throughout the country.

The new $1 billion investment builds on the $1.9 billion investment over five years that Ottawa announced in September 2008 to extend housing and homelessness programs for low-income Canadians. These programs include the Affordable Housing Initiative, Homelessness Partnering Strategy, and housing renovation programs such as the Residential Rehabilitation Assistance Program.

In an interview published shortly after the budget, however, the government reinforced the one-time nature of this investment in social housing. Ottawa emphasized the economic stimulus purpose of the money and cautioned that it did not represent a policy shift to a larger federal role in social housing (Greenaway, 2009). This "clarification" was unfortunate given the need for a strong federal presence in this policy area.

In addition to these general investments, the budget set aside amounts for specific populations over the next two years – $400 million for new housing and retrofit of existing accommodation on First Nations reserves, $400 million for the construction of social housing units for seniors, $200 million for social housing in the North, and $75 million for the construction of social housing units for persons with disabilities.

But a major concern arises from the fact that investment in social housing takes some time to work its way through the system if land must be rezoned in a given community or plans drawn up and tendered. To ensure that the funds get to where they are supposed to be going (and soon), Ottawa must work expeditiously with provinces/territories and municipalities to get these dollars out the door.

Infrastructure

Investment in infrastructure figured prominently in the 2009 federal budget. In addition to the monies allocated for social housing, close to $12 billion was announced for new infrastructure stimulus over the next two years. Funds will be directed throughout the country toward roads, bridges, clean energy, broadband Internet access, and electronic health records. There are two major benefits to this form of stimulus: immediate creation of jobs, especially for so-called "shovel-ready" projects, and long-term economic and social gains, which derive from renewing the vital foundation of cities and communities.

We have supported these investments, having called over the years for infrastructure financing. We have also noted in our own work that the discussion on infrastructure has been fairly narrow, concerned mainly with roads, sewers, water systems, and basic elements that comprise its physical plant. Renewal and environmental upgrading of these elements are essential.

But we have urged a broader definition to include other core components of infrastructure on the social side of the equation – affordable housing, schools, libraries, recreation centres, and museums, which contribute immeasurably to community well-being but often get overlooked in the mix (Torjman, 2009). In addition to providing the physical spaces that can be used for social purposes, social infrastructure includes programs that contribute to positive well-being. There are strong links between participation in recreation and cultural activities, and good physical health, mental health, and social well-being.

This message clearly was received in Budget 2009, with investments over and above those announced for social housing. The budget established a two-year, $4 billion Infrastructure Stimulus Fund to enable provinces/territories and municipalities to repair, renew, and upgrade infrastructure.

Up to $500 million over the next two years was set aside for infrastructure in smaller communities whose resource-dependent economies are being hit hard by the recession. Two new agencies – for northern economic development and for southern Ontario – are being created to bolster economic activity in these regions.

We were especially pleased to see the announcement of $500 million over two years to build and renew community recreation facilities across Canada. Caledon has called for this type of investment over previous budgetary measures that took the form of tax cuts for fitness programs, which were of benefit primarily to middle- and higher-income families – and for so few dollars in tax savings (a maximum $75) that it made no real difference. Nor could these individual tax cuts possibly substitute for the significant investments required to upgrade, repair, and renew community spaces, such as recreation facilities.

In short, the substantial funding for infrastructure is welcome from the perspective of short-term employment and long-term investment in the quality of life in communities. The true test of these measures, of course, will come in the implementation.

The problem, if past practice is any barometer, is that funds earmarked for infrastructure spending barely leave the door. While dollars are announced with press releases and associated fanfare, the actual funds never seem to be (entirely) delivered. They are either lacking or late. Various political and regulatory barriers invariably get in the way of expeditious spending. The latter is crucial given the explicit purpose of infrastructure measures: to counter rising unemployment through the immediate creation of jobs.

The budget itself revealed that nearly $8 billion in unspent infrastructure funding has accumulated on the federal books. In 2007-08, the lapse – the amount of funding appropriated by Parliament but not spent by departments – reached its highest level in recent years at $7.6 billion, or about 9% of appropriated funds. The Federation of Canadian Municipalities estimates that the federal infrastructure fund allocated less than $300 million of the $1.5 billion announced in its first two years of budgeted spending (Brennan, 2009).

Another problem looms large if these funds do not get spent quickly. Delays in implementation mean that the monies could go into the economy at a time when (hopefully) it will be growing again. A big infusion of cash during a period of economic growth could fuel inflation and inadvertently do more harm than good. As in the case of social housing, the funds announced in the "red-ink" budget must be spent with immediacy and intelligence.

Child Care

Early childhood development is the one significant social policy area that was left out of the 2009 budget. The words "child care" did not appear anywhere in the document – at least not together.

There have been decades of effort on the part of parents, researchers, and advocates to convince governments that early learning and child care are crucial to Canada's social and economic health. High-quality early learning and child care services are not just "social policy": they equally are core elements of economic policy because they invest in the critical first years of human capital development and enable parents to work or study.

From an economic perspective, high-quality, affordable child care enables labour market participation, and education and training. It can make the difference between a below- and above-poverty line income for many single parents and couples. High-quality, affordable child care is a good economic investment in light of the many sectors facing severe labour shortages, both now and in the near future.

The large majority of Canadian families, including those with preschool children, have both parents in the labour market. Most single parents work outside the home. Child care is necessary if parents are to participate in the workforce or undertake the education and training that employers demand. Child care is essential for poor families struggling to climb over the welfare wall, and find and keep jobs.

But early learning and child care are not just for families with parents in the workforce. Services such as parental supports and respite also help families that care for their children at home. High-quality early learning and child care can improve children's subsequent performance in school, lessen the learning risks linked to low income, and enhance parents' child-rearing and coping skills.

Canada lags embarrassingly behind other developed nations when it comes to early learning and child care. Even five years ago, the OECD was urging Canadian governments to increase their funding for child care.

The demand for high-quality, affordable child care far outstrips the available supply. Services are uneven between and, in most cases, within provinces and territories. There is nothing approaching a national system – other than in Quebec, which has woven high-quality, affordable child care into its economic and social fabric. Most families in the rest of the country rely on unregulated child care bought or traded on the market (typically from neighbourhood providers) or provided by relatives.

The federal government has a pivotal role to play in contributing to a secure financial base for this crucial investment. Ottawa should make a significant commitment to support this infrastructure, as it did in the federal-provincial/territorial Early Childhood Development Agreement it signed in 2000 and the Agreement on Early Learning and Child Care in 2003.

Canadians need good-quality, affordable child care in order to participate in the labour market. But the child care system itself also creates jobs for early childhood educators. Given the wait list for these services in many parts of the country, the supply of early childhood educators could have been bolstered and their low salaries increased to match the value of the work they do. Equally importantly, a lower educator-to-child ratio would allow for more individualized attention for each child, thereby contributing to the vital child-development objective of these services.

Conclusion

There is no question that deficit financing was required at this time of economic recession. While the 2009 budget made some important social policy investments, it could have directed more assistance to low- and modest-income households in order to have an even stimulative punch.

Of course, a red-ink budget that spends billions to shore up a flagging economy could also be dubbed a red-flag budget for opening the door to years of payout on a higher national debt. The challenge that we face as a nation is to ensure that we embark on an intelligent and strategic deficit reduction plan that is not predicated on the dismantling or destruction of social programs.

References

Battle, K. 2009. *Beneath the Budget of 2009: Taxes and Benefits*. Ottawa: Caledon Institute of Social Policy, February.

Battle, K., M. Mendelson, and S. Torjman. 2006. *Towards a New Architecture for Canada's Adult Benefits*. Ottawa: Caledon Institute of Social Policy, June.

Battle, K. and S. Torjman. 1995. *The Dangers of Block Funding*. Ottawa: Caledon Institute of Social Policy, February.

__________. 2008. *Make Work Pay*. Ottawa: Caledon Institute of Social Policy, September.

Battle, K., S. Torjman, and M. Mendelson. 2008. *The Forgotten Fundamentals*. Ottawa: Caledon Institute of Social Policy, December.

Brennan, R. 2009. "Tories fail to deliver funding, critics say", *Toronto Star*, January 29.

Department of Finance Canada. 2009. *Canada's Economic Action Plan*. Budget 2009. Ottawa: Her Majesty the Queen in Right of Canada.

Girouard, N. and C. André. 2005. "Measuring Cyclically-Adjusted Budget Balances for OECD Countries". Economics Department Working Paper No. 434. Paris: OECD.

Greenaway, N. 2009. "Social housing money one-off", *The Ottawa Citizen*, February 3, A4.

Torjman, S. 2008. *Poverty Policy*. Ottawa: Caledon Institute of Social Policy, October.

__________. 2009. *Put Your Money Where Your Wealth Is*. Ottawa: Caledon Institute of Social Policy, January.

Yalnizyan, A. and D. MacDonald. 2009. *Leadership for Tough Times: Alternative Federal Budget Fiscal Stimulus Plan*. Ottawa: Canadian Centre for Policy Alternatives.

CANADA'S DECLINING SOCIAL SAFETY NET: EI Reform and the 2009 Budget

Lars Osberg, Dalhousie University

In May of 2008, the unemployment rate in Canada was 6.1%. Talk of looming "labour market shortages" dominated labour market policy discussions, and employment insurance reform was not on the policy agenda. By March of 2009, the unemployment rate had risen to 8.0%, and the OECD was predicting a continuing upward trend – to an annual average of 8.8% in 2009 and 10.5% in 2010.[1] Quite suddenly, the global recession arrived, and Canadians looked for a social safety net.

How adequately does Canada's current Employment Insurance (EI) system fill that need? What could or should be done to improve it? How do the initiatives of the 2009 federal budget compare?

The first section of this paper documents the fact that Canada's current EI system offers relatively little income protection compared with the unemployment insurance system in place in other OECD nations and compared with Canada's (Un)Employment Insurance systems of previous years. The second section discusses briefly the changing literature on unemployment and (un)employment insurance, with its new-found emphasis on the benefits, as well as the costs, of insurance for individuals against employment income risk. The third section then discusses the inadequacy of the 2009 budget's response, and the final section speculates on implications.

---

[1]After peaking in October 2008, employment fell by 363,000 (-2.1%) by May 2009.

Canada's Current EI System in Comparative Perspective

Figure 1 plots Canada's seasonally adjusted unemployment rate from 1976 to February 2009. It documents the recessionary surges in unemployment that dominated the early 1980s and 1990s and the brief period (from 2005 to 2008) of unemployment rates under 7%, which started, after a 30-year drought of labour demand, to give Canadians a brief experience of shorter job search and sometimes rising real wages.

If jobs are easily available, the labour market provides the income earning opportunities that people need, and the characteristics of income support programs are relevant only to an unfortunate few. But Figure 2 (taken from the OECD Employment Outlook of September 2009) illustrates that this is not Canada's current and emerging labour market reality.

Compared to the United States and European nations, Canada was a relative "late adopter" of unemployment insurance. As Perry (1989, p. 681) puts it, the passage of the Unemployment Insurance Act of 1940,

Figure 1: The Unemployment Rate in Canada

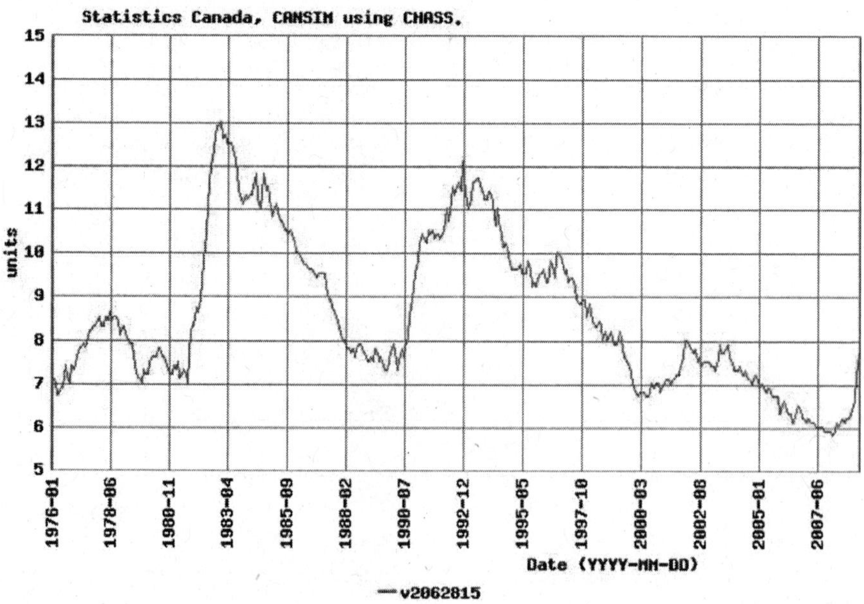

Figure 2: Unemployment Rate Trajectories During Previous Downturns and the Current Downturn

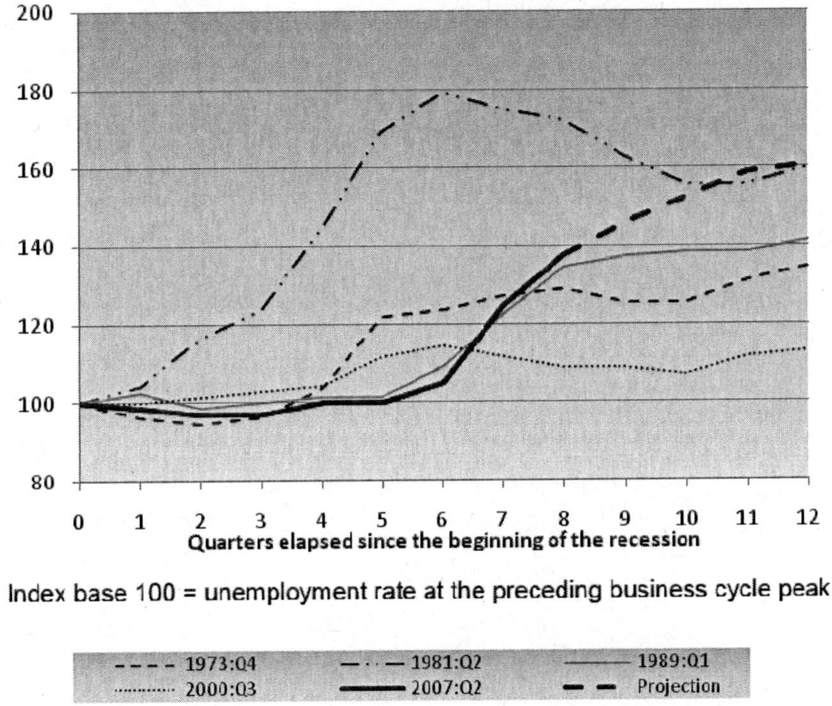

Source: OECD Employment Outlook 2009, at www.oecd.org/dataoecd/62/10/43707194.pdf.

well after the Great Depression of the 1930s, was a belated "recognition of the fact that the historic provincial-municipal relief system was a hopelessly inadequate instrument for dealing with unemployment on a national scale". Changes over the next few decades were relatively modest in scope, but the 1971 revisions were of a different order of magnitude. Figure 3 illustrates both the size of the 1971 revisions and the fairly relentless decline in the benefit replacement rate that has characterized the 38 years since.[2]

[2]The average of the gross unemployment benefit replacement rates for two earnings levels, three family situations. Source: OECD, Tax-Benefit Models. See Martin (1996) for details. At www.oecd.org/document/3/0,3343,en_2649_34637_39617987_1_1_1_1,00.html.

Figure 3: Average Gross Unemployment Benefit Replacement: Canada 1961–2005

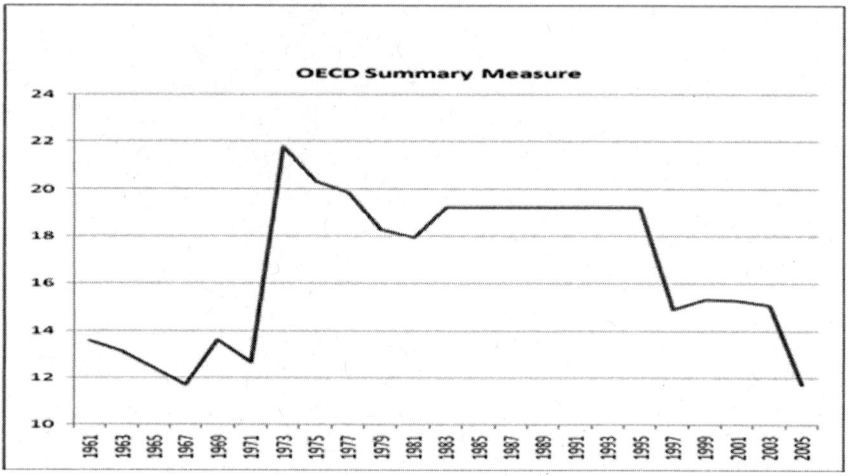

Source: OECD, Tax-Benefit Models. At www.oecd.org/document/3/0,3343,en_2649_34637_39617987_1_1_1_1,00.html.

Because the "replacement rate" (i.e., the ratio of unemployment benefits to employment earnings) varies with the situation of individual workers, and because the accessibility and duration of benefits are hugely important dimensions of any unemployment scheme, a general moral of the international literature is the complexity of real world unemployment income replacement schemes. In looking for an intellectual framework to simplify this real-world complexity, the 1970s and 1980s literature on unemployment insurance in Canada adopted a "labour/leisure choice" perspective. The disincentive effects of unemployment insurance were analyzed in terms of the impact of increased weeks of work per year on benefit duration, while presuming that the option of employment at an unchanging wage was always open to individuals and that unemployment was equivalent to (enjoyable) leisure (e.g., Green and Cousineau, 1976).

The Sargent Index of unemployment insurance incentives has kept this supply-side perspective of voluntary "leisure" choice, but amended the early literature's assumption of an annual accounting framework to reflect the possibility that shorter cycles of work and non-work might be personally optimal. Figure 4 plots the relative value of the index compared to a 1970 base. Although the 1971 revisions produced a sharp

Figure 4: Sargent's Employment Insurance Index: 1976-2002

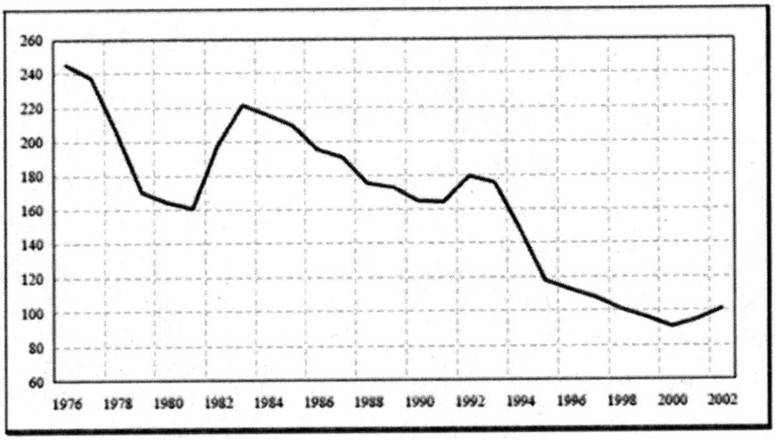

Source: James *et al.* (2007, p. 11).

increase, it has declined to a similar degree as the simpler OECD Summary Measure over the last three decades.[3]

The "replacement rate" can be calculated either as a gross ratio (comparing benefits to employment earnings before tax) or as a net after-tax and after-transfer concept (i.e., after accounting for any changes in income tax or other social transfers and benefits that would be triggered by unemployment or lower annual income). As Figures 5 and 6 illustrate, it makes little difference when comparing Canada to other OECD nations. Canada is close to the lowest by either criterion – as Figure 5 shows, with marginally lower gross replacement than the US average (see also Appendix A Tables A1 and A2).

However, it is not just low-wage Canadians who are exposed to unemployment risk. In thinking about income replacement and economic (in)security, it is important to remember that only insurable earnings up

[3]James *et al.* (2007, p. 11) summarize it as: "This index incorporates a number of the EI parameters, including coverage, benefit levels, benefit duration, and regional differences and is designed to capture the impact of the EI system on unemployment." See also Grey and L'Italien (2001).

Figure 5: Average Gross Unemployment Benefit Replacement

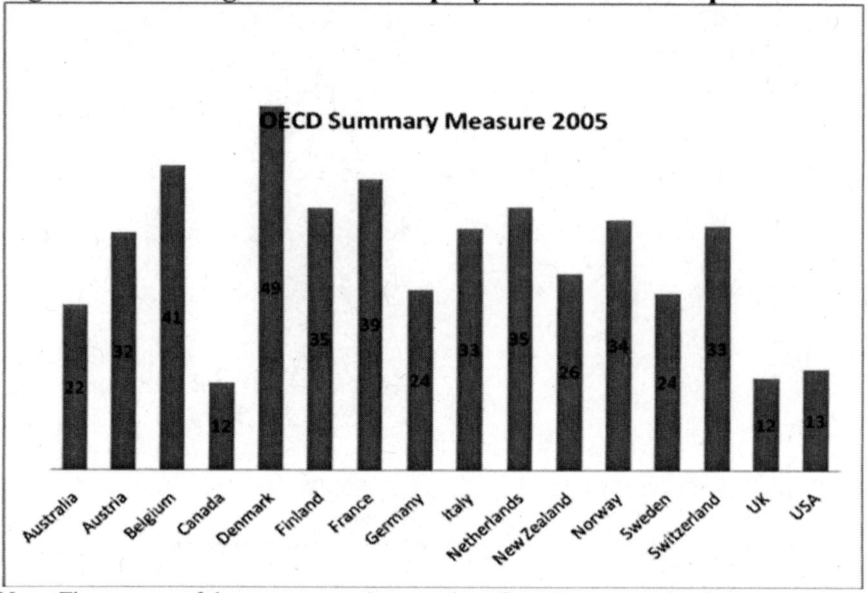

Note: The average of the gross unemployment benefit replacement rates for two earnings levels, three family situations.

Source: OECD, Tax-Benefit Models (see Appendix A for more details), at www.oecd.org/document/3/0,3343,en_2649_34637_39617987_1_1_1_1,00.html.

Figure 6: Net Replacement Rate Over 60 Months of Unemployment, 2006

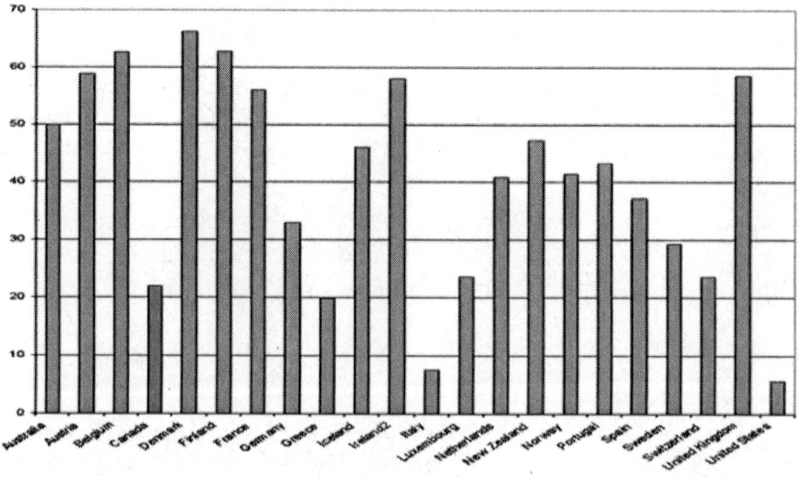

Note: Average over 4 Family types 67% and 100% of AW without Social Assistance.

Source: OECD, Tax-Benefit Models at www.oecd.org/els/social/workincentives.

to the Maximum Insurable Earnings (MIE) are covered by Canada's EI program. The calculations of replacement rates for OECD countries presented in Figures 5 and 6 present an average of the replacement rates for workers at 67% and 100% of average weekly earnings because the OECD is particularly interested in replacement rates for low- and middle-income workers. But because earnings above the MIE (in 2009, $42,300) are not insured, in Canada the replacement rate is substantially lower at the upper end of the earnings distribution.[4] Just under half (in 2009, 44%) (HRSDC 2009) of claims are at the maximum, implying a lower aggregate replacement rate for all such individuals.

EI in Canada in 2009 does not, therefore, replace nearly as much of lost employment income as UI/EI used to in Canada, or as compared to similar unemployed people in the vast majority of OECD nations – even assuming one can get it. But as Figure 7 illustrates, a major problem with Canada's social safety net in this recession, compared to earlier downturns, is how much rarer it is for the unemployed to get regular EI benefits.[5] In January 2009, the seasonally adjusted unemployment rate in Canada was 7.7% – as it also was in February of 1990, near the start of the early-1990s recession – but only a bit over half as many of the unemployed were getting unemployment benefits in 2009, compared to 1990.[6]

A positive feature that Canadian EI has retained from the old UI system is a formula-driven recognition built into program design that the demand side of labour markets does matter. The higher the local unemploy-

---

[4]For example, in the event of unemployment, somebody earning $85,000 (twice the MIE) would have half their earnings replaced at 55%, and the other half replaced at 0%, for an average replacement rate of 27.5%, even before averaging in the impact of the two-week waiting period of zero replacement.

[5]Jones (2004, p. 27) examined alternative EI coverage measures, noting that the "B/U ratio can be used to evaluate program targets, rather than just to evaluate the performance of a program relative to an exogenously given target".

[6]Both the number of beneficiaries and the number of unemployed are volatile and seasonal, so Figure 7 presents a 12-month moving average – by this calculation the B/U ratio for Canada was 83.7% in February 1990 and 43.9% in February 2009. The unsmoothed B/U ratio was 92.3% in February 1990 compared to 52.7% in February 2009. For Ontario, the comparison is 61.9% to 31.5% (smoothed) and 73.5% to 39.9% (unsmoothed). For the United States, the unsmoothed B/U ratio in February 2009 was 38.3%. See www.ows.doleta.gov/unemploy/claims.asp.

Figure 7: UI/EI Beneficiaries to Unemployed Ratio Canada and Ontario: 1976-2009

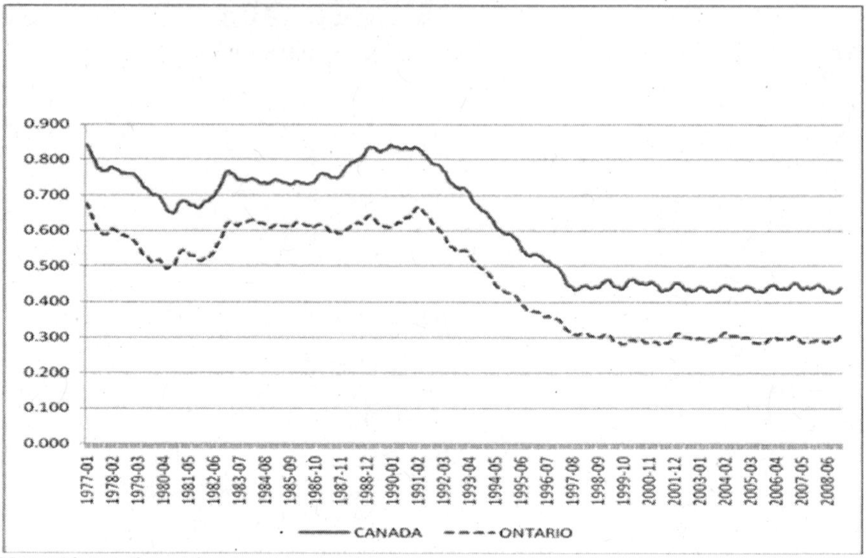

Note: 12 month moving average.
Source: CANSIM V384773, V384807, V2091135, V2094924.

ment rate, the greater the job search difficulties of the unemployed. EI regulations recognize that reality by automatically adjusting entrance requirements and benefit durations – as Table 1 illustrates. In April/May of this year, the minimally qualified EI applicant in Windsor, Ontario, had an entrance requirement that was only 60% of the insurable hours required to qualify in Halifax, Nova Scotia – and would be entitled to benefits for 20% longer – because the local unemployment rate was over twice as high.

Table 1: EI Eligibility and Duration, April 12 to May 9, 2009, Regular Benefits

	Toronto	*Montreal*	*Windsor*	*Halifax*
Unemployment Rate	8.8	8.7	13.2	6.0
Number of Insured Hours Required to Qualify	595	595	420	700
Minimum Weeks Payable	23	23	31	19
Maximum Weeks Payable	47	47	50	41
Unemployed - March 2009	295,300	110,600	42,600	14,100

Source: "Information on EI Economic Regions", at www.hrsdc.gc.ca.

In its *World Economic Outlook* of October 2008, the IMF argued that this design feature of Canada's system should be emulated worldwide. As part of a wider package of counter-recessionary measures, they argued:

> The role of fiscal policy as a macroeconomic stabilizer could be enhanced by strengthening the broader fiscal framework. … First, ... automatic stabilizers could be boosted by making regular tax and transfer programs more cyclically responsive. For example, the generosity of unemployment insurance systems could be automatically increased when the economy is in a downturn and jobs are harder to find. (IMF, 2008a, Foreword, p. xiv)

Although the responsiveness of UI/EI in Canada to local labour market conditions is now recognized internationally as good policy design, it has come at a cost, in political economy terms. Some areas of the country will always have above-average local unemployment, and the rural areas of eastern Canada have fit this description. Table 1 includes both the unemployment rate and the number of unemployed in order to make the point that although Halifax has just under half the labour force of Nova Scotia, in aggregate numbers it is still very small relative to other Canadian local labour markets. Whatever impact UI/EI may or may not have had on unemployment in Atlantic Canada, the population there has never been big enough to have a major impact on Canada's unemployment rate. Furthermore, the urban areas of Atlantic Canada, like Halifax, have throughout the past 30 years had unemployment rates quite similar to comparably sized cities elsewhere in Canada. Nevertheless, regional stereotypes of Atlantic Canada's "dependency" on UI/EI became deeply entrenched in policy discourse in Canada throughout the 1980s and 1990s.[7] The small population base of the rural parts of Atlantic Canada has always implied their quantitative insignificance to Canada's national unemployment problems, but quantitative importance has rarely impeded the political impact of an evocative stereotype. The inherent politeness of Atlantic Canadians usually restrained them from noting that the unemployed of rural Quebec have always outnumbered the unemployed of rural Atlantic Canada, and the rural labour markets of Quebec and Ontario have also had above-average unemployment rates for many years and sometimes similar UI/EI usage patterns. Nevertheless, lasting damage has been done to the sense of national community necessary for Canada's fiscal federalism.

---

[7]Between 2001and 2009, on average 5.8% of Canada's unemployed lived in rural Atlantic Canada. Even considering the data within rural Alantic Canada, there was a continuing confusion between the (sometimes) statistical significance of UI/EI variables and empirically important effect magnitudes.

Changing Perspectives on Unemployment and (Un)Employment Insurance

In the period before Canada's Unemployment Insurance (UI) system morphed into Employment Insurance in 1996, a notable feature of the academic literature on UI[8] was its emphasis on supply-side incentives to individual behaviour. Whether the framework of analysis was labour/leisure choice or optimal choice of reservation wage in a search context, the focus was firmly[9] on how individuals' choices were changed – perhaps distorted – by the provisions of the Canadian UI system and the impact of such distortions on measured unemployment. Part of this emphasis on individual choice was a presumption that unemployment was equivalent to voluntary leisure – that jobs were available to the unemployed and that all non-work time was intrinsically enjoyable.

A large literature in social psychology (e.g., Kelvin and Jarrett, 1985) has long argued otherwise. As Jahoda (1979, p. 423) has put it:

> There are latent consequences of employment as a social institution which match human needs of an enduring kind. First among them is the fact that employment imposes a time structure on the waking day. Secondly, employment implies regularly shared experiences and contacts with people outside the family. Thirdly, employment links an individual to goals and purposes which transcend his own. Fourthly, employment defines aspects of status and identity. Finally, employment enforces activity.
>
> It is these objective consequences of work in complex industrialized societies which help us to understand the motivation to work beyond earning a living; to understand why work is psychologically supportive, even when conditions are bad, and, by the same token, to understand why unemployment is psychologically destructive.

Until fairly recently, this literature had little impact on economics, but the explosion of articles on self-assessed "happiness" and "life satisfaction" in the last decade has begun to remind many economists that people typically do not like being unemployed. Winkelmann (2006, p. 1) is representative of a large literature in saying:

---

[8]For a survey, see Osberg (1996).

[9]There were some exceptions (e.g., Osberg, Erksoy, and Phipps, 1997, 1998a,b).

individual unemployment has a large negative effect on subjective well-being. This mirrors the well documented effect of unemployment on physical health and on mental health. This negative effect appears to be causal: we know from panel data estimators that the association persists once we follow the same individuals over time, and thereby control for individual specific fixed effects. Neither is it the case that unemployed people have a completely different personality, or that they anchor their responses on the well-being scale in a way that is systematically different from the way employed persons anchor theirs. Nor does it seem that there is an instance of reversed causation, i.e., that unhappiness causes unemployment (or, for that matter, that happiness leads to idleness).

It is also clearly understood that the negative effect of unemployment on well-being goes well beyond the effect that the income loss associated with unemployment can bring about. Indeed, the non-pecuniary cost of unemployment seem to exceed the pecuniary cost by far.[10]

Luechinger, Meier, and Stutzer (2008), among others, have also noted that higher unemployment decreases the self-reported well-being of the employed, as well as the unemployed, because "increased *economic insecurity* constitutes an important welfare loss associated with high general unemployment". This accumulation of evidence on the unpleasantness of unemployment has undermined the foundations of perspectives that saw all non-work time as essentially similar, and pleasurable, and the voluntary choice models of unemployment built on those assumptions.

As well, a curious feature of the early academic literature on unemployment insurance was that it never balanced the budget – the impacts of UI benefits on search and labour supply behaviour were discussed without any simultaneous discussion of the behavioural impacts of the premiums necessary to raise the revenue to pay for those benefits. Had both premiums and benefits been jointly considered, the natural question to ask would have been: "Why would rational individuals vote for an Unemployment Insurance system in the first place, knowing that they must expect to pay for any benefits they may receive through payroll or income taxation?"

By looking just at behavioural impacts of UI benefits, the 1980s and 1990s literature on UI focused on one aspect of the system's costs, and it is not entirely surprising that a research agenda that focused solely on

---

[10]See also Frey and Stutzer (2002), Di Tella, MacCulloch, and Oswald (2003), and many others.

costs should come to negative conclusions on impacts. However, if both benefits and costs are considered, then the socially important question is what individuals think they are getting from an unemployment insurance system and how much they will rationally want to purchase. In recent years, a revisionist literature (e.g., Shimer and Werning, 2006; Chetty, 2008) has begun to consider the benefits of unemployment insurance for risk-averse individuals who face some probability of demand-side employment shocks and who may also be liquidity-constrained or otherwise unable to smooth consumption privately when those shocks occur. Given that rational citizens/workers can expect both costs and benefits to vary with the level of income replacement, the issue is how much insurance a typical citizen would like to purchase against the risk of income loss due to unemployment. This new literature therefore asks: "What is the optimal amount of income replacement when unemployed?" – and the basic answer is, "Considerably more than is now available!"

The Federal Budget of 2009

As the Red River flood moved north from the United States to Manitoba in late March of 2009, a repeated theme of Canadian media reports was the contrast between frantic sandbag preparation in US towns and the reassuring readiness of dikes and floodway diversion channels in Canada. The moral drawn was clear: risky and unsatisfactory ad hoc emergency measures are what a society has to do if it has failed to put a system in place to deal with potential looming disasters.

Historically, the United States has reacted to recessions in a somewhat similar way as to floods. In the current recession, as in previous downturns, Congress passed special legislation to extend state unemployment benefits – in 2009, by 13 weeks' additional benefits. This ad hoc, but entirely predictable, aspect of the US unemployment insurance system can be seen as an informal understanding that an inadequate system will be liberalized when a severe recession strikes (see Figure 3). In contrast to a formula-driven system, such as in Canada, ad hoc legislative revisions to unemployment benefits are not necessarily timely, sensitive to local labour market realities, or directed to areas of greatest need. But at least the Americans know how to build a better sandbag dike.

In Canada, the 2009 federal budget extended the maximum duration of EI benefits by five weeks. Entrance requirements and the replacement rate remained unchanged. From the perspective of macroeconomic stimulus, the $575 million that is estimated to be the cost of these five additional weeks of EI benefits amounts to about 1/28th of 1% (i.e., 0.037%) of Canadian GDP.[11] The increase in benefit duration (which is only temporary, for two years) is easily affordable from program revenue – i.e., projected to cost about 3.42% of EI premium income in 2009-10. The IMF may have been saying since October 2008, "The world economy is now entering a major downturn in the face of the most dangerous shock in mature financial markets since the 1930s",[12] but the response of Canada's federal government has been distinctly tepid.

The inadequacy of the federal government's response on EI in 2009 has to be seen in the context of the structural reforms of the mid-1990s to the financing and extent of Canada's social safety net for working-age adults and their families. Historically, provincial social assistance (SA) programs – albeit with low benefit levels and highly invasive asset and family income means testing – have been the backstop to a federally funded UI/EI program. As the C.D. Howe Institute has noted (2008, p. 2):

> macroeconomic conditions have an extremely strong impact on SA rates, and the decline in the unemployment rate from a high of 12% in 1993 to between 6 and 7% at the end of the period of analysis (2005) was the single most important factor in reducing the incidence of SA benefits .... The most significant influence on SA rates appears to be the availability of jobs, and it was the substantial strengthening of the economy after 1996 that had the greatest effect in driving SA rates downward.

But what came down from 1993 to 2005 can now be expected to go back up again, as the unemployment rate rises – and in commenting on the federal budget of 2000, Osberg (2000, p. 226) noted:

> The distribution of fiscal risk from business cycle fluctuations has shifted significantly in recent years. During the recessions of the early

---

[11]See Table 3.5, p. 121, Budget 2009.

[12]IMF (2008a). The IMF has since revised its growth projections significantly downward in two updates – in November 2008 and again in January 2009. And by late April of 2009, as flood waters threatened outlying areas of Winnipeg, the self-congratulatory tone of Canadian media reports on flood preparedness had largely disappeared.

1980s and 1990s, the federal government shared in the costs of cyclical downturn through its responsibility for Unemployment Insurance, and the cost sharing of social assistance under the Canada Assistance Plan.[13] In those recessions, the vast majority of the unemployed got Unemployment Insurance (paid for by the federal government) and those who ran out of UI could sometimes go on social assistance, for which the federal government paid 50% of the cost.

Since the late 1990s, the situation is fundamentally different. A minority of the unemployed are eligible for EI and any increase in social assistance costs produced by a downturn in labour demand will be entirely borne by provincial treasuries. The shift to block funding of transfers to the provinces embodied in the CHST means that the federal government's participation in increased social assistance payments in a recession is now zero. Demands on the social assistance system are likely to be more sensitive to future business cycle downturns because the dramatic decline in eligibility for unemployment insurance payments under EI[14] means that provincial social assistance programs will be called on to carry the burden earlier, and to a far greater degree, than in past recessions.

In addition to "recession proofing" its own fiscal situation at the expense of the provinces, the federal government has backed away from its commitment to the macroeconomic stabilization of output and employment, preferring a commitment to "price stability", with concomitant greater likelihood of output and employment fluctuations. Aggregate cyclical risk has grown and the provinces now have a greater share of that higher risk.

As the daily newspaper headlines are now reminding us, academic talk of a "Great Moderation" in business cycle fluctuations during the late 1990s was decidedly premature. Although the federal government could, and did, reduce its fiscal exposure to business cycle risk in the mid-1990s, that underlying risk remained, although much of its costs were off-loaded to the provinces and to families. Indeed, because both the decline in UI/EI replacement rate on lost earnings and the diminished probability of getting unemployment benefits have worked to weaken the "automatic

[13]In the 1990s recession, federal participation in recessionary costs was greatly limited by the "Cap on CAP", which limited annual increases in Canada Assistance Plan transfers to Ontario, BC, and Alberta to 5% – despite the fact that the recession hit Ontario hardest.

[14]In 1997, the percentage of the unemployed receiving EI benefits was 25%. The beneficiary to unemployed ratio was significantly higher (at 42%), largely because a significant fraction of EI recipients work while on claim (and declare their earnings) and are therefore not counted as unemployed. The decline in UI/EI recipiency in the 1990s has been dramatic – the beneficiary/unemployed ratio in 1989 was 83%. See HRDC (1998, Table 4.1, p. 56).

stabilizer" macroeconomic function of (Un)Employment Insurance, we are now experiencing the consequences – an ensuing increase in the depth of cyclical downturns and accentuated systemic cyclical risk.

The inadequacies of EI and social assistance mean that most of this increased cyclical risk is uninsured and will be borne by families. Since low-wage individuals are especially likely to experience unemployment, the downloading of recessionary risk will have its biggest impacts on disadvantaged Canadians.[15]

Appendix B of this paper presents the references to "Employment Insurance" in the 2009 federal budget. Enhanced training expenditures financed from the EI fund ($2 billion over two years) and the freezing of EI premium rates[16] are the main expenditure items listed in Budget 2009. Neither directly address the needs families have for replacement of lost employment income during a recession.

Until the late 1980s, unemployment insurance in Canada – as in most other OECD nations today – was an unemployment benefits program, in the sense that its costs were the UI benefits it paid to unemployed workers and its revenues came from a payroll tax (the premium income collected from employers and employees). Over the last two decades, however, the federal government has shifted training expenditures, employment service and benefit costs from its Consolidated Revenue Fund expenditures to the UI/EI Account. As well, throughout the late-1990s, premium income greatly exceeded expenditures, and the surplus

---

[15]However, in the 343 pages of Budget 2009, the words "poverty" and "inequality" do not appear, even once. On page 49, "Standard and Poor's Index" is cited as a source reference for housing values, but otherwise, the word "poor" cannot be found either. Budget 2009 does commit to "doubling the tax relief provided by the Working Income Tax Benefit to make work more financially attractive for low-income Canadians", but this omits the most disadvantaged – Canadians who cannot get work – and also begs the question: Are "work incentives" really the big issue, when jobs cannot be found in a recession?

[16]This freezing of the premium rate is described on page 95 as "a projected $4.5 billion stimulus relative to break-even rates", but in Table A1.2 on page 241, only part ($2.449 billion) is booked under "Action to Help Canadians Stimulate Spending". Either way, it seems a bit odd to count something that the government is promising not to do in the future as equivalent to, and an addition to, actual spending initiatives. Should one, with similar reasoning, when one has already counted deficit spending as "stimulus", also count as a "stimulus" the revenue that the government is not raising because it is not increasing income tax rates to balance the aggregate budget?

in EI revenues made a major contribution to the reduction of Canada's general government deficit. In comparing Canada's "social safety net" with that of other OECD nations, one also has to remember that maternity and sickness benefits in Canada have long been paid from the EI account, unlike the situation anywhere else. Whatever one's opinions on the optimality of the expenditures on maternity benefits or human capital formation or deficit reduction funded from the EI account, this funding base for these types of expenditures has been a peculiarity of Canadian political economy, compared to other nations.

Only about 60% of Canada's expenditure on EI account[17] can be currently counted as representing a social safety net in the sense of helping families to meet their immediate cash needs by partially replacing earnings lost due to unemployment. The balance represents a social choice to fund deficit reduction, labour market training programs, and the costs of maternity and family policy from EI premiums – i.e., from a payroll tax base. Retraining programs may (or may not) help improve future employability, but they do not help meet current income needs – and whether or not jobs will materialize to absorb the newly created skills depends heavily on future business cycle recovery, whenever it may occur. Maternity benefits help offset the financial burden of parenthood, but they do not insure against "risk". Although both programs can be defended as appropriate areas of public expenditure, they are not a social safety net for cyclical unemployment risk in any meaningful sense, and both could just as easily be funded from the general tax base (as is normally the case in other OECD nations).

Some of the initiatives of Budget 2009 are eminently sensible. It is entirely reasonable to commit now to not raising payroll taxes (i.e., EI premiums) in 2010, when the business cycle recovery is likely to be as yet fairly faint. As well, it is an overdue good idea to provide "$500 million over two years in a Strategic Training and Transition Fund to support the particular needs of individuals who do not qualify for EI

[17]Canada's Chief Actuary has estimated that total Regular Benefits for 2009 will be $9,545 million, or approximately 54.6% of total EI costs. Maternity, Sickness and Compassionate Benefits are estimated at 22.6% of costs, while Training (Employment Benefits and Support Measures – 12.2%) and Administration costs (9.45%) make up almost all of the remainder. Pro-rating administration costs as proportional to expenditure, Regular Benefits plus their administration costs are 59.8% of total costs. Fishing Benefits (1.58%) and Work-Sharing Benefits (0.08%) blur the picture only slightly (Chief Actuary of Canada, 2009, p. 8).

training, such as the self-employed or those who have been out of work for a prolonged period of time" (p. 94). It has long been a dysfunctional weirdness of Canada's training system that individuals have had to get quite a bit of work in order to get the EI eligibility that would enable access to the training which would help them to get work. As unemployment fell in the period prior to 2008, the resulting escalation of EI entrance requirements meant that the marginally employable who did not get quite enough weeks of work in the reference period were often shut out of training, as well as denied financial benefits – at precisely the time when, if they could have got new skills, their productivity would have been most welcomed by employers.

However, whether or not retraining helps economic efficiency much in a labour market with over 10% unemployment is a harder question. Retraining has its biggest social benefits when it provides the means to reduce structural unemployment by reskilling unemployed workers to enable them to fill job vacancies that would otherwise have stayed empty, costing firms lost sales and production. But 10%+ unemployment signals a generalized cyclical surplus of labour. When workers of all types are unemployed, what exactly is the social benefit of having an even longer queue of qualified potential applicants for any emerging vacancy? Individuals may (or may not) be able to use their shiny new retraining certificate to jump ahead in the job queue, but any such private benefits come at the cost of longer unemployment durations for others. Like digging holes and filling them again, expenditure on training programs can always be counted on as a stimulus to consumer expenditure and macroeconomic demand – but unless new skills are quickly put to work (i.e., unless the recession is short), the outputs of these programs are likely to rust with disuse.

The underlying strategy of Budget 2009 only makes sense if the problems of the Canadian labour market are fundamentally "supply side" in nature and the current recession is just a short, sharp blip in trend. Its overwhelming emphasis on training and improving labour-cost employer incentives at the margin (by freezing EI premiums) is, to be fair, not a set of policies specific to the current government. Retraining, increasing work incentives, and decreasing marginal labour cost have long been the dominant themes of Canadian labour market policy. This is "SOS" – the "Same Old Song" – that has been coming from Ottawa for many years. Budget 2009 just turns up the volume a bit.

However, is same-old good enough? Does it meet the challenge of the times? Budget 2009 may begin Chapter 2 with the statement, "The global economy is in the most synchronized recession in the post-war period and the ongoing financial market crisis is the worst since the 1930s", but it is not about rebuilding a social safety net that can provide Canadians with insurance against unemployment risk in that recession. And as we head deeper into a recession of unknowable length, many Canadians are finding that they need a social safety net more than they ever did before.

Implications

As Anderson and Gascon (2007, p. 1) have noted: "Globalization displaces workers and creates insecurities that increase the demand for social insurance ... As a result, postwar globalization was founded on the principle that the federal government would provide economic security, while free international markets would provide the best aggregate outcomes." Although their context is the United States and their data predate the current recession,[18] their motivation is the observation that "19th century globalization sowed the seeds of its own destruction. Political backlash due to economic insecurity, not economic factors, killed globalization". They note that although aggregate output may expand if trade increases, those gains are at risk if a majority of voters come to feel themselves to be at risk. Their conclusion – "Globalization, by increasing economic insecurity, amplifies workers' demands for social insurance" (p. 17) – is highly relevant to Canada in 2009 given that Canadian EI now arguably provides no more adequate insurance against unemployment risk than US UI now does.[19]

As Green (2009, p. 1) notes: "In general, subjective employment insecurity tracks the unemployment rate" – with the proviso that the secular trend is for any given unemployment rate to produce a somewhat

[18]Using 17 waves of the US General Social Survey 1977-2004 to track subjective insecurity and expectations of cost and probability of job loss, they try to explain why: "According to polls from the 2006 congressional elections, globalization and economic insecurity were the primary concerns of many voters." They conclude: "Our findings verify the economic theory that globalization generates economic volatility leading to worker insecurity."

[19]Because each state administers its own UI system within a federal legislative framework, it is really more accurate to speak of US UI systems. Compared to the average state UI system, Canadian EI provides marginally less adequate initial earnings replacement (see Figure 5 and Table A1), slightly greater probability of entitlement (as measured by the B/U ratio), but shorter average duration of benefits (given the 13-week extension in the United States).

higher level of subjective insecurity (as one might expect in increasingly more "flexible" OECD labour markets). In this context, as the Canadian unemployment rate spikes upward, Budget 2009 is a curious document. At the same time as it was being delivered, the IMF was beginning its update to the World Economic Outlook with the words: "World growth is projected to fall to ½ percent in 2009, its lowest rate since World War II." But there is little sense in Budget 2009 of a recognition that historically bad times are upon us.

(Un)Employment Insurance is the major program by which the Government of Canada has historically helped offset the financial risks of unemployment faced by Canadian families. Unemployment in Canada is now rising at an unprecedented rate and is forecast to stay high for some time to come. Many Canadians are now finding out personally just how little insurance coverage they have. But the response of the Government of Canada has been decidedly meagre. In access, benefit duration, and income replacement levels, EI in Canada is far below OECD norms and the levels of Canadian unemployment insurance in past recessions. Budget 2009 did little to change that. Eligibility and benefit levels remained unchanged, while benefit duration was increased by only five weeks.

Now that they need a social safety net, many Canadians are discovering they do not have much of one. As Table 1 noted, in March 2009 the maximum duration of the EI benefits now being received by the minority who qualify is less than a year. This implies that current EI recipients will run out of benefits sometime before February 2010. What happens then? The OECD estimates that Canadian unemployment in 2010 will be substantially higher (10.5%) than it currently is – a quick rebound in labour demand seems most unlikely.

Reforms to Canada's EI system need to remedy its inadequacies as a safety net for both short-term unemployment and longer-duration unemployment spells. In the current context, Canadians need (1) a plausible expectation that they can get unemployment benefits if laid off – i.e., an easing of entrance requirements, and (2) a safety net for the possibility of a longer-duration recession – i.e., a "second tier" of unemployment benefits (combined with counselling and retraining) to deal with the problems of the long duration unemployed. The question for Canada's political economy is – if the recession drags on – what happens if that is not forthcoming.

Appendix A

Table A1: The OECD Summary Measure of Benefit Entitlements, 1961-2005[1]

	1961	*1971*	*1981*	*1991*	*2001*	*2003*	*2005*
Australia	17	14	22	26	25	22	22
Austria	20	23	29	31	32	32	32
Belgium	42	41	45	42	38	42	41
Canada	14	13	18	19	15	15	12
Denmark	20	34	54	52	51	50	49
Finland	5	8	24	39	35	36	35
France	25	24	31	38	44	39	39
Germany	30	29	29	29	29	29	24
Italy	4	2	1	3	34	34	33
Netherlands	13	48	48	53	53	53	35
New Zealand	42	26	29	30	28	28	26
Norway	4	5	29	39	43	34	34
Sweden	4	6	25	29	24	24	24
Switzerland	2	1	13	22	38	33	33
United Kingdom	24	25	24	18	13	13	12
United States	7	11	15	11	14	14	13

[1]The OECD summary measure is defined as the average of the gross unemployment benefit replacement rates for two earnings levels, three family situations and three durations of unemployment. For further details, see Martin (1996). Pre-2003 data have been revised.

Source: OECD, Tax-Benefit Models, at www.oecd.org/els/social/workincentives.

Table A2: Average of Net Replacement Rates over 60 Months of Unemployment, 2006 (for Four Family Types and Two Earnings Levels, in Percentage)[1]

	Without Social Assistance				
	No Children		*2 Children*		
	Single Person	*One-Earner Married Couple*	*Lone Parent*	*One-Earner Married Couple*	*Overall Average*
Australia	38	33	59	69	50
Austria	51	53	65	66	59
Belgium	58	58	70	65	63
Canada	11	12	32	33	22
Denmark	60	61	72	71	66
Finland	51	60	72	68	63
France	51	52	61	61	56
Germany	24	25	42	41	33
Greece	16	17	23	24	20
Iceland	39	37	58	51	46
Ireland[2]	40	63	62	67	58
Italy	7	7	8	8	8
Luxembourg	17	17	31	30	24
Netherlands	41	39	40	44	41
New Zealand	45	38	61	45	47
Norway	26	27	69	44	41
Portugal	40	40	48	46	43
Spain	36	35	39	39	37
Sweden	15	15	47	40	29
Switzerland	22	22	25	25	24
United Kingdom	49	49	65	71	59
United States	6	6	5	5	6
Average	**34**	**35**	**48**	**46**	**41**

[1]Unweighted averages, for earnings levels of 67% and 100% of AW. Any income taxes payable on unemployment benefits are determined in relation to annualized benefit values (i.e., monthly values multiplied by 12) even if the maximum benefit duration is shorter than 12 months. For married couples, the percentage of AW relates to one spouse only; the second spouse is assumed to be "inactive", with no earnings. Children are aged four and six, and neither child care benefits nor child care costs are considered.

Note: Former Eastern bloc and non-European nations excluded.

Source: OECD, Tax-Benefit Models, at www.oecd.org/els/social/workincentives.

Appendix B

Excerpts from Budget 2009

1. Increasing for two years all regular Employment Insurance (EI) benefit entitlements by five extra weeks and increasing the maximum benefit duration to 50 weeks from 45 weeks. (p. 94)
2. Providing $500 million over two years to extend EI income benefits for Canadians participating in longer-term training, benefiting up to 10,000 workers. (p. 94)
3. Increasing funding for training delivered through the Employment Insurance program by $1 billion over two years. (p. 94)
4. Investing $500 million over two years in a Strategic Training and Transition Fund to support the particular needs of individuals who do not qualify for EI training, such as the self-employed for those who have been out of work for a prolonged period of time. (p. 94)
5. Freezing EI premium rates at $1.73 per $100 for both 2009 and 2010 – their lowest level since 1982 – a projected $4.5 billion stimulus relative to break-even rates. (p. 95)
6. For 2011 and beyond, the Canada Employment Insurance Financing Board (CEIFB) – announced in Budget 2008 – will begin setting premium rates on a break-even basis. In order to ensure that premium rate increases are gradual enough to support a strong economic turnaround, the CEIFB will be mandated not to recover any EI deficits as a result of the two-year $2.9 billion of enhanced EI benefits and training announced in Budget 2009. (p. 106)
7. On the expense side, as the economic slowdown raises unemployment, more people will claim Employment Insurance (EI) benefits. This will support the economy and those most affected by the slowdown. Furthermore, the Government has announced in this budget that the EI premium rate will remain frozen at $1.73 per $100 of insurable earnings in 2010, when the economic recovery is expected to remain fragile, rather than rising to the level needed for the program to break even. Together with the below break-even premium rate in 2009, this will provide an additional $4.5 billion in economic stimulus in 2009 and 2010. (p. 208)
8. Transfers to persons are expected to be higher by $0.9 billion in 2009-10, $1.0 billion in 2010-11, and $0.3 billion in 2011-12, as higher projected unemployment rates result in higher Employment Insurance benefits. Transfers to persons are expected to be $0.4 billion lower in 2013-14, once the economy has recovered. (p. 215)
9. Employment Insurance benefits are projected to increase by 9.0 per cent to $15.6 billion in 2008-09, reflecting higher unemployment, as well as the growth in the maximum weekly benefit, which is indexed to the growth in the average industrial wage. In 2009-10, Employment Insurance benefits are projected to increase by 21.4% to $18.9 billion, and remain at that level in 2010-11, largely due to the two-year $2.9 billion of enhanced EI benefits and training proposed in this budget. (p. 226)

References

Anderson, R.G. and C.S. Gascon. 2007. "The Perils of Globalization: Offshoring and Economic Insecurity of the American Worker", Working Paper 2007-004A, Federal Reserve Bank of St. Louis. At research.stlouisfed.org/wp/2007/2007-004.pdf.

C.D. Howe Institute. 2008. "Dramatic Decline in Welfare Dependency in Canada, Several Factors Responsible", *Communiqué*, Thursday, June 19.

Chetty, R. 2008. "Moral Hazard vs. Liquidity and Optimal Unemployment Insurance", Working Paper 13967. National Bureau of Economic Research. At www.nber.org/papers/w13967.

Di Tella, R., R. MacCulloch, and A. Oswald. 2003. "The Macroeconomics of Happiness", *The Review of Economics and Statistics* 85(4), 809-827.

Frey, B.S. and A. Stutzer. 2002. *Happiness and Economics: How The Economy and Institutions Affect Well-Being.* Princeton: Princeton University Press.

Green, C. and J. Cousineau. 1976. *Unemployment in Canada: The Impacts of Unemployment Insurance.* Ottawa: Economic Council of Canada.

Green, F. 2009. "Subjective Employment Insecurity Around the World", *Cambridge Journal of Regions, Economy and Society*, 1-21.

Grey, A. and F. L'Italien. 2001. "The Sargent Index of EI/UI Behavioural Effects: The Impact of Uncertainty", Applied Research Branch, Strategic Policy, Human Resources Development Canada Research Paper R-02-6E, August.

Human Resources Development Canada (HRDC). 1998. "An Analysis of Employment Insurance Coverage in Canada?" Applied Research Branch, Research Paper W-98-35E, Ottawa, October.

Human Resources and Social Development Canada (HRSDC). 2009. "Report of the Chief Actuary to the Employment Insurance Commission on the Employment Insurance Premium Rate and Maximum Insurable Earnings". At www.rhdcc-hrsdc.gc.ca/eng/employment/ei/premium_rate/2009/transf/ei-ae_2009.pdf.

International Monetary Fund (IMF). 2008a. *World Economic Outlook: A Survey by the Staff of the International Monetary Fund.* Washington, DC: International Monetary Fund.

__________. 2008b. *World Economic Outlook: Update.* November 6.

Jahoda, M. 1979. "The Psychological Meaning of Unemployment", *New Society*, 422-425.

James, S., T. Sargent, R. Barnett, and C. Lavoie. 2007. "The Canadian Labour Force Participation Rate Revisited: Cohort and Wealth Effects Take Hold", Working Paper 2007-01, Finance Canada.

Jones, S.R.G. 2004. *Review of the Employment Insurance Coverage Measures, Final Report for HRSDC,* Contract 9431-04-0004 / 00 October 21.

Kelvin, P. and J. Jarrett. 1985. *Unemployment: Its Social Psychological Effects.* Cambridge: Cambridge University Press.

Luechinger, S., S. Meier, and A. Stutzer. 2008. "Why Does Unemployment Hurt the Employed? Evidence from the Life Satisfaction Gap between the Public and Private Sectors", Public Policy Discussion Paper No. 08-1. Federal Reserve Bank of Boston.

Martin, J.P. 1996. *Measures of Replacement Rates for the Purpose of International Comparisons: A Note*, OECD Economic Studies No. 26.

Osberg, L. 1996. "Unemployment Insurance and Unemployment-Revisited", in B. MacLean (ed.), *The Unemployment Crisis: All for Naught.* Montreal & Kingston: McGill-Queen's University Press, 75-106.

Osberg, L., S. Erksoy, and S. Phipps. 1997. "Unemployment, Unemployment Insurance and the Distribution of Income in Canada in the 1980's", in P. Gottschalk, B. Gustafsson, and E. Palmer (eds.), *Changing Patterns in the Distribution of Economic Welfare – An International Perspective.* Cambridge: Cambridge University Press, 84-107.

__________. 1998a. "How to Value the Poorer Prospects of Youth in the Early 1990s?" *Review of Income and Wealth* 44(1), 43-62.

__________. 1998b. "The Distribution of Income, Wealth and Economic Security: The Impact of Unemployment Insurance Reforms in Canada", in S. Jenkins, A. Kapetyn, and B.M. van Praag (eds.), *The Distribution of Welfare and Household Production: International Perspectives.* Cambridge: Cambridge University Press, 321-345.

__________. 2000. "Poverty Trends and the Canadian Social Union", in H. Lazar (ed.), *Canada: The State of the Federation 1999/2000: Toward a New Mission Statement for Canadian Fiscal Federalism.* Montreal & Kingston: McGill-Queen's University Press, 213-231.

Perry, J.H. 1989. *A Fiscal History of Canada – The Post-War Years.* Toronto: Canadian Tax Foundation.

Shimer, R. and I. Werning. 2006. "Reservation Wages and Unemployment Insurance", Working Paper 12618. At www.nber.org/papers/w12618. National Bureau of Economic Research, October.

Winkelmann, R. 2006. "Unemployment, Social Capital, and Subjective Well-Being", IZA DP No. 2346, September.

ENDING POVERTY THROUGH CHILD BENEFITS: HITTING THE WALL?

Frances Woolley, Carleton University

The direction of social policy in Canada has changed fundamentally since the Conservative government took office in 2006. The National Child Benefit (NCB) program was the cornerstone of social policy under the previous Liberal government. The fatal attraction of NCB was that one program achieved two policy goals. It supported families with children, "ensuring that all of our children have a strong start in life" (HRDC, 1997, p. 1). And it was designed to help parents climb over the so-called welfare wall, promoting "attachment to the workforce ... by ensuring that families will always be better off as a result of working" (HRDC, 1997, p. 6). To get some sense of the strength of the Liberal commitment to the NCB program, one needs only to note that between the first NCB payments in 1998 and the last Liberal budget in 2005, the maximum per-child payment increased more than 160% in real terms.[1]

Since their election into office in 2006, the Conservatives have allowed the NCB program to stagnate. Child policy and income support policy are being divided. There is a trend toward universal recognition of the cost of children: every Canadian child now generates some tax benefits for his or her parent(s). Support for low-income adults is being separated

---

Kevin Milligan's CTaCS parameter database (Milligan, 2009a) was a useful reference for tax-benefit parameters. Mary Rita Holland provided research assistance and Alan Macnaughton helpful comments.

[1]The first year that the NCB Supplement was paid, 1998 (for the 1997 tax year), the nominal benefit was $605. The 2006 payment (for 2005) was $1,945 in nominal values (taken from CTaCS database; see Milligan, 2009a). Adjusted for inflation to 2008 dollars using CPI, the benefit levels are $764 (1998 payment) and $2,034 (2006 payment).

from support for children: the Conservative government's Working Income Tax Benefit provides the same benefits regardless of the number of children a person has. While the NCB program still exists, the real value of payments to the lowest-income families has remained unchanged since the Conservatives took office.

Each one of the new Conservative programs can be dismissed, in the infamous words of Scott Reid, as "beer and popcorn money". Yet taken together, they represent a deep philosophical shift. This essay begins by showing how benefits for families with children have evolved in recent years. Some family types, particularly families with an at-home parent, are particularly advantaged by the policy changes, as is also documented in the Milligan (2009b) paper in this volume. Mothers and fathers are not affected equally by the new policies: some benefits are only available to mothers; other benefits are available only to a parent with taxable income. The new policies do address some problems inherent to the NCB approach. Yet the present policy changes are, in some ways, less significant than the signal they provide as to the likely evolution of policy in the future.

Policies reflect philosophies. The policies introduced by the Conservative government are consistent with a belief in the importance of personal responsibility, a social conservativism that values intact families, parental child care, and a concern with men's social roles. They also reflect efficiency concerns and practical, get-the-vote politics. The Conservative programs provide relatively more benefits to the demographic groups who are generally thought to be more likely to vote conservative, such as married men.

There are a number of serious issues with the Conservative approach to ending poverty and helping children. But at the same time, it can be argued that the Liberal approach had hit the wall in the sense of reaching the limits of its effectiveness. The new policies fill some significant gaps. In particular, they introduce greater horizontal equity into the tax system, have potential efficiency benefits, and begin to address the situation of a large – but largely ignored – group of low-income individuals: unattached non-elderly adults.

Child Policy: Toward Universality

Prior to the election of the Harper Government in 2006, the only broad-based recognition of children in the income tax system was the income-tested Canada Child Tax Benefit. Figure 1 shows the child benefit structure for families with children over six as it was at the time that the Liberal government was defeated in 2006, adjusted for inflation to 2009 (dollar values and details on calculations and sources are provided in Appendix Table A1). The Liberal government's child benefits were income-tested, refundable tax credits, concentrated on low- and moderate-income families. Benefits were reduced or taxed back when income exceeded certain thresholds or cut-offs, shown as Cut-Off A in Figure 1. If the Liberal structure had been kept in place, a typical two-parent family – average income,[2] two children, two earners – would be receiving just over $400 in child benefits this year, or about $35 per month. To put this number into historical perspective, 25 years ago, in 1974, that same family would have been receiving $480 in family allowance payments, or over $2,000 in 2009 dollars.[3]

The Conservative government has, through successive budget initiatives, extended recognition of children up the income scale. Figure 1 shows, in the lightest shade of grey, the net effect of Conservative initiatives that are available to all families with children: the Amount for Children non-refundable credit (introduced in 2007) and the increase, from Cut-Off A to Cut-Off B, in amount of income a family can earn before child benefits begin to be taxed back (in the 2009 budget). These initiatives provide no benefits for the lowest-income families. Given the other non-refundable credits available to these households (personal, eligible dependant, employment, CPP/EI, public transit, and so on), they are unlikely to pay enough taxes to benefit from a non-refundable tax credit. If their incomes are below Cut-Off A, they will not benefit from the increase in the tax-back threshold. However, as Figure 1 shows, for an average two-earner family, non-refundable tax credits are now more

---

[2]With children over seven. Incomes = 2007 average market income (economic families), taken from www40.statcan.gc.ca/l01/cst01/famil22a-eng.htm.2007 incomes adjusted to 2008 by using CPI factor 114.1/111.5 taken from www40.statcan.gc.ca/l01/cst01/econ46a-eng.htm. April 2009 CPI data shows no inflation in 2009. The overwhelming majority of two-parent families have at least two earners: www.statcan.gc.ca/pub/75-202-x/2007000/t205-eng.htm.

[3]1974 family allowance figure and CPI taken from CTaCS parameter database.

Figure 1: Child Benefits for Families with Two Children, 2009

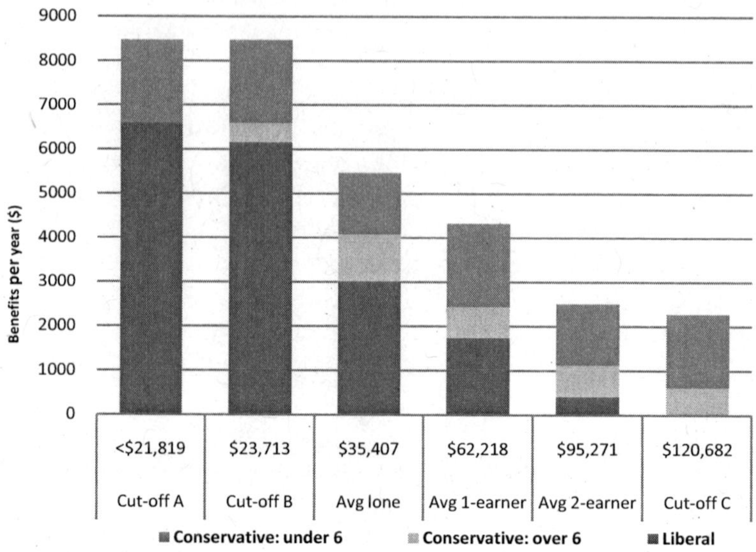

important than child tax benefits. If Figure 1 included the programs announced in the 2008 budget – Fitness Amount generating tax savings of up to $75 per child[4] and the $100 increase in the Canada Education Savings Grant to match parental Registered Education Savings Plan contributions – there would be even more tax recognition of the cost of children at higher income levels.

Families with children under the age of seven have been most affected by Conservative child benefit policies, as shown in the medium-grey bar in Figure 1.[5] In the 2006 budget, the Conservatives eliminated the NCB supplement for children under seven and abandoned the Liberals' planned national child care strategy. Instead, a Universal Child Care

---

[4]I have excluded it because there is, as yet, no data available on the take-up of the Fitness Amount.

[5]For simplicity sake, children aged six are not shown in Figure 1. Six-year-olds were eligible for the NCB Supplement for children under seven, but are not eligible for the UCCB. Hence, these families experienced additional losses of about $260 per child in 2009 dollars as a result of the Conservative policy changes.

Benefit (UCCB) of $1,200 per child under the age of six, taxable in the hands of the lower-income parent, was introduced. Like other Conservative policies, the UCCB tends to make benefits for children more universal. As Figure 1 shows, for average-income and above two-parent families, the UCCB represents a major change in the financial recognition of the cost of children. If it is "beer and popcorn" money, where does that leave the pre-UCCB set of benefits?

From "Attachment to the Workforce" to Choice in Child Care

The Conservative Party is committed to efficiency in government:

> The Conservative Party believes the government should implement de tailed processes to streamline government services and eliminate waste, unnecessary overlap and duplication between the levels of government. (www.conservative.ca/media/2008-PolicyDeclaration-e.pdf)

So why create new programs for families with children? Wouldn't it have been administratively simpler (eliminating waste, unnecessary overlap, and duplication) to achieve the policy outcomes shown in Figure 1 just by changing the rate at which child benefits are taxed back from higher-income families?

A possible reason why the administratively simpler option was not chosen is that the Conservative government wished to target benefits toward particular types of families making particular types of choices. Figure 2 compares the net effect of the child benefit policy changes on various family types: lone-parent, two-parent one-earner, and two-parent two-earner families at moderate and high income levels.[6] These families are not intended to be representative – there are not many lone parents with two children under six and a net family income of $120,000. They simply serve to make two points. First, high-income families typically benefited more from the UCCB than other family types. Low-income and average-income families lost their income-tested benefits when the UCCB was introduced; high-income families did not.

---

[6]In calculating marginal tax rates, I assumed a 1/3: 2/3 income split for two-earner families.

Figure 2: Impact of Conservative Policy Changes by Family Type, Two Children Under Six

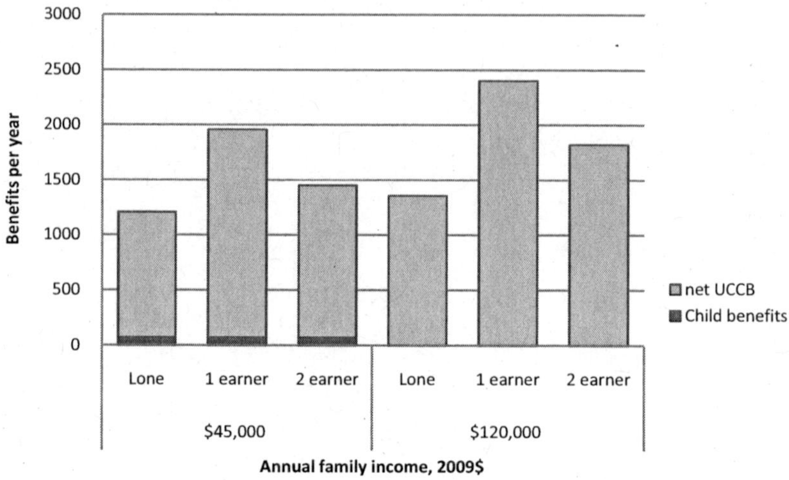

Second, one-earner two-parent families gain substantially more from the UCCB than other family types. The UCCB is taxable in the hands of the lower income earner or, for lone parents, in the hands of the lone parent. One-earner two-parent families pay no tax on UCCB payments. At any given level of family income, lone-parent families pay the most tax on UCCB. By way of contrast, the reduction in the Child Tax Benefit tax-back rate in the 2009 budget, shown as the small black bar in Figure 2, has the same value to each family type at a given income level.

The 2006 budget framed the UCCB in terms of choice: "Through the proposed UCCB, parents will be able to choose the child care option that best suits their families' needs – whether that means formal child care, informal care through neighbours or relatives, or a parent staying at home" (Department of Finance, 2006, p. 57). But the design of the UCCB makes one particular choice, parental care for children, more attractive than others. In 1999, while still in opposition, the Conservative Party moved: "That, in the opinion of this House, the federal tax system should be reformed to end discrimination against single-income families with children".[7] The design of the UCCB is consistent with the

[7]Bevilacqua and Discepola (1999), www2.parl.gc.ca/HousePublications/Publication.aspx?DocId=1031602&Language=E&Mode=1&Parl=36&Ses=1&File=12.

Conservatives' long-term commitment to reducing the taxes paid by single-earner families relative to two-earner families at the same income level.

However it is important to realize that any program that replaces child care subsidies, such as those planned by the Liberals, with cash transfers, like the UCCB, would be predicted to decrease female labour force participation. Figure 3 makes this point with basic microeconomic analysis, by comparing a hypothetical child care subsidy with a cash transfer that provides the same per-person transfer. Child care subsidies have the same effect as an increase in the wage rate. They make working for pay more worthwhile and cause substitution toward paid employment and away from time at home. A cash transfer has no substitution effect, only an income effect. Because a higher income means people want to spend more on things that they like, a cash transfer will tend to increase time spent at home, as long as people like spending time with their children.

Figure 3: Comparison of Child Care Subsidies and Cash Transfers on Time in Household

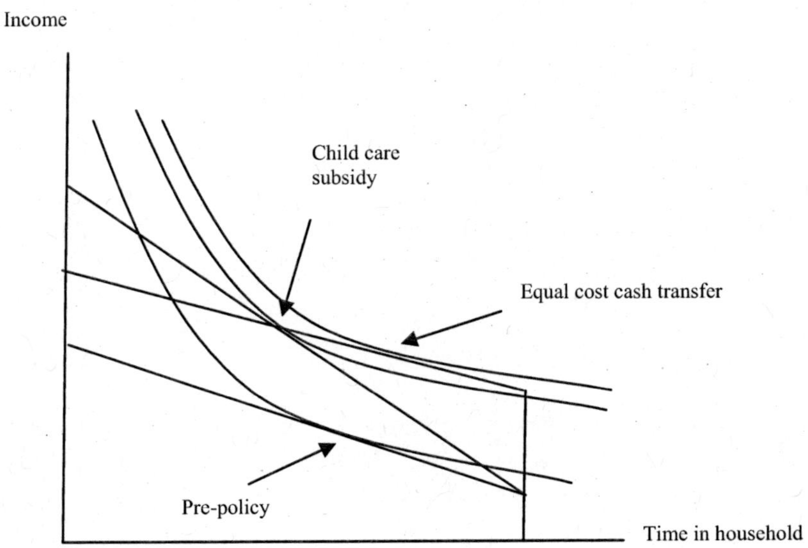

Figure 3 may also provide some additional insight as to why the Liberal government lost in 2006 despite running on a platform that included up to $11 billion in child care spending.[8] My analysis suggests that a parent is better off – on a higher indifference curve – with a cash transfer than with a child care subsidy. There may be good reasons to subsidize child care – as a proven way of lifting single parents out of poverty, for example (Kimmel, 1995). But Figure 3 suggests that it is far from obvious that child care subsidies are the best way to make parents and children happy.

Policy Framing: From "Investing in Canada's Children" to Parental Responsibility

The decision to substitute the UCCB for an expanded NCB can be explained by the Conservative commitment to parental care. But what about the new Amount for Children non-refundable credit? Refundable credits and non-refundable credits have the same net effect on family income, so, from an economic point of view, there is no difference between the two. And surely increasing the size of already existing child benefit cheques would have involved lower administrative costs than further complicating Canada's income tax system?

One explanation for the introduction of the Amount for Children non-refundable credit is the way in which policies are framed. One of the founding principles of the Conservative Party is:

> A belief that it is the responsibility of individuals to provide for themselves, their families and their dependents, while recognizing that government must respond to those who require assistance and compassion.[9]

Marjorie Kornhauser (2009) argues that the means by which benefits are delivered "frames" the policy in a particular way. She argues, in the American context, that benefits delivered through the income tax system are congruent with a world view that "favors individualism, autonomy, and self-reliance". Non-refundable tax credits convey the message: we

---

[8] www.cbc.ca/story/canadavotes2006/national/2005/12/06/elxn-martin-childcare.html.

[9] www.conservative.ca/EN/4679/.

recognize that the income you earn goes to support your family, and adjust your taxes accordingly.

Refundable credits can be framed in a way that is appealing to Conservative voters, as the case of the UCCB suggests. Kornhauser (2009) argues that Conservative norms tend to value equal opportunity and levelling the playing field, and these values can be harnessed in support of universal human capital programs, for example. The first line of the policy pamphlet introducing the NCB program is "investing in children" (HRDC, 1997, p. 1), so clearly there was an attempt to use a human capital frame to support Liberal policies. Yet because NCB was also being framed as an anti-poverty program, possibly the human capital investment message was lost. In addition, because child benefits were and are targeted, many families receive very small cheques – as noted earlier, the average two-earner, two-parent family receives a cheque of about $35 per month. It is hard to frame such a small cheque as a significant investment in children.

Gender Politics

Economists are often (rightly) skeptical of psychological explanations, preferring to think about incentives – for example, politicians having an incentive to design policies in ways that maximize votes. Gender politics – and vote maximization – does indeed provide an alternative explanation of why the Conservatives would introduce a new non-refundable tax credit rather than increasing the existing child benefit programs.

The National Child Benefit and Child Tax Benefit are paid to the person "primarily responsible for the care and upbringing of a child" (www.cra-arc.gc.ca/E/pbg/tf/rc66/rc66-08e.pdf). Generally, this is assumed to be the mother: "If there is a female parent who lives with the child, we usually consider her to be this person." The Universal Child Care Benefit is also generally paid to mothers.

The new credits introduced in Conservative budgets are, ostensibly, gender-neutral. The "Amount for Children" non-refundable credit could, in theory, be claimed by either parent as long as the parent has some amount of tax payable. As a tax credit (as opposed to a deduction), its value is independent of the parent's income. The same is true of the Fitness Amount Tax Credit.

Unfortunately, the income taxation statistics that would allow us to know who claims the new tax credits are not yet available. Yet we can make some inferences about the likely distribution of benefits by examining existing tax credits. There are other non-refundable credits that, like new tax credits, are generally only claimed by one spouse, but can be freely transferred between spouses: education amounts transferred from children to parents, the charitable donations credit and the caregiver amount.

Canada Revenue Agency's income taxation statistics (CRA, 2008) do not separate own-account education claims from claims transferred from parents to children. However, for adults in the 45-to-60 age range, it seems reasonable to expect that the education amounts claimed will primarily be amounts transferred from children. In this age range, women receive 38% of education tax credits; men receive 62%.[10] Charitable donations tell a similar story. A couple can reduce taxes by consolidating their charitable donations on one tax return – but except for people in Ontario, Nova Scotia, PEI and Yukon subject to provincial/territorial surtaxes – it doesn't matter which one.[11] According to the National Survey of Giving, Volunteering and Participating, 51% of charitable donations are made by men, 49% by women (Hall *et al.*, 2006, p. 17). However, according to Canada Revenue Agency's taxation statistics, 67% of charitable donations claimed on income tax returns are claimed by men, 33% by women (CRA, 2008). The Caregiver amount, that claimed by those caring for disabled or aged relatives, conforms to the same pattern. In 2006, 60% of the Caregiver amounts were claimed by men.

It is not simply that men earn more than women or that men pay more in taxes, although this is the case. The employment amount tax credit, even though it was introduced as part of a package of tax relief for trades-people, goes to women and men in almost exactly equal proportions – 49% to women, 51% to men.[12] Women actually benefit more from the public transit amount tax credit than men. Looking at the distribution of tax credit claims, a clear pattern emerges: when a credit can be claimed

---

[10]All figures in this paragraph are calculated from CRA (2008), interim statistics, Table 4A.

[11]Because of the graduated structure of the charitable donations tax credit (a 15% credit on the first $200 or so claimed, a 29% credit on amounts over and above $200), consolidating donations saves (.29-.15)*$200, or $28 federally.

[12]Department of Finance (2006), at www.fin.gc.ca/budget06/bp/bpc3b-eng.asp#tradespeople.

by both men and women, it is. When a credit can be claimed by only one spouse, most often it is claimed by men.[13]

There are a number of reasons why credits may end up on male returns. First, as Lars Osberg suggested at the JDI conference, some tax preparation software has "maximize benefit" routines that allocate credits to the higher-income spouse, even if the value of the credit is independent of the spouse's income. Given that some provinces have surtaxes that make credits more valuable to the higher-income spouse, overall this is a good strategy. Usually, women earn less than their partners, hence are less likely to have credits allocated to them. Second, Canada's tax system is complex. Most people do not understand exactly how their taxes are calculated and, being influenced by American media, may assume that Canadian credits, like American deductions, are worth more to higher-income earners. (And one can see why politicians might be in no hurry to educate taxpayers. A $500 Fitness Amount Tax Credit sounds much more impressive than a $75 tax refund.) Third, fathers might have some sense that they pay the bills and thus they deserve the non-refundable tax credit.

Whatever forces determine the allocation of credits between men and women, one thing is clear: it matters. Lundberg, Pollak, and Wales (1997) find, using UK data, that the substitution of a refundable child credit for a non-refundable tax deduction had a real impact on household spending patterns. Burton, Phipps, and Woolley (2007) find real effects from the change in the intra-household distribution of income created by women's receipt of Old Age Security. There is a considerable literature that finds that payments made to women have a different effect on family spending than payments made to men. In particular, they are more likely to be spent for the direct benefit of children – for example, for chldren's clothing or for gifts. So why not put funds in women's hands? One explanation is that the Conservative government wants to deliver results to people more likely to vote Conservative; another is that there is a deeper agenda.

---

[13]One exception is the medical expenses tax credit, which may be maximized by being placed on the lower-income spouse's return. More women than men claim medical expenses; this may reflect either tax minimizing allocation of expenses or women's longer life expectancy, and the concomitant greater probability of having long-term care or other expenses.

"Non-Working Women Are Mothers; Non-Working Men, a Blight"

A 1996 article in *The Economist* warned that men could become tomorrow's second sex because of female success and male failure in education and in the labour market. It painted a dire picture:

> Consider for a moment a neighbourhood in which most working-age women are not in paid jobs. This may conjure up a picture of tidy homes, children at play and gossip. Now think of a neighbourhood in which most men are jobless. The picture is more sinister. Areas of male idleness are considered, and often are, places of deterioration, disorder and danger. Non-working women are mothers; non-working men, a blight. (*The Economist*, 1996)

The Economist then goes on to argue, "When men find it impossible to provide, they also seem to find it difficult to learn the nurturing bits." According to this view of the world, men's involvement in family life – fatherhood – is intrinsically linked to men's ability to find employment and contribute to their family.

The connections between lack of family, joblessness, and poverty identified by *The Economist* over ten years ago are still relevant. In Canada in 2007, non-elderly unattached individuals were the most economically vulnerable group in Canada, with 29.7% of unattached men living with low incomes and 35.1% of unattached women.[14] Ironically, the relative vulnerability of the unattached may reflect the success of the NCB. In 1997, when the NCB was introduced, lone parents were more likely than unattached men to have incomes below the low-income cut-off; in 2007, unattached non-elderly men were 40% more likely to be in a low-income situation than lone parents (unattached non-elderly women continue to have the highest rate of low incomes of any group). This reversal is exactly what we would expect given the Liberal government's decision to focus social policy on child benefits: the aim of the policy was to take children out of poverty, and that involved taking lone parents out of poverty.

One of the best features of the Working Income Tax Benefit (WITB) is that it can be claimed by single or childless adults, as well as parents, and hence goes some way toward reducing the vulnerability of adults living

---

[14]Statistics Canada (2009), Table 13.1, at www.statcan.gc.ca/pub/75-202-x/2007000/t202-eng.htm.

alone. Yet even after the enrichments announced in the 2009 benefit, the maximum benefit is only $925 for a single person, $1,680 for a couple. To put these numbers into perspective, Statistics Canada (2009) estimates that the average low-income single male had an income $7,400 below the low-income cut-off in 2007. The WITB alone will not take an average low-income single out of poverty.

But perhaps what matters is not the absolute amount of the WITB, but rather the incentives that the WITB creates. The WITB was introduced in the 2006 federal budget because "Reducing barriers to paid employment is essential to fostering opportunities and economic growth." The benefit aimed to "improve incentives to work for low-income Canadians" (Department of Finance, 2006). One key difference between the WITB and other social programs is that receipt is conditional upon participation in paid work. WITB is not paid until earnings reach $3,000. Benefits are gradually phased in between earnings of $3,000 and (for singles) $6,700, providing a 25% subsidy to earnings within this range. Once income (that is, earnings plus employment insurance or other benefits) exceeds $10,500 (for singles), the WITB is gradually taxed back.

The design is consistent with the rhetoric of personal responsibility. But what about the reality? To find out how many people had improved work incentives as a result of the WITB, I used the 2006 public-use version of the Survey of Labour and Income Dynamics to estimate the earnings and incomes of unattached adults under 65 (identified as those living in a one-person census family) who were not students. Of these unattached adults, just 2% had earnings in the range where the WITB was being phased in. A much greater number, 14%, had after-tax incomes in the WITB phase-out range so face reduced work incentives as a result of the program. A more serious concern is that another approximately 14% of unattached individuals have earnings below $3,000, yet are not eligible for the WITB.

A little thought reveals a reason why a policy-maker might want to exclude these very low-earning adults from the WITB. Many individuals with no earnings receive CPP/QPP disability payments, workers compensation payments, Employment Insurance, welfare or other social payments – or live at home with their parents. If WITB is added to those payments, work incentives are not improved. Rather, life on the dole becomes less painful. When the NCB was introduced, provinces had the option of reducing welfare payments by the amount of the NCB, and a number of provinces did, in an attempt to lessen the difference between income on welfare and income in work. One could see integration of the WITB with other social programs as a long-term social policy goal.

Given the diversity of programs supporting unattached adults, such integration may be even more difficult to achieve than for the NCB. In the meantime, it is best to think of the WITB "work incentives" as essentially a way of excluding people on existing social programs, rather than something that will create positive incentives for employment.

The WITB as currently structured has a limited potential to increase work incentives. But it differs from the NCB in a number of key respects, all of which could potentially be associated with other sorts of incentive effects. First, the WITB can be claimed by only one adult in a two-adult family – but the government does not specify which one must claim. This is, in some ways, an odd policy choice: if the aim of the policy is to increase work incentives, wouldn't it make more sense to tie an individual's benefits to his or her own earnings? Unfortunately, there is no published information on the gender breakdown of WITB recipients – by which I mean who actually receives the cheque – or the recipients of a similarly structured credit, the GST credit. But because WITB can be claimed by fathers, it potentially reinforces paternal contributions to the family. The message is "Dad contributes" rather than "I have enough income to go it alone."

A second key difference between the WITB and the NCB is that WITB payments are independent of the number of children one has. Any adult is eligible, except for students. By way of contrast, generous child benefits could conceivably cause more people (especially poor people?) to conceive. "Family values" have not, as far as I am aware, ever been mentioned as a motivation for WITB. However, it is interesting that the WITB removes the incentive to have more children that is present in child benefit programs.

A third difference between the WITB and the NCB is the timeliness of benefit delivery. Child benefits received from July 2009 to June 2010 will be based on income in the 2008 taxation year. When an economy is growing and incomes are rising, this lack of responsiveness may not be a problem. When the economy contracts – as is happening at present – and families see large reductions in incomes, the child benefit's lack of responsiveness may become an issue. The WITB, unlike the NCB, can be paid in advance. It is not clear to what extent this will relieve the timeliness problem, however. US experience with the Earned Income Tax Credit finds that people tend not to take up advance payment options, in part because repaying overpayments is so difficult for very low-income individuals (Romich and Weisner, 2000).

A final difference between the NCB and the WITB is the incentives for marriage or divorce. The NCB uses the same family income threshold, regardless of the number of adults in a family. Consider, for example, a two-child family in which each parent has a net income of $20,000 per year before tax. If one parent leaves, the increase in NCB payments (for a two-child family, $3,747 in 2009), together with the possibility of claiming a dependent amount tax credit as a single parent (worth $1,440 federally and $446 in Ontario), replace one third of the departing parent's after-tax income. Child support (with a guideline amount of $308 per month) replaces another third. Taking into account the savings in groceries and other costs from having one less adult in the household, it is easy to see how parents would be better off apart than together. The WITB is, at present, so small that it makes a trivial difference to the marriage or separation decision. But because benefits are higher and taxed back more slowly in two-adult families, WITB does not create as many incentives for divorce or separation as the NCB does.

I am not aware of any policy statement that presents the WITB as pro-family values. However, if someone had been trying to come up with an alternative-benefit design that created positive incentives for parents to stay together, reinforced the role of fathers within families, and discouraged reckless child-bearing, they might well have ended up with a program that looked something like the WITB.

Doing the Right Thing – But for the Wrong Reasons?

A number of years ago, Nick Rowe and I wrote a paper entitled "The Efficiency Case for Universality" (Rowe and Woolley, 1999). In this paper, we made a straightforward argument for universal benefits. If, say, child benefits are targeted toward low- and middle-income families, they must at some point be taxed back. The tax-back of benefits means that people with children face higher marginal tax rates than people without children. Unless there is some reason to believe that parents have particularly inelastic labour supplies, efficiency can be increased by universalizing benefits. Horizontal equity also suggests that a taxpayer with children has a lower ability to pay taxes than a childless taxpayer at the same income level and should have their tax liabilities adjusted accordingly. Hence, for both efficiency and equity reasons, the Conservative move to universalize benefits for children is the right thing to do.

It is, however, unfortunate that the Conservative government placed child benefits in the hands of the higher-income earner through the Amount for Children non-refundable credit, rather than the person primarily responsible for the care of the child, or divided equally between both parents. It is also unfortunate that the new programs introduced further complicate the tax system when a simple alternative – enriching existing child benefits – was available. As it is, the government has the cost of implementing new programs *and* the cost of mailing out numerous child benefit cheques for trivial amounts to middle class families.

Perhaps the Conservative government was searching for what are in Ottawa-speak called "announcables" – new initiatives that can be announced by the Finance Minister on budget day. The Fitness Amount Tax Credit in the 2008 budget giving a non-refundable tax credit for children's participation in physical activities is a typical "announcable". The amount of the credit is so small – the $500 tax credit lowers taxes owing by $75 – relative to the cost of issuing and verifying receipts, changing tax software, and so on, or relative to the time and money costs of having a child in, say, hockey, that it is hard to believe it has substantial economic effects. It is sad to think that votes can be bought so cheaply.

Appendix Table A1: Data for Figure 1 Comparing 2005 (Liberal) and Current (Conservative) Child-Related Benefits

Two children value of credits (2009)			Female lone parent, one earner	Two parent, one earner	Two parent, mean income	CTB eliminated (new)
	<$21,819 Cut-off A	$23,713 Cut-off B	$35,407	$62,218	$95,271	$120,682
NCB (2005)	3913	3477	352	0	0	0
CTB (2005)	2680	2680	2680	1745	422	0
Change NCB		436	436	0	0	0
Change CTB				76	76	0
Child <18			627	627	627	627
UCCB	2400	2400	2400	2400	2400	2400
NCB <7	518	518	518	518	518	0
MTR	0	0	0.21	0	0.21	0
Net UCCB	1882	1882	1377	1882	1377	1652

Child benefit amounts taken from www.budget.gc.ca/2009/plan/bpc3b-eng.asp#24.

CTB and NCB are indexed for inflation, so their real value does not change over time.

Child under 18 tax credit evaluated at 2009 parameter values taken from CTaCS parameter database.

Incomes = 2007 average market income (economic families), taken from www40.statcan.gc.ca/101/cst01/famil22a-eng.htm.

2007 incomes adjusted to 2008 by using CPI factor 114.1/111.5, taken from www40.statcan.gc.ca/l01/cst01/econ46a-eng.htm.

April 2009 CPI=13.9 according to www40.statcan.gc.ca/l01/cst01/dsbbcan-eng.htm.

UCCB amount verified from www.cra-arc.gc.ca/bnfts/uccb-puge/fq_pymnts-eng.html.

2005 NCB amount = 243 per child. Adjusted for inflation using www40.statcan.gc.ca/l01/cst01/econ46a-eng.htm 2005=107, 2008=114.1, no inflation to date in 2009.

UCCB is taxed at lower earner's MTR. Estimated at zero for net family incomes of $23,713 (by estimating value of spousal/dependant/employment/CPP/EI amounts).

MTR on UCCB for incomes $35,407 is sum of federal and provincial (Ontario) rates, as UCCB does not reduce NCB or CTB amounts.

References

Bevilacqua, M. and N. Discepola. 1999. *For the Benefit of Our Children: Improving Tax Fairness: Nineteenth Report of the Standing Committee on Finance*. Ottawa: House of Commons: Standing Committee on Finance. At www2.parl.gc.ca/HousePublications/Publication.aspx?DocId=1031602&Language=E&Mode=1&Parl=36&Ses=1.

Burton, P., S. Phipps, and F. Woolley. 2007. "Inequality Within the Household Reconsidered", in J. Micklewright and S. Jenkins (eds.), *Inequality and Poverty Re-Examined.* Oxford: Oxford University Press.

Canada Revenue Agency (CRA). 2008. *Income Statistics, 2008.* Ottawa: Canada Revenue Agency. At www.cra-arc.gc.ca/gncy/stts/menu-eng.html.

Department of Finance. 2006. *Restoring Fiscal Balance in Canada: Focusing on Priorities: Budget 2006.* Ottawa: Department of Finance. At epe.lac-bac.gc.ca/100/200/301/finance/budget_2006/restoring-e/pdf/fp2006e.pdf.

Hall, M., D. Lasby, G. Gumulka, and C. Tryon. 2006. *Caring Canadians, Involved Canadians: Highlights from the 2004 Canada Survey of Giving, Volunteering and Participating.* Ottawa: Statistics Canada. At www.statcan.gc.ca/pub/71-542-x/71-542-x2006001-eng.pdf.

Human Resources Development Canada (HRDC). 1997. *The National Child Benefit: Building a Better Future for Canadian Children.* Ottawa: Human Resources Development Canada.

Kimmel, J. 1995. "The Effectiveness of Child-Care Subsidies in Encouraging the Welfare-to-Work Transition of Low-Income Single Mothers", *American Economic Review* 85(2), 271-275. At www.jstor.org/stable/2117931.

Kornhauser, M. 2009. "Cognitive Theory and the Delivery of Welfare Benefits", *Loyola University Chicago Law Journal* 40(2), 253-296. At www.luc.edu/law/activities/publications/lljdocs/vol40_no2/kornhauser_welfare.pdf.

Lundberg, S.J., R.A. Pollak, and T.J. Wales. 1997. "Do Husbands and Wives Pool Their Resources? Evidence from the United Kingdom Child Benefit", *Journal of Human Resources* 32(3), 463-480. At www.jstor.org/stable/146179.

Milligan, K. 2009a. Canadian Tax and Credit Simulator. Database, software and documentation, Version 2009-1.

__________. 2009b. "What Have Four Conservative Budgets Done to Personal Income Taxes?" This volume.

Romich, J. and T. Weisner. 2000. "How Families View and Use the EITC: Advance Payment versus Lump Sum Delivery", *National Tax Journal* 53(4).

Rowe, P.N. and F. Woolley. 1999. "The Efficiency Case for Universality", *Canadian Journal of Economics* 32(2), 613-629.

Statistics Canada. 2009. *Income in Canada.* Ottawa: Statistics Canada, Catalogue No. 75-202-XWE.

The Economist. 1996. "Men: Tomorrow's Second Sex", 28 September. Cover Story.

Session Six
THE FEDERAL BUDGET AND THE ENVIRONMENT

THE 2009 FEDERAL BUDGET AND THE ENVIRONMENT: MISSED OPPORTUNITIES AND MISGUIDED DIRECTIONS

Nancy Olewiler, Simon Fraser University

Introduction

The environment was a minor element in the federal budget of 2009. While there were some new initiatives, many were recycled or repackaged from previous budgets. I examine the 2009 budget in the context of the 2007 and 2008 federal budgets. I then assess the environmental high and low points in Budget 2009 in four areas:

- Infrastructure investment
- Energy efficiency
- GHGs and climate change
- Meeting environmental targets.

To the extent that infrastructure investment is targeted at environmental projects, the budget is good news, but there are many areas for concern, and I highlight those in the form of missed opportunities and misguided directions.

The Federal Budgets of 2007 and 2008: Building Canada Plan

The 2007 budget introduced or reintroduced a number of environmental initiatives that could help build and sustain a more resilient environment. The government announced that they would soon bring in a number of environmental regulations, particularly in the area of greenhouse gas (GHG) emissions and air pollutants. They committed to bringing in targets for GHG reductions and regulations to help achieve the targets. More stringent fuel efficiency standards would be announced for new passenger vehicles and light duty trucks beginning with the 2011 models. These lofty promises largely did not materialize, at least not in a form that signalled significant progress on tackling climate change or air pollution. However, investment in the environment was a component of the 2007 budget, with minor updates in the 2008 budget, as part of the Building Canada Plan, an infrastructure investment program of $33 billion to be spent over seven years. There were two key environmental features in the 2007 budget: the $4.5 billion Clean Environment investment plan over seven years and the extension of the Gas Tax Fund.

There are three main components to the Clean Environment program: air, water, and lands.

Clean Air. The goals of the Clean Air program are to reduce GHGs and encourage investment by the provinces and territories in clean energy via a $1.5 billion Canada ecoTrust for Clean Air and Climate Change. The Trust is to support projects that include provincial technology and infrastructure development, such as carbon sequestration, and clean coal and electricity transmission. Specific components included the phase-out of accelerated capital cost allowances (ACCA) for oil sands investment and the extension of ACCA to industries that invest in equipment that improves energy efficiency and equipment acquired prior to 2020 for renewable energy, including wave, solar, tidal, and waste-to-energy technologies. Additional programs include an incentive that provided up to $2,000 to purchase a fuel-efficient vehicle (a fund of $160 million over two years), a fund of $36 million for the subsequent two years to buy back older vehicles that had low fuel efficiency, a levy on gas-guzzling vehicles, and $2 billion over seven years to subsidize the production of renewable fuels. The 2008 budget extended funding created in the 2006 budget for public transit. The 2006 budget allocated up to $1.3 billion to support public transit infrastructure, while the 2008 budget announced that the government would put up to $500 million into a third-party trust for public transit infrastructure. Provincial transit infrastructure would be eligible for funding on a per capita basis if a public commitment to a project was made before March 31, 2008. These funds represented one-time money, not a sustained program. The 2008 budget also included the Automotive Innovation Fund, which was to provide up to $250 million over five years to support large-scale R&D in the automotive sector to develop innovative and more fuel-efficient vehicles, thereby reducing air contaminants and GHGs.

A ***National Water Strategy*** was announced in the 2007 budget, with goals to improve protection of drinking water and decrease untreated waste water. Programs included $11 million to be spent over two years to remove contaminated sediments in parts of the Great Lakes; $12 million and $7 million to clean up lakes Simcoe and Winnipeg, respectively; $19 million over two years to protect oceans and support pollution prevention along the coasts; $39 million for fisheries science research; providing First Nations with clean drinking water; and improving water and waste-water infrastructure as part of the long-term infrastructure plan. The 2008 budget provided $10 million over two years for repairs and environmental cleanup of small-craft harbours. The goal of this program was not to improve environmental quality per se, but to ready these harbours for transfer to interested parties.

Clean Land. The goal was to decrease solid-waste disposal and encourage efficient land use. However, few concrete programs were announced in 2007 and no additional ones in 2008. In 2007, the key funding was $225 million for the Nature Conservancy of Canada to conserve ecologically sensitive land in southern Canada; $30 million in funding to support an innovative model of sustainable land and resource management development in the Great Bear Rainforest on the central coast of British Columbia; and $110 million was allocated to support the new Species at Risk Act. The 2007 budget was also to provide funds to hire 50% more environmental enforcement officers. The 2008 budget added $10 million over two years to Natural Resources Canada to promote Canada's forestry sector in international markets as a model of environmental innovation and sustainability.

Gas Tax Fund. The Gas Tax Fund emanates from the 2005 budget of the Liberal government, under their *New Deal for Cities and Communities*. A share of the federal excise tax on motive fuels was allocated to the provinces to be spent at the municipal level to support sustainable environmental infrastructure projects. These projects could include public transit, water and waste-water treatment, community energy systems, and solid waste treatment. The initial size of the fund was $600 million, distributed to the provinces on a per capita basis. The fund was to increase in size until it reached $2 billion in 2009-10 (equivalent to five cents per litre of the fuel excise tax). The 2007 Conservative government budget extended the fund for an additional four years to 2013-14, and the 2008 budget made the fund permanent at a level of $2 billion annually.

Budget 2009: Green Infrastructure Fund and Miscellaneous Small Programs

The "big news" of the 2009 budget was the $33 billion major infrastructure spending program, covered in detail by other papers in this volume. The intent of the program was to support "shovel ready" projects that would infuse dollars into the economy and create employment to help address the recession. Eligible infrastructure could include projects that improved environmental quality, such as public transit and "clean energy" projects. While these shovel ready projects could have environmental attributes, there was not a requirement. The government targeted the environment with two funds of $1 billion each to be spent over five years – the Green Infrastructure Fund and a fund for clean energy. Budget 2009 was rather vague on what the Green Infrastructure Fund would cover, noting that it "includes infrastructure that supports a focus on the creation of sustainable energy" (Budget 2009, p. 144). The only example of sustainable infrastructure was energy transmission lines that "will contribute to improved air quality and lower carbon emissions" (Budget 2009, p. 144).

The Clean Energy Fund will support "the development and demonstration of technologies, including large-scale carbon capture and storage projects" (Budget 2009, p. 179). Allocation within this fund is broken down into $150 million for research (for unspecified topics) and $850 million for the development and demonstration of "promising" technologies, including carbon capture and storage (CCS) projects. The government has been very supportive of CCS, providing $375 million since 2006, including $250 million in Budget 2008 for full-scale commercial demonstration in Saskatchewan's coal-fired generators, carbon storage in Nova Scotia, and economic and technological issues. An additional $125 million is available for CCS under the ecoENERGY Technology Initiative of Natural Resources Canada.

The balance of the environmental aspects of the 2009 budget included a number of small programs that included:

- Increasing funding by $80 million over two years to manage and assess federal contaminated sites.
- Improving the government's annual reporting on key environmental indicators such as clean air, clean water and greenhouse gas emissions with expenditures of $10 million in 2009–10.
- Continuation of the grants to homeowners for the Eco-energy Retrofit program – an additional $300 million over two years.
- Increased funding of $407 million to VIA Rail Canada to improve passenger rail services.
- Nuclear power R&D and safety: $351 million to Atomic Energy of Canada Limited.
- Upgrades to water and sewer systems across the province of Quebec;
- Water treatment projects in Yukon.
- Safe drinking water for First Nations.

A number of regulatory changes that affect the environment were also introduced in Budget 2009. The government announced that it would revise the *Canadian Environmental Protection Act* to streamline environmental impact assessment (EIA) procedures. The stated goal of the regulatory reform was "to drive efficiencies in assessing environmental and other impacts of infrastructure projects without compromising protection of the environment". The basic premise was to require only one EIA of projects rather than have both federal and provincial assessments. As long as the provincial assessment process was no less binding than the federal process, the federal process could be waived. The provision was controversial because environmental proponents feared that there would be less oversight over projects than in the past and, hence, weaker EIA processes. The government also announced changes to the *Fisheries Act* and *Navigable Waters Protection Act*, again to "streamline" application of the regulations. These changes were introduced as part of the budget bill (Bill C-10) and came as a surprise to the environmental community because of the lack of consultation.

Assessment of the 2009 Budget

There are features in the 2009 budget that can promote improvements in environmental quality, but the budget can also be characterized by opportunities missed and directions that do not help sustain our natural environment. This section assesses the 2009 budget in the four areas of focus – infrastructure investment, GHGs and climate change, energy efficiency, and meeting environmental targets.

The "Good" (Maybe)

Infrastructure investments

The Gas Tax Fund (GTF) is one program that can improve environmental quality if the funds are used to improve public transit and, by doing so, convince more people to switch from private vehicles to transit. If the mode switch occurs, GHG emissions will decline, as will air contaminants. As transportation is a major source of GHGs, attempts to reduce emissions from vehicles will contribute to meeting GHG reduction targets. Fewer air contaminants will mean less smog. More transit ridership also means less traffic congestion – leading to both a higher quality of life as well as lower economic costs for transport and time lost. The GTF can also be used for investment in environmental infrastructure. It is too soon to tell what the mix of investment projects will be because the fund can be used to build roads and bridges as well as public transit and environmental infrastructure. A full accounting of expenditures is not yet available, but Infrastructure Canada's Web page lists the projects funded by the GTF through to December 2009.[1] These include a third SeaBus for Vancouver (public transit), and bridge and road construction in Ontario and Quebec (does not support mode-shifting to transit).

The Green Infrastructure Fund can support a wide range of environmental infrastructure projects ranging from producing renewable energy to water and sewage treatment. Projects underway so far include a transmission line in Yukon ($71 million federal contribution), a transmission line in northern British Columbia ($130 million), a groundwater treatment plant in Saskatchewan (up to $5 million), waste-water treatment upgrades near Winnipeg ($11 million), and a series of biomethanization projects in Quebec that build anaerobic digesters and composting facilities to turn organic waste into biogas for vehicles (a total of $171 million).[2] Transmission lines move electrons that can be generated from "clean" renewable sources, such as hydroelectric and wind generation, or "dirty" power from coal- or diesel-fired generators (thermal plants). New transmission may make it possible to open up regions of each province to renewable power, such as in northwest British Columbia or Quebec. But these lines may also increase the ability of thermal plants to move their

[1]See www.infc.gc.ca/media/news-nouvelles/gtf-fte/2009/gtfnews-nouvellesfte-09-eng.html. Accessed February 26, 2010.

[2]See www.actionplan.gc.ca/initiatives/eng/index.asp?mode=7&initiativeID=115. Accessed February 26, 2010.

electricity to other regions. With over one third of the fund now allocated, it appears that at least a quarter of the funds are being used to directly improve environmental quality.

Energy efficiency incentives

The federal government has put much emphasis on incentives to increase energy efficiency to help reduce GHG emissions and put less strain on the environment. It is hard to be opposed to energy efficiency. If we can lower our energy consumption per dollar of GDP, we reduce the trade-offs between economic activity and adverse environmental impacts.[3] The $300 million over two years that the budget allocated to finance energy retrofits of homes would allow 200,000 homes to reduce their energy costs and consumption (GBC, 2009, p. 3). However, in the next section, I argue that these sorts of programs would be much more effective if they were combined with environmental pricing.

Reducing GHGs

The Clean Energy Fund will be allocated to the commercial development of CCS technology. Economically viable CCS would reduce GHG emissions and allow coal- and fossil-fuel-fired electricity generation to be sustained in a carbon-constrained world. However, there is no guarantee that cost-effective CCS will be developed any time soon. Current pilot projects are underway, but results thus far indicate that the technology will be expensive and only viable if carbon emissions are priced and/or the technology is heavily subsidized. Estimates of the costs of CCS will likely fall as more investment into the technology occurs. A study by the International Energy Agency (IEA, 2004, p. 20) estimated the costs of CCS at US $50 to $100 per ton of CO_2 and would add 30 to 100% to capital costs for coal-fired power plants and 25 to 100% to operating costs. These numbers would translate into a 10 to 20% increase in consumer prices of electricity generated by thermal plants. Pouring millions of dollars into CCS may be a good strategy, but this investment would make more sense (and likely be cheaper to taxpayers) if there was a price on carbon to help stimulate private investment.

---

[3]Improvements in energy efficiency not only reduce GHGs per unit GDP, but will also reduce the impacts of energy production on ecosystems through reduction in the extraction of fossil fuels per unit GDP, less land converted to renewable energy production, and thus all the associated environmental impacts on air and water quality as well as land use.

Helping to meet environmental targets

Funds to clean up toxic waste sites help to improve environmental quality and meet targets for cleaner drinking water and restore brownfields to productive use. Canada has been woefully slow in addressing its many toxic sites, so any funding for toxic cleanup is a good thing. The problem is that $80 million is a "drop in the bucket", so to speak. Environment Canada estimated the cost of restoring the 4,000 contaminated sites on the Federal Contaminated Sites Inventory at $3.5 billion in 2005.[4] The 2004 budget provided for this level of funding, but since then the government changed, and it is difficult to ascertain how quickly progress is being made. Similarly, it is good to see funding to help provide cleaner water and waste-water treatment for First Nations, Yukon, and Quebec, but again, the expenditures are small relative to the problems. Finally, funding for data collection and dissemination is essential to see where we are and progress toward targets. The $10 million funding for environmental indicators covered only one year, and there are no guarantees that the funding will be sustained. Environmental indicators were an integral part of the Green Plan in the early 1990s and a number of initiatives, but will be terminated when the funding ends.

The "Bad": Missed Opportunities and Misguided Directions

Infrastructure investments

The Economic Action Plan's multi-billion-dollar infrastructure spending program, with its focus on "shovel ready" projects, has environmental infrastructure projects as one of its foci, but it is not clear how much funding will flow to environmental infrastructure. It is difficult to tell what share environmental infrastructure makes up of the $7.6 billion that has been committed by the federal government for more than 4,700 provincial, territorial, and municipal projects. The sample shown on the government's Canada's Action Plan Web site highlights road projects (summing to about $180 million), environmental infrastructure ($444 million), $30 million for ports, and about $10 million for community infrastructure such as arts centres.[5] Each province has its own priorities, and again, it is difficult to tell what the relative shares are. Of the $444

---

[4]See Environment Canada's Web pages on contaminated sites, www.ec.gc.ca/media_archive/press/2005/050802_b_e.htm. Accessed February 26, 2010.

[5]See www.actionplan.gc.ca/eng/feature.asp?pageId=153. Accessed February 28, 2010.

million for environmental projects, $350 million goes to water and waste-water treatment in Quebec. Whether the other provinces have similar expenditures remains to be seen.

Public transit is an important component of an environmental infrastructure program. What the Action Plan misses is any federal contribution to operating expenses of transit systems and in some provinces the debt service costs for the portion of the capital funded by the transportation authority. Public transit is subsidized; fares cannot be high enough to pay for the total operating plus debt service costs. None of the federal programs help pay the wage bill or fuel costs. This is especially the case for bus services, where the fare box covers at most about 60% of total operating costs. Municipalities have been seeking federal support for operating transit for years, to no avail. If the transit authorities cannot operate the system, there is little point in seeking infrastructure funds. In addition, the infrastructure fund may bias provincial transit/transportation planning to large capital projects regardless of whether they have the highest net present value for the transit system.

Energy efficiency incentives and subsidies

The missed opportunity from an environmental perspective is that the price of virtually all energy consumed in Canada does not reflect the environmental costs associated with its production, distribution, and consumption. Energy prices are either set by regulators on world markets, as in the case of oil, as for electricity and natural gas in many provinces, or by local/regional markets (electricity in some provinces). Canada does not price pollution or GHGs or other deleterious attributes of energy production and consumption. Hence, the social cost of energy use exceeds its private cost, often by substantial amounts. The upshot is that prices for energy are low in Canada because we have large endowments of energy sources, weak environmental regulation, and virtually no environmental pricing. The benefit of energy efficiency subsidies is that they lower the cost to consumers and may give them incentives to buy windows and heating systems that use less energy. The problem is that this policy is second best to social cost pricing of energy.

Other difficulties arise from subsidizing energy efficiency investments. First, the programs do not discriminate among emissions intensity of different energy sources. Electricity may have very few adverse environmental impacts if it is generated by existing hydroelectric dams.[6] If electricity is generated by coal-fired plants, there are large environmental impacts. Programs that then induce consumers (households and firms) to substitute away from, say, fuel oil and natural gas to electricity may or may not improve environmental quality. Second, subsidizing the investment in energy-efficient goods may lead to what is known as the "rebound effect". By lowering the operating cost of these goods, the consumer may respond by consuming more energy-using goods in total. The prime example is that the increase in fuel efficiency of motor vehicles lowers the marginal cost of driving and may lead to more kilometres travelled. Third, the programs may contribute to what is called "free riding" – consumers who would have purchased the energy-saving equipment even without the subsidy. Estimates of free ridership vary considerably, from a low of around 12% to almost 90%.[7] Fourth, the programs simply may not be all that effective. Studies of demand-side management programs in the United States found that subsidies to the purchase of energy-efficient equipment led to very little take-up and may be quite expensive per unit of energy saved. Finally, these programs may simply not be necessary because energy efficiency has already increased significantly in our homes, appliances, vehicles, and other equipment. Homes built after 2000 are about 35% more energy-efficient than ones built in the 1970s. Energy-efficient household appliances are way more efficient in 2005 in that they consume less electricity per hour of use than those produced in 1990. For example, refrigerators are more than twice as efficient, clothes washers almost three times, and dishwashers more than three times, comparing 1990 to 2005.[8] If the federal government had introduced policies to price GHGs, it is arguable that none of these subsidies would be needed. The market would work to induce substitution to energy-efficient equipment.

The 2009 budget also did nothing to end subsidies that shouldn't exist at all. Subsidies to ethanol production were introduced in the 2007 budget as part of $2 billion funding announced for biofuels. These programs were augmented by a 2008 amendment to the *Canadian Environmental Protection Act* that requires 5% ethanol in gasoline by 2010. The impact

---

[6]The construction of the dams and reservoirs may have had large environmental impacts, but those are now sunk costs, and incremental environmental damage is low.

[7]Eto *et al.* (2000) found free ridership of 12.2% for commercial DSM programs, while Malm (1996) estimated it at 89% for heating system subsidies.

[8]Natural Resources Canada (2009) is the source for these energy efficiency estimates.

of ethanol subsidies has led to all sorts of unintended and not always welcome consequences, including the conversion of food crops (corn and other grains) to fuel. Studies of the "cradle to grave" environmental impacts of ethanol production are all over the map in terms of their estimates, in part depending on the type of plant used to produce ethanol. Some find the total energy cost of ethanol (e.g., from corn) to exceed its energy output when combusted, but this would not be the case for cellulosic ethanol (e.g., from switchgrass). Ethanol may also be no better than burning gasoline in vehicles in terms of air contaminants released into the atmosphere.[9] So the jury is still out on ethanol. The even more misguided subsidy related to ethanol is that given to E85 vehicles. These are vehicles that can use up to 85% ethanol fuel. The absurdity is that there are only a handful of gas stations in the whole country that sell E85 fuel. A Google search could confirm only three stations in Canada, all in Ontario. These subsidies waste public funds with no discernable impact on environmental quality.

The government also missed opportunities to remove some of its archaic subsidies to the mining and energy sector. See the Green Budget Coalition (2009) for details.

Reducing GHGs

Canadian federal governments have an abysmal record when it comes to reducing GHG emissions; the current government is no exception. With the exception of a slight dip in 2006, GHG emissions have risen inexorably over the period from 1991 to the present. Figure 1 shows the time path of Canada's GHG emissions. Our target set for the Kyoto Protocol was to reduce emissions to just over 558 megatonnes CO_2e by 2012. Our prime minister and his environment ministers have categorically said that Canada will not meet its Kyoto commitments. The current target set by the federal government is a reduction of 17% below the 2005 CO_2e levels, as shown in Figure 1.

---

[9]One of the studies of ethanol fuels was done by Environment Canada, who, in testing four vehicles, found no statistically significant difference in GHG emissions between regular unleaded gasoline and gasoline containing 10% ethanol. Carbon monoxide emissions were lower with ethanol fuel, but emissions of other hydrocarbons increased with ethanol. I cannot find a reference to this study on the Environment Canada Web site, but the report was widely quoted in the media in 2008. See, for example, the CBC at: www.cbc.ca/technology/story/2008/05/12/tech-ethanol-faq.html. Accessed February 28,2010.

Figure 1: Canada, Total GHG Emissions, 1990 to 2007

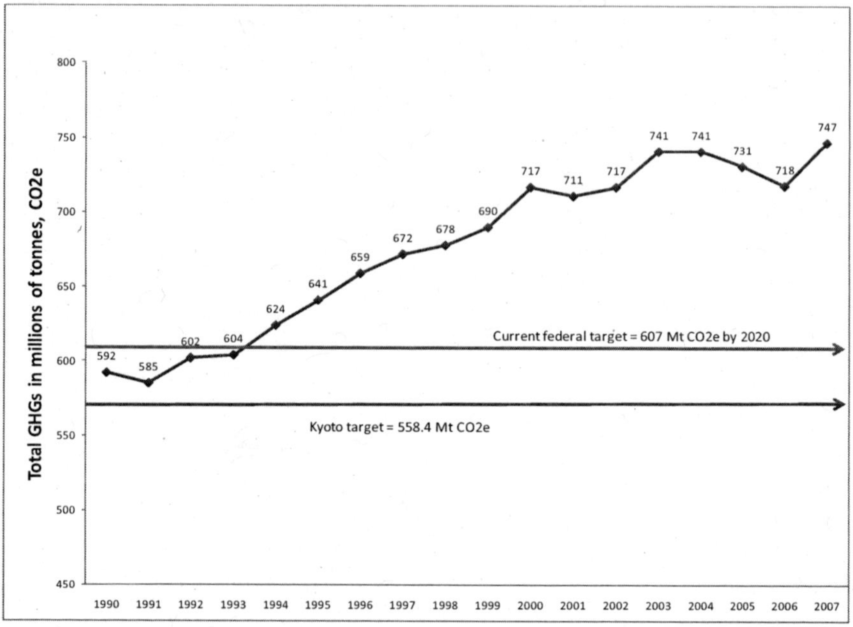

Data source: Environment Canada, *National Inventory Report: Greenhouse Gas Sources and Sinks in Canada, 1990-2007.*[10]

The federal government's stated tools to reduce GHG emissions are to regulate emissions, enhance energy efficiency, increase the share of renewable energy in the overall energy mix, and promote and accelerate technology development and deployment. Based on these approaches, Budget 2009 is right on track. The provisions in the 2009 budget, combined with the previous budgets of this government and its predecessors, contain policies and expenditure programs that consist of three of the four approaches. Figure 1 shows how well these approaches have been working in the past. The missing link is regulation of emissions in any meaningful way: the federal government has simply failed to introduce concrete policies to regulate the emissions of GHGs. The current stance is as follows: "The Government of Canada is working in collaboration with the provinces and territories towards the development of a cap-and-trade system that will ultimately be aligned with the

---

[10]Available at Environment Canada's Web site: www.ec.gc.ca/pdb/ghg/inventory_e.cfm. Note that aggregate data is not available for years beyond 2007.

emerging cap-and-trade program in the United States."[11] In other words, we have no explicit plan to regulate GHG emissions, at least not until the United States brings in their program.

This policy stance is misguided for a host of reasons. The list is large, and I can only touch on the issues here. Canada needs to put a price on GHGs to enhance all the other policies in the government's arsenal to reduce GHGs. Previous policies have not priced GHG emissions. As noted above, energy efficiency incentives work better the higher the price of the good you are using as an incentive for people to move away from. Investment in substitute fuels, new technologies to sequester carbon, or alternative processes that are less energy-intensive will have a higher payoff the higher the price of carbon. A cap-and-trade system will put a price on carbon, but we won't know what that price will be or how it will change over time until we have a functioning cap-and-trade system. The design of a cap-and-trade system is anything but simple. The European Union brought in its first cap-and-trade system with a three-year experimental phase that ended last year. The experiment provided many insights into how not to run the market. In North America, the Western Climate Initiative has been working for at least three years on the design of a system that would include a number of western US states and, in Canada, British Columbia, Manitoba, Ontario, and Quebec. The system is slated to be installed in 2012, but that may not occur. No one expects a US federal system to be in place until 2015, even if a bill can be passed in the US Congress in 2010, and it is looking like that possibility is receding. The list of design issues is daunting. A partial list includes the following:

- What entities will be covered by the system? Cap and trade cannot possibly address emissions from every source – for example, households can only be covered indirectly by including the "mid-stream" producers (e.g., wholesalers of fuels who then pass along the cost of the GHG permits to their customers).
- How will permits be allocated – by auction or based on other criteria (e.g., past production, type of industry)?
- Will the government address potential price volatility by installing price ceilings or floors? The Alberta cap-and-trade system, which applies only within that province, is based not on actual emissions, but emissions intensity. It has an implicit price ceiling in that covered sources can either buy permits at the prevailing price or

[11] Canada's Action on Climate Change, www.climatechange.gc.ca/default.asp?lang=En&n=D43918F1-1. Accessed February 28, 2010.

contribute to a technology fund for each tonne of carbon emitted at a fixed price of $15 per tonne.

- What about the potential for market manipulation – think of the new "products" that can be sold such as derivatives for carbon? The financial sector is gearing up for what could become a multi-billion-dollar business, with the majority of the rents from the market going to the financial intermediaries.
- What counts as a legitimate offset? An offset is a means of sequestering carbon, most commonly in the form of absorption by forests or other land forms. Under the Clean Development Mechanism of the Kyoto Protocol, an offset must be truly incremental to business as usual, verifiable, and so on. Will offsets be allowed only within Canada or abroad? Who will verify them? Will there be a limit on the number of offsets allowed in total and/or per covered source?
- How will the federal system be integrated with existing GHG policies at the provincial level, e.g., BC's carbon tax, Quebec's tax, and Ontario's new programs?
- How will we integrate our system with that of the United States? Will it be identical in all respects? What if we allocate permits differently than does the United States because of our oil sands development? Is there the potential for US interests to challenge Canada's "unfair" subsidies to its energy sector?
- How will we deal with differing regional impacts of the policy? Will equalization have to be re-examined?

Each of these questions merits a paper on its own. The list gives one a flavour of all the complexity in the design of a cap-and-trade system, and Canada is waiting for the United States to design one for us. This policy stance smacks of more of the same inaction on GHG emissions that has typified federal policy in the past. The obvious alternative to a cap-and-trade system is a carbon tax to regulate carbon emissions in combination with the existing policies. We have a perfectly good working model of a carbon tax right here in Canada: the BC carbon tax. That policy went from concept to implementation in under one year. A carbon tax is thus relatively simple to design and implement and, as British Columbia has shown, can be completely revenue-neutral – every dollar collected is returned to the province in the form of lower taxes and programs to address hardship regions and low-income households. The tax revenue gives the government the ability to address regional and industry-specific concerns, but keeps the marginal price of carbon the same for all. The tax can apply to all domestic emissions because it is based on where the fuel is combusted. A carbon tax puts a price on carbon that is set by the government, not the market. The uncertainty is then over the amount of emission reduction, so changes in the tax rate will likely be needed as the government measures the impact of the tax on emission levels. As in British Columbia, one way to address this issue is to announce an escalating tax rate over time. The first tranche of the BC tax ends in 2012, when the price will be $30 per tonne of CO_2e. Prior to 2012, the BC government will announce the price schedule for the next tranche. The obvious solution of a carbon tax is currently anathema to our federal government. But it is not outside the realm of possibility that the United States will bring in a carbon tax rather than a cap-and-trade system. Canada should be prepared.

Helping to meet environmental targets

Areas of missed opportunity and misguided policy include the failure to eliminate industry subsidies that contribute to environmental degradation, concern over the changes to environmental regulation, and the failure to address protection of Canada's threatened ecosystems and their biodiversity.

The government extended to March 2010, rather than cancelled, the Mineral Exploration Tax Credit (or "super flow-through shares program"), which subsidizes mineral exploration. This is a subsidy that is not needed, and one hopes that the 2010 budget removes it. As the Green Budget Coalition notes, the government also "did nothing to address the imbalance between the tax benefits and expenditures provided to promote the virgin extraction of minerals versus much more environmentally sound alternatives of conservation and recycling of metals" (GBC, 2009, p. 4). Pouring additional funding into the CANDU nuclear reactor program is also inconsistent with promoting renewable energy and minimizing environmental harm that occurs from uranium mining and nuclear waste disposal problems. It also seems inconsistent that a government with a "free enterprise" philosophy should subsidize what should be a private sector product.

The environmental community is highly suspicious of the proposed changes to the *Fisheries Act* and *Navigable Waters Protection Act,* as well as changes to the environmental impact process, fearing a weakening in the protection of the environment. There was no prior consultation on these changes, and groups such as the Green Budget Coalition (GBC) found it disturbing that the government would include these measures in a budget bill prior to its announced plans to consult widely on changes to the *Canadian Environmental Protection Act* and because the government announced in the budget that "environmental protection will not be compromised".[12]

In general, the 2009 budget did very little to protect or enhance Canada's natural capital. The conservation of our natural areas is essential to sustain the ecosystem goods and services that flow from nature and to reduce the need to substitute more costly human-made alternatives. Stresses to our natural capital come from economic activity (urban sprawl, road construction, industrial development), and studies estimate that we need to protect more land and water than we currently do. Provisions in the budget to improve degrading infrastructure in national parks is commendable, but fails to address the need to protect lands outside parks, the most threatened of which are near urban areas.

Summary and Overall "Scorecard"

My assessment of Budget 2009's environmental scorecard is as follows:

- Clean Air
  - ↓GHGs – no (also nothing on climate adaptation)
  - ↑ green energy – maybe
  - ↓ air contaminants – only by funding public transit

- Clean Water
  - Source water protection – no
  - ↓ untreated waste water – probably yes
  - ↑ clean drinking water – probably yes
  - Protecting oceans and their resources – no

- Clean Land
  - ↓ solid waste – possibly yes
  - Encourage efficient land use – no
  - Protecting natural capital — no.

What is missing in Budget 2009 is the sense of environmental leadership in the areas of climate change and protecting our valuable natural capital. Environmental initiatives are present basically only if they are part of

[12]As quoted in the Green Budget Coalition (2009, p. 6) and Budget 2009, p. 143.

infrastructure spending and programs to enhance energy efficiency. As the evidence on GHG emissions shows, federal climate programs to date have failed to reduce emissions. As our natural areas diminish, we lose the ability of our ecosystems to provide clean drinking water and absorb the waste products of society. The economy was a mess in 2009, and economic stimulus was required, but we need to move beyond the rhetoric that pitches the economy against the environment. Without the natural environment, there is no economy.

References

Eto, J., S. Kito, L. Shown, and R. Sonnenblick. 2000. "Where did the Money Go? The Cost and Performance of the Largest Commercial Sector DSM Programs", *Energy Journal* 21(2), 23.

Government of Canada. 2009. *Budget 2009.*

Green Budget Coalition (GBC). 2009. "Budget 2009: Environmental Impact, Summary and Analysis". At www.greenbudget.ca/pdf/GBC%20 Environmental%20Impact%20Summary%20of%20Budget,%20March%20 2009.pdf. Accessed February 25, 2010.

International Energy Agency (IEA). 2004. "Prospects for CO_2 Capture and Storage". IEA: Paris.

Malm, E. 1996. "An Actions-Based Estimate of the Free Rider Fraction in Electric Utility DSM Programs", *Energy Journal* 17(3), 41.

Natural Resources Canada. 2009. "Improving Energy Performance in Canada", Report to Parliament under the *Energy Efficiency Act* for the Fiscal Year, 2007-2008.

Session Seven

WRAP-UP PANEL: THE BIG PICTURE

BUDGET PRIORITIES FOR CANADA: Time for Some Big Ideas?

Robin Boadway, Queen's University

Introduction: Time for Some Big Ideas?

Federal budgets tend to oscillate among various types. They can be primarily transformative or visionary in nature, such as when fundamental policy changes of a far-reaching and foresighted measure are introduced. They can reflect periods of consolidation and responses to crises, when more or less sound economic policies are enacted. And they can represent episodes of political compromise and, in the extreme, pure populism. Or they can contain elements of all three. In Canada, notable periods of transformative change included extended periods in the 1950s and 1960s, and again in the late 1980s and 1990s. The former period witnessed the establishment of universal social programs and the basic architecture of federal-provincial fiscal relations. The latter period was notable for a number of market-oriented reforms of trade relations, taxation, and public indebtedness.

Populist budgets are politically tempting. Indeed, political constraints are sometimes offered as an excuse for compromised policies. Good policies are typically unpopular with some influential segment of the population and take political courage to implement. The examples of the Goods and Services Tax (GST) and the Free Trade Agreement (FTA) come to mind. It is a bit of a mystery why sound policies sometimes get enacted in the face of public opposition and sometimes not. The immense literature on political economy provides little guidance. Presumably, it has to do with the quality and persuasiveness of politicians, the foresight and ideas

---

Some of the issues discussed in this paper are presented in more detail in my paper entitled "Fiscal Priorities for Canada: Building on the Legacy of David Dodge", prepared for a *Festschrift* for David Dodge (Boadway, 2009a).

coming from the bureaucracy, and the role of outside critics. In any case, it seems apparent that political constraints are endogenous, and ought not to be taken as given. That being so, one can argue that our responsibility as students and advocates of economic and social policy is to propose the best policies relatively unencumbered by perceived political constraint. (Political constraints may not be the only relevant ones. David Watters suggested at this conference that the capacity of the bureaucracy to deal with the enormous climate change problems we face might be inadequate.)

In fact, we have gone through a period of relatively populist, politically driven budgets and, most recently, one that was crisis-driven. Kevin Milligan, in his presentation, used the apt phrase "boutique tax changes" to characterize some of the tax changes in recent budgets. The exception might be the infrastructure programs recently introduced, and discussed at this conference by Paul Hobson and Tracy Snoddon. However, recent budgets have done little to address some of the big challenges that lie ahead. My theme is that it is now time for another episode of transformative and visionary policy changes. Before turning to what these challenges and policy options to deal with them might be, it might be worth briefly recalling the past episodes mentioned above.

Transformative Reforms of the 1950s/1960s and 1980s/1990s

The 1950s and 1960s saw a number of major policies enacted that established the Canadian version of the welfare state and have stayed with us since. Universal public medical and hospital services were instituted with the assistance of shared-cost federal grants. For the elderly, the system of Old Age Security and Guaranteed Income Supplement provided considerable protection to the needy. The Canada and Quebec pension plans instituted a partly funded occupational public pension. The Unemployment Insurance system was made universal, and the provincial welfare programs were introduced, with some encouragement by the federal government through the Canada Assistance Plan. In addition to federal funding for provincial health and welfare programs, the basic architecture of federal-provincial fiscal relations was put in place with the institution of the Equalization program, based on the representative tax system approach and the Tax Collection Agreements for individual and corporate income taxes. The income tax system itself was reformed following the monumental Carter Report (Royal

Commission on Taxation, 1966). And, significantly, despite the role played by the federal spending power to induce provinces to institute major social programs, the process of gradual decentralization of the Canadian federation was soon begun.

The major reforms of the 1980s and 1990s were of an entirely different nature. Whereas the reforms of the earlier period established and consolidated the welfare state, those of the 1980s and 1990s accepted and fostered the primacy of private markets rather than government direction as the main determinants of economic activity. The historic Canada-US Free Trade Agreement, subsequently expanded to include Mexico by the North American Free Trade Agreement (NAFTA), ended a century of protectionist industrial policy that had begun virtually with Confederation. Of course, NAFTA was facilitated by the system of social protection that was in place. As a complementary policy, the GST replaced the inefficient Manufacturers Sales Tax and effectively put Canadian producers on an even playing field with their competitors abroad. Eventually, the retail sales tax in some provinces was replaced with value-added taxes and harmonized with the GST as a Harmonized Sales Tax (HST) in three of the Atlantic Provinces and with the Quebec Sales Tax (QST) in Quebec. These innovations remain the models for further sales tax harmonization of the sort that has finally got underway with BC's and Ontario's acquiescence. Even more than the FTA, the GST was a highly unpopular policy reform, but most policy watchers would agree that it was the right one.

A third major area of reform in this latter period was in the broad area of bringing public indebtedness under control. From a narrow perspective, this involved quickly running down the public debt by eliminating deficit financing. Although the objective was successfully achieved, it was not without side effects. One in particular was that a disproportionate amount of the burden of deficit reduction was effectively passed on to the provinces through reduced transfers (and subsequently to some extent to their respective municipalities). In addition to simply transferring debt from one level of government to another, this set off the acrimonious debate on vertical imbalance that was eventually partly redressed by federal transfers, but remains a source of distrust. Public indebtedness includes more than the actual public debt. It includes implicit liabilities in other parts of the public budget, such as public pensions and expenditure obligations for elderly persons. These too were addressed by policy actions. Policy reforms to the CPP went some distance to improving its solvency. Moreover, reforms to the tax system encouraged Canadians to save more for their own retirement, thereby reducing any commitment the government might have. All these reforms were both successful and timely. Canada's debt-to-GDP ratio, as well as the balance of its generational accounts, became among the best in the OECD. Given what has happened to the macro-economy in recent months, and what is predicted to happen demographically in coming years, these reforms put Canada in a much more favourable position to respond than most countries.

Other less sweeping fiscal innovations were also instituted in this period. Refundable tax credits were introduced, which, as we shall discuss, have the potential for repairing some pending problems in coverage of the needy. The consolidation of federal-provincial social transfers into block grants with minimal conditions completed the transformative use of the spending power of the earlier period. The Equalization system has also been subject to some rationalization following the advice of the O'Brien Report (Expert Panel on Equalization, 2006). And the Tax Collection Agreements have evolved to enable more provincial discretion while at the same time retaining harmonization. The main disappointment of the era was the inability of the federal government to reform the system of business taxation, despite the reasonable advice offered by the Mintz Committee (Technical Committee on Business Taxation, 1997).

Circumstances have changed since this raft of fiscal reforms. New challenges are emerging. In what follows, five major fiscal challenges are outlined and policy options suggested. Each of them will involve some return to the transformative budget-setting of the past and away from the more populist recent budgets. The five challenges to be discussed briefly, taken in increasing order of their difficulty (from both a policy and a political perspective) though not of their urgency, are as follows: inequality and poverty, income tax reform, human capital investment, natural resources policy, and carbon pricing. Each of these is discussed in turn.

It is important to bear in mind the underlying context of the need for fiscal restraint in the wake of the recent severe recession and the coming fiscal pressures that will result from the aging of the Canadian population. These factors will constrain future policies, but will not dictate them.

Inequality and Poverty

Recent evidence (National Welfare Council, 2008; OECD, 2008) indicates that income, earning and wealth inequality as well as poverty rates have been increasing in Canada in recent years and now are above the OECD average. At the same time, tax-transfer policies have become less redistributive. The income tax system has become less progressive, especially at the top. Real incomes received by welfare recipients (including refundable tax credits) have been declining since 1989, especially since 1994, and are now 60-70% less than poverty cut-off levels, measured in both relative and absolute terms. Decentralization of fiscal responsibilities seems to have been an important factor. Social assistance and disability transfers provided by the provinces have not kept pace with transfers provided by the federal government to families with children (Canada Child Tax Benefit, Universal Child Care Benefit), to the elderly (Old Age Security and the Guaranteed Income Supplement), and to low-income workers (Working Income Tax Benefit [WITB]). This reflects in part the stagnation of the Canada Social Transfer, as discussed in the Snoddon and Hobson paper in this volume.

A number of policy options suggest themselves, given budget constraints into the near future and the apparently deteriorating demographics. From a general point of view, the tax-transfer system could be made more effective as a redistributive tool by putting much more emphasis on targeting and less on universality as a matter of principle. Special emphasis could be put on poverty reduction. For a start, *all* tax credits could be made refundable and income-tested, thereby turning the federal tax system into a proper negative income tax. To accomplish this, marginal tax rates would have to be quite steep at the bottom, at least after the WITB income range (despite some adverse incentive effects). Welfare and disability assistance reform could be used in a complementary fashion, with rates benchmarked at least to surmount poverty lines and indexed to the CPI. As well, asset limitations should be relaxed so that welfare recipients are able to do more self-insurance, and work incentives should be made more attractive. For example, the WITB work eligibility hurdle could be reduced from $3,000 per annum. Provincial transfer programs could be harmonized, perhaps encouraged by an imaginative use of the Canada Social Transfer (CST). Credits for charitable donations could be improved to reflect the fact that voluntary donations are a more cost-effective way of financing support to the poor than tax dollars. The social infrastructure could be improved, including especially the provision of child care services on a targeted basis. Finally, a potential problem with low incomes among the elderly could be averted by taking action now to repair the decline in availability of occupational pensions, especially defined-benefit ones. An imaginative solution, which is an attractive option, is the provision of public pensions as an alternative to private employee-based pensions, which persons are automatically enrolled in unless they choose to opt out (Ambachtscheer, 2007).

Income Tax Reform

The Canadian income tax has gone through a long period of incremental changes (including Kevin Milligan's so-called "boutique" tax reforms). The system has lost some of its focus. What used to be the guiding principle of a comprehensive income tax system has long since lost its relevance. Basic income tax reform is long overdue. Economic circumstances have changed considerably, especially the increase in mobility of income and other consequences of globalization. Major reform initiatives have been launched elsewhere, particularly the European Union, and some far-reaching new approaches have been adopted. Moreover, thinking about tax policy has evolved considerably since the days of the Carter Report (Royal Commission on Taxation, 1966). This has been reflected in major documents, such as the report of the President's Advisory Panel on Federal Tax Reform (2005) in the United States and the Mirrlees Review (Mirrlees *et al.*, 2010) for the Institute of Fiscal Studies in the United Kingdom. Major reform of the income tax system would complement sales tax harmonization in improving the competitiveness of the Canadian economy. The time is ripe for a thorough rationalization of the income tax system.

Nowadays, there is little support for the comprehensive income tax that was the model until the mid-1970s. Today there are two camps. Advances in both tax theory and innovative thinking by the Meade Report (Report of a Committee Chaired by Professor J.E. Meade, 1978) and the US Treasury (1977) initially led to widespread support for progressive consumption or expenditure taxation in which asset income is fully sheltered from taxation. Direct consumption taxation has not been introduced in any OECD country, presumably owing to the difficulty of exempting capital income from taxation. Instead, there has been growing support for a schedular income tax system, such as the one introduced first into some of the Nordic countries and subsequently taken up elsewhere in the European Union, in which earnings and capital income are subject to different rate schedules. In the Nordic system of so-called dual income taxation, earnings and transfers are subject to a progressive rate structure, while capital income is taxed at a flat rate corresponding to the lowest positive rate of earnings taxation (Boadway, 2004). This dual income tax was one of the options recommended by the President's Advisory Panel in the United States and is an option being considered by the Mirrlees review. It has much to recommend it.

A dual income tax addresses earnings inequality, which is the main source of income inequality. It removes the constraint on progressivity of earning taxation that applies when capital income is part of the base. It recognizes that the optimal taxation of capital income is less than that of labour income, while still imposing some tax on capital income from inherited assets, which would otherwise go untaxed under direct consumption taxation. Moreover, some taxation of capital income is also desired on theoretical grounds, for example, because of an observed tendency for savings to be correlated with earning ability because of either saving habits or steeper age-earnings profiles (Banks and Diamond, 2008) and because of earnings uncertainty that is uninsured. At the same time, the flat rate of tax on capital income has administrative advantages, given the mobility of capital and the ease of avoiding or even evading taxes on capital income. A uniform rate, for example, allows capital income tax to be collected through withholding by financial institutions. The uniform rate also makes integration with the corporate tax simpler and more accurate. The dual income tax would also have an advantage in a federal context. The earnings tax could be jointly occupied by the federal and provincial governments, with tax collection agreements applying for harmonization. The capital income tax would then be ideally allocated to the federal government alone.

A dual income tax reform could be accompanied by other measures. It would still be possible to shelter savings for retirement, housing, and human capital accumulation from the capital income tax. Given that the rate would be preferentially low, there would be less distortion than under the current system. Ideally, an inheritance tax would serve as a useful complement to the dual income tax to address inequality of wealth at the upper end, as in various EU countries, though that might be a difficult sell in Canada. Similarly, refundable tax credits could be used to preserve equity at the lower end. Finally, it would still be desirable to pursue business tax reform. Following some of the ideas of the Mintz Committee Report (1997) would remove existing inefficiencies affecting business decisions. At the same time, the business tax system could be much more effectively used to collect rents from those industries, such as the resources industries, where rents are prominent. We return to this issue later.

Human Capital Investment

The fiscal treatment of human capital accumulation raises a number of important issues because of its importance for economic prosperity, for equal opportunity, and for earnings distribution. Its current treatment in the tax system is uneven at best: reform is long overdue.

Human capital investment has a number of features that distinguish it from other forms of asset accumulation. Individuals are endowed with some initial amount of human capital, but endowments and the ability to accumulate further are unevenly distributed and correlated with one another. Human capital accumulation is significantly affected by one's social environment, especially family circumstances, so opportunities differ. Accumulation is risky, and liquidity constraints may affect access to human capital investment. These features lead to various reasons for government policy interest in human capital investment. There are efficiency concerns arising from market failure: uninsured risk, liquidity constraints, and externalities of knowledge creation and diffusion associated with human capital investment. There are possibly behavioural reasons for underinvestment in human capital, for example, as a result of bounded rationality, myopia, or time-inconsistent preferences. There are equity reasons arising from unequal market outcomes because of differences in initial endowments and in abilities to accumulate human capital. And related to this, there are equality-of-opportunity arguments, such as the obligations set out in section 36(1) of the Canadian constitution. Together, these rationales provide some motivation for government to enact policies to encourage human capital investment, especially by disadvantaged persons, and to redistribute its proceeds.

A number of policy observations follow the rationale for government intervention. Note, first, that the tax treatment of human capital accumulation is already fairly generous. At least some of the costs of human capital investment – those that are due to forgone earnings – as well as revenues are treated on a cash-flow basis as in a consumption tax system, while financial costs such as tuition, books, and the like are offered partially refundable tax credits. Moreover, education at all levels is heavily subsidized. There are also a number of special features in the tax system that further reduce the cost of human capital investment, at least for some families, including student grants and loans and the Registered Education Savings Plan, which effectively subsidizes saving to finance human capital investment. At the same time, the progressive nature of the tax system works against the incentive to invest.

However, the system should be harmonized to better achieve the objectives of efficiency, equity, and equality of opportunity. To fully shelter the returns to human capital investment in a way that treats forgone earnings and financial costs on a par, existing credits for tuition, books, and education, which are poorly targeted to the most needy, could be replaced by full deductions, and equality of opportunity could be addressed by more focused means. The existing Canada Student Loan program offers a sound starting point in terms of structure, but its size is nowhere near large enough to address equality-of-opportunity objectives. To deal with the inefficiencies arising from uninsured risk and liquidity constraints, a system of income-contingent loans would be appropriate. With these measures in place, the case for subsidizing saving for education through the RESP program could be abolished. Moreover, with suitable levels of generosity of targeted assistance to students from low-income families, tuition fees could rise to provide much needed financial support for post-secondary institutions.

More generally, some rationalization could be achieved in the respective roles of the federal and provincial governments. There is far too much overlap in programs at the moment in areas ranging from student assistance and loans to grants to universities for infrastructure to faculty appointments through federally funded research chairs. As well, provincial policies are highly non-harmonized, and there are growing incidents of beggar-thy-neighbour policies in fees, admissions, and retention of graduates within provinces. One possible institutional way to address these issues of rationalization between the federal government and the provinces, as well as among provinces, is to separate the post-secondary grant component from the CST and use it in imaginative and co-operative ways to encourage harmonization.

Natural Resources

Canada's natural resource wealth is an enormous windfall for Canadians, but it also poses enormous challenges for the federation. As discussed elsewhere (Boadway, 2009b), there are two major challenges posed by natural resource wealth (oil and gas, uranium, timber, etc.). One is the potential for so-called Dutch disease, or the resource curse, that arises from the diversion of factors of production from other sectors of the economy with more long-run potential for innovation and technical progress (e.g., information technology, biotechnology, manufacturing). This is exacerbated to the extent that the rents accruing to the public sector are not saved, especially if they are not saved in international assets. Some countries, such as Norway, have minimized the consequence of natural resource wealth by saving virtually all the rents from their offshore petroleum wealth in a fund that holds foreign assets (with the risk that entails). Only the income from the fund is used for current spending.

The second major challenge arises from the fact that natural resources are owned by the provinces, and natural resource wealth is found disproportionately in a small number of less populous provinces. These facts lead to complications over and above the natural resource curse. First, large horizontal fiscal imbalances occur, as discussed by Michael Smart in a paper in this volume, and this poses almost insuperable challenges for the Equalization system. Partly because of this, the equalization of natural resources has been watered down by recent changes proposed by the O'Brien panel and recently implemented. Despite that, the system is viewed by some as unaffordable, leading to ad hoc measures like caps of growth of the system.

Second, for whatever reason, the provincial governments seem unable or unwilling to save natural resource rents. This alone exacerbates the natural resource problem. However, it is not just the absence of saving that poses a problem, but also the way in which the resource revenues are spent. They provide resource-rich provinces with the means to engage in competitive province-building through the provision of infrastructure and the like. It is far from clear from an economic geography point of view that developing diversified economies on the basis of where natural resource wealth happens to be found will lead to an efficient pattern of regional development. This is especially true if the pattern of development is the result of unequal fiscal abilities to diversify.

Policy options for dealing with the challenges of natural resources are limited, and not all are politically easy, especially given the well-known political fallout from the National Energy Policy of an earlier era. Nonetheless, there are some options that would be supported on economic policy grounds. There are measures that could be taken to address at least some of the fiscal imbalances induced by natural resource revenues. While it would be difficult to convert the Equalization system itself into one that directly redistributed from have to have-not provinces, there are reforms that can have the equivalent effect. For example, the system of social transfers (CHT/CST) could be integrated with the Equalization system such that payments are made contingent of fiscal capacity. Although this would violate the oft-espoused edict that equalization should be restricted to the Equalization system, this is essentially what is done in Australia. Complementary to this, the size of the vertical fiscal gap could be increased. The argument against this is usually posed in terms of affordability and accountability, but these have little force in my view. Affordability is an artificial argument in this context and may even be viewed as ingenuous. A change in the fiscal gap can be engineered with no net effect on the taxpayer, since it really only involves a reallocation of revenues from one level of government to the other. Similarly, accountability is a bit of a red herring when it comes to the raising of revenue. Governments simply do not use the revenue system to fine-tune the size of their budgets, and in any case, both levels of government would retain scope for marginal adjustments to their revenues over the longer run. The move toward a harmonized GST has the potential to facilitate a readjustment of the vertical gap (Tremblay, 2009). A national GST is precisely the vehicle used in Australia to achieve fiscal balance.

Other specific measures could be contemplated that would counter the consequences of provinces having unequal access to resource revenues. The federal government could increase its own access to resource revenues in a constitutionally sanctioned way by obtaining more federal taxes from resource firms. The existing corporate tax could be reformed so that it is more effective at extracting rents from natural resource firms. Options exist, like cash-flow-type taxes, that would be suitable for this purpose. In Europe, various countries have implemented so-called Allowance for Corporate Equity (ACE) corporate taxes, which are similar to cash-flow taxes, and effectively, tax rents. As it stands, the existing corporate tax is overly generous to resource firms, as documented by, among others, the Mintz Committee. Another measure that could be taken would be for the federal government to counter-balance province-building investments. To some extent, the federal infrastructure program offers such an opportunity. There might be incentives contemplated, inducing the provinces to save more of their resource revenues, although any such move might be viewed as an unwarranted form of intrusion into provincial fiscal priorities.

Finally, it should be noted that natural resource extraction and processing often carries significant environmental consequences. While this is the topic of our final issue, one prior comment is in order. According to the Stern Review (2007), the known reserve of low-cost oil is sufficient in itself to cause carbon dioxide emissions to exceed what they view as reasonable target levels. To the extent that one accepts these target levels, that would suggest that oil from high-cost sources like the tar sands should not be extracted at all unless extremely effective means of carbon capture can be devised in the meantime. At the least, one might advocate a moratorium on further exploitation, though that would require extreme political persuasion.

Carbon Pricing

Despite what has been happening in many other OECD countries, especially those in Europe, carbon pricing has been shunned in Canada, including in recent budgets. The evidence is mounting that global warming is a serious issue. The Stern Review put it aptly when it said that global warming is the biggest market failure we have ever known. It represents a global externality with potentially catastrophic consequences in which policy correction necessarily involves action by almost all countries in the world, in which the costs are borne by current generations and in which the main benefits accrue to future generations. In the absence of a world government, this is a difficult problem indeed, and it requires that all countries voluntarily do their part. This is a much more difficult problem in international coordination than the recent one dealing with national fiscal policies and the incentive to free-ride there.

There are many challenging and almost intractable policy issues involved, all of them with fiscal consequences. It would be a shame to let populist politics dictate the outcome. The primary issue is whether pricing and emissions policies should mimic those recommended by the Stern Review. This called for a rapidly rising and substantial carbon price, combined with heavy investment in technology to reduce emissions as well as to facilitate adaptation. Moreover, the carbon price should be worldwide, and aid should be provided to developing countries to enable them to participate fairly. The pricing scheme could in principle be based on a carbon tax or on cap and trade, or some combination of both, country by country. The advantage of taxation is that it leads to more stable carbon pricing, and it might be easier to share the burden across developed and developing countries. It might also be easier to harmonize if countries implement their own carbon tax schemes. (The case for carbon taxation in Canada is developed by Mintz and Olewiler, 2008; and Courchene and Allan, 2008). On the other hand, cap-and-trade systems lead to more certainty about the quantity of emissions, and such schemes have already been established in the European Union and seem to be the policy of choice in the United States. In principle, either system could be adopted and lead to a suitable system of carbon pricing. Indeed, a combination of cap and trade and taxation could be deployed to avoid excessive fluctuations of both price and quantity (e.g., Roberts and Spence, 1976).

Whatever system is adopted, there are many issues of design quite apart from harmonization. With a tax system, revenues are generated that could be used for various purposes, including general tax relief (the so-called double dividend). With a cap-and-trade system, the issue is more whether the value of the cap will accrue to the public sector at all rather than simply being given away to producers as their property rights. Political feasibility aside, the case for selling the caps by auction or other means is compelling. There are a number of other issues that would have to be settled. One is the coverage: whether to include all of industrial, agricultural, and household carbon emissions. At what stage of production should carbon pricing apply, or should it apply at multiple stages analogous to the GST, as proposed by Courchene and Allan (2008)? How should exports and imports be treated? What should be the role of the federal government versus the provinces in implementing carbon taxation? There is also the complementary issue of the role of technology and adaptation. Should the revenues from the carbon-pricing scheme be earmarked for these purposes? On strictly economic grounds, there is no reason why that should be the case.

Finally, there are a number of supply side issues that some observers have suggested are potentially important. We have already mentioned the prediction of the Stern Review that the known reserves of low-cost oil are already sufficient to take the level of CO_2 in the atmosphere to dangerous levels and the implications this might have for oil sand extraction. Sinn (2008) has made the point that in the absence of virtually universal co-operation in carbon pricing, it is practically impossible to control all suppliers of oil and gas. If the suppliers cannot be controlled, they will find ways to sell their products. Moreover, he cautions that the kind of policies that the Stern Review recommends, such as accelerating carbon pricing to reflect the social cost of emissions as the stock in the atmosphere increases, can have a perverse effect. If producers expect the carbon price to rise, their response may be to accelerate the rate of extraction, and this would hasten global warming. This is what Sinn refers to as the "green paradox".

Clearly, policies for carbon pricing are challenging and require a degree of international co-operation that we have not witnessed in the past. It requires countries to behave in the interest of international welfare, with the interest of future generations in mind, rather than to free-ride on other nations, as has been our practice to date.

Concluding Remarks

Some important fiscal challenges lie ahead, at least comparable in magnitude to what we have faced in the past. The challenge is for policy-makers and politicians to take a proactive role in ensuring that the good policies are implemented. Loss aversion in the minds of voters tends to lead to political opposition to reasonable policies for which there are some losers. This loss aversion tends to deter lazy or populist-oriented governments from pursuing far-sighted and well-conceived policies. Obviously, the enactment of good policies relies on the integrity of politicians and their advisors in the bureaucracy. However, they rely equally on the unsolicited advice of the policy research community. In my view, we should also stubbornly insist on basing our policy research and prescriptions on principles and not be deterred by issues of political feasibility.

References

Ambachtscheer, K.P. 2007. *Pension Revolution: A Solution to the Pensions Crisis.* John Wiley and Company.

Banks, J. and P. Diamond. 2008. *The Base for Direct Taxation.* Prepared for the Report of a Commission on Reforming the Tax System for the 21st Century, chaired by Sir James Mirrlees. London: Institute for Fiscal Studies.

Boadway, R. 2004. "The Dual Income Tax System – An Overview", *CESifo DICE REPORT, Journal for Institutional Comparisons* 2(3), 3-8.

__________. 2009a. "Fiscal Priorities for Canada: Building on the Legacy of David Dodge", *Festschrift in Honour of David Dodge's Contributions to Canadian Public Policy.* Ottawa: Bank of Canada.

__________. 2009b. "Natural Resource Shocks and the Federal System: Boon or Curse?" in J.R. Allan, T.J. Courchene, and C. Leuprecht (eds.), *Canada: The State of the Federation 2006/07– Transitions: Fiscal and Political Federalism in an Era of Change.* Montreal & Kingston: McGill-Queen's University Press, 107-130.

Courchene, T.J. and J.R. Allan. 2008. "Climate Change: The Case for a Carbon Tariff/Tax", *Policy Options* 29(3), 59-64.

Expert Panel on Equalization and Territorial Formula Financing (the O'Brien Report). 2006. *Achieving a National Purpose: Putting Equalization Back on Track.* Ottawa: Department of Finance.

Mintz, J. and N. Olewiler. 2008. *A Simple Approach for Bettering the Environment and the Economy: Restructuring the Federal Fuel Excise Tax.* Prepared for the Sustainable Prosperity Initiative, University of Ottawa Institute of the Environment.

Mirrlees, J., S. Adam, T. Besley, R. Blundell, S. Bond, R. Chote, M. Gammie, P. Johnson, G. Myles, and J. Poterba, eds. 2010. *Tax by Design: The Mirrlees Review.* Oxford: Oxford University Press.
National Welfare Council. 2008. *Welfare Incomes, 2006 and 2007.* Ottawa: National Welfare Council.
Organisation for Economic Co-operation and Development (OECD). 2008. *Growing Unequal: Income Distribution and Poverty in OECD Countries.* Paris: OECD.
President's Advisory Panel on Federal Tax Reform. 2005. *Simple, Fair and Pro-Growth: Proposals to Fix America's Tax System.* Washington.
Report of a Committee Chaired by Professor J.E. Meade (Meade Committee). 1978. *The Structure and Reform of Direct Taxation.* London: George Allen and Unwin.
Roberts, M.J. and M. Spence. 1976. "Effluent Charges and Licenses under Uncertainty", *Journal of Public Economics* 5, 193–208.
Royal Commission on Taxation (Carter Commission). 1966. *Report.* Ottawa: Queen's Printer.
Sinn, H.-W. 2008. *The Green Paradox – Appeal for an Illusion-Free Climate Policy*. Berlin: Econ Verlag.
Stern Review. 2007. *The Economics of Climate Change*. Cambridge: Cambridge University Press.
Technical Committee on Business Taxation (Mintz Committee). 1997. *Report.* Ottawa: Department of Finance.
Tremblay, J.-F. 2009. "Fiscal Balance and Revenue-Sharing", in J.R. Allan, T.J. Courchene, and C. Leuprecht (eds.), *Canada: The State of the Federation 2006/07 – Transitions: Fiscal and Political Federalism in an Era of Change*. Montreal & Kingston: McGill-Queen's University Press, 131–143.
US Treasury. 1977. *Blueprints for Basic Tax Reform.* Washington: Treasury of the United States.

LOOKING FORWARD: SOME IMMODEST PROPOSALS

Thomas J. Courchene, Queen's University

Introduction

In the John Deutsch Institute's long and venerable history of mounting budget conferences, this 2009 version has to rank with the very best. Part of this may be due to the fact that the 2009 budget bordered on the spectacular – politically, economically, and, of course, fiscally. Nonetheless, it need not have followed that the roster of speakers would read like a Who's Who of Canadian public policy academics/analysts in our profession. For this, our collective thanks go out to Charlie Beach and his co-editors, Bev Dahlby and Paul Hobson. Indeed, this volume is a most fitting way to congratulate and to pay tribute to Charlie for his outstanding contribution to Canadian public policy as the Director of Queen's John Deutsch Institute for the Study of Economic Policy.

The theme of this final section of the volume is, as the conference agenda indicated, to focus on the "big picture". I have interpreted this as a call to provide a forward-looking public policy perspective or context relating to an admittedly arbitrary selection of issues drawn from the above papers. In more detail, the second section focuses on aspects of the global financial collapse and on how and why Canada fared so well in international perspective. Attention is then directed toward a recent proposal to rework aspects of Canadian financial regulation. The third section highlights the rapid-fire transition of the budget from surpluses to stimulus and arguably to fiscalamity (especially if one includes the provinces). This is followed by some observations relating to the allocation of deficits between Ottawa and the provinces. The fourth section argues that while the budgetary infrastructure stimulus may well be appropriately "shovel ready", it is inappropriately "shovel heavy". In other words, the stimulus should have been more "transformative", i.e., more directed toward human capital than physical capital. The section concludes with an assertion that the Harper government's "open federalism" is offside with the new global order, given that the new reality is that many of the key issues/areas that are in the national interest also happen to be under provincial jurisdiction. The rest of the paper focuses in turn on proposals for reforming or rethinking three policy areas: climate change, enhancing horizontal fiscal equity, and Employment Insurance. A brief conclusion completes the paper.

Anatomy of the Financial Collapse

The spectacular boom leading up to the financial debacle was unique in that, despite its intensity and duration, interest rates remained uncharacteristically and inappropriately low. One of the principal causes is not hard to find: China, the global workshop, with access to an effectively unlimited unskilled/low-skilled labour force and with its exchange rate pegged to the US dollar, ensured that US CPI inflation remained low and stable. In turn, and unlike a normal boom where rising interest rates would have served to temper the economic expansion, low inflation during the 2000s boom kept interest rates correspondingly low, especially so in light of the insatiable demand for loans and credit spurred on by "irrational exuberance". (By way of an important analytical aside here, in such a scenario where inflation is kept in check by Chinese imports, CPI inflation targeting is arguably a defective strategy unless it takes into account asset inflation.) In any event, in this booming economy/low-interest-rate environment, the search was on to find some reasonably high-interest-rate financial instrument suitable for leveraging. The fateful solution was to privilege sub-prime (i.e., unqualified) borrowers with mortgages that were then successively leveraged via collateralized debt obligations and credit default swaps.[1] Moreover, the explosion of these mortgages was certainly not independent of the reality that mortgage interest payments are tax deductible in the United States. When these underlying mortgages fell

[1]Credit default swaps have been termed "financial instruments of mass destruction" because they take the form of insurance policies on leveraged debt obligations. The incredibly destructive feature here, apart from the lack of regulation, is that third parties can take out insurance policies for or against the default of these obligations. As a result, the value of credit default swaps dwarfed the value of the underlying obligations.

into default and were foreclosed (in part because the typical mortgage embodied an initial two-year, low-interest period with a much higher interest rate for the renewal and in part because the economic collapse clobbered housing prices), this huge inverted pyramid of credit came crashing down with devastating consequences for the financial and real economy alike.

Some mighty icons have fallen (disappeared, effectively nationalized, or taken over) – Bear Sterns, Lehman Brothers, and the Royal Bank of Scotland on the financial side and the Detroit-Three and Stelco on the real side. In the process, Wall Street has (temporarily, at least) surrendered financial leadership to the sovereign wealth funds and the petro-dictatorships. Moreover, the international financial community is pressing for a new international financial architecture (led by France) and a substitute for the dollar as the global currency (led by China).

If there is any good news here, it is that the Canadian banking sector remains alive and well – indeed, spectacularly well in international comparative context. With the collapse of the US banking/finance sector, Toronto now qualifies as one of the premier financial centres in North America; this will be a key asset in terms of our recovery and of our ability to market our exports. Indeed, the latest Top Ten ranking of North American banks by assets now includes four Canadian banks – holding positions seven through ten are RBC, TD Canada Trust, BNS, and Bank of Montreal – compared with only RBC a year ago. Moreover, with the US banking system likely to continue consolidating, major opportunities south of the border will arise for Canada's banks since branch banking is their forte.

OSFI to the Rescue

How did Canada come to escape the US financial carnage? My version of the story begins during the mid-1980s FTA negotiations. In part because of overly restrictive provincial ownership rules, the largely Ontario-based Canadian securities industry was in deep trouble. Specifically, the entire capital of the Canadian securities industry was less than that of the then existing US-based Salomon Bros. In a surprise move, Quebec indicated that it intended to relax its ownership rules for the securities industry, including allowing institutions from other financial pillars to own Quebec-based securities firms. In response, some Ontario-based securities firms publicly mused about moving their headquarters to Montreal, and at least one chartered bank indicated that it would be interested in establishing a securities presence in Quebec. Almost immediately, David Peterson's Ontario countered by throwing the ownership of Ontario securities firms wide open. However, federal Finance Minister Michael Wilson was none too happy with all of this because allowing US investors to take an ownership position in the Canadian securities industry was supposed to be a key bargaining chip in the ongoing FTA negotiations and Ontario had just delivered this chip to the United States on a platter. Presumably in response to the finance minister's concerns, Ontario modified its proposal to allow Canadian institutions a full year to purchase these firms or to open their own securities firms before foreigners would be allowed entry. Ottawa then accommodated Ontario's revised position by altering the *Bank Act* to allow the chartered banks to become owners of securities firms.

The fortuitous result was that the chartered banks gobbled up most of the Canadian-based securities firms – the Bank of Nova Scotia ended up with Scotia McLeod, RBC with Dominion Securities, CIBC with Wood Gundy, BMO with Nesbitt Burns, and Banque Nationale with Lévesque Beaubien. For its part, TD chose to "build rather than buy" by establishing Greenline, which, over time and after mergers/takeovers, became TD Waterhouse.

In roughly the same time frame, the Canadian Commercial Bank and the Northland Bank failed, Canada's first bank failures since the collapse of the Home Bank in 1923. This led to the inquiry into these failures chaired by Justice Estey, which, in turn, led to the merger of the Office of the Inspector General of Banks and the Department of Insurance to form OSFI (Office of the Superintendent of Financial Institutions). In the process, OSFI emerged as a much more effective institution in terms of financial regulation and supervision. Therefore, when Canada's recapitalized securities industry was effectively gobbled up by the chartered banks, it also fell indirectly[2] under the conservative regulatory eye of OSFI, which, in turn, kept our securities industry within a "banking culture" rather than the more or less free-for-all "securities-industry culture" of the United States. For example, when the United States followed us by relaxing the *Glass-Steagall Act* (which allowed banks to own securities firms), the result was that some major US banks (e.g., Citibank) essentially abandoned their banking charter to focus on the much less regulated securities activities or largely unregulated hedge-fund activities.

---

[2]"Indirectly" because the regulation of the securities industry rests with the provinces. However, in regulating the banks, OSFI will obviously be concerned with the financial viability of any securities firm that is a subsidiary of a bank.

All in all, a Canadian success story, although we did suffer through our own financial fiasco with ABCP (asset-backed commercial paper).

The Bank of Canada as the Super-Regulator?

A policy issue that has arisen in the wake of the financial collapse is the Bank of Canada's expression of interest in taking over OSFI, i.e., taking over the regulation of all federally regulated financial institutions, including the chartered banks. (By way of an aside, the US Fed is also intent on obtaining overarching regulatory powers.) The rationale for this new role for the Bank is that while OSFI focuses on the prudential oversight of each and every financial institution, the current financial collapse dictates that attention also needs to be directed to "system stability", or what the G20 has called the "macro-prudential" role. Arguably, the Bank does have an advantage over OSFI when it comes to assessing system stability, and indeed it has been monitoring system stability all along. But this is not where the concern lies. Rather it is whether OSFI's prudential function, the CDIC's deposit insurance role, and the Bank's monetary policy and system stability roles are best placed under a single omnibus regulator. My answer is "no": these institutions deal with financial/prudential objectives that can on occasion be in conflict, and, as such, they need independent institutional and advocacy status. An obvious compromise would take the form of embracing the status quo, but with the additional feature that OSFI and the Bank be required to hold monthly or quarterly meetings where system stability or macro-prudential issues would be on the table. Indeed, one presumes that some version of this has long been in place. Hence, I support the recent (post-conference) announcement by Finance Minister Flaherty that responsibility for Bank regulation and supervision will remain under Finance and not be transferred to the Bank of Canada. Respected academics in the United States and in international financial institutions are also recommending against increasing the Fed's financial regulatory powers.

Reflections on the Fiscal Front

From Surpluses to Deficits to Fiscalamity

In his November 27, 2008, *Economic and Fiscal Statement*, Finance Minister Flaherty decreased the earlier proposed program spending for

2009-10 from the levels contained in the February 2008 budget in order to ensure that surpluses would be the order of the day, not only for fiscal year 2009-10 but as well for the following three fiscal years. So offside was this budgetary stance with the emerging on-the-ground reality and with Canadians' expectations that the Conservative minority government survived only by virtue of the Governor General's budgetary mulligan, with the result that the ensuing January 27, 2009, budget landed safely in the fairway, economically and politically. Part of the success of the re-launch, especially on the political front, was no doubt a result of the impressive consultation process undertaken by the Conservative government, including the appointment of a Blue Ribbon committee headed by former BC Finance Minister Carole Taylor. In our joint assessment of the 2009 budget (Courchene and Allan, 2009a), we noted that not since Sir John A. installed himself in a Toronto hotel room and invited industrialists to create the tariff schedule for the National Policy has this sort of "reverse rent-seeking" been elevated to such a level. Indeed, we suggested "No Consultee Left Behind" as the preferred title for the 2009 budget.

However appropriate the 2009 budget may have been when delivered, the march of events has not been kind to its forecasts. In early June of 2009, TD Economics projected the five-year cumulative deficit to be $170 billion, twice the $85 billion in Flaherty's budget forecast. As important, in the fifth year out (fiscal 2013-14), the 2009 Budget projected a small surplus, whereas the TD forecasts still have the fiscal balance deep in the red by $20 billion. Over the same interval, the loonie has risen by roughly 20% (from 76 US cents in March, to the low 90-cent range in early June, and further to 96 cents in mid-October as this is being written), leading the Governor of the Bank of Canada and the business community generally to become quite concerned that this rapid appreciation will create problems for exports as well as for the recovery. The message here is that economic recovery alone is not likely to be strong enough to return the system to budget balance, i.e., the deficit has become structural and will require additional taxes and/or spending restraint. In passing, one might note that the one voice that was most prescient in terms of the evolving budget imbalance and that was willing to speak truth to power was Kevin Page, the parliamentary budget officer. One hopes that this recently created role will become a permanent and adequately funded position, but history is against the survival of these separation-of-powers-type initiatives in Westminster systems unless they come fully under the auspices of Parliament.

Deficit Downloading and the EI-Welfare Nexus

In the 1990s recession, the aggregate provincial and federal deficits for fiscal year 1989–90 were $4.3 and $28.9 billion, respectively, and for 1992–93, they were $24.7 and $41.0 billion. In other words, while Ottawa's deficit increased by $12.1 billion, the aggregate provincial deficit rose by $20.4 billion, thanks in part to Ottawa's cap on the Canada Assistance Plan, and selected caps and freezes on other transfers, on the one hand and increases in UI premiums to ameliorate the federal deficits on the other. In contrast, while Australia underwent a similarly severe recession in the early 1990s, Canberra took action to ensure that the aggregate state budgets remained in surplus throughout, although individual states did go into the red. Moreover, much of Paul Martin's acclaimed deficit slaying, beginning with his landmark 1995 budget, was the result of downloading the deficit to the provinces via the one-third absolute cut in CHST transfers (albeit with some reconstitution during the mid-1990s-to-early-2000s boom). Apparently, the provinces make great foul weather friends!

In the current time frame, this deficit downloading is again alive and well. The 2009 budget's claim of $51 billion of stimulus over the two-year period (fiscal 2009–10 and 2010–11) includes nearly $12 billion of "required" or "shared-cost" provincial money – $8.9 billion (or 50%) of the budget's allocation for provincial and municipal infrastructure, $1.475 billion (or 42%) of the budget's allocation for municipal housing, and a 33% contribution from Ontario as its share of the federal bailout for the Detroit-Three. One wonders whether the revenue capacity exists for provinces (and municipalities) to contribute to the federal stimulus package to the degree anticipated by the budget.

Arguably, the most serious (albeit perhaps not yet fully obvious) downloading issue relates to the rising unemployment rates. Thus far, Parliament's attention has been riveted on whether and how to revamp the EI formula in order to make benefits more responsive to the needs of workers who have lost their jobs. Given the severity of the recession, even without increasing the duration of benefits, the EI system is likely to run deficits in the billions. However, these deficits would still be but a fraction of the roughly $60 billion or so that Ottawa (inappropriately, if not illegally) diverted over the years from EI surpluses to its Consolidated Revenue Fund as part of the Liberals' deficit-slaying strategy. Figure 1 traces this run-up to $60 billion in the cumulative EI surplus through to 2008 and then estimates the projected decrease over the next few years and then the return to the $60+ range in cumulated

Figure 1: Unemployment/Employment Insurance Financing

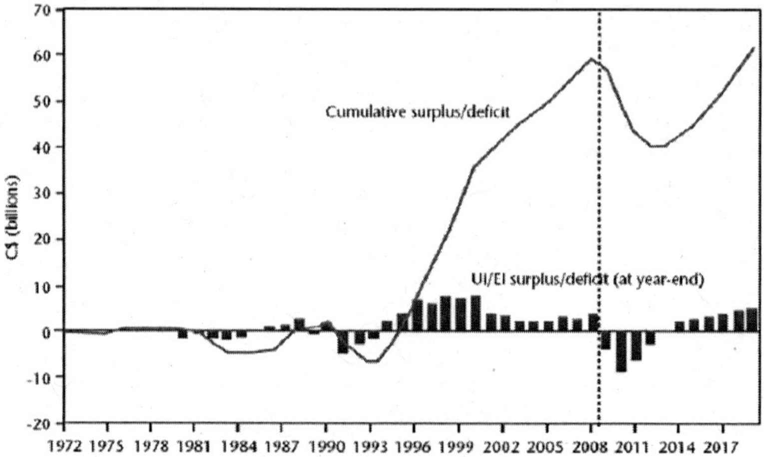

Note: 2009 deficit nets out budgeted $2.9 billion EI reserve.
Source: TD Economics, HRSDC, Library of Parliament. Reproduced from Courchene and Allan (2009b).

surplus. This return to the $60 billion range occurs in part because i) benefits will eventually decrease and contributions increase as employment increases; ii) the legislation requires EI premiums to rise in order to eliminate any deficit for the forthcoming year; iii) the premium rate can rise or fall by no more than .15% relative to the rate for the previous year; and iv) upswings tend to be longer than downturns. Working together, these factors impart a tendency for the cumulated surplus to rise over time. Intriguingly, there is no commitment to return to an overall zero cumulative balance.[3] Hence, as in the post-1995 period, the return to economic growth, replete with rising EI contributions, falling EI benefits, and a downward-sticky contribution rate will eventually offset the EI component of the deficit and will then begin to contribute to achieving overall budget balance.

What has not been mentioned in all of this is the impending fiscal nightmare for the provinces when these unemployed Canadians exhaust their EI benefits and are forced to turn to provincial welfare. For

[3]However, a class action suit (initiated in Quebec) against Ottawa with respect to this diversion of excess EI premiums is now working its way up to the Supreme Court.

example, in May of 2009, there were 778,000 Canadians and their families receiving EI benefits. But there were 800,000 unemployed Canadians and their families who were without benefits, many of whom would be on welfare. And as of now (October), many of the May EI beneficiaries may well have exhausted their benefits and joined the ranks of the welfare recipients. Unlike the case for Ottawa, there is no set of premiums that the provinces can use to recoup their soon-to-be mushrooming spending on welfare. This indirect version of deficit shifting is just one of the ways in which the EI program serves to interact with the rest of social policy to prevent Canada from developing a state-of-the-art social envelope. A "big bang" approach to EI reform will be addressed in the penultimate section of this paper.

Infrastructure Spending: Shovel Ready Versus Shovel Heavy

From Boards and Mortar to Mortarboards

The Dale Orr (2008) criteria for an effective stimulus package – timely, targeted, temporary, and cost-efficient – have been generally accepted, and they lead rather naturally to a focus on upgrading Canada's physical infrastructure (roads, rail, bridges, public and private structures, and the like). Now it is certainly true that Canada does have a physical infrastructure deficit, and it is also true that upgrading this infrastructure will make us more competitive. However, given the sheer magnitude of the stimulus and the reality that the global economy is undergoing dramatic and profound changes in areas like the knowledge-based economy, climate change, and the relationship between the citizen and the state, there is a further requisite for any stimulus package: it ought to be *transformative.* Specifically, just as physical and financial capital underpinned the Industrial Revolution, human capital will be the principal driving force underpinning the knowledge/informatics revolution. It is this reality that led to our comment that the budget's approach to infrastructure, while appropriately "shovel ready", is inappropriately "shovel heavy" (Courchene and Allan, 2009a).

Phrased differently, the infrastructure program in the budget focuses too much on boards and mortar and not enough on mortarboards or, more generally, not enough on those areas that will lead to success in the new global order – early childhood development, daycare, K-12 and PSE, health, climate change. In contrast, with President Obama's focus on health, education, and even providing fiscally challenged states with equalization-like transfers, the United States seems intent on moving in the direction of a continental European social economy, Congress willing. And the Australian budget, in its "Building the Education Revolution", directed very significant monies on K-to-12 education – e.g., 500 new science labs, monies for library upgrades, $200,000 for each school for renewal of infrastructure, a $950-per-child Back To School bonus to support 2.8 million children from low- and middle-income families as well as a similar grant to students and persons outside the labour force for study or training.

To be sure, Canada's 2009 budget does address aspects of infrastructure needs for universities and provides training funds through EI as well as on a stand-alone basis. But if our goal as a society is, as I outlined in *A State of Minds* (2001), to provide equality of opportunity for all Canadians to develop and enhance their human capital, then Ottawa cannot shy away from privileging areas like early childhood education. Data from the OECD (*Starting Strong II*, 2006) indicate that for some key areas of ELCC (early-learning child care), such as ELCC spending on children 0–6 as a percent of GDP and the percent of children 0–3 years in regulated facilities, Canada ranks at or near the bottom of OECD countries. Why are we not following more in Australia's footprints here? Presumably, one aspect of the Harper Conservatives' answer would be "open federalism". Since I view this as a wholly inadequate response in an era where society is undergoing dramatic economic and social evolution, some elaboration is in order.

Open Federalism and the National Interest

Open federalism is a principled approach to federalism, the principle being a respect for constitutional division of powers, replete with a commitment to restrain the exercise of the federal spending power in areas of exclusive provincial jurisdiction. No doubt what lent open federalism some of its appeal in the 2006 federal election was the seemingly excessive manner in which Prime Minister Paul Martin, as *maître d'* in charge of what *The Economist* referred to as his "fiscal cafeteria", struck bilateral deals with the provinces across a wide range of areas falling under provincial jurisdiction. Moreover, it did not go unnoticed that principal among the reasons why the provinces were so cash-starved and, therefore, so willing to be party to these deals was Martin's CHST cuts in his 1995 budget.

Nonetheless, Martin was on to something fundamentally important – namely, that success in the new global order will increasingly depend on excelling in some areas that, in Canada at least, fall under provincial jurisdiction – e.g., ensuring dynamic cities in addition to the areas highlighted in the previous paragraph. In other words, an increasing number of areas that are now in the *national interest* happen also to be within *provincial jurisdiction*. This being the case, it seems to me that the Harper Conservatives must be careful that their embracing of "open federalism" is not just a reversion to the old "watertight compartments" approach to federalism. While it is true that Prime Minister Martin's "fiscal cafeteria" can be viewed as an unprincipled reliance on the federal spending power, our federal history is nonetheless full of creative ways in which Ottawa has privileged key areas and policies that are in the national interest but under provincial jurisdiction, and where we did this in a manner consistent with respecting provincial jurisdiction – i.e., with the provinces on board. What is the principle that allows the federal budget to engage in shared-cost, boards-and-mortar infrastructure projects in provincial areas but not shared-cost mortarboards infrastructure?

The underlying message here, and one that will be increasingly important for success in the knowledge-based economy and society, is that federalism must ultimately be about increasing the welfare of citizens, not just of governments!

In the remainder of the paper, attention is directed to three specific policy issues/areas – carbon pricing, equalization, and EI – each of which features prominently in the earlier chapters of this volume.

Climate Change and Carbon Pricing

Until recently in both Canada and the United States, it was the provinces and the states, not the federal governments, that drove the climate change agenda. With its $30/tonne carbon tax, British Columbia can claim the title of Canada's carbon-pricing star. In the United States, this title belongs to California, with its vehicle emissions standards, its limits on the carbon footprint of imported fossil fuel, and its quarterbacking of the Western Climate Initiative (WCI), an association of seven US states and four provinces (BC, Manitoba, Ontario, and Quebec) that is committed to implementing a cross-border cap-and-trade (C&T) regime. However, it seems most likely that the US component of the WCI, as well as the US northeast RGGI (Regional Greenhouse Gas Initiative), will be folded into a national US C&T system, a system that the Harper government has committed to associate itself with. Were this to come to fruition, it would be intriguing indeed, given that the cross-border C&T regime would involve a Kyoto non-signatory and a Kyoto signatory but non-implementer. Nonetheless, it would also be impressive since leadership on the carbon-pricing file in both countries would be transferred to the federal governments.

Given this, it is passing strange that the provisions of the Clean Energy Fund in the 2009 federal budget focus primarily on CCS (Carbon Capture and Storage/Sequestration), a strategy that parallels the climate change policies of Saskatchewan and Alberta. This is not to say that a CCS focus is inappropriate, since both the International Energy Agency and the Intergovernmental Panel on Climate Change suggest that any successful transition to a carbon-constrained future will require a significant CCS contribution. This is especially the case since improving the technology for CCS will be essential in light of the reality that countries such as China will continue to build coal-fired electricity-generation plants and will need access to an effective version of CCS to mitigate the associated CO_2 fallout.

Rather, the concern is that support for CCS ought to have been part of a larger portfolio of policies. For example, although the Clean Energy Fund may benefit the renewable energy industry, the words "renewable energy" are not even mentioned in the budget. Indeed, the successful program ecoEnergy for Renewable Power was not renewed. This is in sharp contrast to the $55 billion proposed by President Obama in his "recovery and investment" program to promote renewable energy and efficiency. As Figure 2 reveals, Canada places rather low in the national rankings of the percentage of the fiscal stimulus packages that is allocated to "green themes".[4] This is hardly good news for a country that is already viewed as an outlier in terms of economic greening.

Since climate change issues are likely to loom large in our policy future, it seems appropriate to highlight three areas[5] where Canada should play the role of lead advocate in the end-of-year Copenhagen run-up to Kyoto II.

---

[4]Even though China comes off looking "green" in Figure 2, it is at the same time rapidly increasing its reliance on coal-fired generators in order to satisfy its growing demands for electrical energy.

[5]The following three areas are elaborated upon in more detail in Courchene and Allan (2010).

Figure 2: Green Stimulus, Regional Ranking as a Percent of Total Stimulus

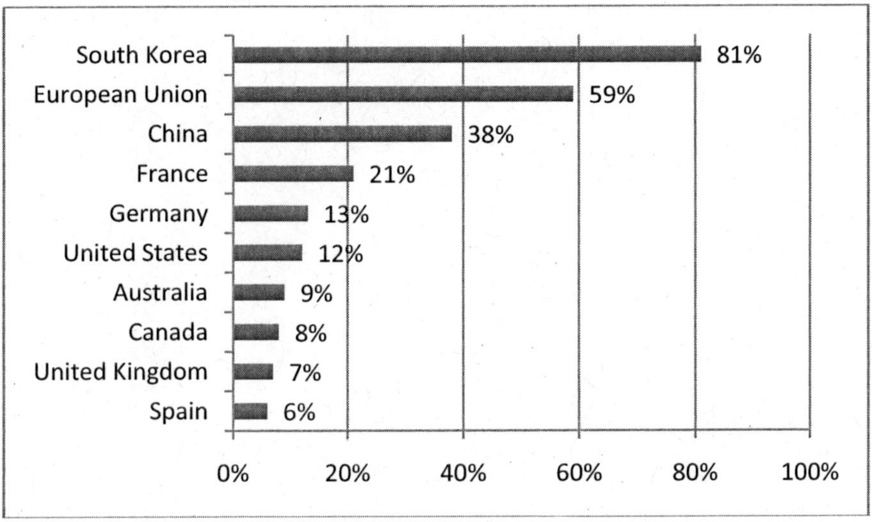

Source: HSBC "Climate Changer Global", February 25, 2009.

Population-Sensitive Emissions Targets

The first of these is that the Kyoto emissions caps should take account of population change. From Table 1, Canada's emissions growth from 1990-2004 was 26%, the highest of the countries in the table. However, corrected for the population growth data in the middle column, our per capita emissions growth was 8.2% (column 3), still the highest, but not far off Australia and the "rest of EU" (EU minus UK and Germany). Clearly, population growth matters, and the longer the time frame for the emission targets, the more it matters. Given the lengthy time frames of the Kyoto process, it seems imperative that population growth be an integral part of Kyoto II emissions policy and targets.

Assigning Carbon Footprints

The second issue relates to natural-resource and energy-producing countries like Canada. Kyoto assigns the carbon footprint arising from Canada's *production* of commodities (oil, gas, cement, etc.) to Canada,

Table 1: Comparison of Greenhouse Gas Emission Trends (in Percent)

Country	*Emissions Growth (Without LULUCF) 1990 to 2004*	*Population Growth 1990 to 2004*	*Increase in Emissions (Without LULUCF) per capita, 1990 to 2004*
Australia	+24.3	+17.0	+6.3
Canada	+26.6	+17.0	+8.2
Japan	+6.5	+3.1	+3.4
Russia	-33.1	-3.0	-31
United States	+15.8	+17.1	-1.2
EU 15	-1.0	+4.5	-5.3
Germany	-17.4	+3.8	-20.3
United Kingdom	-14.3	+4.8	-18.2
Rest of EU	+12.8	+4.7	+7.8

Note: LULUCF is Land-Use, Land-Use Change and Forestry.
Source: Emissions data from UN FCCC emissions profiles (unfccc.int/ghg_emissions_data/items/38954.php). Population data from US Census Bureau (www.census.gov/ipc/www/idbrank.html). Reproduced from Harrison and Sundstrom (2007, Table 4).

whether they are consumed domestically or exported. This is wrong. The carbon footprint *up to the point of export* arising from the production and transformation of our energy exports to the United States or of our cement exports to China should be assigned to the Americans and Chinese, respectively, and not to Canada. As matters now stand, the raw-material-exporting countries are making the importing countries appear to be much more environmentally benign than they actually are. For example, the United Kingdom is currently under its Kyoto targets for 2008–12. But if the United Kingdom had to incorporate the carbon footprint associated with the production in the exporting country of its energy and resource imports, it would not be (Harrison and Sundstrum, 2007). Without this change in emissions assignments, and with a growing India and China increasing the demands for our resources, Canada is unlikely to be able to meet *any* Kyoto II targets.

Marine Shipping

The final issue is along the same general lines. The carbon footprint of marine shipping is not included in Kyoto, nor is it included in any carbon pricing or C&T regime of which I am aware. Marine shipping produces about 5% of CO_2 emissions, more than double the aviation total, with potential to rise much higher. Moreover, in a feature article in *The Globe and Mail,* Mittelstaedt (2009) noted that marine shipping accounted for about two thirds of sulphur dioxide emissions from the transportation sector in 2002, headed for well above 90% by 2020 without control measures. For example, under international standards, ships can burn fuel containing up to 45,000 parts per million of sulphur. By comparison, gasoline for motor cars must have under 80 ppm. (Note that Canada and the United States are proposing 1,000 ppm as the new standard for shipping.) If one focuses on all GHGs, not only CO_2, the surprising reality is that marine transportation emits more GHGs than all other modes of transportation combined. Were shipping emissions to be integrated into Kyoto, one could expect some creative solutions, e.g., shipping "hybrids" with solar panels as the top deck. Of particular relevance to Canada and especially to Alberta is that any comparison of GHG emissions from the oil sands and from oil from the Gulf States should include the footprints from shipping. If Copenhagen fails to include the carbon footprints from shipping, then our exports to the United States will be discriminated against in comparison with exports from overseas. Phrased differently, ignoring the carbon footprint of shipping, especially ocean shipping, means that all countries are equidistant under Kyoto, which is certain to wreak havoc with our "carbon competitiveness" in NAFTA economic space.

The bottom line here is that there is a strong case for Canada to take these issues to Copenhagen this December (en route to Kyoto II) and, perhaps more important, to press the case for them to be considered in any joint Canada-US carbon pricing system. In all three cases, one wonders what our political masters and our negotiators were actually doing in Kyoto in 1997.

Introducing More Horizontal Equity into Equalization

From Michael Smart's excellent paper (this volume) on the post-O'Brien changes to equalization:

> With the 2009 Equalization changes, the federal government now operates three distinct lump-sum grants as its major transfers, each allocated based on different principles and each legislated to grow at a different rate – the Canada Health Transfer (CHT) at 6% annually, the Canada Social Transfer (CST) at 3%, and now Equalization at the growth rate of nominal GDP. Grappling with fiscal arrangements in coming years is therefore going to require decisions about the relative priority of vertical versus horizontal grants and an articulation of what each of the grants is intended to achieve.

This is a most creative take on the evolution of the federal-provincial transfer system of cash transfers, and it provides the backdrop for proposing an "overarching" approach to interprovincial horizontal equity, one that involves all three transfers. I hasten to add that Michael Smart may not agree with what follows.

The starting point for what I shall refer to as overarching horizontal equity, or OHE, is the observation that the sum of last year's own-source revenue capacity plus equalization generated just over $13,000 per capita for Alberta, $11,000 for Newfoundland and Labrador, $8,400 for Saskatchewan, $8,100 for BC, with the remaining provinces in the low- to mid-$7,000 range.[6] Perhaps Saskatchewan and BC are not outliers in terms of the s.36(2) constitutional provision calling for "reasonably comparable levels of public services at reasonably comparable levels of taxation", but Alberta and Newfoundland and Labrador surely are. One way to bring the per capita provincial revenue positions more in line with the constitutional provision would be to bring the other federal provincial cash transfers (CHT and CST) within the equalization framework writ large.

To see how OHE might work, it is instructive to note that, for 2009-10, Equalization was projected to equal $14.2 billion, the CHT to equal $24 billion, and the CST to equal $10.9 billion. These latter two transfers are effectively allocated on an equal per capita basis. Conveniently for purposes of the ensuing analysis, the CHT and CST transfers sum to $35.9 billion, or roughly $1,000 per capita. The essence of OHE is straightforward: since virtually every other federal cash transfer is income-tested, the rationale for OHE is to apply income testing (or, more correctly, "revenue-testing") to these CHT/CST transfers.

---

[6]With falling energy prices recently, these differentials will presumably be smaller. However, the principle in play carries through.

One version of revenue-testing would be along the following lines. For each dollar that a province's sum of own-source revenue and equalization exceeds, say, 110% of the all-province average of own-source revenues and equalization, that province's CHT/CST cash transfer would decrease by, say, 25 cents. The revenues clawed back would then be allocated again in the same fashion until the entire $35.9 billion has been distributed; i.e., Ottawa would not gain from this exercise. What this means is that if a province has per capita own-source revenues plus Equalization equal to $4,000 above the threshold (i.e., four times the $1,000 per capita value of the CHT/CST, then its entire CHT/CST will be fully clawed back. If the clawback were 20%, then a province's current $1,000 CHT/CST transfer would be fully clawed back if its revenues above the threshold were five times the value of the CHT/CST. And so on.

This proposal will presumably not meet with favour from the rich provinces. However, if the constitutional provisions are not to be ignored, revenue-testing the cash transfers (i.e., OHE) would be among the more effective ways to increase horizontal fiscal equity in the federation. My intention is to use current data to implement this model and to assess its implications, but if others wish to apply the model, so much the better.

Toward a State-of-the-Art Social Canada: Reforming EI [7]

The 1940 constitutional amendment that enshrined unemployment insurance as an exclusive federal power – s.91(2A) – represented a key turning point in Canada's social, political, and regional history since it provided Ottawa with an instrument that, over time, allowed it not only to end-run "property and civil rights" – s.92 (13) – but, as well, to fragment the internal social and economic union as long as the areas in question could be linked somehow to unemployment insurance. Hence, through UI and later EI, Ottawa became a key player in industrial Canada (seasonal benefits as well as UI for self-employed fishers but not farmers, for example), in regional policy (variable entrance requirements and benefit duration periods based on regional unemployment rates), in violating horizontal equity since otherwise identically situated Canadians are treated differently (again, VERs and different benefit durations across

[7] This section draws heavily from Courchene and Allan (2009b).

regions), in achieving Canada's fiscal balance in the wake of Paul Martin's 1995 budget (by diverting nearly $60 billion in excess EI premiums to Ottawa's Consolidated Revenue Fund, as Figure 1 above reveals), and finally but not exhaustively in creatively enlarging Canada's social envelope (maternity, parental, sickness, and compassionate benefits).

Arguably, the overall result of this omnibus EI program, with its tentacles extending hither and yon, is that Canada is unable and will continue to be unable to develop a state-of-the-art social envelope suitable for knowledge-based society unless and until we undertake a fundamental reform of EI. My version of this reform draws from joint work with John Allan (2009b) and would include the following four tenets:

- Returning the contributions-benefits nexus to insurance principles.
- Introducing a negative income tax (NIT) or guaranteed annual income (GAI) for adults.
- Making the "employment benefits" of EI more accessible to all Canadians.
- Introducing incentives to increase labour-force participation.

These four elements are interdependent in that all are essential for a state-of-the-art social envelope. Each of these components merits elaboration.

Returning EI to Insurance Principles

Table 2 presents the relationship among contribution hours (or weeks), benefit weeks, and unemployment rates in EI regions. Reading across the rows, for any given range of hours worked, each 1% increase in the unemployment rate generates two additional weeks of benefit (until the maximum 50 weeks is reached). And reading downward, for any given unemployment rate, it takes 70 hours (or two weeks at 35 hours per week) (up to 1,435 hours) to generate an additional week of benefits beyond which each additional 35 hours (one week) of contributions generates an additional week of benefits. At unemployment rates of 6% or lower, one needs 700 hours (20 weeks) to qualify for EI and be eligible for 19 weeks of benefits. However, in areas where the unemployment rate is 16% or above, 420 hours (or 12 weeks) will generate 37 weeks of benefits. To qualify for 37 weeks in the lowest unemployment

Table 2: Benefit Duration by Hours Worked and Regional Unemployment Rates

	Unemployment rate in economic region											
Hours of work	6% or less	6% to 7%	7% to 8%	8% to 9%	9% to 10%	10% to 11%	11% to 12%	12% to 13%	13% to 14%	14% to 15%	15% to 16%	+16%
420-54	0	0	0	0	0	0	0	0	31	33	35	37
455-89	0	0	0	0	0	0	0	29	31	33	35	37
490-524	0	0	0	0	0	0	28	30	32	34	36	38
525-59	0	0	0	0	0	26	28	30	32	34	36	38
560-94	0	0	0	0	25	27	29	31	33	35	37	39
595-629	0	0	0	23	25	27	29	31	33	35	37	39
630-64	0	0	22	24	26	28	30	32	34	36	38	40
665-99	0	20	22	24	26	28	30	32	34	36	38	40
700-69	19	21	23	25	27	29	31	33	35	37	39	41
770-839	20	22	24	26	28	30	32	34	36	38	40	42
840-909	21	23	25	27	29	31	33	35	37	39	41	43
910-79	22	24	26	28	30	32	34	36	38	40	42	44
980-1,049	23	25	27	29	31	33	35	37	39	41	43	45
1,050-119	24	26	28	30	32	34	36	38	40	42	44	46
1,120-189	25	27	29	31	33	35	37	39	41	43	45	47
1,190-259	26	28	30	32	34	36	38	40	42	44	46	48
1,260-329	27	29	31	33	35	37	39	41	43	45	47	49
1,330-399	28	30	32	34	36	38	40	42	44	46	48	50
1,400-434	29	31	33	35	37	39	41	43	45	47	49	50
1,435-469	30	32	34	36	38	40	42	44	46	48	50	50
1,470-504	31	33	35	37	39	41	43	45	47	49	50	50
1,505-539	32	34	36	38	40	42	44	46	48	50	50	50
1,540-574	33	35	37	39	41	43	45	47	49	50	50	50
1,575-609	34	36	38	40	42	44	46	48	50	50	50	50
1,610-644	35	37	39	41	43	45	47	49	50	50	50	50
1,645-679	36	38	40	42	44	46	48	50	50	50	50	50
1,680-714	37	39	41	43	45	47	49	50	50	50	50	50
1,715-749	38	40	42	44	46	48	50	50	50	50	50	50
1,750-784	39	41	43	45	47	49	50	50	50	50	50	50
1,785-819	40	42	44	46	48	50	50	50	50	50	50	50
1,820+	41	43	45	47	49	50	50	50	50	50	50	50

Note: Table includes the five additional benefit weeks from the 2009 federal budget. Note that for each column (excluding the zeros), until 1,435 hours worked, each 70 hours increases benefits by one week. Thereafter, each 35 hours increases benefits by one week.

Source: HRSDC, *Employment Insurance Act, Employment Insurance Regulations*. Produced from Courchene and Allan (2009b).

rate area would require 1,680 hours, or 48 weeks of work (see column 1).[8]

Equity issues argue for a common or uniform entry requirement, while insurance principles suggest that the duration of benefits should be based largely or entirely on contribution hours/weeks. This means that any of the "filled in" columns (see footnote 8) can play this role. My preference is one of the leftmost columns, say column 1. Note that under this altered entry requirement, a worker would need 420 hours, or 12 weeks, in order to qualify for 15 weeks of benefits. However, since regional unemployment rates are no longer driving benefits, entry qualification periods could be lowered: again following the formula in footnote 8, eight weeks of contributions would generate 14 weeks of benefits. In addition, there is no reason that the maximum duration cannot be higher, up to some higher maximum, as long as this is driven by longer contribution hours/weeks. Obviously, many other alternatives can also work. However, the underlying theme would be that longer-term benefits should only be able to be earned through longer-term contributions.

It would of course be possible, indeed desirable, if in severe downturns the above contributions-benefits relationship became more generous across the board, and vice versa, for substantial economic upswings.

An NIT/GAI for Adults

This rather dramatic shift to an insurance-compatible EI program can only be viable if accompanied by an alternative form of income support. With the refundable Child Tax Benefit and the OAS/GIS for the elderly, we effectively have NITs for our seniors and our children. What we lack is a GAI/NIT for adults. This we can and should introduce, preferably by converting the personal and spousal amounts/credits (under the federal income tax) into refundable and income-tested benefits and payable monthly to adults, with any reconciliation occurring at tax-filing time. Since the income-support component of welfare spending by provinces is likely to fall, Ottawa could reallocate to the GAI/NIT some or all of these

---

[8]It is convenient at this juncture to use the information in the previous two sentences to "fill in" the zeros in Table 2. Hence, the values in the first column would be, reading downward, 15, 15, 16, 16, 17, 17, 18, and 18, which then links up with the 19 in the table. Reading across for the first row would yield 15, 17, 19, 21, 23, 25, 27, 29, and then the 31 that appears in the table. Readers can readily replace the remaining zeros.

savings from the Canada Social Transfer. And, of course, since EI premiums would fall under this system, this would create tax or revenue room that could be applied to the GAI/NIT. Beyond this, the provinces may wish to augment the federal GAI/NIT by piggy-backing their provincial PITs onto the federal program.

The key social policy point here is that *there needs to be a greater federal presence in income support* because only Ottawa can internalize the many interprovincial externalities – e.g., Alberta and Saskatchewan are becoming the provinces of employment for many out-of-province workers while their home provinces become the locus for welfare when the economy turns sour.

Increasing Access to "Employment Benefits"

One of the very important roles of EI has been to expand the social envelope through what are referred to as "employment benefits", i.e., maternity, parental, sickness, training, and compassionate benefits. However, most of these benefits are preferably viewed as part of the larger social envelope, and, as such, they should be funded from general revenues and be available to all Canadians, rather than available on a highly subsidized basis to those who are EI-eligible. We run the risk of falling into the US vision and version of social policy, where access to the full social envelope requires access to a "good" job. Along these lines, many EI-eligible mothers do not take full advantage of maternal and parental benefits because the benefit rates arising from their jobs are not high enough to qualify as "liveable". At the very least, the system ought to allow mothers to take the total amount of benefits and to distribute them (appropriately discounted) over fewer weeks so that the benefit levels do become liveable. Without this and related initiatives to broaden access, maternal and paternal benefits, especially in tough economic times, will tend to be associated with employment in the public sector and in large corporations. We must do better.

Recently, Prime Minister Harper has proposed extending maternal and parental benefits of the self-employed. The details of his proposals are yet to be released, but his earlier electoral platform promised to introduce a voluntary program that would deliver full maternity and parental benefits provided that the self-employed had contributed to EI for six months prior to making a claim. As John Allan and I have noted (2009b), "such an approach would be so rife with moral hazard and so devoid of any insurance principle that it would surely lead to a demand to remove these benefits from EI and make them citizen based". Mischievously, I conclude this section by thanking Saskatchewan for its leadership in making medicare citizen-based because, otherwise, we might now be in the position of trying to wrest medicare from EI and to make it available for all Canadians by virtue of their citizenship. Quebec seems to be taking the lead here by mounting its own more expansive (but much more expensive) program for maternal and parental leave.

Increasing Labour-Force Participation

The final component of a reconstituted EI is some expanded version of Canada's WITB (Working Income Tax Benefit) or the US earned income tax credit. This will be important not only in its own right but also in terms of addressing Canada's looming labour shortage. One of the challenges will be to integrate the WITB with the tax-back provision of the NIT/GAI. This is part of the larger "notch" problem, whereby the many income-tested programs can interact to trigger inordinately high marginal tax rates at low levels of market income. One approach to this would be for Ottawa to set the maximum federal marginal tax rate, inclusive of clawbacks, equal to the top federal marginal tax rate. The rate would remain there until the actual combined tax-cum-clawback rate fell below the top marginal rate. Other programs that also serve to increase labour-force participation could also be included here – training and programs devoted to labour-force adjustment.

Obviously, there are far too few details provided here for any meaningful assessment of this reworking of EI/welfare. However, the role of the above analysis is to make the case that the ongoing rethinking of EI should embrace the overall income support system, including assessing the pros and cons of some version of an NIT/GAI.

Conclusion

If there is a theme that runs through these comments, it is the need for *transformation.* Yet as I read and listen to the public policy commentary (mostly from the financial community), I hear much about retrenching, efficiency, restoring budget balance, and the like, which I recognize as important for any future but which are in effect really a call for the good old days and ways. The reality is that this would deliver a future, socially and economically, that will leave us short of our potential.

In the context of achieving this potential, I labelled the budget "shovel heavy" and failing on the transformative front. The massive stimulus package was a once-in-a-lifetime opportunity to chart a new course and to embrace the dictates of a knowledge-based economy and society. By focusing on boards and mortar infrastructure, we effectively ignored mortarboards infrastructure (*à la* Australia), and ignored economic greening (*à la* China and South Korea), and instead riveted our attention on what worked in the previous paradigm.

Transformation is especially needed on the social and institutional fronts. I tried to make the case that "open federalism" has to be reconciled with the reality that some key policy areas essential for success in the knowledge-based era are under provincial jurisdiction. For example, my view is that provincial fortunes are so uneven and uncertain that Ottawa needs to play a larger role in income distribution and especially in income support. Moving in the direction of a GAI/NIT addresses this and does so in a way that respects provincial jurisdiction. In some areas, however, immodest proposals need to be aired. Given that access to comparable provincial public goods and services is increasingly a key component of what it will mean to be a Canadian in this emerging era, it is unacceptable to have the existing degree of per capita revenue inequality, post-Equalization, across the provinces. This is the rationale for the OHE proposal, as controversial as it will surely be. On the EI front, my argument is that the program is preventing us from having a state-of-the-art social policy. The Canadian way has been to ensure that key social programs are citizen-based and not employment-based, and EI is moving us in the direction of the latter (i.e., in the US direction). Finally, with respect to carbon pricing, we are spending too much effort on the specifics of this versus that program when there are some framework parameters that are cast in ways that are certain to create problems for us under any pricing scenario – namely, the need for population-sensitive emissions targets, for appropriate carbon assignments for exports, and for including the carbon footprints from marine shipping (indeed, all shipping) so that climate change policies do not disadvantage us in the US and global marketplace.

References

Courchene, T.J. 2001. *A State of Minds: Toward a Human Capital Future for Canadians.* Montreal: IRPP.

Courchene, T.J. and J.R. Allan. 2008. "Climate Change: The Case for a Carbon Tariff Tax", *Policy Options/Options politiques* (March), 59-64.

__________ 2009a. "Finding a Balance: Assessing Budget 2009", *Policy Options/Options politiques* (March), 12-18.

__________ 2009b. "A Short History of EI, and a Look at the Road Ahead", *Policy Options/Options politiques* (September), 19-28.

__________ 2010. "Carbon Pricing and Federalism", in T.J. Courchene and J.R. Allan (eds.), *Carbon Pricing and Environmental Federalism* (the 2009 edition of *Canada: The State of the Federation*), Montreal & Kingston: The Institute of Intergovernmental Relations, Queen's University and McGill-Queen's University Press.

Harrison, K. and L. Sundstrom. 2007. "The Comparative Politics of Climate Change", *Global Environmental Politics* 7(4) (November), 1-18.

Mittelstaedt, M. 2009. "The High Cost of Blowing Smoke on the High Seas", *The Globe and Mail* (April), A1.

OECD. 2006. *Starting Strong II: Early Childhood Education and Care.* Paris: OECD Publishing.

Orr, D. 2008. "Stimulus: What Works, What Doesn't", *Financial Post* (December 15), op. ed.

CONTRIBUTORS

Editors

Charles M. Beach	Department of Economics, Queen's University
Bev Dahlby	Department of Economics, University of Alberta
Paul A.R. Hobson	Department of Economics, Acadia University

Authors

Ken Battle	Caldeon Institute of Social Policy, Ottawa
Robin Boadway	Department of Economics, Queen's University
Thomas J. Courchene	School of Policy Studies, Queen's University
Robert Fairholm	Centre for Spatial Economics, Milton
Janice MacKinnon	Department of History, University of Saskatchewan
Chris Matier	Parliamentary Budget Office, Ottawa
Kevin Milligan	Department of Economics, University of British Columbia
Nancy Olewiler	Public Policy Program and Department of Economics, Simon Fraser University
Lars Osberg	Department of Economics, Dalhousie University
Christopher Ragan	Department of Economics, McGill University
William Scarth	Department of Economics, McMaster University
Michael Smart	Department of Economics, University of Toronto
Tracy Snoddon	Department of Economics, Wilfrid Laurier University

Stephen Tapp	Parliamentary Budget Office, Ottawa
Lindsay M. Tedds	School of Public Administration, University of Victoria
Sherri Torjman	Caldeon Institute of Social Policy, Ottawa
Frances Woolley	Department of Economics, Carleton University

Queen's Policy Studies

Recent Publications

The Queen's Policy Studies Series is dedicated to the exploration of major public policy issues that confront governments and society in Canada and other nations.

Our books are available from good bookstores everywhere, including the Queen's University bookstore (http://www.campusbookstore.com/). McGill-Queen's University Press is the exclusive world representative and distributor of books in the series. A full catalogue and ordering information may be found on their web site (http://mqup.mcgill.ca/).

John Deutsch Institute for the Study of Economic Policy

Discount Rates for the Evaluation of Public Private Partnerships, David F. Burgess and Glenn P. Jenkins (eds.), 2010. Paper ISBN 978-1-55339-163-0 Cloth ISBN 978-1-55339-164-7

Retirement Policy Issues in Canada, Michael G. Abbott, Charles M. Beach, Robin W. Boadway and James G. MacKinnon (eds.), 2009. Paper ISBN 978-1-55339-161-6 Cloth ISBN 978-1-55339-162-3

The 2006 Federal Budget: Rethinking Fiscal Priorities, Charles M. Beach, Michael Smart and Thomas A. Wilson (eds.), Policy Forum Series no. 41, 2007. Paper ISBN 978-1-55339-125-8 Cloth ISBN 978-1-55339-126-6

Health Services Restructuring in Canada: New Evidence and New Directions, Charles M. Beach, Richard P. Chaykowski, Sam Shortt, France St-Hilaire and Arthur Sweetman (eds.), 2006. Paper ISBN 978-1-55339-076-3 Cloth ISBN 978-1-55339-075-6

A Challenge for Higher Education in Ontario, Charles M. Beach (ed.), 2005. Paper ISBN 1-55339-074-1 Cloth ISBN 1-55339-073-3

Current Directions in Financial Regulation, Frank Milne and Edwin H. Neave (eds.), Policy Forum Series no.40, 2005. Paper ISBN 1-55339-072-5 Cloth ISBN 1-55339-071-7

Higher Education in Canada, Charles M. Beach, Robin W. Boadway and R. Marvin McInnis (eds.), 2005. Paper ISBN 1-55339-070-9 Cloth ISBN 1-55339-069-5

Financial Services and Public Policy, Christopher Waddell (ed.), 2004. Paper ISBN 1-55339-068-7 Cloth ISBN 1-55339-067-9

The 2003 Federal Budget: Conflicting Tensions, Charles M. Beach and Thomas A. Wilson (eds.), Policy Forum Series no. 39, 2004. Paper ISBN 0-88911-958-9 Cloth ISBN 0-88911-956-2

School of Policy Studies

Mission Critical: Smaller Democracies' Role in Global Stability Operations, Christian Leuprecht, Jodok Troy, and David Last (eds.), 2010. Paper 978-1-55339-244-6

Canada's Isotope Crisis: What Next? Jatin Nathwani and Donald Wallace (eds.), 2010. Paper 978-1-55339-283-5 Cloth 978-1-55339-284-2

Pursuing Higher Education in Canada: Economic, Social, and Policy Dimensions, Ross Finnie, Marc Frenette, Richard E. Mueller, and Arthur Sweetman (eds.), 2010. Paper 978-1-55339-277-4 Cloth 978-1-55339-278-1

Canadian Immigration: Economic Evidence for a Dynamic Policy Environment, Ted McDonald, Elizabeth Ruddick, Arthur Sweetman, and Christopher Worswick (eds.), 2010. Paper 978-1-55339-281-1 Cloth 978-1-55339-282-8

Taking Stock: Research on Teaching and Learning in Higher Education, Julia Christensen Hughes and Joy Mighty (eds.), 2010. Paper 978-1-55339-271-2 Cloth 978-1-55339-272-9

Architects and Innovators: Building the Department of Foreign Affairs and International Trade, 1909–2009/Architectes et innovateurs : le développement du ministère des Affaires étrangères et du Commerce international,de 1909 à 2009, Greg Donaghy and Kim Richard Nossal (eds.), 2009. Paper 978-1-55339-269-9 Cloth 978-1-55339-270-5

Academic Transformation: The Forces Reshaping Higher Education in Ontario, Ian D. Clark, Greg Moran, Michael L. Skolnik, and David Trick, 2009. Paper 978-1-55339-238-5 Cloth 978-1-55339-265-1

The New Federal Policy Agenda and the Voluntary Sector: On the Cutting Edge, Rachel Laforest (ed.), 2009. Paper 978-1-55339-132-6

The Afghanistan Challenge: Hard Realities and Strategic Choices, Hans-Georg Ehrhart and Charles Pentland (eds.), 2009. Paper 978-1-55339-241-5

Measuring What Matters in Peace Operations and Crisis Management, Sarah Jane Meharg, 2009. Paper 978-1-55339-228-6 Cloth ISBN 978-1-55339-229-3

International Migration and the Governance of Religious Diversity, Paul Bramadat and Matthias Koenig (eds.), 2009. Paper 978-1-55339-266-8 Cloth ISBN 978-1-55339-267-5

Centre for the Study of Democracy

The Authentic Voice of Canada: R.B. Bennett's Speeches in the House of Lords, 1941-1947, Christopher McCreery and Arthur Milnes (eds.), 2009. Paper 978-1-55339-275-0 Cloth ISBN 978-1-55339-276-7

Age of the Offered Hand: The Cross-Border Partnership Between President George H.W. Bush and Prime-Minister Brian Mulroney, A Documentary History, James McGrath and Arthur Milnes (eds.), 2009. Paper ISBN 978-1-55339-232-3 Cloth ISBN 978-1-55339-233-0

In Roosevelt's Bright Shadow: Presidential Addresses About Canada from Taft to Obama in Honour of FDR's 1938 Speech at Queen's University, Christopher McCreery and Arthur Milnes (eds.), 2009. Paper ISBN 978-1-55339-230-9 Cloth ISBN 978-1-55339-231-6

Politics of Purpose, 40th Anniversary Edition, The Right Honourable John N. Turner 17th Prime Minister of Canada, Elizabeth McIninch and Arthur Milnes (eds.), 2009. Paper ISBN 978-1-55339-227-9 Cloth ISBN 978-1-55339-224-8

Bridging the Divide: Religious Dialogue and Universal Ethics, Papers for The InterAction Council, Thomas S. Axworthy (ed.), 2008. Paper ISBN 978-1-55339-219-4 Cloth ISBN 978-1-55339-220-0

Institute of Intergovernmental Relations

Canada: The State of the Federation 2009, vol. 22, *Carbon Pricing and Environmental Federalism*, Thomas J. Courchene and John R. Allan (eds.), 2010.
Paper ISBN 978-1-55339-196-8 Cloth ISBN 978-1-55339-197-5

Canada: The State of the Federation 2008, vol. 21, *Open Federalism and the Spending Power*, Thomas J. Courchene, John R. Allan, and Hoi Kong (eds.), forthcoming.
Paper ISBN 978-1-55339-194-4

The Democratic Dilemma: Reforming the Canadian Senate, Jennifer Smith (ed.), 2009.
Paper 978-1-55339-190-6

Canada: The State of the Federation 2006/07, vol. 20, *Transitions – Fiscal and Political Federalism in an Era of Change*, John R. Allan, Thomas J. Courchene, and Christian Leuprecht (eds.), 2009. Paper ISBN 978-1-55339-189-0 Cloth ISBN 978-1-55339-191-3

Comparing Federal Systems, Third Edition, Ronald L. Watts, 2008.
Paper ISBN 978-1-55339-188-3

Canada: The State of the Federation 2005, vol. 19, *Quebec and Canada in the New Century – New Dynamics, New Opportunities*, Michael Murphy (ed.), 2007.
Paper ISBN 978-1-55339-018-3 Cloth ISBN 978-1-55339-017-6

Spheres of Governance: Comparative Studies of Cities in Multilevel Governance Systems, Harvey Lazar and Christian Leuprecht (eds.), 2007. Paper ISBN 978-1-55339-019-0
Cloth ISBN 978-1-55339-129-6

Canada: The State of the Federation 2004, vol. 18, *Municipal-Federal-Provincial Relations in Canada*, Robert Young and Christian Leuprecht (eds.), 2006.
Paper ISBN 1-55339-015-6 Cloth ISBN 1-55339-016-4

Our publications may be purchased at leading bookstores, including the Queen's University Bookstore (http://www.campusbookstore.com/), or can be ordered online from: McGill-Queen's University Press, at **http://mqup.mcgill.ca/ordering.php**

For more information about new and backlist titles from Queen's Policy Studies, visit http://www.queensu.ca/sps/books or visit the McGill-Queen's University Press web site at: **http://mqup.mcgill.ca/**